THE·ROMAN·GODDESS
CERES

BARBETTE·STANLEY·SPAETH

UNIVERSITY OF TEXAS PRESS · *Austin*

Requests for permission to reproduce material from this work should be sent to
Permissions, University of Texas Press, Box 7819, Austin, TX 78713-7819.

Library of Congress Cataloging-in-Publication Data

Spaeth, Barbette Stanley.
　　The Roman goddess Ceres / Barbette Stanley Spaeth.
　　　　　p.　　cm.
　　Includes bibliographical references and index.
　　ISBN 0-292-77692-6 (cloth : alk. paper).—ISBN 0-292-77693-4
　(paper : alk. paper)
　　　1. Ceres (Roman deity)　2. Rome—Religion.　I. Title.
　BL820.C5S63 1995
292.2'114—dc20　　　　　　　　　　　　　　　　　95-13112

Paperback cover image: The central figure of the relief of the southeastern corner of the Ara
Pacis Augustae. Courtesy Deutsches Archäologisches Institut, Rome. Neg. 86.1454.

THE·ROMAN·GODDESS

CERES

Matri et Sorori

CONTENTS

CONTENTS

ILLUSTRATIONS

Illustrations follow page 32

PREFACE

Recently there has been considerable interest in "Goddess religion," an interest that derives from a feminist desire to reimage the concept of the divine in female as well as male form. The impulse, I believe, is natural, given the long exclusion of women from patriarchal monotheistic religion. Although I find the goals of proponents of Goddess religion to be laudable, their approach is at times problematic.[1] The basic difficulty arises from their theory that in the ancient past there existed one great Mother Goddess from whom all other goddesses derived.[2] This female divinity was the supreme power in a society that was both egalitarian and peaceful, and, if not actually matriarchal, certainly matrifocal. This belief is often combined with another problematic assumption: that the goddesses of ancient society were archetypes, models for the behavior and personality of women both in the past and today.[3] Such models pointed the way to the liberation of women, for the goddesses represented the power of the female elevated to the status of the divine.

These two concepts, I believe, have seriously distorted our understanding of the role of goddesses in antiquity and our picture of ancient religion and society as a whole. I am concerned that in their search to find precedents for their vision of a religion in which women are equal in importance to men and in which female needs are met, proponents of Goddess religion have both obscured what the ancient goddesses meant to the people who actually worshipped them and ignored the basically patriarchal structure of ancient society. I have no quarrel with those who would invent a new religion in which women may participate equally; indeed, I support their endeavor. My difficulty lies with those who would argue that their inventions represent historical reality. I feel that this emphasis on problematic historical precedents can harm the cause of creating a new feminist-oriented religion, for if it turns out that such constructs have no basis in historical fact, then the new creations may be discarded along with their discredited prototypes.

The goddesses of antiquity, I argue, can be understood only in their cultural context. By studying the literary and artistic representations of these divinities that were created by the men and women who worshipped them, we can recreate, at least partially, the meaning of those divinities within their society. This meaning is extraordinarily complex, and it is that very complexity, the web of associations represented in the figure of a single divinity, that I am interested in recovering. My interest is in religious ideology, the way in which a divinity embodies certain ideas of a people. This ideology, of course, is not static; it changes over time and is dependent on social context. Therefore, the study of a particular divinity must always be placed within a chronological and social framework to enable us to reconstruct, as best we can from the limited evidence remaining to us, a picture of that divinity's ideological significance.

I have chosen to study the Roman goddess Ceres. This divinity is usually known as the goddess of grain, from whom our word "cereal" derives, but her significance is much more complex than this simple association would indicate. Ceres has already been the subject of a number of interesting studies in Roman religion. Early scholarship focused on both her relationship to the Greek goddess Demeter and her association with the Italic earth goddess Tellus.[4] In 1958 Le Bonniec published a comprehensive study of her cults down to the end of the Roman Republic: *Le culte de Cérès à Rome des origines à la fin de la République*.[5] He traced the development of three aspects of her worship: the native Italic cult in which she was worshipped as a fertility deity together with Tellus; the triadic cult of Ceres, Liber, and Libera, which was closely tied to the social class of the Roman plebs; and the imported Greek cult of Ceres and her daughter, Proserpina, in which women played an important role. Le Bonniec's study was chronologically oriented, and his focus was largely on literary evidence for the various cults of the goddess. Since the appearance of Le Bonniec's study, scholarship has been directed primarily to challenging, explicating, or expanding his views on these three cults.[6]

In this book I offer a new examination of the goddess Ceres that focuses on her ideological significance, rather than the historical development of her cults. I take a thematic approach by studying the various concepts and categories connected with the goddess. I ground this approach in a chronological study of the development of her ideological associations in the various periods of Roman history, from prehistoric Italy to the Late Roman Empire. The methodology is interdisciplinary: I employ literary, epigraphical, numismatic, and artistic sources to reconstruct a picture of Ceres and her meaning to the Romans. I have made use of a variety of collections to obtain the data for my study. For instance, I compiled an extensive list of references to the goddess in Latin literature from the computer data base prepared by the Packard Humanities Institute and the Pandora search program developed at Harvard University. I collected numismatic representations of Ceres from Crawford's study of Roman Republican coinage and Mattingly and Sydenham's of Roman imperial coinage.[7] My gathering of artistic representations was made much easier by De Angeli's recent article on Demeter/Ceres in the *Lexicon Iconographicum Mythologiae Classicae*.[8] Once I had accumulated all this information, I carefully evaluated it to determine what ideas and categories the Romans connected with Ceres over time. In the course of this evaluation, I discovered that often these ideological associations were used in a political context; the goddess herself became a symbol in the repertoire of Roman political propaganda. I felt this discovery revealed both the historical significance of the underlying themes that I had recognized in her character and the way in which a female divinity could be used by a male-dominated power structure to reinforce the status quo.

In this book, I present the results of my investigation into the ideological significance of Ceres to the Romans. In the first chapter, "Historical Overview," I present the chronological development of the various concepts and categories that were connected with the goddess. The next four chapters examine each of these ideas in detail.

The second chapter, "Fertility," looks at the most basic concept linked to the goddess, which is contained in the root of her name. "Ceres" derives from the Indo-European root *ker-, which means "to grow, bring increase," and the goddess represents the power that causes both plants and humans to grow— that is, agricultural and human fertility. The goddess' relation to both types of fertility is examined, along with the significance of her most common association, the growth and harvesting of grain.

Chapter 3, "Liminality," explores Ceres' connection to religious rituals of transition. The term "liminality" refers to crossing the threshold or boundary from one state of being to another. Liminal rituals may be divided into two categories: rites of passage and rites of intensification. The first category comprises those rites by which an individual passes from one social status to another, e.g., from single to married. Ceres is especially involved with the final stage of these rituals, in which the individual is reincorporated into society after a period of separation. The second category, the rites of intensification, includes those rituals that bond the members of a society together and preserve the society as a whole, e.g., the ritual that renews social ties after an attempt has been made to overthrow the government. I call Ceres' place in this second set of rituals her "liminal/normative" role, for through them she operates to preserve the status quo of society. Ceres' connection to liminality, which has never been recognized before, forms an essential aspect of her character.

Ceres has ties to the social category known as the plebs, a group which existed in opposition to the patricians, or aristocracy, of Rome. Chapter 4 examines her connection with this class as revealed through the associations of the plebeian political organization with her temple and the opposition of her triadic cult to the patrician cults of Jupiter, Juno, and Minerva and of Cybele.

The fifth chapter considers the association of the goddess with Roman women, particularly women of the upper class. The role of these women in the Greek cult of Ceres is explored, as is the way in which that cult reflected their social roles. Ceres became identified with the ideal Roman woman of this class and her virtues of chastity and motherhood. The identification of the goddess with these female virtues is shown to be significant for our understanding of how religious ideology supported the patriarchal foundations of Roman society.

At the end of each of these topical chapters, I present a discussion of the use of that concept or category in Roman political propaganda. This discussion illustrates how that ideological association manifested itself in a particular period and demonstrates the practical significance of the symbol of Ceres. I examine the propagandistic use of her connections with agricultural and human fertility under the Empire, the appeal to her liminal/normative role in the events surrounding the death of Tiberius Gracchus in 133 B.C., the manipulation of her ties to the plebs in the numismatic propaganda of the Late Republic, and the political significance of her identification with women of the imperial family from Livia to Julia Domna.

In the final chapter I discuss in detail one image of the goddess that combines all of her various ideological associations and appears on a famous relief panel from the Ara Pacis Augustae, an important monument from Rome in the Augustan period. This representation, I argue, shows how the various aspects of the goddess are interrelated and illustrates their significance in Roman political symbolism.

Two appendixes to the book provide additional information pertinent to my study. Appendix 1 contains the original texts of the longer passages I have translated in the book. All the translations in the book are mine, unless otherwise specified. I have tried to be as literal as possible, without losing the sense. Appendix 2 offers a catalogue of the evidence that I have collected for the identification of women of the imperial family with Ceres.

This study of Ceres offers the reader a detailed picture of one Roman goddess. I hope that it will suggest the incredible diversity and complexity that the entire pantheon of female divinities presented in antiquity. Understanding that diversity and complexity is critical both for reconstructing the ancient past and for applying our knowledge of the past to the needs of women's spirituality today.

ACKNOWLEDGMENTS

This book originated in my doctoral dissertation, written in 1984–1987 at The Johns Hopkins University in Baltimore and at the American School of Classical Studies in Athens. I thank my adviser, John Pollini, and second reader, Frank Romer, for their careful direction. With the aid of the Oscar Broneer Fellowship of the Luther L. Replogle Foundation and a Junior Faculty Research Sabbatical from Tulane University, I conducted additional research in 1990–1991 at the American School in Athens and the American Academy in Rome. In 1993 and 1994, I received a grant from the Committee on Research of Tulane University to cover the costs of obtaining photographs for this publication.

Many people have assisted me in the research and writing of this book, including especially: Nancy Bookidis, John Camp, Jane Carter, Ileana Chirassi-Colombo, Diskin Clay, Kevin Clinton, Karl Galinsky, Dennis Kehoe, Diana Kleiner, Vasilios Manthos, John Pedley, Elizabeth Pemberton, Joe Poe, Michael Putnam, Linda Reilly, and Amy Richlin. I also am grateful for the expert guidance and assistance of the staff of the University of Texas Press, including Joanna Hitchcock, Kerri Cox, Tayron Cutter, Bruce Bethell, and Frankie Westbrook.

Finally, I wish to thank my family and friends, without whose patience, support, and encouragement this book would not have been completed.

THE·ROMAN·GODDESS
CERES

Chapter 1

HISTORICAL OVERVIEW

1.1 *Ancient Italy*

The oldest written evidence we have of any Roman divinity mentions the goddess Ceres. An inscription bearing her name appears on a spherical impasto urn dated to c. 600 B.C.[1] The urn was found in a grave in the necropolis of Civita Castellana, ancient Falerii, not far from Rome. The inscription runs three times around the circumference of the vessel. At its beginning appear the words "Let Ceres give grain (*far*)." The dialect of the inscription is Faliscan, closely related to Latin and spoken by the people who lived to the north of Latium, the land of the Romans. The inscription shows that in this early period a divinity by the name of Ceres was worshipped by the Faliscans, who associated her with *far*, or spelt, an ancient cereal crop.

The name of the goddess itself provides us with further information about her ancient past. It is derived from an Indo-European root, **ker-*, and so the origin of Ceres' name dates back to the period before the split of Proto-Indo-European into the different languages of the Indo-European family.[2] The meaning of this root may be deduced from its later derivatives, such as the Latin verbs *crescere*, "to come forth, grow, arise, spring, be born," and *creare*, "to bring forth, produce, make, create, beget." The root is also found in the name of the Roman divinity Cerus, who was associated with Janus, the god of beginnings in the ritual hymn of the Salian priests.[3] The Roman lexicographer Festus reports that the phrase *Cerus manus* from the hymn may be interpreted as "the Good Creator" (Fest., s.v. *Cerus*, 109 Lindsay). The name is rare, and the masculine divinity seems not to have been a competitor of Ceres among the Romans. The interpretation given by Festus, however, again links the root of Ceres' name with the concept of creation. From this etymological analysis, we can see that in origin Ceres was the divine power that produced living things and caused them to grow.

Ceres' name also links her with several ancient Italic divinities, such as Kerrí, Keri Arentikai, Regina Pia Cerria Iovia, and Anaceta Ceria. These divinities were worshipped by the the Osco-Umbrians or Sabellian-Umbrians, peoples of the central and southern regions of Italy.[4] These groups belonged to a single linguistic stock of Indo-European origin different from Latin and represent a fundamental element of the history and culture of pre-Roman Italy. Our knowledge of their divinities is based almost exclusively on local epigraphical evidence, which is limited, fragmentary, and difficult to date. Often at issue is the extent to which the individuals named in these inscriptions are "pure" Italic divinities, or have already been assimilated to the pantheons of the Greeks and Etruscans. Concerning the later inscriptions, the question also arises as to whether the Romans themselves may have influenced the conception of these Italic goddesses. Nevertheless, the inscriptions relating to these divinities give us some tantalizing glimpses into elements of the character of the original Italic Ceres.

Perhaps our most detailed evidence for this Italic divinity comes from the Tablet of Agnone, a small brass tablet found in Capracotta near Agnone.[5] The tablet is inscribed in Oscan on both sides and is dated to c. 250 B.C. on the basis of letter forms. The Oscan words can be translated into their Latin and English equivalents, although some problems of interpretation remain. The inscription describes a series of rituals held in a "sacred grove of Ceres" for a list of seventeen divinities, many of whom are described as "Cerealis" or "belonging to Ceres." The names of these Oscan divinities suggest links to the same concepts that we will see tied to the Roman Ceres. Certain of these divinities are connected to motherhood and children, and hence human fertility: the Daughter of Ceres (Filia Cerealis), Nurse of Ceres (Nutrix Cerealis), and the Divine Progenitress (Diva Genitrix).[6] Others are associated with agricultural fertility, in that they are associated with the water that crops require to grow or with qualities of vegetation: the Nymphs of Ceres (Lymphi Cereales); the Rain Showers of Ceres (Imbres Cereales); the Dispensers of Morning Dew (?) of Ceres (Mati Cereales); Jupiter the Irrigator (Jupiter Rigator); She Who Opens Up (the grain hull?) (Panda Pinsitrix); and She Who Flowers of Ceres (Flora Cerealis).[7] Other divinities may be associated with the liminal/normative aspect of Ceres: She Who Stands Between (?) (Interstita) and She Who Bears the Laws Between (?) (Legifera Intera). Four of those named have Roman counterparts who are connected with Ceres in Roman cult: Liber Pater (Euclus Pater); Hercules (Hercules Cerealis); Jupiter (Jupiter Vergarius and Jupiter

Rigator); and Flora (Flora Cerealis).[8] The Agnone tablet thus suggests a variety of connections between the Oscan divinity Kerrí and the Roman goddess Ceres.

Inscriptions from other Oscan sites also mention divinities who may be associated with Ceres. In a necropolis at Capua was found a curse tablet that mentions Keri Arentikai, or Ceres Ultrix, the Avenger.[9] This epithet identifies the goddess as an avenging deity, usually connected with the underworld and the spirits of the dead. The Roman Ceres also has associations with the world of the dead in her liminal capacity, through the ritual of the opening of the mundus Cereris and with the funerary rituals of the porca praesentanea and praecidanea.[10] From Rapino in the territory of the Marrucini comes a dedication to Jupiter Pater and to Regina Pia Cerria Iovia.[11] The inscription points to an identification of Ceres with the spouse of Jupiter, known to the Romans as Juno Regina. Inscriptions from Sulmo and Corfinium in the territory of the Peligni mention a divinity called Anaceta Ceria or Angitia Cerealis.[12] Scholars have suggested that this being may be identified with the Roman goddess Angerona, who was associated with childbirth, pointing to a connection with human fertility. Finally, another Pelignan inscription from Corfinium names a *Cerfum sacracirix semunu*, or *Cererum sacerdos semonum*, which may be translated as "priestess of the Cereres and the divinities of sowing."[13] The association with the divinities of sowing indicates a connection with agricultural fertility. The Cereres, a plural of Ceres, may perhaps be interpreted as Ceres and her daughter Proserpina.[14] On the other hand, other Pelignan inscriptions mention a dual priesthood of Ceres and Venus, and so perhaps the term refers to these two divinities.[15] In any case, the evidence clearly supports the hypothesis that these Oscan divinities are closely related to the Roman Ceres.

I find more problematic the proposed associations of Ceres with the divinities of the Italic Umbrians and the Etruscans. The Iguvine Tablets from Gubbio in Umbria, dated to the second century B.C., name the divinities Çerfo Martio, Prestota Çerfia, and Torsa Çerfia.[16] These divinities are particularly associated with war: Çerfo Martio is equivalent to the Roman Mars, the god of war; Prestota Çerfia is described as defending the citizens of the city; and Torsa Çerfia is the goddess who puts its enemies to flight. These martial divinities seem to have little in common with the Roman Ceres. Dumézil has suggested their names do not necessarily imply a connection with Ceres: the Umbrian -*rf*- may not be equivalent to the Oscan and Latin *-rs-*.[17]

Similarly, evidence for connections of Ceres with Etruscan divinities seems weak. Several late Latin authors state that Ceres was worshipped by the Etruscans, but no specific Etruscan divinity has ever been identified definitively with Ceres.[18] Archaeological evidence has been adduced to support the limited lit-

3

erary evidence. On a terracotta plaque from the sanctuary of Poggio Civitate (Murlo) south of Siena appear six figures, whom Gantz hypothesized represent two triads of divinities: the Capitoline triad of Jupiter, Juno, and Minerva, and the Aventine triad of Ceres, Liber, and Libera.[19] The divinities, he has proposed, may be recognized by their attributes: Jupiter holds a lituus; Minerva has a sword and spear; Juno makes a traditional wedding gesture with her veil; Ceres holds a stalk that terminates in poppy capsules; Liber has a double axe; and Libera holds a stalk with pomegranates. The iconography of the plaque remains problematic, however.[20] For example, five of the figures are seated, suggesting an equality among them; the one identified as Minerva, however, stands like the servants represented on the plaque. The double axe is hardly a common attribute of Liber; Jupiter is missing his most common attribute, the thunderbolt. The identity of the plant the Ceres figure holds is uncertain.[21] Libera's connection with the pomegranate depends on her identification with Proserpina, the evidence for which is quite late in Roman sources.[22] Since no other solid evidence for these triads among the Etruscans has been found, the interpretation of the Murlo plaque remains open to question.[23] At present, therefore, the putative Umbrian and Etruscan forerunners of Ceres must be considered unproven.

1.2 Regal Rome

At Rome itself, there is evidence for the worship of Ceres as far back as the regal period, traditionally dated to 753–509 B.C. First, the festival of the goddess, the Cerialia, is listed in capital letters in the pre-Julian calendar of the Roman Republic. The Romans ascribed this calendar to King Numa, and many modern scholars, following Mommsen, have accepted a date in the regal period for the festivals marked in capitals in this calendar.[24] In addition, the priest of her cult in Rome, the flamen Cerealis, belonged to the most ancient class of priests, the flaminate, whose foundation was again ascribed to Numa.[25] These features of the archaic cult of Ceres are tied to agricultural fertility. The Cerialia was celebrated on April 19 as part of a cycle of agricultural and pastoral festivals in the month of April.[26] The central ritual of this festival, in which torches were tied to the tails of foxes, has been associated with magical rites to protect the crops.[27] This ritual was performed in the Circus Maximus in the Vallis Murcia, where cults of several other archaic agrarian divinities were also celebrated.[28] The flamen Cerealis celebrated a ritual called the sacrum Cereale, in which were named twelve minor divinities specifically connected with agricultural work (Serv. on Verg. *G*. 1.21). Scholars have also ascribed other agricultural rites connected with Ceres to this early period, including: the sacrifice of the porca praecidanea, performed before the harvest; the offering of the first fruits of the harvest; the festival of the Ambarvalia, associated with the lustration of the fields in May; the Feriae Sementivae, associated with the protection of the seeded crops in the latter half of January; and the feast day of Ceres and Tellus on December 13, associated with the end of the sowing season, cited in the Roman calendar.[29] The latter two festivals link Ceres and Tellus, another Italic goddess, and Le Bonniec has suggested that the ancient Italic cult adopted by the Romans was dedicated to these two divinities.[30] The principal festivals of these two divinities, the Fordicidia of Tellus on April 15 and the Cerialia of Ceres on April 19, also reveal a connection between them. The interval of four days that separates these two festivals was customary for related festivals in the ancient Roman calendar.[31]

Other aspects of the cult of Ceres in the regal period may be attributed to her role as a liminal divinity. The ritual of the opening of the mundus Cereris allowed the spirits of the dead to roam the world, breaking down the boundaries between living and dead.[32] This ritual represents an example of the second category of liminal rites, rites of intensification for society as a whole. By eliminating temporarily the distinction between the living and the dead, the ritual ultimately reaffirmed this distinction and allowed the members of Roman society to pursue their everyday lives free from fear of the dead. If the site of the mundus Cereris is to be identified with the circular bothros in the Roman Forum, which according to tradition Romulus had established at the foundation of Rome (Plut. *Vit. Rom.* 11.2), then this ritual of the goddess is tied to the very origins of the city.[33]

Another liminal association of Ceres in this early period is the law regulating divorce (Plut. *Vit. Rom.* 22.3), an example of the first type of liminal rite associated with the goddess, a rite of passage for the individual.[34] This law is attributed to the first king of Rome, Romulus. Ceres' association with marriage, another rite of passage, is seen in a note by Festus saying that the wedding torch was carried in honor of the goddess (Fest., s.v. *facem*, 87 Müller).[35] This association of the goddess has been attributed to the regal period on two grounds.[36] First, it may be related to Ceres' role in divorces, which is traditionally assigned to this period. Secondly, we know from Servius that Tellus was also named in Roman marriage ceremonies (Serv. on Verg. *Aen.* 4.166). As we noted above, the connection of Tellus and Ceres has been associated with an ancient Italic cult, and Ceres' association with the marriage ceremony is thought to derive from her connection to Tellus. I remain sceptical, however, of the idea that Ceres' connection with weddings dates to the regal period, since the evidence we have for this connection is much later than the period in question. The ritual sacrifice of the porca praesentanea (Fest., s.v. *praesentanea porca*, 250, Müller) and porca praecidanea (Varr. in Non. Marc., 240 Lindsay) may also be considered in this context.[37] These sacrifices were conducted as part of funerary ceremonies and thus also have a liminal significance. Again, because Tellus is named along with Ceres in the latter ritual, these funerary rituals too have been assigned to the regal period.[38]

1.3 *The Early Republic*

With the foundation of the Roman Republic, traditionally dated to 509 B.C., a new association of Ceres arose, in which the goddess was connected with a particular social class, the plebeians, or plebs. The plebs existed in opposition to another class, the patricii, or patricians. Both plebeians and patricians were members of the society of regal Rome; indeed several of the early kings had plebeian names. The origins of the distinctions between patricians and plebeians remain obscure, although scholars have proposed a variety of possibilities, including ethnic, economic, and political differences between the two orders.[39] By the foundation of the Republic, the patricians had become the ruling class in the state, and the plebeians engaged in a political struggle with them throughout the period of the Early Republic (late sixth–early third centuries B.C.) that was called the Conflict of the Orders. This struggle ended in the early third century B.C. with the plebs as a whole obtaining political equality and with certain plebeian families sharing power with the patricians, creating a new ruling class. It is in the context of this conflict that the plebeian associations of Ceres are most clearly manifested.

The origin of Ceres' association with the plebs is tied to the foundation of a new temple devoted to a triad of divinities: Ceres, Liber, and Libera. During the Early Republic this temple became the nucleus of the plebeian political organization in its struggle against the patricians.[40] As we shall see, the temple served as the office of the plebeian magistrates, the archives of the plebs, and possibly the plebeian treasury and grain distribution center. The plebeian magistrates, the tribunes and aediles of the plebs, were closely associated with Ceres, and indeed the aediles seemed to have served as priests of the triadic cult.[41] The cult of Ceres, Liber, and Libera became the focal point for the development of the class consciousness of the plebeians.[42] It stood in opposition to the patrician cult of Jupiter, Juno, and Minerva, and later to another patrician cult, that of Cybele.

The establishment of the plebeian cult is traditionally dated to soon after the foundation of the Roman Republic. According to the Greek historian Dionysius of Halicarnassus (6.17.2–4), in 496 B.C. the Roman dictator Aulus Postumius consulted the Sibylline Books, a collection of Greek oracles acquired by the Romans, because a grain shortage had brought famine to the city before a major battle was to be fought with the Latins. The Books recommended that the divinities Demeter, Kore, and Dionysus (the Greek equivalents of Ceres, Liber, and Libera) be propitiated, and so Postumius vowed a temple to them before the battle. After the Romans won a major victory in this battle, the temple was constructed, and the consul Spurius Cassius dedicated it in 494/3 B.C. (Dion. Hal. 6.94.3). This date is also that of the First Secession of the plebs, in which the plebeians withdrew from the city until the patricians met certain demands for their political recognition. The synchronism in the traditional dates suggests a correspondence between plebeian political and religious recognition, to which we shall return in chapter 4. Although the exact dating of these events is contested, scholars generally agree that they took place in the first half of the fifth century.[43] The location of the Temple of Ceres, Liber, and Libera, however, is still in dispute (fig. 1). Simon, Nash, Le Bonniec, Van Berchem, and Giovenale identify the remains of a tufa podium underneath the Church of Santa Maria in Cosmedin in the ancient Forum Boarium with the Temple of Ceres, Liber, and Libera.[44] Richardson, Coarelli, Platner-Ashby, and Merlin have argued, rightly I believe, that this podium belongs to another structure, possibly the Ara Maxima of Hercules, and that the literary evidence points to a location of the temple of the triadic cult on the lower slopes of Aventine Hill, facing the Circus Maximus.[45] In any case, the temple stood outside the pomerium, the sacred boundary of the city, which may mark it as "foreign," since only native Roman cults were allowed inside the pomerium.[46] The new triadic cult was connected to the ancient Ceres cult, for in the calendar of the Roman Republic the names of Liber and Libera were added to that of Ceres for the festival of the Cerialia.[47]

Scholars have disputed the origins of the new triadic cult, variously proposing Etruscan, Greek, or Italic precedents.[48] As I have demonstrated, the evidence for an Etruscan origin is weak, since neither Ceres herself nor the triad can be proven to have existed in ancient Etruria. More substantial are the claims for a Greek origin, especially those which point to the Greek colonies of Southern Italy (Magna Graecia) as the source for the Roman cult. The three Greek divinities named by Dionysius (Demeter, Kore, and Dionysus) were worshipped in the cities of Magna Graecia. The Romans believed that the Sibylline Books, which ordered the propitiation of these divinities, came from the Greek city of Cumae in this region. According to the scholar Pliny the Elder (*HN* 35.154), the temple of Ceres, Liber, and Libera in Rome was decorated in the Greek style by Greek artists, Damophilus and Gorgasus, who probably came from one of the Doric West Greek colonies in Southern Italy. These factors point to important associations of the new cult with Magna Graecia.

As Le Bonniec has demonstrated, however, the triadic cult itself was a new creation at Rome, based on Italic precedents.[49] It was composed by linking two dyads of Italic divinities, Ceres/Liber and Liber/Libera. The relationship among the three divinities is unique, for in Greece proper and her colonies in Magna Graecia, the goddesses Demeter and Kore always formed a pair, to which a male divinity could be added, but only as a subsidiary to the main couple of mother and daughter. In contrast, in Roman sources the identification of Libera as the daughter of Ceres is rather late, and Ceres tends rather to form a pair with the god Liber. Liber is linked with Libera in an etymological duality that has several parallels in early Roman religion, such as Faunus and Fauna.[50] According to later sources, Liber was associated with male fertility and Libera with female, so the dyad presided over human sexual union.[51] Further evidence for this association is provided by the ancient phallic cult of Liber, practiced originally in Lavinium and later brought to Rome.[52] This connection with human fertility parallels Ceres' own association with the concept and suggests a native Italic rationale for the linkage of the three divinities. The triadic cult therefore must be considered a Roman creation based on Italic precedents, but with Greek influence in its formation.

This Greek influence represents the first steps in the "Hellenization" of the goddess Ceres. Like the other divinities of the Roman pantheon, Ceres came to be identified by the Romans with her Greek counterpart, the goddess Demeter. Eventually, Ceres took on the iconography and mythology of Demeter in Roman art and literature. Simon and De Angeli wish to date the transferral of Greek characteristics to Ceres to the establishment of the triadic cult.[53] They cite in this connection the decoration of the temple with terracotta plaques and paintings by the Greek artists Damophilus and Gorgasus (Pliny *HN* 35.154) and the erection of a bronze statue dedicated to the goddess in her temple in 485 B.C. (Dion. Hal. 8.79.3; Pliny *HN* 34.15), possibly done by these same artists. They propose that these representations would have portrayed Ceres in the type and iconography of the Greek Demeter. No physical evidence for this hypothesis exists, however, since the first images of Roman Ceres to come down to us date to the third century B.C. Similarly, the first mentions of Ceres in Latin literature are much later than this early period, and so we cannot tell for sure when the mythology and iconography of Greek Demeter were adopted for the representation of the Roman Ceres. This must have taken place, however, sometime during the period of the Early Republic, for by the Middle Republic there is clear evidence for Ceres being represented in the guise of Demeter.

We are left with the problem of explaining the reason for the choice of Ceres and her cult companions as the tutelary divinities of the plebs. A variety of proposals have been made, none of which is entirely satisfactory. One theory suggests that these divinities, who were particularly associated with agricultural fertility, originally belonged to the Latin farmers, who formed the nucleus of the Roman plebs.[54] The patricians, who may have represented a different ethnic element in the Roman state, adopted the Latin cult in order to incorporate the plebs more completely into the fledgling state in the face of threats from other Latin peoples. This theory depends on an original ethnic distinction between patricians and plebeians that is problematic, to say the least. Another theory points toward the evidence for Greek elements in the triadic cult and to the location of its temple outside the pomerium.[55] These factors suggest that the new cult was considered "foreign," and hence not subject to patrician control. The urban plebs therefore chose this cult as camouflage for their political and social ambitions. This hypothesis, I believe, overemphasizes the Greek elements in the cult and ignores the problem of why Aulus Postumius, who as dictator in 496 B.C. was a patrician magistrate, would have deliberately created a cult intended to subvert patrician control.

Another proposal suggests that the new cult was particularly concerned with grain importations, which came from the region of Magna Graecia, the source also of the Greek elements in the cult.[56] The urban plebs especially depended on these importations, and so they chose this cult as their own. One problem with this theory is that the evidence for associating the grain supply with the temple of the triadic cult is late, as we shall see below. In addition, the notion that the grain supply was significant only to the plebeians seems unlikely, and indeed is contradicted by the fact that Postumius, a patrician, vowed the temple of the triadic cult because of a grain shortage. Perhaps the reason for the linkage of the cult with the plebeians is overdetermined, that is, it results from a combination of various factors. I believe that one of these factors may be Ceres' liminal/normative role. In the period in which the cult was established, the plebeians were in conflict with the patricians, threatening the stability of the state, in fact, literally standing outside of it, as the tale of the First Secession shows. What divinity is more appropriate to reincorporate them into the state, to move them from a liminal position to a stable one, than Ceres, who is, as we shall see, the goddess who presides over the final stage of liminal transition, incorporation?

Ceres' connection with liminality may also be seen in two laws dated to the Early Republic. First, the law on the violation of sacrosanctitas, the principle that protected the person of the tribune of the plebs, is dated to the First Secession of the plebs in 494/3 B.C., and may be connected both with the plebeian and liminal/normative aspects of Ceres (Dion. Hal. 6.89.3 and Livy 3.55.7–8).[57] This law, which provided that those who violated the sacrosanctitas of a tribune, a political officer of the plebs, be put to death and their goods confiscated for the benefit of Ceres, protected both the rights of the plebs and also the compromise whereby the Roman state reincorporated the plebeians into the community as a whole. Secondly, by its similiarities to this law, another that punished anyone who attempted to set himself up as a tyrant may also be connected with the goddess Ceres.[58] The law on attempted tyranny is attributed by Livy (2.1.9; 2.82) and Plutarch (*Vit. Publ.* 12.1) to L. Junius Brutus and P. Valerius Publicola, the first consuls of the Roman Republic in 509 B.C. Evidence for its association with Ceres may be seen in the story of Sp. Cassius, who was executed in 485 B.C. for attempting to set himself up as a tyrant and had his goods consecrated to Ceres.[59]

Ceres' connection with agricultural fertility may also be discerned in the period of the Early Republic. A law belonging to the Twelve Tables, cited by Pliny the Elder (*HN* 18.3.13), provides that a person who damaged the harvest be put to death in honor of Ceres. The Twelve Tables represent the earliest codification of Roman law and are dated to 451–450 B.C. This law also may be connected with the liminal/normative aspect of Ceres, for it punishes the person who violates the institution of family property rights through the division of the fields, which was the foundation of the new social and economic order of the Early Republic.[60] Finally, De Angeli, Dumézil, and Le Bonniec date the association of Ceres with the frumentationes, the distributions of grain to the urban poor, and the annona, the administration of the grain supply, to this early period.[61] Although the evidence for these connections is late—a passage from Varro (in Non. 63 Lindsay) dated to the Augustan period and a fragment of Lucilius (200 Marx) dated to the Late Republic—these scholars argue that as Ceres came to be closely associated with the plebs of the city of Rome in the Early Republic, her connections with rural agricultural activities would have become less significant in the new urban setting. The focus of her powers in agricultural fertility then would have shifted from the sowing, growth, and harvesting of crops to the protection of the grain supply and the assurance of its distribution to the plebs. This theory is unprovable on current evidence.

1.4 The Middle Republic

In the period of the Middle Republic (early third–late second centuries B.C.), Ceres became increasingly Hellenized and developed a new connection with another social group, women. The earliest representations we have of Ceres date to this period and show considerable Greek influence.[62] From a sanctuary at Ariccia in the Alban hills near Rome comes a terracotta protome, or bust, dated to c. 300 B.C. (fig. 2).[63] The protome represents a mature woman, wearing a diadem and a corona spicea, or crown made of wheat stalks, a necklace open in front, the ends of which terminate in the heads of two snakes, and a pair of earrings consisting of a rosette and a pyramidal shape. The representation is very similar to images of the goddess on coins from Lucera, dated to 211–208 B.C., and also resembles images on the more ancient coinage of Capua, dated to 268–218 B.C.[64] The corona spicea identifies the figure of the Ariccian protome as Ceres, for as we shall see, this crown was a primary attribute of the Roman goddess. This crown, however, was borrowed from the iconography of Greek Demeter, as numerous coins from the Greek colonies of Southern Italy and Sicily show.[65] The snake is also an attribute of both Ceres and Demeter in Greek and Roman literary and artistic sources. The type of earrings shown on the Ariccian bust and the use of the protome shape suggest further connections with the art of Magna Graecia.[66] The representation from Ariccia can be identified as Demeter/Ceres, that is, the Roman goddess Ceres shown in the type and iconography of Demeter as represented in Magna Graecia. The sanctuary at Ariccia has yielded other terracotta sculptures of Demeter/Ceres and also representations of a younger female figure also wearing stalks of wheat in her hair. The latter has been identified as the daughter of Demeter/Ceres, that is, Persephone/Proserpina. The association of these two figures points to a new development in the Roman conception of Ceres that is also reflected in literary sources.

These sources indicate that a new cult dedicated to Ceres and Proserpina was established in Rome sometime during the latter part of the third century B.C.[67] The first evidence we have for this cult is from the time of Hannibal's attack on Italy in the Second Punic War. According to Livy (22.56.4), the "yearly rite of Ceres," or *sacrum anniversarium Cereris*, celebrated by the matronae, or married women of Rome, had to be interrupted because of the mourning imposed on these women by the disastrous defeat of the Romans at Cannae on August 2, 216 B.C. Festus (s.v. *Graeca sacra*, 97 Müller) tells us that this festival, which he calls the Graeca sacra festa Cereris, was celebrated "on account of the finding of Proserpina," thus linking it with the story of the rape and return of Ceres' daughter, known from sources dating back to the *Homeric Hymn to Demeter*. Festus also informs us in this passage that the festival was imported "from Greece," which may be interpreted as either mainland Greece itself or Magna Graecia. The latter interpretation is supported by Cicero (*Balb.* 55), who reports that the priestesses for this cult generally were from the Greek colonies of Naples and Velia in Southern Italy. As we shall see in chapter 5, other literary and epigraphical evidence for this cult indicates that it was celebrated by women alone, who were both the officiants and participants in the cult. The Roman festival seems closely related to the Greek festival of Demeter known as the Thesmophoria, which was especially important in Magna Graecia. The participants in both festivals ritually reenacted the myth of rape of Persephone/Proserpina and her return to her mother, Demeter/Ceres. The myth and rituals of these festivals had particular significance for women, in that they symbolized the two primary roles of women in upper-class Roman society: the young, chaste maiden and the mature, fertile mother. The themes of fertility and chastity expressed in this cult of Ceres and Proserpina represented the "female virtues" encouraged in Roman women, especially during the period of the Empire.[68] The connection of Ceres with women, however, is much earlier than this, dating back to the Middle Republic and associated with the introduction of the Greek cult of the goddess and her daughter.

Again, the problem arises of why this cult was established at Rome at this particular time. We should note first of all that the second half of the third century B.C. and the first half of the second century include several instances of religious innovation.[69] For example, the cult of Venus Erycina was imported from Sicily in 215 B.C. and that of Cybele from Asia Minor in 204 B.C. The cult of the Bacchanalia that had been imported from Greece also grew very popular in this period. The Senate came to view the latter cult as dangerous, given its appeal to upper-class women and the rumors of promiscuity and sedition attached to it, and so ordered the suppression of the Bacchanalia in 186 B.C. These innovations represented a challenge to traditional Roman religion. The challenge may be connected with the military reverses the Romans suffered in the latter part of the third century B.C., including an invasion of

Gallic tribes in 226 B.C. and the crushing defeats inflicted by Hannibal in 218–211 B.C. As Livy reports (25.1.6–7), the latter in particular led to religious hysteria at Rome, where traditional rites and religious customs were abandoned, especially by women, in favor of prayers and sacrifices to foreign gods. The acceptance of the Graeca sacra Cereris seems to fit a pattern in which foreign religious practices were adopted by the Romans in this period.

We may postulate that the liminal/normative aspect of Ceres may have played a role in the adoption of this cult. As Chirassi-Colombo has demonstrated for the Greek festival of the Thesmophoria, its rituals integrated women into the state by recognizing their importance in preserving and maintaining the fertility on which the state depended.[70] So too, I propose, the cult of Ceres and Proserpina valorized the contributions made by women to the continuity of the state and thus reintegrated them into Roman society at a time when the basis of that society was threatened both by outside forces and by internal hysteria. This cult, as we shall see, encouraged the virtues of fertility and chastity among upper-class women, and thus may be contrasted with the Bacchanalic cult, which the Senate believed was encouraging promiscuity and other vices among these women. It is for this reason, I suggest, that the cult of Ceres and Proserpina was allowed to flourish among Roman women of this social class, while the Bacchanalic cult was suppressed. The cult of the two goddesses reinforced the status quo and returned Roman women to their proper role in society, as defined by the male ruling class.

A passage from Cicero (*Balb.* 55) supports the hypothesis that the cult emphasized the civic importance of the actions of its female officiants. The orator reports that the priestess of the Greek cult of Ceres was to "perform the rites as a citizen on behalf of citizens," and that she was to "pray to the immortal gods with a foreign and external knowledge, but with a domestic and civil intention." The passage also indicates that the state recognized the civic significance of the actions of these women, for the Senate deliberately made the woman who performed these rituals into a Roman citizen so that she could act on behalf of the state.

Valerius Maximus (1.1.15) provides further evidence for the importance the Roman state attached to these rituals conducted by women. He notes that the Senate ordered after the Battle of Cannae that mourning be limited so that the annual festival of the Greek cult could be celebrated by the matronae.[71] The disastrous battle had resulted in so many deaths that all the women of the city were in mourning and thus ritually impure and unable to participate in the festival. Valerius Maximus says that the women were compelled to wipe away their tears and set aside their emblems of mourning so that they could put on the white robes of celebration and offer incense on the altars. Besides indicating the significance the state attached to the cult, the passage may also point to another meaning. The Senate's order compelling the women to curtail their mourning may indicate that it found these actions disruptive to the state.

Holst-Warhaft has suggested that the state-decreed limits to mourning in fifth-century Athens were tied to the need to transform the lament over the loss of individuals by their female relatives into official praise of the sacrifice of those individuals on behalf of the state of the whole.[72] This new attitude toward the mourning of the dead is demanded by a state that must recruit a standing army if it is to survive. After the Battle of Cannae, the Senate had to demand further sacrifice of individuals in the war against Hannibal, and so it may have found a need to silence the disruptive laments of women, who were crying out for peace rather than compliantly accepting further personal loss. Holst-Warhaft goes on to note that such attempts to restrict mourning in Athens had to be accompanied by a substitute for the laments of women if they were to gain popular support. In Greece, funerals represented a unique occasion for women to raise their voices in public, and depriving them of this outlet might have had serious social consequences. In the case of the Romans, the performance of the rituals of the Greek cult of Ceres offered to Roman women a socially acceptable public role and substituted for the potentially disruptive funerary laments. These rituals thus reintegrated these women into society and appropriated their actions for the benefit of the state.

The atmosphere of crisis surrounding the Second Punic War also may help to explain other innovations in the cult of Ceres. According to Livy (22.10.9), in 217 B.C., at the time of Hannibal's invasion of Italy, a special ritual, called a lectisternium, was held at Rome in honor of the twelve great divinities, honored for the first time as a group in Rome. These divinities were grouped into couples, including the pair of Mercury and Ceres. The ritual of the lectisternium, in which a meal was offered to the statues of divinities that were exhibited on special couches, was in origin a Greek rite.[73] It had been celebrated in Rome for the first time in 399 B.C. after a severe epidemic had occasioned a consultation of the Sibylline Books, which prescribed the new rite in honor of six divinities (Livy 5.13.4–6). The context suggests that originally the ritual was especially concerned with a time of crisis, when special circumstances indicated a need to propitiate the gods. Another ritual, the *ieiunium Cereris*, or "fast of Ceres," was instituted in a similar situation. According to Livy (36.37.4–5), after a series of terrible prodigies in 191 B.C., the Senate ordered that the Sibylline Books be consulted, and these ordered that a fast be instituted for Ceres, to be repeated every five years. Later, the fast became an annual ritual, for it is reported in the Roman calendar for October 4.[74] This fast may have become part of the rites of the Greek cult of Ceres celebrated by women.[75] In any case, this ritual again associates Ceres with a time of crisis. The appearance of prodigies signals a breakdown in the natural order, which can only be repaired by appealing to the gods. In later years, Ceres and Proserpina come to be named regularly among the divinities propitiated when prodigies occurred.[76] This association, I shall argue, derives from the liminal/normative aspect of Ceres.

The ritual of the *ieiunium Cereris* points to another association of Ceres during the period of the Middle Republic: her connection with the plebs. The date of the institution of this ritual is significant; it comes soon after the establishment of the cult of the Magna Mater on the Palatine Hill in Rome in 204 B.C. The cult of the Magna Mater was particularly associated with the patricians, and, as we shall see, seems constituted deliberately in opposition to the plebeian cult of Ceres, Liber, and Libera. Le Bonniec has argued that the institution of a ritual in honor of Ceres soon after the importation of the new patrician goddess may represent a concession to plebeian religious sensibilities.[77] Certainly, other events during the Middle Republic indicate the continued importance of Ceres to the plebs. On four separate occasions, in 296, 210, 208, and 197 B.C., the plebeian aediles dedicated gifts in honor of the goddess in the temple of the triadic cult.[78] In 176 B.C., the plebeian aedile C. Memmius introduced a new celebration into the festival of the Cerialia: a set of games involving dramatic productions, or ludi scaenici.[79] These games were in honor of the plebeian triad, Ceres, Liber, and Libera, and were celebrated during the period of April 12–18, before the traditional games in the Circus, or ludi circenses, of April 19. The plebeian associations of the goddess thus remain strong throughout the Middle Republic.

The first references to Ceres in contemporary Latin literature also date to this period. The birth of Latin literature is a relatively late development in Roman culture; the earliest extant authors are from the late third century B.C. The references to Ceres in this early literature point to her connections with human and agricultural fertility and may reflect the Hellenization of the cult. The playwright Plautus mentions the *vigilia Cereris*, or night festival in honor of the goddess (*Aul.* 36, 795), and the *nuptiae Cereris*, or wedding of Ceres (*Aul.* 354). It is unclear whether these are actually Roman rites in honor of Ceres, or Greek ones in honor of Demeter. Both references to the *vigilia Cereris* concern the sexual violation of a virgin at the festival, possibly suggesting a connection with human fertility in the ritual. We have no other evidence for a "wedding of Ceres," although perhaps this festival is to be connected with the *nuptiae Orci*, known from other sources.[80] In any case, the festival points to an association of the goddess with weddings, which we have seen may date back to the regal period.

Another mention by Plautus (*Rud.* 146) connects Ceres with grain, pointing to her role in agricultural fertility. This meaning also is to be attached to the playwright Terence's quotation (*Eun.* 732) of the proverb "Without Ceres and Bacchus, Venus grows cold" (sine Cerere et Libero friget Venus), i.e., without food and wine, love grows cold. The metonymic identification of Ceres with food comes from her connection with bread and grain. Finally, we have the description of the sacrifice of the porca praecidanea to Ceres in Cato's treatise on agriculture (*Agr.* 134), a fertility ritual which is to be conducted by the farmer before harvesting the grain. The other associations of Ceres are not manifested in extant Latin literature of this period, but much of the early writings has been lost.

1.5 *The Late Republic*

By the time of the Late Republic (late second century B.C.–late first century B.C.), all the various associations of Ceres are in place: her connection with fertility, both agricultural and human, liminality, the plebs, and women. These associations are manifested in both literary and artistic sources of this period. In literary sources the goddess is frequently associated with agricultural fertility. She is identified with the earth, from which crops spring, with the agricultural work necessary to produce crops, and with the crops themselves, especially grain and the bread produced from it.[81] In visual representations as well of the Late Republic, Ceres is associated with agricultural work and with its product, grain. On two coin types, the bust of Ceres is shown on the obverse while the reverse depicts a yoke of oxen.[82] On other coin and gem types, she wears the corona spicea, is shown with wheat and barley grains, or holds stalks of wheat in her hands.[83] Thus, on the obverse of a denarius of Q. Cornificius dated to 44–42 B.C., Ceres appears wearing the corona spicea (fig. 3).[84] She is also linked directly to the annona, or grain supply, now of great importance in this period. On one coin, she seems to wear a *modius*, or grain measure, on her head.[85] On another coin, the head of Ceres is shown on the obverse (fig. 4a) and on the reverse appear two seated male figures with a wheat stalk to their right, representing the official distributions of grain to the people, the frumentationes (fig. 4b).[86] Alföldi has argued that the frequent appearance of Ceres on the coinage of this period is generally connected with the grain supply and with the agrarian reforms proposed by popularis politicians.[87] Ceres' connection with the grain supply is also reflected in a fragment of Lucilius dated to this period (200 Marx), a quotation of Varro (in Non. 63 Lindsay), and in Julius Caesar's creation of two new officials, whom he called the aediles Ceriales and put in charge of the grain supply (Dio Cass. 43.51.3). Ceres' role in agricultural fertility is also prominent in a new cult dedicated to her in Roman Africa: the cult of the Cereres, generally interpreted as Ceres and her daughter Proserpina. The Roman cult was a revival of a Greek cult of Demeter and Persephone imported to Carthage from Syracuse in the fourth century B.C. and continued by the Numidian king Masinissa as part of a program to encourage his nomadic subjects to take up agriculture.[88] The cult became especially significant under the Empire, when Africa served as one of Rome's principal granaries.

Other authors of the Late Republic point to Ceres' association with human fertility. Lucretius (*RN* 4.1168) describes a big-breasted woman as like Ceres with Iacchus at her breast (at tumida et mammosa Ceres est ipsa ab Iaccho). This description suggests that the poet was familiar with an artistic representation of the goddess as a nursing mother. Varro (*Rust.* 2.4.2) also points to a connection with human fertility when he indicates associations among the pig sacrificed at the ritual of Ceres, the one sacrificed at the beginning of a wedding, and the common use of the term "pig" to refer to female genitalia.[89]

The latter passage also points to Ceres' connection with liminality, for Varro connects the pig sacrificed in the ritual of Ceres, the one offered at the beginning of a wedding, and the one sacrificed at the conclusion of a peace treaty by saying that all these ceremonies are initia, that is, beginnings. According to Cicero (*Verr.* 2.5.187; cf. Varr. *Rust.* 3.15.5), Ceres is a goddess of beginnings, for it is she who provided the laws that enabled humankind to establish civilization, especially the law that provided for the division of the fields and led to the adoption of agriculture and hence to civilized life. The goddess is connected with the transition from a lawless state to an ordered one, from a society based on hunting and gathering to one based on agriculture, from barbarism to civilization. Again according to Cicero (*Leg.* 2.35–36), this transition does not have merely a historical and societal significance, but also a personal mimetic meaning. By becoming initiated into the mysteries of the goddess, the individual is tamed and cultivated. The mystery initiation itself thus represents another liminal aspect of the goddess, for such a ceremony is a rite of passage.[90]

The mysteries to which Cicero refers in this passage are another foreign cult of Ceres that became increasingly significant during the Late Republic: the Eleusinian Mysteries. These mysteries of Demeter had been conducted from time immemorial at Eleusis, a sacred site near Athens. In the Late Republic, we hear of prominent Romans being initiated into this cult, including Sulla (Plut. *Vit. Sulla* 26) and Cicero and his friend Atticus (Cic. *Leg.* 2.35). Bayet has proposed that the growing interest in this cult among the Romans is reflected in the coinage of this period, in which Ceres is shown with attributes which he identifies as Eleusinian, such as torches and a snake-drawn chariot.[91] For example, on the reverse of a denarius of C. Vibius Pansa Caetronianus dated to 48 B.C., Ceres, wearing a wheat crown, stands in a chariot drawn by two serpents; she holds the reins in her right hand and a torch in her left (fig. 5).[92] These symbols point to the myth of Ceres' search for her daughter Proserpina, which was an integral element of the Eleusinian cult. Bayet has further seen the appearance of these symbols with Ceres in coinage of the Late Republic as evidence that the Roman festival of the Cerialia had been contaminated by Eleusinian cult of Demeter during this period. It is difficult to be sure, however, whether these symbols refer to the Eleusinian or the Thesmophoric cult of the goddess, for as we have seen the latter was also associated with the myth of Ceres and Proserpina and had been imported to Rome during the Middle Republic. Arguing against the Eleusinian interpretation is the fact that Cicero, who is our first source in Latin literature to relate the myth of the two goddesses, does not mention Eleusis, but rather focuses on a Sicilian locus for the events in the story (Cic. *Verr.* 2.4.106–107, 111). Moreover, as we shall see, Cicero links the Sicilian cult associated with the myth specifically with women, while the Eleusinian cult was open to both men and women.[93] Whatever their cultic reference, the appearance of the new symbols in the coinage of the Late Republic indicates a further Hellenization of the Roman concept of the goddess. For the Romans, Ceres was becoming more and more equivalent to Demeter.

The Eleusinian cult may be related to Ceres' association with liminality in another way. According to Cicero (*Leg.* 2.35–36), believers in the cult benefited from their initiation into the Eleusinian cult of Ceres not only in this life, but also in the next. The goddess was thought to offer her believers a blessed afterlife, to which they would be admitted if they had undergone initiation into her cult in the current life. The belief suggests a link between the world of the living and the world of the dead that is presided over by Ceres, similar to the link suggested by the ritual of the opening of the mundus Cereris. The Eleusinian cult thus fits into the ancient Roman ideological construct surrounding Ceres, one reason why, I believe, the cult was accepted by the Romans. We shall return to the relationship between this cult and Ceres' association with liminality in chapter 3. There, we shall also explore two other examples of this association which are dated to the Late Republic: Ceres' involvement in prodigies and their expiation (e.g., Cic. *Verr.* 2.4.107), and her connection with the law on attempted tyranny and its application in the Senate's reaction to the murder of Tiberius Gracchus in 133 B.C. (Cic. *Verr.* 2.4.108).[94]

Ceres' associations with the plebs are also prominent in the Late Republic. The referent of this term, however, had changed by this period. After the Conflict of the Orders was settled at the end of the Early Republic, the term "plebeian" came to be applied to those of the lower social and economic orders, the citizens who made up the "urban mob" of Rome, and for whose support those of the ruling class competed in their struggles for political power. Le Bonniec has suggested that the Late Republican coin types representing Ceres appealed to the sympathies of the plebs and garnered their support for the issuing authorities.[95] We have seen that these coin types may be interpreted in other ways as well, but nonetheless I believe that Le Bonniec's hypothesis helps to explain certain coin types in their political context.

For example, a denarius issued in 46 B.C. honoring Julius Caesar bears on its obverse the head of Ceres and the legends COS. TERT. (*consul tertium*, "consul for the third time") and DICT. ITER. (*dictator iterum*, "dictator for the second time" (fig. 6a); on the reverse are the priestly emblems of the augurate and pontificate (*culullus*, *aspergillum*, lituus, and jug) and the legends AUGUR, PONT. MAX. (pontifex maximus) and either D (*donatium*, "donative") or M (*munus*, "gift") (fig. 6b).[96] The legends indicate that the coin was struck on behalf of Julius Caesar, who held the offices specified in 46 B.C. The reference to a donative or gift indicates that the coin was a special issue given out free in honor of a public celebration. The occasion was probably Caesar's victory over the remnants of the party of the Pompeians at Thapsus in Africa on April 6, 46 B.C. Ceres then may appear on this coin as the protectress of the plebs, with whose support Caesar had founded his dictatorship. If the coin was indeed issued soon after the Battle of Thapsus, then it could have been timed to coincide with the ludi Ceriales and the Cerialia, held on April 12–19, a festival highly significant to the plebs. Caesar would then have been honoring Ceres as the goddess of the plebs, whom he intended to flatter with the issue. As we shall see in chapter 4, a variety of other coin types from the Late Republic may also be interpreted as political appeals for plebeian support.[97] The connection between Ceres and the plebs is also suggested by the fragment from Lucilius (200 Marx) mentioned above, which states "Nourishing Ceres is failing, and the plebs does not have bread" (deficit alma Ceres, nec plebs pane potitur).

Finally, Ceres' association with women is also evident in the Late Republic.

In the works of Cicero, several passages link the goddess with women.[98] In the Verrine orations, for example, the orator cites the myth of Ceres and her daughter Proserpina, which we have seen was connected with the Greek cults of Ceres, including the Graeca sacra Cereris, a cult limited to women.[99] Indeed, Cicero specifically notes that in the cults of the goddess at Catena and Enna in Sicily, only women were allowed to enter the shrine, to approach the statue of the goddess, and to perform the rituals of the cult.[100] At Rome itself, Cicero notes in another oration (*Balb.* 55), the rituals of Ceres (sacra Cereris) were performed by priestesses, that is, female officiants. Finally, in a philosophical treatise on the ideal state (*Leg.* 2.21, 34–37), Cicero provides that among the rituals to be permitted to women in this state would be the mysteries of Ceres (initia Cereris), provided that they were conducted in broad daylight so as to safeguard the reputation of the women who participated in them. The passage suggests that, like the rites of the Bona Dea, the mysteries of Ceres were open only to women. The conduct of these rites was designed to reinforce cultural norms for the behavior of upper-class women in Rome. Cicero indicates the nature of the women who officiated at such rituals when he says that they were "older women respected for their noble birth and character" (*Verr.* 2.4.99) and that they conducted the rituals "with the greatest chastity of maidens and women" (*Verr.* 2.4.102). He thus connects the rituals of Ceres with the female virtue of chastity, an association we shall explore further in chapter 5.[101]

1.6 *The Augustan Period*

The Late Republic ends with the accession to power of the princeps Augustus, whose reign (27 B.C.–A.D. 14) marks the transition from Republican Rome to Rome of the Empire. In the Augustan period, all the associations of Ceres we have already examined continue: her connections with fertility, liminality, the plebs, and women. The association with agricultural fertility is especially prominent in this period. In literary sources, Ceres is connected with the earth and the fields; with farming, farmers, and those who dwell in the country; with crops, especially grain; and with bread and food in general.[102] She is given a variety of epithets by Augustan authors which signal this association: *fecunda*, "fecund"; *fertilis*, "fertile"; *flava*, "golden" (referring to the color of grain); *frugifera*, "bearer of crops"; *genetrix frugum*, "progenitress of crops"; *potens frugum*, "powerful in crops"; *rubicunda*, "ruddy" (referring to the color of grain).[103] In Augustan literature, moreover, the metonymic use of Ceres' name to mean "grain" or "bread" is common.[104] The literary identification of Ceres with grain, I believe, explains certain artistic representations of the goddess dated to this period that show her rising up out of the earth or emerging from vegetation. For example, on an Augustan architectural terracotta relief the bust of Ceres is shown emerging from the earth, holding poppies and stalks of wheat in her hands, and bearing snakes wrapped around her arms (fig. 7).[105] The goddess is implicitly identified here with the grain that grows out of the earth.[106] In other visual representations of the Augustan Age, Ceres appears with the corona spicea or holding stalks of wheat, again signaling a connection with agricultural fertility.[107] Her associations with human fertility in this period are signaled by literary references to her role in wedding ceremonies and by the dedication of an altar to her as Ceres Mater, Ceres the Mother.[108]

Her connections with weddings may also be related to her liminal role as the divinity who presides over this rite of passage for the individual. Ceres' association with liminality is also evoked in Augustan literature by references to her connection with funerary rites, the mundus, prodigies, the law on attempted tyranny, and the Eleusinian Mysteries.[109] The sources for the latter suggest that in the Augustan period the Eleusinian and Thesmophoric cults of the goddess were conflated. As I have suggested above, the Thesmophoric cult may be connected with the Sicilian setting for the myth of Ceres and Proserpina, while the Eleusinian cult should point to the site of Eleusis itself. In literary sources from this period for the myth, Eleusis is mentioned for the first time. In Ovid's relating of the story in the *Metamorphoses*, Ceres visits Eleusis to give grain to the Attic prince Triptolemus after she has recovered her daughter (*Met.* 5.642–647). The visit to Eleusis thus takes place outside the main narrative of the myth. In the later version in the *Fasti*, the visit to Eleusis (*Fast.* 4.502–560) is made part of Ceres' wanderings in search of her daughter. The conflation of the two settings, I believe, reflects a conflation of the two cults, as Ceres becomes ever more completely the same as Demeter: Ceres Eleusina, as Vergil calls her (*G.* 1.163). A terracotta relief from the Augustan period also indicates the assimilation of Ceres to Eleusinian Demeter (fig. 8).[110] The relief shows the goddess holding a torch and stalks of wheat and standing in front of a *kiste*, around which a snake is curled. The *kiste* is a special symbol of the Eleusinian Mysteries, for it was in this sacred chest that the sacra, or sacred emblems of the cult, were carried in procession from Eleusis to Athens and back again during the festival of the Greater Mysteries.[111] The importance of the Eleusinian cult of the goddess in this period is also signaled by Augustus' own initiation at Eleusis (Suet. *Aug.* 93).

Ceres' connection with the plebs is evident in several references in the histories of Rome by Livy and Dionysius of Halicarnassus, both published during the Augustan period, which we have previously examined.[112] Although these references are to earlier periods in Rome's history, they indicate that the idea of the plebeian associations of Ceres was still current at the time of their publication. Given the close connections of the Temple of Ceres, Liber, and Libera with the plebs, Augustus' restoration of this temple (Tac. *Ann.* 2.49) may have political significance, representing an appeal to plebeian sympathies. Le Bonniec has suggested also that the appearance of Ceres on coin types of this period may signal that the issuer wished to present Augustus as the heir to the claim to be defender of the common people.[113]

As we have seen, Livy mentions Ceres' historic connections with women when he relates the tale of the interruption of the festival of the goddess after the Battle of Cannae (Liv. 22.56.4; 34.6.15).[114] These associations also underlie Ovid's description of two festivals of the goddess, in which only women take part (Ov. *Am.* 3.10; *Met.* 10.431–436). These festivals emphasize the chastity of the women who participate in the rituals of the goddess. The story of the Rape and Return of Proserpina, which we have noted was closely tied to the cult of the goddess limited to women, is told in detail twice by Ovid.[115] As Simon has pointed out, although Ovid associates the myth as told in the *Fasti* with the festival of the Cerialia, it seems more suitable to the annual festival of the matronal cult in August.[116] This may again reflect conflation of the various cults of Ceres, as we have noted above for the Thesmophoric and Eleusinian cults. Further evidence for Ceres' association with women is provided by the epithets that Augustan authors provide her: *alma*, "nuturing, cherishing"; *genetrix*, "progenitress, mother"; and above all, *mater*, "mother;" as we have seen, also a cultic epithet of Ceres in this period.[117] These epithets link the goddess with motherhood, which, like chastity, was one of the primary virtues ascribed to Roman women, as we shall see in chapter 5. Chirassi-Colombo has argued that Ceres in fact became "specialized" to the female world in the Augustan period.[118] She connects this also with the increased emphasis on Ceres' role in agricultural fertility, which she terms the "rusticization" of the goddess. These two factors, she believes, caused Ceres to lose her political dimension under the Empire.

In my view, however, the political dimension of the goddess is not lost under the Empire, merely transformed. To be sure, as both Chirassi-Colombo and Le Bonniec have noted, Ceres' association with the political aspirations and class consciousness of the plebs during the Early and Middle Republics and the use of her image to appeal for the political support of the plebs during the Late Republic and Augustan period are little in evidence by the time of the Empire.[119] This phenomenon was inevitable, as the constitution of the Republic gave way to that of the Empire, and the old political rivalries gave way to new ones. However, Ceres acquires a new political meaning during the period of transition: she is attached to the figure of the princeps and to his family.[120] Through his association with the goddess, the princeps receives the benefits of her benevolence, which he then transmits to the people of the Empire as a whole. Ceres thus comes to serve as a symbol of "integration propaganda," in Ellul's terminology, for she serves to unite the people behind their ruler.[121] This propagandistic use of the goddess in the imperial period operates through the associations we have already uncovered for her during the Republic: her connections with fertility, liminality, women, and the plebs.

We first see Ceres' association with the princeps during the Augustan period. We have already noted Augustus' involvement in the various cults of Ceres during this period: his consecration of the altar of Ceres Mater and Ops Augusta, his initiation into the Eleusinian Mysteries, and his restoration of the Temple of Ceres, Liber, and Libera.[122] The first of these links the princeps to the fertility aspect of Ceres, the second to her liminal role, and the third to her association with the plebs. Augustus' tie to Ceres as a fertility goddess is signaled even more clearly by his adoption of the corona spicea. Augustus is represented wearing the crown in a marble portrait bust dated to the late first century B.C. or early first century A.D. (fig. 9)[123] The assumption of this iconographic emblem symbolizes the assimilation of Augustus to Ceres and signals his guarantee, through her benevolence, of the agricultural fertility of the Empire.

More commonly, however, we see Augustus' wife Livia identified with Ceres in Roman art. She appears on several gems and coin types of the Augustan period and later wearing the corona spicea or holding wheat stalks and poppies.[124] For example, in a cameo dated to the first half of the first century A.D., Livia appears wearing the crown of Ceres, here consisting of poppy capsules as well as the usual wheat stalks (fig. 10).[125] The assimilation of Livia to Ceres again signals a connection of the princeps to the goddess, this time expressed indirectly through a female member of his family. The mediation here of a female figure also suggests Ceres' associations with Roman women. We shall see this type of association continued under the Empire, as various women of the family of the princeps are associated with or assimilated to Ceres.[126]

In Augustan literature, the princeps is again tied to Ceres, through her association with the restoration of peace to the Roman world, a function of her liminal/normative aspect.[127] Two passages from Ovid's *Fasti* illustrate the point.[128] In Book 1, the poet addresses the princeps with the words:

> Thanks to the gods and to your house! Bound in chains, for a long time now wars lie under your foot. Let the cow come under the yoke, let the seed come under the ploughed earth. Peace nourishes Ceres, Ceres is the nursling of Peace.
>
> (Ov. *Fast.* 1.701–704)

Augustus has brought peace to the Empire, and so now the fertility that Ceres symbolizes can flourish. The goddess thus presides over the transition from the time of war and destruction in the Late Republic to the peaceful, fertile period under Augustus. In a passage from Book 4 (407–408), the links among Ceres, peace, and the princeps are made even more explicit:

> Ceres is joyful in Peace, and pray, you farmers, for perpetual peace and a peace-making leader.
>
> (Ov. *Fast.* 4.407–408)

The "peace-making leader" is Augustus, who brings with him peace and the blessings of the goddess of fertility. The associations of Augustus with Ceres and peace are visually represented in a famous relief from the Ara Pacis Augustae (fig. 11). In chapter 6, I present the argument for identifying the central figure of this relief as Ceres and discuss her role in the sculptural program of the altar as a whole.

1.7 The Early Roman Empire

In the period of the Early Roman Empire (early first century A.D.–late third century A.D.), the trends that we have noted in the Augustan principate continue. Ceres' associations with fertility and liminality are frequently expressed in literary, artistic, and epigraphic sources. Her connections with the plebs also appear, although much less commonly. Her association with women is much in evidence. All these associations of the goddess are tied to the ruling princeps, who thus serves as mediator between her and the people of the Empire.

In this period Ceres is most frequently associated with fertility, chiefly agricultural rather than human. The greatest number of literary references of the period are to this aspect of the goddess. She is connected with the fields and the countryside, with those who dwell in the country, with farming, with crops in general and grain in particular, and with food, especially bread.[129] Again, the metonymic use of her name to mean "grain" or "bread/food" is common.[130] Her literary epithets also indicate her fertile aspect: *flava*, "golden" (referring to the color of grain); *frugifera*, "bearer of crops"; and *larga*, "abundant." [131] She is represented in various artistic media (coins, gems, sculpture, wall painting, reliefs) with general symbols of fertility, including the poppy, pomegranate, pig, *kalathos* (fruit-basket), plate of fruits, and cornucopia. For example, a bronze statuette dated to the second–third century A.D. shows the standing goddess with a *kalathos*, diadem and veil on her head; she holds stalks of wheat in her left hand and in her right she may have originally held a torch (fig. 12).[132]

Other attributes of the goddess point to her specific connection with grain and the grain supply: the corona spicea (crown of wheat or wheat and poppies), stalks of wheat, the ant (an insect often connected with grain), the *modius* (used to measure grain), and a ship's stern (symbolizing grain importation by sea). Thus, on a wall painting from Pompeii dated to the Neronian period, the seated goddess holds a bundle of wheat stalks in her left hand and a torch in her right; her head is crowned with wheat and to her left appears a basket filled with wheat (fig. 13).[133] The goddess Annona, the personification of the grain supply, appears with Ceres on several imperial coin types.[134] For example, on the reverse of a coin of Nero dated to A.D. 64–66 a seated Ceres appears; she holds stalks of wheat and a torch; in front of her stands Annona with a cornucopia in her left hand; between them is a garlanded altar on which sits a *modius*; in the background at the right is the stern of a ship (fig. 14).[135] The legend reads ANNONA AUGUSTI CERES. The symbolism is clear: the ship represents the transport of grain by sea, the *modius* its distribution to the people, and Ceres and Annona are the presiding deities of that distribution.

The scenes on gems and reliefs that show Ceres presenting grain to Triptolemus also reflect the goddess's association with agricultural fertility.[136] For example, on a gem dated to the second century A.D., Ceres stands to the right, holding stalks of wheat and a platter of fruit; to the left appears Triptolemus, also holding wheat stalks and a patera (fig. 15).[137] The epigraphical evidence that we have for the cults of Ceres under the Empire also points to her connection with agricultural work. In Rome itself, the ancient Italic cult of the goddess continued at least to the period of Vespasian.[138] This inscription mentions the flamen Cerealis, who, as we saw above, celebrated the sacrum Cereale which was directly associated with various aspects of agriculture.[139] In North Africa, the cult of the Cereres flourished under the Empire, a cult that we have seen was especially tied to the cultivation of grain. Elsewhere, Ceres was honored by votive inscriptions of people connected with the grain trade.[140]

Ceres' connection with agricultural fertility was directly linked with the ruling princeps.[141] First, the goddess appears on the reverse of a large number of imperial coin types, while the portrait of the princeps is found on the obverse. The connection between the two is made even more obvious by those types which give the goddess the epithet "Augusta." For example, on a bronze dupondius of Claudius, dated to A.D. 41, the head of Claudius appears on the obverse (fig. 16a); on the reverse appears a seated Ceres, veiled and holding a torch in her left hand and two stalks of wheat in her right, with the legend CERES AUGUSTA (fig. 16b).[142] The epithet of the goddess here ties her directly to Claudius himself and suggests that he operates with her approval and support. Scholars have generally interpreted the association between Ceres and the princeps to refer to her role in agriculture, especially the cultivation and importation of grain.[143]

In certain examples this meaning is explicit. We have already examined the Neronian sestertius that shows Ceres and Annona with a *modius* and the stern of a ship (fig. 14). The obverse of the type is the head of Nero, suggesting that he oversees the grain distribution indicated by the reverse type with the help of the divinities depicted there. The propagandistic message is even more direct on a bronze sestertius from the brief reign of Vitellius, dated to between July and December of A.D. 69 (fig. 17).[144] The obverse shows the head of Vitellius; the reverse shows the princeps in military dress, standing with a spear in his right hand. Facing him is a seated Ceres, holding a patera and torch; between them appears an altar and in the background the stern of a ship. The whole scene deliberately recalls the Neronian sestertius, but on this reverse Vitellius himself is substituted for the figure of Annona, and thus is conceived of directly as lending his protection to the grain supply along with that of Ceres. Moreover, as we saw with Augustus, several of the emperors were portrayed wearing the corona spicea of Ceres, including Antoninus Pius, Marcus Aurelius, Lucius Verus, and Hadrian, again indicating their connection with the goddess.[145] All of these images link the ruling princeps with the agricultural fertility that Ceres both produced and personified.

The liminal aspect of the goddess is also in evidence during the Early Roman Empire. In this period Ceres is connected with four rites of passage: birth, divorce, death, and initiation. The first connection is implied by artistic representations that show her accompanied by the birth goddess Eileithyia at the birth of another divinity.[146] For example, on a cameo dated to the imperial period, Ceres stands to the right, holding stalks of grain in her right hand; in the center is the seated Proserpina, who hands over the newborn child Iacchus to the standing Eileithyia on the left (fig. 18).[147] These representations may also

ERRATA

MODELS: K7S8X (R3.0) / K7S8XE (R3.0) / K7VT4-4X (R3.0) /
K7VT4-8X (R3.0) / K7VM4

The FID adjustment table contained in the User Manuals within the Support CDs for K7S8X
(R3.0) / K7S8XE (R3.0), K7VT4-4X (R3.0) / K7VT4-8X (R3.0), and K7VM4 is incorrect (K7S8X (R3.
0) / K7S8XE (R3.0): page 14; K7VT4-4X (R3.0) / K7VT4-8X (R3.0): page 14; K7VM4: page 13). For
the correct adjustment, please refer to the updated table below. As to the function and the
detailed information about FID adjustment, please refer to the User Manuals within the
Support CDs of these five models (K7S8X (R3.0) / K7S8XE (R3.0): page 14; K7VT4-4X (R3.0) /
K7VT4-8X (R3.0): page 14; K7VM4: page 13).

Multiplier	FID0	FID1	FID2	FID3	FID4
5x	2-3	2-3	1-2	2-3	2-3
5.5x	1-2	2-3	1-2	2-3	2-3
6x	2-3	1-2	1-2	2-3	2-3
6.5x	1-2	1-2	1-2	2-3	2-3
7x	2-3	2-3	2-3	1-2	2-3
7.5x	1-2	2-3	2-3	1-2	2-3
8x	2-3	1-2	2-3	1-2	2-3
8.5x	1-2	1-2	2-3	1-2	2-3
9x	2-3	2-3	1-2	1-2	2-3
9.5x	1-2	2-3	1-2	1-2	2-3
10x	2-3	1-2	1-2	1-2	2-3
10.5x	1-2	1-2	1-2	1-2	2-3
11x	2-3	2-3	2-3	2-3	2-3
11.5x	1-2	2-3	2-3	2-3	2-3
12x	2-3	1-2	2-3	2-3	2-3
12.5x	1-2	1-2	2-3	2-3	2-3
13x	2-3	2-3	1-2	2-3	1-2
13.5x	1-2	2-3	1-2	2-3	1-2
14x	2-3	1-2	1-2	2-3	1-2
15x	2-3	2-3	2-3	1-2	1-2
16x	2-3	1-2	2-3	1-2	1-2
16.5x	1-2	1-2	2-3	1-2	1-2
17x	2-3	2-3	1-2	1-2	1-2
18x	1-2	2-3	1-2	1-2	1-2
19x	1-2	2-3	2-3	2-3	1-2
20x	1-2	1-2	2-3	2-3	1-2
21x	1-2	1-2	1-2	2-3	1-2
22x	1-2	2-3	2-3	1-2	1-2
23x	2-3	1-2	1-2	1-2	1-2
24x	1-2	1-2	1-2	1-2	1-2

NOTE: The correct FID adjustment table is also available from ASRock web site.
Please refer to http://www.asrock.com

ERRATA

MODEL: K7VM2 (R3.0)

The FID adjustment table contained in the User Manual within the Support CD for K7VM2 (R3.0) is incorrect (see page 13). For the correct adjustment, please refer to the updated table below. As to the function and the detailed information about FID adjustment, please refer to the User Manual within the Support CD of K7VM2 (R3.0) (see page 13).

For multiplier adjustable CPU whose default value is in the range of 5.0x to 12.5x, the maximum multiplier can be adjusted is 12.5x. Please refer to the following table.

Multiplier	FID0	FID1	FID2	FID3
5.0x	1-2	1-2	2-3	1-2
5.5x	2-3	1-2	2-3	1-2
6.0x	1-2	2-3	2-3	1-2
6.5x	2-3	2-3	2-3	1-2
7.0x	1-2	1-2	1-2	2-3
7.5x	2-3	1-2	1-2	2-3
8.0x	1-2	2-3	1-2	2-3
8.5x	2-3	2-3	1-2	2-3
9.0x	1-2	1-2	2-3	2-3
9.5x	2-3	1-2	2-3	2-3
10.0x	1-2	2-3	2-3	2-3
10.5x	2-3	2-3	2-3	2-3
11.0x	1-2	1-2	1-2	1-2
11.5x	2-3	1-2	1-2	1-2
12.0x	1-2	2-3	1-2	1-2
12.5x	2-3	2-3	1-2	1-2

Note: FID4 is at CPU default setting.

For multiplier adjustable CPU whose default value is in the range of 13.0x to 16.0x, the maximum multiplier can be adjusted is 24.0x. Please refer to the following table.

Multiplier	FID0	FID1	FID2	FID3
13.0x	1-2	1-2	2-3	1-2
13.5x	2-3	1-2	2-3	1-2
14.0x	1-2	2-3	2-3	1-2
15.0x	1-2	1-2	1-2	2-3
16.0x	1-2	2-3	1-2	2-3
16.5x	2-3	2-3	1-2	2-3
17.0x	1-2	1-2	2-3	2-3
18.0x	2-3	1-2	2-3	2-3
19.0x	2-3	1-2	1-2	1-2
20.0x	2-3	2-3	1-2	1-2
21.0x	2-3	2-3	2-3	1-2
22.0x	2-3	1-2	1-2	2-3
23.0x	1-2	2-3	2-3	2-3
24.0x	2-3	2-3	2-3	2-3

Note: FID4 is at CPU default setting.

NOTE: The correct FID adjustment table is also available from ASRock web site.
Please refer to http://www.asrock.com

point to Ceres' role in human fertility. The goddess' role in divorce is cited by Plutarch, an author of this period, in his life of the first Roman king, Romulus (*Vit. Rom.* 22.3). Ceres' connection with death is indicated by a number of sources of the imperial period. Aulus Gellius (*N.A.* 4.6.8) mentions her role in the funerary sacrifice of the porca praecidanea. Statius (*Theb.* 4.460, 5.156) also connects her with funerals, referring to the goddess as *inferna* and *profunda*, both epithets related to the underworld. Ceres is shown with other divinities of the underworld in certain artistic representations, such as the marble relief from the architrave of the Tomb of the Haterii, dated to the Trajanic period, where the goddess appears, holding wheat stalks, with the deities Hermes, Proserpina, and Pluto (fig. 19).[148]

Ceres' role in initiations is indicated by the numerous literary references and artistic representations related to the Eleusinian Mysteries. In this period there are frequent literary allusions to the Eleusinian Mysteries and to the story of the Rape and Return of Proserpina, which was associated with these rites.[149] In art, Ceres appears in the so-called Eleusinian triad, with Proserpina and Iacchus/Dionysus, in scenes that seem to reflect details of the initiation at Eleusis.[150] For example, on the famous Lovatelli urn, which portrays the initiation of Hercules in the Eleusinian Mysteries, Ceres appears to the left, seated on a *kiste* around which a snake is curled; she holds stalks of wheat in her right hand and a long torch in her left and wears a corona spicea on her head; Proserpina stands to the left and Iacchus in front (fig. 20).[151] Representations of the Rape of Proserpina, which again may refer to the Eleusinian Mysteries, are common in marble sarcophagi of the second–third centuries A.D.[152] In a sarcophagus dated to 220–230 A.D., Ceres appears to the left, holding two torches, and standing in a chariot drawn by two snakes; to the right are Hades and Proserpina, fleeing in a chariot drawn by four horses (fig. 21).[153] The torch, snake-drawn chariot, and *kiste*, which are attributes of Ceres in a variety of media during the imperial period, probably refer to her connection with the Eleusinian Mysteries. These rites are often tied to the ruling princeps. Literary sources inform us that Claudius tried to import the Eleusinian Mysteries to Rome (Suet. *Claud.* 25) and that Hadrian actually did so (Aur. Vict. *Caes.* 14). Hadrian, Antoninus Pius, Commodus, Lucius Verus, M. Aurelius, Septimius Severus, and Gallienus were all initiated, and many commemorated their initiation in coin types.[154]

Other sources of imperial date point to Ceres' liminal/normative aspect. In literary sources she is associated with the laws that established civilization, the law on attempted tyranny, and the expiation of prodigies.[155] This aspect of the goddess may also explain certain details of the plot to assassinate Nero, as detailed by Tacitus. The conspirators planned the assassination to take place at the Circus during the games that were the high point of the Cerialia (*Ann.* 15.53). The plot was to be carried out "for the benefit of the Republic" (pro re publica) (*Ann.* 15.52). The weapon to be used for the murder was a dagger taken from the Temple of Salus (Safety) at Ferentinum, which was consecrated (sacrum) for the task (*Ann.* 15.53). I believe that the conspirators intended to portray their act as the consecration to Ceres of a person who had set himself up as a tyrant in contravention of the law which protected the nascent Republic.[156] The plot was foiled, however, and Nero in celebration increased the number of horse races at the Cerialia, decreed that the month of April in which this festival took place was to have his name, and ordered that a new temple to Salus be erected (*Ann.* 15.74). He thus implicitly rejected the conspirators' claim that he was an attempted tyrant, took the protection of the goddess Ceres for his own, and reaffirmed the social order that she and the goddess Salus protected.

The connection between Ceres and the return to social order is also reflected in the imperial period by the assimilation to her of a number of personifications that symbolize this concept. Concordia (harmony), Fides Publica (public trust), Pax (peace), and Salus (safety) all appear in Roman imperial coin types with the attributes of Ceres, such as stalks of wheat, *modius*, poppies, and basket of fruits, and sometimes with the additional epithet Augusta, linking them to the ruling princeps.[157] On other types appear only the symbols of these divinities, signaling the strong linkage among them.[158] For example, on the reverse of a denarius from the period of the Civil Wars is portrayed the caduceus of Pax, the clasped hands of Concordia, and the wheat stalks and poppies of Ceres; above these symbols is the legend PAX (fig. 22).[159] With this type, the princeps reassured the populace that he would secure for them all the blessings that the return of social order would bring: Pax herself, an end to war; Concordia, harmony among the peoples of the Empire; and Ceres, fertility nourished by peace.

In contrast to her associations with fertility and liminality, Ceres' association with the plebs is not much in evidence under the Empire. Literary sources mention the Temple of Ceres, Liber, and Libera, which certainly was connected with the plebs during the Republic; we may surmise that this connection may have continued in the imperial period.[160] The festival of the Cerialia, with its ludi circenses and ludi scaenici, is also mentioned in sources of this period.[161] Aulus Gellius (*N.A.* 18.2.11) notes that the plebeians customarily issued banquet invitations to one another for this festival, thus indicating a continued link between Ceres and the plebs in the imperial period. Although Ceres is represented in imperial art with Dionysus/Liber, her cult companion in the plebeian triad, the reference is generally to the Eleusinian cult or to Ceres and Liber as gods of the countryside, rather than to the plebeian cult.[162] One coin type of Nerva links the princeps and the plebs and may also refer indirectly to Ceres. The laureate head of Nerva appears on the obverse of the coin (fig. 23a); the reverse shows a *modius* containing six stalks of wheat and a poppy with the legend PLEBEI URBANAE FRUMENTO CONSTITUTO, "with the grain having been established for the urban plebs" (fig. 23b).[163] The legend indicates the concern of the princeps for the grain supply of the urban plebs, while the symbols used suggest a connection with Ceres as grain goddess, and perhaps also as goddess of the plebs. The connection between the plebeians and Ceres is thus mediated through the person of the princeps. This example reflects the transformation of Ceres' political associations under the Empire that I have mentioned above. Instead of being associated directly with the political aspirations of the plebs, the goddess is connected with the princeps, and through him to the plebs.

Ceres' connection with women is much in evidence under the Empire, and it too is associated with the princeps. Both literary and epigraphical sources in-dicate the continued existence of the cult of Ceres practiced by women, the Graeca sacra Cereris.[164] Juvenal (6.50–51) links this cult specifically with the female virtue of chastity.[165] As we have seen, references to the Rape and Return of Proserpina are common in both literary and artistic sources of the imperial period, and this myth was connected to the Graeca sacra Cereris as well as to the Eleusinian Mysteries.[166] Representations of Ceres and Proserpina alone are also found in this period and may refer to the cult associated with women.[167] Thus, on a sardonyx cameo dated to the first century A.D., in the foreground appears the bust of Ceres, veiled and crowned with wheat; in the background is the bust of Proserpina with a diadem (fig. 24).[168]

Bieber has identified three statue types of the imperial period that are used to represent contemporary women in the guise of Ceres and her daughter: the Ceres type, the Large Herculaneum Woman (= Ceres), and the Small Herculaneum Woman (= Proserpina).[169] These types are directly associated with the goddesses in those examples that have stalks of wheat and poppies as attributes. The heads of these statues have portrait features and indicate the identification with Ceres or Proserpina of the women represented.[170] For ex-ample, a statue dated to A.D. 140–150 holds a torch in her right hand and a bundle of wheat stalks and poppies in her left; her features identify her as Faustina the Elder, wife of Antoninus Pius (fig. 25).[171] The Large and Small Herculaneum Woman types are also found on Roman imperial sarcophagi and funerary stelae, where the first represents the wife of the deceased and the latter, his daughter.[172] For example, in a relief from Athens dated to the late

Antonine period, the Large Herculaneum Woman type is used for the older woman to the left, and the Small Herculaneum Woman type for the younger woman to the right (fig. 26).[173] The identification with the two goddesses is variously interpreted. De Angeli and Bieber believe it signals that the women so represented were priestesses or at least worshippers of the goddess.[174] Wrede, however, suggests a more general interpretation: the two goddesses represent the ideal types of the mother and daughter, and so the women are identified with them in these two roles.[175]

These statue types along with representations in other media, such as gems and coins, are often used to portray female members of the family of the princeps: his wife, daughter, mother, or sister.[176] For example, in an aureus from the reign of Claudius, his mother, Antonia Minor, appears on the obverse, wearing the corona spicea of Ceres; the legend reads ANTONIA AUGUSTA (fig. 27).[177] We shall examine this practice in detail in chapter 5, and a catalogue of identifications of women of the imperial family with Ceres is presented in appendix 2. Here, it is sufficient to note that the identification of these women with Ceres associated them with her connections with fertility, both agricultural and human, and with female virtue, especially chastity and motherhood. These women became symbols of the prosperity and moral rectitude of the Empire, and through them the princeps himself was tied to these concepts.

1.8 *The Late Empire and Afterward*

In the period of the Late Roman Empire (late third–fourth centuries A.D.), Ceres slips into obscurity. Julia Domna, the wife of Septimius Severus (ruled A.D. 193–211), is the last member of the imperial family to be associated with Ceres in official coinage.[178] Ceres herself appears for the last time in Roman coinage during the reign of Claudius Gothicus (A.D. 268–270).[179] Her cult, to be sure, continued for some time. Her temple in Rome was still standing in the fourth century, and an inscription of the fifth century mentions a *mystes Cereris*.[180] The story of the Rape and Return of Proserpina also endured; Claudian made it the subject of an epic poem, *De Raptu Proserpinae*, in the late fourth century. The goddess is mentioned in other late literary sources, such as the commentary by Servius on Vergil, dated to the fourth century, which preserves much interesting information from earlier periods.[181] However, the changing circumstances of the Empire, particularly the conversion of the emperor to Christianity and its spread among the upper classes of Roman society in the fourth century, guaranteed the gradual disappearance of Ceres.

Nevertheless, the goddess was not completely obscured, even after the end of the Empire. Berger has done a study of how the various Christian saints took the place of Ceres as grain protectresses in the medieval period: Saints Radegund, Macrine, Walpurga, Milburga, and Brigid were all connected with grain.[182] The Virgin Mary, too, was connected with grain, particularly in the story of the Grain Miracle.[183] According to this story, during the Flight into Egypt, the Holy Family passed by a field that a farmer had just sown with grain. The Virgin told him that if soldiers should come and ask if he had seen a mother and child pass by, he should say that he had seen them when he had first sown the seed. As the Holy Family passed through the field, the grain miraculously sprouted, grew tall, and was ready to be harvested. When Herod's soldiers arrived soon thereafter, they asked the farmer if he had seen a mother and child go by. He replied that he had done so, when the seed was first sown in the field. They assumed that this had happened long ago, and so gave up the search. The scene is represented in medieval art, as in an illustration from the Grandes Heures de Rohan, dated to the first quarter of the fifteenth century, where the Virgin and Child watch over the scene of the farmer in the grain field confronted by the soldiers of Herod (fig. 28).[184] Mary here is associated with the miraculous growth of grain, and thereby assumes the role of the ancient grain goddess.

The story of the Grain Maiden of Milan also connects Mary with the grain goddess.[185] A medieval merchant had a vision of the Virgin Mary dressed in a robe sewn with stalks of wheat. The merchant was so grateful for this promise of prosperity that he commissioned a painting of the vision for the cathedral of Milan, where worshippers hung flower garlands to secure the fertility of the image for themselves. The story indicates that Ceres' associations with fertility were transferred to the Virgin Mary, as is also the case for other female divinities, such as Isis.

The connection between the Virgin Mary and Ceres is also signaled by the depiction of Mary in both the Ceres type and the Large Herculaneum Woman type.[186] Bieber mentions a miniature of the ninth century that shows the Virgin in the Ceres type, holding stalks of wheat in her hand.[187] The ancient Italic goddess Ceres, who was such a powerful symbol to the Romans throughout their history, thus lived on into the Christian era in a new form.

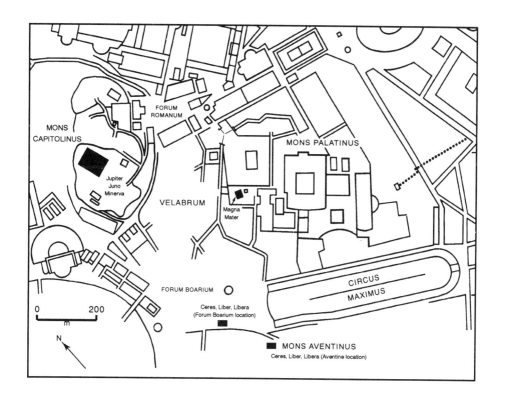

MONS
CAPITOLINUS

FORUM
ROMANUM

MONS PALATINUS

Jupiter
Juno
Minerva

VELABRUM

Magna
Mater

FORUM BOARIUM

CIRCUS
MAXIMUS

0   200
        m

N

Ceres, Liber, Libera
(Forum Boarium location)

◼ MONS AVENTINUS
Ceres, Liber, Libera (Aventine location)

1 · Map of the center of Rome. After
Talbert (1985) 121.

2 · Ceres of Ariccia. Terracotta bust. Rome, Museo Nazionale, inv. 112375. After Borda (1951) pl. 98a. (Courtesy of Washington University, St. Louis)

3 · Head of Ceres with the corona spicea. Denarius of Q. Cornificius (obverse). London, British Museum. *RRC* 509.5; *BMCRR* Africa 27. (Courtesy Trustees of the British Museum)

4a

4b

5

4 · Denarius of M. Fannius and L. Critonius: (a) head of Ceres with the corona
spicea (obverse); (b) seated aediles with
wheat stalk (reverse). London, British Museum. *RRC* 351.1; *BMCRR* Rome 2463.
(Courtesy Trustees of the British Museum)

5 · Ceres with torches riding in chariot.
Denarius of C. Vibius Pansa (reverse).
London, British Museum. *RRC* 449.3a;
BMCRR Rome 3973. (Courtesy Trustees
of the British Museum)

6a   6b

7

6   Denarius in honor of Julius Caesar:
(a) head of Ceres with the corona spicea
(obverse); (b) priestly emblems (reverse).
London, British Museum. *RRC* 467.1a;
BMCRR Africa 21. (Courtesy Trustees of
the British Museum)

7 · Ceres rising from the earth. Terracotta
relief. Rome, Museo Nazionale Romano
delle Terme, inv. 121313. (Courtesy Ali-
nari/Art Resource, NY, S0072060/AL
28364)

8 · Eleusinian Ceres. Terracotta relief. Copenhagen, Glyptotek Ny Carlsberg, inv. 1480. (Courtesy The Ny Carlsberg Glyptotek, Copenhagen)

9 · Augustus with corona spicea. Marble
bust. Rome, Vatican Museums, inv. 715.
(Courtesy Direzione Generale Musei Vaticani, neg. XXXV.6.49)

10 · Livia/Ceres with wheat and poppy
crown. Onyx cameo. Florence, Museo
Archeologico inv. 26. (Courtesy Soprintendenza Archeologica per la Toscana, Fi-
renze. Gabinetto Fotografico. Fot. 13417/n.
Inv. N. 1h5h9)

11 · Ceres and the nymphs. Relief panel
from the southeast corner of the Ara Pacis
Augustae. (Courtesy Deutsches Archäologisches Institut, Rome, neg. 86.1449)

12 · Standing Ceres with *kalathos* and
wheat stalks. Bronze statuette. Paris,
Bibliothèque Nationale. (Courtesy Bibliothèque Nationale de France, © cliché
Bibliothèque Nationale de France, Paris)

13 · Seated Ceres with corona spicea, wheat stalks, and basket of wheat. Wall painting from Pompeii. Naples, Museo Nazionale, inv. 9457. (Courtesy Museo Nazionale, Naples, Fotografia della Soprintendenza Archeologica della Province di Napoli e Caserta—Napoli, neg. 76140)

14

15

16a

16b

14 · Ceres and Annona. Sestertius of Nero (reverse). *RIC* 1²:161.136; *BMCRE* Nero 127. London, British Museum. (Courtesy Trustees of the British Museum)

15 · Ceres and Triptolemus. Sardonyx. London, British Museum, inv. 1306. (Courtesy Trustees of the British Museum)

16 · Dupondius of Claudius: (a) head of Claudius (obverse); (b) Ceres Augusta seated with torch and wheat stalks (reverse). London, British Museum. *RIC* 1²: 127.94; *BMCRE* Claudius 137. (Courtesy Trustees of the British Museum)

17 · Ceres and Vitellius. Sestertius of Vitellius (reverse). London, British Museum. *RIC* 1²: 275.131, 277.166; *BMCRE* Vitellius 47. (Courtesy Trustees of the British Museum)

18 · Ceres and Proserpina in a birth scene with Iacchus and Eileithyia. Sardonyx cameo. Paris, Bibliothèque Nationale. (Courtesy Bibliothèque Nationale de France, © cliché Bibliothèque Nationale de France, Paris)

19 · Ceres with divinities of the underworld. Marble relief from the Tomb of
the Haterii. Rome, Vatican Museums inv.
10.018. (Courtesy Direzione Generale
Musei Vaticani, neg. XXXI.11.94)

20 · Proserpina, Ceres, and Iacchus. Terra-
cotta relief from the Lovatelli urn. Rome,
Museo Nazionale delle Terme. (Courtesy
Alinari/Art Resource, NY, S0061030/
AN2023)

21 · Ceres pursuing Hades and Proserpina. Marble sarcophagus relief. Aachen, Münster G3. (Courtesy Aachen Cathedral. © Domkapitel Aachen. Photo by Ann Münchow, Aachen)

22 · Wheat stalks and poppies of Ceres, clasped hands of Concordia, caduceus of Pax. Aureus of Gialba (reverse). London, British Museum. *RIC* 1²:206.34; *BMCRE* Civil Wars (Spain) 6. (Courtesy Trustees of the British Museum)

23a

23b

23 · Sestertius of Nerva: (a) head of Nerva (obverse); (b) *modius* with stalks of wheat and poppy (reverse). London, British Museum. *RIC* 2:229.89, 230.103; *BMCRE* Nerva 115. (Courtesy Trustees of the British Museum)

24 · Busts of Ceres and Proserpina. Sardonyx cameo. Paris, Bibliothèque Nationale. (Courtesy Bibliothèque Nationale de France, © cliché Bibliothèque Nationale de France, Paris)

25 · Faustina the Elder in the Ceres type.
Marble statue. Paris, Musée du Louvre,
inv. MA 1139. (Courtesy Musée du Louvre, © Photo R.M.N.)

26 · Large and Small Herculaneum
Woman types. Relief inserted into the
small Metropolis at Athens. (Courtesy
Deutsches Archäologisches Museum, Athens. Neg. nr. Ath. Var 1271)

27 · Head of Antonia Minor with the corona spicea. Aureus of Claudius (obverse).
London, British Museum. *BMCRE* Claudius 109. (Courtesy Trustees of the British
Museum)

28 · The Grain Miracle, Flight into Egypt.
Illustration from the Hours of the Rohan
Master. Paris, Bibliothèque Nationale.
(Courtesy Bibliothèque Nationale de
France, © cliché Bibliothèque Nationale
de France, Paris)

29 · Ceres rising out of floral scroll. Architectural terracotta acquired at Rome. Copenhagen, Glyptotek Ny Carlsberg, inv. 1716. (Courtesy The Ny Carlsberg Glyptotek, Copenhagen)

30

31

32

30 · Ceres, Antoninus Pius, and Victoria. Medallion of Antoninus Pius. Naples, Museo Nazionale, inv. *Fiorelli* 15994. (Courtesy Museo Nazionale, Naples, Fotografia della Soprintendenza Archeologica della Provincedi Napoli e Caserta—Napoli, neg. 118115)

31 · Ceres Augusta with wheat stalk, poppy, and caduceus. *As* of Galba (reverse). London, British Museum. *RIC* 1²: 246.292; *BMCRE* Galba 140. (Courtesy Trustees of the British Museum)

32 · Pax with wheat stalks, poppy, and caduceus. Aureus of the Civil Wars (reverse). London, British Museum. *RIC* 1²: 212.144; *BMCRE* Civil Wars 58. (Courtesy Trustees of the British Museum)

33a

33b

34a

34b

33 · Denarius of L. Cassius Caeicianus: (a) head of Ceres with corona spicea (obverse); (b) yoke of oxen (reverse). London, British Museum. *RRC* 321.1; *BMCRR* Rome 1725. (Courtesy Trustees of the British Museum)

34 · Denarius of C. Memmius: (a) head of Quirinus (obverse); (b) seated Ceres with torch, wheat stalks, and snake (reverse). London, British Museum. *RRC* 427.2; *BMCRR* Rome 3940. (Courtesy Trustees of the British Museum)

35a   35b

36a   36b

35 · Denarius of C. Vibius Pansa Caetronianus: (a) head of Liber (obverse);
(b) Ceres walking with torches in either
hand (reverse). London, British Museum.
RRC 449.2; *BMCRR* Rome 3976. (Courtesy Trustees of the British Museum)

36 · Aureus of Q. Caepio Brutus and
L. Sestius: (a) bust of Ceres with corona
spicea (obverse); (b) priestly emblems (reverse). London, British Museum. *RRC*
502.2; *BMCRR* East 41. (Courtesy Trustees of the British Museum)

37a

37b

38a

38b

37 · Quinarius of Q. Caepio Brutus:
(a) bust of Ceres with corona spicea (obverse); (b) Victory with palm branch and wreath (reverse). London, British Museum. *RRC* 502.3; *BMCRR* East 46. (Courtesy Trustees of the British Museum)

38 · Aureus of L. Mussidius Longus:
(a) head of Ceres with corona spicea;
(b) wreath of wheat stalks. London, British Museum. *RRC* 494.44a; *BMCRR* Rome 4233. (Courtesy Trustees of the British Museum)

39a

39b

40a

40b

39 · Denarius of P. Clodius: (a) head of
Octavian (obverse); (b) Ceres with wheat
stalk and sceptre (reverse). London, British
Museum. *RRC* 494.19; *BMCRR* Rome
4282. (Courtesy Trustees of the British
Museum)

40 · Aureus of Augustus: (a) head of Augustus (obverse); (b) Ceres with sceptre
and wheat stalks. London, British Museum. *RIC* 1^2:56.219; *BMCRE* Augustus
544. (Courtesy Trustees of the British
Museum)

41a

41b

42a

42b

41 · Aureus of Claudius: (a) head of Divus
Augustus (obverse); (b) Ceres/Livia with
sceptre and wheat stalks (reverse). London, British Museum. *RIC* 1²:128.101;
BMCRE Claudius 224. (Courtesy Trustees
of the British Museum)

42 · Aureus of Antoninus Pius: (a) bust
of Faustina the Elder (obverse); (b) Ceres
standing with torch and sceptre (reverse).
London, British Museum. *RIC* 3:70.356;
BMCRE Antoninus Pius 395. (Courtesy
Trustees of the British Museum)

43

44

43 · Agrippina the Younger with corona spicea. Aureus of Claudius (reverse). London, British Museum. *RIC* 1²:126.80; *BMCRE* Claudius 72. (Courtesy Trustees of the British Museum)

44 · Messalina holding wheat stalks. Local coin of Alexandria (reverse). London, British Museum. *BMCRE Alexandria* 73. (Courtesy Trustees of the British Museum)

45 · Livilla/Ceres with poppy and wheat crown and two children. Agate cameo. Berlin, Staatliche Museen, inv. FG11096. (Photo Jutta Tietz-Glagow. Courtesy Antikensammlung, Staatliche Museen zu Berlin, Stiftung Preussischer Kulturbesitz)

46 · Head of central figure with corona
spicea. Detail of relief panel in figure 11.
(Courtesy Deutsches Archäologisches Institut, Rome, neg. 86.1455)

47 · Flowers and wheat stalks. Detail of relief panel in figure 11. (Courtesy Deutsches Archäologisches Institut, Rome, neg. 86.1458)

48 · Fruits in the lap of the central figure. Detail of relief panel in figure 11. (Courtesy Deutsches Archäologisches Institut, Rome, neg. 86.1454, detail)

49 · Demeter with pomegranate. Statuette from the Demeter Malophoros sanctuary at Selinus. Palermo, Museo Regionale, inv. 395. (Courtesy Museo Regionale, Palermo, neg. 6307)

50 · Demeter with child in lap. Statuette from the Demeter Malophoros sanctuary at Selinus. After Gàbrici (1927) pl. 59.8. (Courtesy Accademia Nazionale dei Lincei)

51 · Goddess nursing two children. Lime-
stone statue from Megara Hyblaea. Syracuse, Museo Nazionale. After Langlotz-
Hirmer (1965) pl. 17. (Courtesy Hirmer
Verlag)

52 · Nereid on *ketos*. Detail from the carved mantle of the cult statue of Demeter from Lycosura. Athens, National Museum, inv. 1737. (Courtesy TAP Service, Ministry of Culture, Hellenic Republic)

53 · The nymph Kamarina on a swan. Didrachma from Kamarina. London, British Museum. *BMC Sicily* 36–37.16–18. (Courtesy Trustees of the British Museum)

54 · Demeter and Persephone with the
nymphs and Pan. Votive relief from the
Ilissos. Berlin, Staatliche Museen, inv. Sk
709. (Courtesy Antikensammlung, Staatliche Museen zu Berlin, Stiftung Preussischer Kulturbesitz, neg. Sk 3259)

55 · Head of Livia. Detail of figure from
the south processional frieze of the Ara
Pacis Augustae. (Courtesy Deutsches
Archäologisches Institut, Rome, neg.
86.1511)

Chapter 2

FERTILITY

2.1 *Introduction*

The concept of fertility is both essential and original to Ceres. It was the basis for Roman attitudes to the goddess, was present in her cult from its origins, and remained an important aspect of her nature until the end of paganism. The Romans believed that Ceres' essential nature was connected with fertility and that her basic function was to cause things to grow, to produce fruit. As the Augustan poet Ovid says of Ceres, "This one provides the cause for fruits" (haec praebet causam frugibus) (*Fast.* 1.674). In this chapter, I shall survey Ceres' association with fertility, both agricultural and human, and examine the use of this association in the political symbolism of the Empire.

The ancient etymologies for Ceres' name illustrate the Roman belief that fertility was essential to her. The most ancient and widely attested etymology for "Ceres" associates the name with *gerere*, "to bear, bring forth, produce." The Augustan scholar Varro quotes the earlier poet Ennius as saying, "She, because she bears (*gerit*) fruits, (is called) Ceres" (quae quod gerit fruges, Ceres) (*Ling.* 5.64).[1] Varro goes on to explain: "Because for the ancient writers what is now G (was written) C" (antiquis enim quod nunc G C). An alternate etymology is given by Servius, a commentator on the Augustan poet Vergil from the Late Empire. He connects the name with *creare*, "to produce, create": "Ceres, called so from *creando* (creating)" (Ceres a creando dicta) (Serv. on Verg. *G.* 1.7).[2] Clearly, to the Romans "Ceres" meant "the force which produces or creates," hence, fertility.

The accepted modern etymology of the term proves that the ancient association of the name "Ceres" with fertility is sound. Modern scholars derive the name from the Indo-European stem *ker-*, "to grow, cause to grow, nourish," which they recognize also in the Latin words *creare* and *crescere*, though not in Ennius' proposed *gerere*, which Varro approved.[3] The stem also appears in the names of other ancient Italic deities, like the Latin deity Cerus and the various Samnite deities designated Kerriai in the Tablet of Agnone.[4] These divinities, too, seem linked with fertility. The lexicographer Festus interprets Cerus as meaning "the Creator" (Fest., s.v. *Cerus manus*, 109 Lindsay). Festus dates to the late second century A.D., but his source is a lexicographer of the Augustan period, Verrius Flaccus. The divinities named in the Tablet of Agnone, dated to the third century B.C., include Ammaì Kerríiaí (Nutrix Cerealis, Nurse of Ceres) and the Fluusaí Kerríiaí (Flora Cerealis, She Who Flowers of Ceres). The first of these is associated with nursing children and hence is related to the growth of human beings; the second is connected to flowering plants and thus to the growth of vegetation. As we shall see, both these aspects of fertility are also linked to the Roman goddess Ceres.

If Ceres' name marks her association with fertility, the antiquity of the name indicates the historical primacy of this association. As we have seen, the goddess was already known by this name in the regal period (traditionally 753–509 B.C.).[5] Her festival, the Cerialia, is listed in Rome's oldest calendar.[6] The existence of a flamen Cerialis also points to an early date for the name of the goddess, since this priesthood is among the six minor flaminates which tradition ascribed to King Numa.[7] Direct evidence for the antiquity of the name is provided by a Faliscan inscription naming Ceres and belonging to the late seventh century B.C.[8] Ceres' name and therefore her cultic function were associated with fertility from earliest times. This connection was still foremost in the minds of writers like Ennius, Varro, and Servius, all of whom lived long after the cult of Ceres had been established at Rome.

Ceres was linked especially to certain aspects of fertility. First, the goddess was connected with the growth of vegetation and its cultivation for human consumption, which I call "agricultural fertility." From this comes Ceres' special connection with the growth and cultivation of grain. In addition, the goddess was connected with human fertility and the product of that fertility, children.

2.2 *Agricultural Fertility*

2.2.1 GENERAL

In her capacity as a deity of agricultural fertility, Ceres had strong affinities with Tellus (or Terra Mater), the goddess of the earth. Tellus was also a fertility goddess who oversaw reproduction and growth of both animals and crops: "Tellus, fertile in crops and herds" (fertilis frugum pecorisque Tellus)

FERTILITY

(Hor. *Carm. Saec.* 29–30). Together the two goddessess were the "mothers of crops" (*frugum matres*) (Ov. *Fast.* 1.671). Ovid explains:

> Ceres and Terra serve a common function: the one provides the cause for crops, the other their place.
>
> (Ov. *Fast.* 1.673–674)

The ancient rites in which the two goddesses were jointly worshipped indicate their close ties to agricultural fertility. These rites include the Feriae Sementivae and the Sacrum Cereale.

The Feriae Sementivae was a moveable feast celebrated in January. The name of the festival, according to Varro (*Ling.* 6.26), was derived from *semente*, "sowing," because the festival was held at the time of sowing the seed.[9] The purpose of this festival was to assure the growth of crops:

> The Feriae Sementivae had been established, thinking that on account of this [festival] the crops were able to grow.
>
> (Fest., s.v. *Sementivae*, 337 Müller)

In the *Fasti*, a poetical calendar of the Roman year, Ovid describes the rituals of the Feriae Sementivae (*Fast.* 1.659–674). The offerings at this festival were dedicated to both Tellus and Ceres and consisted of spelt and a pregnant sow. The pregnant victim is a common offering to female fertility divinities and was apparently intended, on the principle of sympathetic magic, to fertilize and multiply the seeds committed to the earth.[10] The central prayer of this festival, dedicated to Tellus and Ceres, provides further evidence for their close association with the growth and protection of the crops.

> Partners of labor, through whom the ancient days were corrected and the oaken acorn was conquered by a more useful food, satisfy the eager farmers with boundless crops, so that they may receive the rewards worthy of their cultivation. Give perpetual growth to the tender seeds and do not let the new stalks be chafed by the cold snows. When we sow, make the sky clear with fair winds; when the seed lies hidden, sprinkle it with water from heaven. Take care lest the birds, grievous to the tilled land, lay waste the fields of Ceres with their injurious flock.
>
> (Ov. *Fast.* 1.675–684)

The rite of the sacrum Cereale also ties Tellus and Ceres to agriculture and agrarian fertility.[11] The little we know of this rite comes from a passage in Servius (on Verg. *G.* 1.21) reporting information from Fabius Pictor, a historian of the late third century B.C.: a flamen conducted the rite (probably the flamen *Cerealis*) and dedicated it both to Ceres and to Tellus. In his prayers, the flamen also invoked twelve minor deities: Vervactor (the Plower), Reparator (the Preparer of the Earth), Inporcitor (the Maker of Pigs), Insitor (the Planter of Seeds), Obarator (the Tracer of the First Plowing), Occator (the Harrower), Serritor (the Digger), Subruncinator (the Weeder), Messor (the Reaper), Convector (the Carrier of the Grain), Conditor (the Storer of the Grain), and Promitor (the Provider of the Grain).[12] Ceres and Tellus oversee the agricultural work that is specified in the names of these twelve lesser gods.

Other agricultural rites focus on Ceres alone, although these rites may also have been dedicated originally to her cult companion Tellus.[13] We know from Cato's treatise on farming, dated to c. 160 B.C., that a *porca praecidanea*, literally "a pig that is killed before," was offered to Ceres before the harvest:[14]

> Before you harvest, it is necessary for the porca praecidanea to be made in this manner. To Ceres, a female pig as a porca praecidanea, before you store these crops: spelt, wheat, barley, beans, rapeseed.
>
> (Cato *Agr.* 134)

Again Ceres appears as an agricultural deity whose help must be sought, and whose power propitiated, before ordinary agricultural work can take place. Ceres' other agricultural rites include ritual cleansing of the fields, or lustration, a rural harvest festival with ritual singing and dance, and an offering of the first fruits from the harvest.[15]

In addition, her principal festival, the Cerialia, was part of a cycle of agrarian festivals that occupied the last half of the month of April in the Roman calendar.[16] These festivals, which were dedicated to assuring agricultural and animal fertility, include the Fordicidia on the 15th of April, the Cerialia on the 19th, the Parilia on the 21st, the Vinalia on the 23rd, the Robigalia on the 25th, and the ludi Florales on the 28th. In the *Fasti* (4.679–682; 703–712), Ovid describes the rites of the Cerialia. He mentions a horse race in the Circus Maximus and then describes a peculiar rite that may also have taken place there. In this rite burning torches were tied to the tails of foxes, which were then allowed to run loose.

Ovid follows his description of the rituals of the festival with an interesting aetiological myth. A boy on a farm in Carseoli once trapped a fox that had been stealing chickens. He wrapped it in straw and hay and set it afire. The fox escaped, however, and ran through the fields, burning the crops. Therefore a fox is burned at the Cerialia to punish the species in the same way in which it destroyed the crops. The exact significance of the ritual burning of the foxes has been disputed. Frazer, Wissowa, and Reinach believed that the ritual is negative in character, intended to keep harm away from the crops.[17] The fox represents vermin, blight, or excessive heat from the sun. Bayet, Le Bonniec, and Köves-Zulauf argued that it is a positive rite, intended to encourage the growth of the crops.[18] The fox with its red color and burning tail symbolizes fire and signals that warmth and vitality are being attracted to the crops. The latter interpretation seems the more likely to me. In any case the connection of this rite with agriculture is clear.

Ceres is thus closely linked with the general concept of agricultural fertility. Literary sources from the Late Republic to the Early Roman Empire connect her with crops, the work that produces them, and those who do that work.[19] By extension she is also connected to the fields, the countryside, and the earth, where the crops are planted and grow.[20] The goddess is given epithets in literature that signal her association with fertility, especially as related to agriculture: *fecunda*, "fecund"; *fertilis*, "fertile"; *frugifera*, "she who brings the crops"; *genetrix frugum*, "progenitress of crops"; *larga*, "abundant"; and *potens frugum*, "powerful in crops."[21] In Roman art Ceres is represented as a plant growing out of the earth in a number of architectural reliefs that have been dated to the Augustan period, or the first century A.D..[22] For example, in an Augustan relief the bust of the goddess emerges from the earth; she holds bunches of poppies and stalks of wheat in her upraised hands; around her arms are wrapped two snakes (fig. 7).[23] In another relief, probably from a Roman villa near Albano, the head of the goddess, crowned with a *kalathos*, or fruit-basket, emerges from a network of intertwining vines and flowers (fig. 29).[24] Both of these images point to Ceres' connection with the earth and the growth of vegetation, identifying her as a divinity of agricultural fertility.[25]

2.2.2 GRAIN

Ceres is also associated with a particular product of agricultural fertility: grain. Numerous literary references connect her with various types of grain.[26] I have mentioned previously the Faliscan inscription, dated to c. 600 B.C., that states "Let Ceres give spelt."[27] As we have seen, Cato connects the goddess with spelt (*far*), wheat (*triticum*), and barley (*hordeum*) (*Agr.* 134). The limited mythology of the goddess in Latin literature also associates her with grain. Ceres is said to have first discovered grain and to have taught its cultivation to mankind, as in the following passage from Ovid:[28]

> Ceres was the first to change the acorn for a more useful food when humankind had been called to better sustenance. She compelled the bulls to offer their necks to the yoke: then for the first time did the exposed earth see the sun.
>
> (Ov. *Fast.* 4.401–405)

Elsewhere Ovid links this story to one familiar from Greek sources, in which Ceres gives the seeds of grain to the Attic hero Triptolemus, who then distributes them to mankind:[29]

> Then the fertile goddess attached the twin snakes to the chariot and restrained their mouths with the reins and she was carried through the air between the sky and the earth and she sent her light chariot to the Tritonian city. She gave seeds to Triptolemus and ordered him to sprinkle some on the untilled ground and some on earth cultivated again after a long time.
>
> (Ov. *Met.* 5.642–647)

The scene of Ceres' gift of grain to Triptolemus is represented in art of the Empire.[30] In a gemstone dated to the second-third centuries A.D., Ceres stands to the right and Triptolemus to the left; both hold stalks of wheat (fig. 15).[31]

Indeed, the most common attribute of the goddess in Roman art is the wheat stalk.[32] In Roman imperial art she is frequently shown holding stalks of wheat in her hand or with wheat represented by her side.[33] Another frequent attribute of Ceres is the corona spicea, or crown made of wheat stalks.[34] She wears this crown in a variety of artistic media of both Republican and Imperial date.[35] In Latin literature also Ceres is frequently described with the corona spicea, as in the following lines of the Augustan poet Tibullus: "Golden Ceres, for you may there be a crown of wheat stalks from our fields" (flava Ceres, tibi sit nostro de rure corona // spicea) (Tib. 1.1.15–16).[36] The epithet "golden" (*flava*) suggests the color of ripened wheat. Other Latin authors use this epithet, and another, "ruddy" (*rubicunda*), to point to Ceres' association with grain.[37]

Ceres is viewed at times as a personification of grain, and her name is used by metonymy for grain. The Latin glossarians define "Ceres" as "crops, grain, or the goddess of grain" (fruges, frumentum, vel dea frumenti.)[38] The use of the divine name for grain is common in the Latin poets.[39] For example, Vergil writes:

> Then, exhausted from circumstances, they get ready the grain [Ceres] spoiled by the water and the tools of Ceres, and they prepare to parch the recovered grain with flames and to crush it with a rock.
>
> (Verg. *Aen.* 1.177–179)

The term "Ceres" may also used for the primary product of grain, bread, as Festus explicitly notes:[40]

> Naevius says, "The cook produces Neptune, Venus, [and] Ceres." By "Ceres" he means bread, by "Neptune" fish, by "Venus" vegetables.
>
> (Fest., s.v. *cocum*, 58 Müller)

Her name even comes to stand for food in general, as for example when Ovid says:

> Not the need of Ceres [= food] nor of sleep was able to draw him away from the place.
>
> (Ov. *Met.*, 3.437–438

The association of Ceres and grain is also seen in her cult. The *praemetium*, literally a "measuring out beforehand" (*prae* + *metior*), was an offering of the first fruits of the grain harvest, made exclusively to Ceres:

> They were accustomed to sacrifice to Ceres the *praemetium* of grain stalks that they had harvested first.
>
> (Fest., s.v. *sacrima*, 319 Müller)

Its purpose was to propitiate the goddess before the harvest.[41] Festus defines the term as follows: "*Praemetium* [is] that which was measured out beforehand for the sake of tasting it beforehand" (praemetium quod praelibationis causa ante praemetitur) (s.v. *praemetium*, 235 Müller). That is, the offering of the first fruits was made before the harvest, so that the goddess could taste of the harvest first. This interpretation is supported by Pliny the Elder, who states:

> They did not even taste the new fruits or wine before the priests had made the offering of first fruits [*primitias*].
>
> (Pliny *HN* 18.2.8)

The *praemetium* was apparently very ancient and belonged to the native Italic cult of Ceres.[42] Ovid remarks on the antiquity of this offering to Ceres:

> The ancients, nevertheless, were accustomed to sow spelt, reap spelt, and give the cut spelt as first fruits to Ceres.
>
> (Ov. *Fast.* 2.519–520)

We know that in the historical period the offering was made at the Temple of Ceres, probably by the flamen Cerialis.[43]

Ceres also presides over the distribution of grain to the urban poor, the frumentationes, and over the grain supply, the annona. Varro, quoted by Nonius, reports:[44]

> Those who lacked wealth and had fled to the asylum of Ceres were given bread.
>
> (Varr. in Non. 63, Lindsay)

The phrase "asylum of Ceres" probably refers to the Temple of Ceres as a place of refuge for the plebs.[45] The passage therefore indicates that a free distribution of bread (or perhaps the grain with which to make bread) took place at the Temple of Ceres. This in turn suggests that the temple may have been a location for the frumentationes. A fragment from Lucilius also indicates a connection between Ceres and the distribution of bread: "Nourishing Ceres is failing, and the plebs do not have bread" (deficit alma Ceres, nec plebs pane potitur) (200 Marx). Inscriptions from the Empire indicate that various officials of the grain trade considered Ceres as their protective divinity.[46] Coins also attest to Ceres' connection with the grain supply, as we shall see in the section below on the goddess' role as a fertility symbol under the Empire.

It has also been suggested that the Temple of Ceres served as the headquarters for the administration of the grain supply.[47] The temple served from early times as the headquarters for the principal officers of the plebeians, the aediles plebis. The original function of these officials seems to have been to guard the temple itself, but they soon took on other functions, among which was the cura annonae.[48] It would therefore seem likely that the annona too was administered from the Temple of Ceres. Archaeological evidence has been adduced to support this theory. The Church of Santa Maria in Cosmedin in the Forum Boarium contains ruins of a podium that has been identified as belonging to the Temple of Ceres, Liber, and Libera (fig. 1). Adjacent to this podium in the fourth century A.D. was built a portico, the remains of which are also preserved in the modern church. Near the portico have been found a number of inscriptions giving the names of the praefecti annonae, the administrators of the grain supply under the Empire.[49] On the basis of these inscriptions, the portico has been identified as the *statio annonae*. Rickman has suggested that the portico was simply a late addition to the Temple of Ceres, and that the administrative offices of the praefectus annonae were located originally within the temple itself.[50] The Temple of Ceres would have served therefore from an early period as headquarters for the grain supply.

There are numerous difficulties with this theory, however. The identification of the podium with the Temple of Ceres remains highly problematic. As we shall see, other evidence suggests that this temple was located on the Aventine Hill, not in the Forum Boarium.[51] Even if we accept a location in the Forum Boarium for the temple, the adjacent portico was built much later than this building, and its function may have nothing to do with the earlier temple. Even the identification of this portico as the *statio annonae* is in doubt. The inscriptions that mention the praefecti annonae, although found near the portico, may in fact have nothing to do with this building. Perhaps they were simply set up in this area or were brought in from elsewhere and reused here. In any case, although the archaeological evidence used to support the identification of the

Temple of Ceres as the *statio annonae* remains problematic, the link to the grain supply of the officers of this temple, the aediles of the plebs, is certain, as is Ceres' own connection with grain.

It is interesting to note that the connection of Ceres and grain is paralleled by a similar relation between Liber, her male cult companion, and wine. For example, in his philosophical treatise on the nature of the gods, Cicero states, "Crops [grain] we call Ceres; wine, however, Liber" (fruges Cererem appellamus, vinum autem Liberum) (*Nat. D.* 2.60). The divine power of Liber was considered to be incarnate in the vine, as that of Ceres in grain, as Saint Augustine states:

> Let the god be [called] Jupiter in the heavens . . . Liber in the vines, and Ceres in the grain.
>
> (Aug. *Civ. D.* 4.11)

A special offering of the first fruits of the wine harvest was made to Liber; this offering was called the *sacrima* and parallels the offering of the *praemetium* of grain to Ceres. Festus draws attention to this similarity:

> They used to call *sacrima* the new wine, which they were accustomed to sacrifice to Liber in order to preserve the vineyards and the vessels and the wine itself; just as they were accustomed to sacrifice the *praemetium* of grain ears, which they had harvested first, to Ceres.
>
> (Fest., s.v. *sacrima*, 319 Müller)

It may be that the specialization of the agrarian function of Ceres to grain was reinforced with the establishment of the triadic cult of Ceres, Liber, and Libera. At this time Ceres was to some extent assimilated to the Greek goddess Demeter, and her cult companion Liber to Dionysus.[52] These Greek divinities were already closely associated with grain and wine, respectively, and transference of these Greek associations would have further defined the provenience of their Roman counterparts. It must be noted, however, that Ceres' connection with grain predates the establishment of the triadic cult in the Early Republic. The Faliscan inscription that links Ceres with *far* (spelt) dates to c. 600 B.C. Ceres' connection with Dionysus/Liber may have strengthened her ties with grain, but it did not create those ties.

2.3 *Human Fertility*

In addition to her connection with agricultural fertility and grain, Ceres is also connected with human fertility and its product, children. The transference of powers of agrarian fertility to the human sphere is neither unprecedented nor unnatural, for a goddess of birth and growth in plants has obvious relevance for human life and might be expected to extend her benevolence into other aspects of birth and growth among the human community. Indeed, comparative evidence from anthropology shows that female divinities frequently took this dual role. As Preston points out in his study of mother goddesses, the function of these divinities in both agricultural and human fertility remains active in folk religion in many areas of the world.[53] For example, in South Asia female divinities link the fecundity of the crops with the human womb, and European farmers still place "Corn Mother" dolls in the fields to assure fertility.[54] The association of Ceres with human fertility is revealed in two areas: her role as a mother deity and her connection with weddings.

2.3.1 MOTHERHOOD

Ceres appears as a mother goddess in both Roman cult and Latin literature. She was worshipped with the epithet "Mother" in the altar of Ops Augusta and Ceres Mater, erected in Rome in A.D. 7.[55] Latin poets of the Empire also use the term "mater" to refer to the goddess.[56] Other epithets of Ceres connected with human fertility are *alma*, "nourishing," and *genetrix*, "progenitress, she that has borne (children)."[57] The Late Republican poet Lucretius presents an image of the goddess as a mother deity: "But [if] she is swollen and big-breasted, she is Ceres [suckled] by Iacchus" (at tumida et mammosa Ceres est ipsa ab Iaccho) (*RN* 4.1168).[58]

Lucretius' image of the goddess may have been influenced by the portrayal of Ceres' counterpart, Demeter, by Greek writers and artists.[59] Demeter is given a variety of epithets that point to her role as the nurturer of young children: *kourotrophos* and *paidotrophos*, "child-nourishing"; *trophos*, "nourishing"; *polytrophos*, "many-nourishing"; and *paidophile*, "loving of children." [60] In mythology, Demeter is the mother not only of Persephone, but also of Artemis, Iacchus, Plutus, and Bromius, and the foster mother of Demophöon or Triptolemus.[61] The image of Demeter with her daughter in her lap is common in Eleusinian iconography, as is her depiction with a young male child, generally identified as Dionysus, Iacchus, or Plutus.[62] The *kourotrophos* type of a woman holding a child found at sanctuaries of Demeter in Greece, Asia Minor, Magna Graecia, and Sicily may be a representation of Demeter Kourotrophos.[63] This evidence indicates that Ceres' connections with human fertility and motherhood was certainly strengthened by her identification with Demeter.

Nevertheless these connections may well predate Ceres' assimilation to the

Greek goddess. Evidence from the ancient Italic divinities related to Ceres also suggests a connection with human fertility. In the Tablet of Agnone appear the Daughter of Ceres (Futreì Kerríiaí = Filia Cerealis), Nurse of Ceres (Ammaì Kerríiaí = Nutrix Cerealis) and the Divine Progenitress (Deívaí Genetaí = Diva Genetrix).[64] The Pelignan divinity Anaceta Ceria or Angitia Cerealis has been identified with the Roman goddess Angerona, who was associated with childbirth.[65] These divinities are all closely tied to Ceres, and their association with motherhood suggests that Ceres also in origin may have been connected with human fertility.

The image of Ceres as a mother goddess is seen in Roman art. The goddess is shown frequently with Proserpina, often with Ceres in desperate pursuit as Hades carries away her daughter.[66] In a sarcophagus dated to the early third century A.D., Ceres appears to the left, holding two torches and standing in a chariot drawn by two snakes; to the right is Hades, holding Proserpina, and fleeing in a chariot drawn by four horses (fig. 21).[67] The image points to Ceres' long search for her daughter after she had been taken by Hades. In Ovid's portrayal of the Rape of Proserpina in the *Metamorphoses*, he links this search with Ceres' role as a mother goddess: "O progenitress of the maiden sought throughout the world and progenitress of crops" (o toto quaesitae virginis orbe // et frugum genetrix) (Ov. *Met.* 5.489–490).

Ceres may also be represented with a male youth, either Triptolemus or Iacchus.[68] Thus, she appears on the gem cited earlier, with Triptolemus to the left (fig. 15),[69] and on the Lovatelli urn with Iacchus standing in front of her (fig. 20).[70] These images are related to the representations of Demeter mentioned above, which show the goddess as the mother/foster mother of a male child. So, too, in Ovid's description of Ceres' meeting with Triptolemus in the *Fasti*, she nurtures the child like a mother:

> Nurturing Ceres abstains and gives to you, boy, poppies with warm milk to drink, the causes of sleep. It was in the midst of the night and the silences of placid sleep: she took Triptolemus in her lap and stroked him three times with her hand. . . .
>
> (Ov. *Fast.* 4.547–551)

Ceres' connection with motherhood and human fertility may also explain her appearance in a number of scenes depicting the birth of a divinity.[71] For example, on a cameo of imperial date Ceres stands to the right with wheat stalks in her hand; in the center is the seated Proserpina who hands over the newborn child Iacchus to the standing Eileithyia on the left (fig. 18).[72] Eileithyia is the goddess of childbirth, and her presence here with Ceres suggests the connection of the latter with human fertility.

Finally, as I shall argue in chapter 6, in a relief of the Ara Pacis Augustae Ceres appears, holding in her lap two children who may be identified on one level with Liber and Libera (fig. 11). Cicero calls these cult companions of the goddess the children of Ceres (*Nat. D.* 2.62). According to Saint Augustine, Liber was connected with male fertility and Libera with female: "Let him preside in the name of Liber over the seed of men, and in the name of Libera over that of women" (*Civ. D.* 4.11). If this interpretation is correct, then the two children in the Ara Pacis relief may be meant to point to human fertility and to suggest Ceres' connections with this concept. The image of the goddess on the Ara Pacis, then, combines her roles in both agricultural and human fertility, for she wears the corona spicea, has grain and poppies growing beside her, and holds both fruits and the two children in her lap.

2.3.2 WEDDINGS

Ceres' role in weddings may also be related to her connection with human fertility.[73] As Pomeroy points out, the chief objective of Roman marriage was procreation, so the wedding ceremony may well be associated with the encouragement of fertility.[74] Ceres' association with weddings emerges from two sources. First, Ceres is closely associated with the goddess Tellus (the Earth) in ancient Italic cult, and Tellus is generally recognized as the tutelary divinity of the Roman wedding ceremony.[75] Secondly, literary evidence points to a direct connection of Ceres in weddings and suggests a link between that connection and human fertility.

The links between Ceres and Tellus in ancient Italic cult are well established.[76] They were worshipped together in the Feriae Sementivae and in a festival on December 13, connected with the end of the sowing season.[77] The principal festivals of these two divinities, the Fordicidia of Tellus on April 15 and the Cerialia on April 19, are separated by four days, the customary interval for related festivals. In Latin literature, as well, the two are closely linked, as in the following lines from the Augustan poet Horace:[78]

> Let Tellus, fertile in fruits and herds, present Ceres with a crown of wheat stalks; let the healthy waters and breezes of Jupiter nourish the offspring.
>
> (Hor. *Carm. Saec.* 29–32)

Indeed, at times Ceres and Tellus are identified as one and the same.[79] Cicero cites this identification in his philosophical treatise on the nature of the gods:

> Indeed if she is Ceres from bearing [*gerendo*]—for so you said—the earth itself is a goddess (and so she is considered; for what is she but another Tellus?).
>
> (Cic. *Nat. D.* 3.52)

Given this close association between the two divinities, Tellus' role in the Roman wedding ceremony is especially revealing. Servius reports the cultic acts that connected Tellus and weddings:

> Some . . . hold that Tellus is present at weddings; for she is also invoked in the auspices of weddings: for maidens, either when they first go to the house of their husband, or when they are already established there, make sacrifice to her under diverse names or rite.
>
> (Serv. on Verg. *Aen.* 4.166)

The biographer Plutarch mentions a "law of Numa" that specifies that a widow desiring to remarry before the expiration of her mourning period should sacrifice a pregnant cow (*Vit. Num.* 12.3). Since a pregnant cow was the proper sacrifice at the Fordicidia, the principal festival of Tellus, it seems reasonable to infer that the sacrifice for the wedding of a widow was dedicated to this same goddess.[80] Tellus is thus clearly connected with the Roman wedding ceremony, and we might well expect Ceres to have a similar association.

The literary evidence supports this hypothesis. Vergil gives explicit testimony for Ceres' role in weddings in Book 4 of the *Aeneid*, when Dido and Anna sacrifice to win the gods' favor for the queen's proposed marriage to Aeneas:

> In the beginning they approach the shrines and they seek peace through the altars; they sacrifice sheep chosen according to custom to Ceres who bears the laws and to Phoebus and to Father Lyaeus, and before all to Juno in whose care are the chains of marriage.
>
> (Verg. *Aen.* 4.56–59)

Servius, commenting on this passage, notes:

> Some say that Ceres favors weddings, because she was the first to wed Jove, and she is in charge of the founding of cities, as Calvus teaches: "She taught the sacred laws and she joined the loving bodies in weddings and established the great cities."
>
> (Serv. on Verg. *Aen.* 4.58)

Calvus is a poet of the Late Republic. In the fragment quoted here by Servius, he implies that Ceres established the laws for weddings as well as for other aspects of civilized life. We will return to Ceres' connection with the establishment of laws in chapter 3. Here, we note the role of the goddess in promoting marriage rituals. This role suggests that Ceres was also connected with weddings in Roman belief.[81]

Other evidence connects Ceres with specific aspects of the Roman wedding ceremony. Festus notes: "They were accustomed to carry the torch in weddings in honor of Ceres" (s.v. *facem*, 87 Müller).[82] In addition, the bridegroom threw nuts to the children accompanying the bride to her new home.[83] This rite also may have been conducted at the Cerialia and therefore may have been dedicated to Ceres in the wedding ritual.[84] Finally, Varro mentions an ancient rite in which the bride and bridegroom sacrificed a pig at the beginning of the marriage. The context of this passage seems especially significant:

> The Greek name for the pig is ὗς, once called θῦς from the verb θύειν, that is "to sacrifice"; for it seems that at the beginning of making sacrifices they first took the victim from the swine family. There are traces of this in these facts: that pigs are sacrificed at the initial rites of Ceres; that at the rites that initiate peace, when a treaty is made, a pig is killed; and that at the beginning of the marriage rites of ancient kings and eminent personages in Etruria, the bride and groom, in the ceremonies which united them, first sacrificed a pig. The ancient Latins, too, as well as the Greeks living in Italy, seem to have had the same custom. . . .
>
> (Varr. *Rust.* 2.4.9–10 Loeb trans.)

Although the deity to whom the wedding sacrifice of a pig was made is not specified, Ceres seems likely, since she customarily received the sacrifice of a pig in rituals dedicated to her.[85] Varro also mentions Ceres earlier in this passage when he mentions the pig sacrificed at the mysteries of Ceres, and he may well have had her in mind here.[86]

The evidence thus suggests that Ceres had a role in the wedding ceremony. This role may be linked to the encouragement of human fertility. The wedding torch that Festus notes was "carried in honor of Ceres" seems to have been a fertility symbol.[87] Pliny notes that the most auspicious wood for wedding torches came from the *spina alba*, the may tree, which bore many fruits and hence symbolized fertility (*HN* 30.75). The ritual casting of nuts is also a fertility ritual, similar to the throwing of rice at weddings today.[88] Moreover, the continuation of the passage from Varro quoted above suggests a direct connection between the pig sacrificed at a wedding ceremony and the fertility of women. The passage reads:

> For also our women, and especially nurses, call that part which in maidens is the mark of their womanhood *porcus*, as Greek women call it *choeron*, signifying that it (that is, the sacrifice of the pig) is a worthy mark of weddings.
>
> (Varr. *Rust.* 2.4.10)

In this passage Varro explains why pigs are sacrificed at weddings. The pig symbolizes the untouched sexual organs of the bride, and its sacrifice represents the ritual consummation of the marriage.[89] The pig is therefore a human fertility symbol and the goddess to whom it is dedicated watches over that fertility. If Ceres is indeed the recipient of the pig at weddings, as I have suggested above, then Varro's account proves her function in human fertility.

2.4 *Ceres and Fertility in Roman Imperial Political Symbolism*

Ceres' connection with fertility was used in the political symbolism of the Empire in various ways. First, she was identified with female members of the imperial household: the wives, sisters, daughters, and mothers of the ruling princeps. For example, Livia, the wife of Augustus, appears wearing the corona spicea of Ceres in a cameo dated to the first half of the first century A.D. (fig. 10).[90] Faustina the Elder, the wife of Antoninus Pius, holds the torch, wheat stalks, and poppies of Ceres in a statue dated to A.D. 140–150 (fig. 25).[91] Antonia Minor, the mother of Claudius, appears with the corona spicea in a coin of Claudian date (fig. 27).[92] These representations signal that the women were being identified with Ceres in her role as goddess of agricultural and human fertility, especially motherhood. These women were the mothers of the heirs to the imperial throne and came also to be considered the "mothers" of the people of the Empire just as the princeps was their "father," the pater patriae.[93] We shall explore this practice in more detail in chapter 5.

Secondly, Ceres' function in agricultural fertility was associated with the princeps himself. Several of the Roman emperors were represented wearing the corona spicea, as Augustus is shown in a marble portrait bust dated to the late first century B.C. or early first century A.D. (fig. 9).[94] The assumption of this attribute of the goddess by the princeps symbolizes his assimilation to Ceres, and signals his guarantee of the agricultural fertility of the Empire with the blessing of the goddess. Ceres is frequently shown on the reverse of imperial coin types with the image of the ruling princeps on the obverse. For example, a bronze dupondius dated to A.D. 41 has the head of Claudius on the obverse (fig. 16a); on the reverse appears Ceres, seated and veiled, holding a torch in her left hand and two stalks of wheat in her right, with the legend CERES AUGUSTA (fig. 16b).[95] The epithet of the goddess, Augusta, ties her directly to the princeps and suggests that he operates with her approval and support. Such coin types are generally interpreted as signaling the interest of the princeps in the grain supply.[96]

In certain examples this meaning becomes more explicit. On the reverse of a sestertius of Nero, dated to A.D. 64–66 appears a seated Ceres, holding a torch and wheat stalks. In front of her stands Annona, the personified grain supply, with a cornucopia in her left hand; between them is a garlanded altar on which sits a grain measure, or *modius*. In the background at the right is the stern of a ship. The legend reads ANNONA AUGUSTI CERES (fig. 14).[97] The symbolism is clear: the ship represents the transport of grain by sea, the *modius* its distribution to the people, and Ceres and Annona are the presiding deities of that distribution. Its propagandistic significance is given by its association with the obverse type, a portrait of Nero. The message is that Nero guarantees the grain supply to the people through his association with the divinities who protect that supply. This type is copied or adapted for the coinage of Domitian, Nerva, and Septimius Severus.[98]

The propagandistic message is even more direct on another coin, a sestertius of Vitellius dated to between July and December of A.D. 69 (fig. 17).[99] The reverse shows Vitellius, depicted in military dress, standing with a spear in his right hand; facing him is a seated Ceres, holding a patera and torch; between them appears an altar and in the background the prow of a ship. The legend reads ANNONA AUG(usti). The whole scene deliberately recalls the Neronian sestertius already discussed. However, the princeps himself is substituted for the figure of Annona, and thus is conceived of directly as lending his protection to the grain supply along with that of Ceres. The greater explicitness of this image may reflect a greater need for reassurance for the populace as a whole during the turbulent period of the Year of the Four Emperors.

Finally, the reverse of a medallion of Antoninus Pius dated to A.D. 153–154 shows the emperor seated in the center. Behind him appears Victoria, crowning him with a wreath; in front is the goddess Ceres, handing him a sheaf of wheat (fig. 30).[100] The propagandistic message signals that the emperor, through victory in battle, brings agricultural fertility to the Empire. The image links Ceres, peace, and princeps in a combination that recalls the following lines from the *Fasti* of Ovid:

> Thanks to the gods and to your house! Bound in chains, for a long time now wars lie under your foot. Let the cow come under the yoke, let the seed come under the plowed earth. Peace nourishes Ceres, Ceres is the nursling of Peace.
>
> (Ov. *Fast.* 1.701–704)

We shall explore again the connections among Ceres, peace, and the princeps in the final chapter of this book on Ceres in the Ara Pacis Augustae, the Altar of Augustan Peace.

2.5 Conclusion

The goddess Ceres is connected with the concept of fertilty in a number of different ways. First, her name associates her with the general concept of fertility. In Roman cult, art, and literature, the goddess is connected frequently with agricultural fertility—the generation and growth of plants, particularly those cultivated for human consumption. The goddess is also tied to a particular product of agricultural fertility, the growth and harvesting of grain. Her name indeed becomes synonymous with grain itself; "Ceres" is the equivalent by metonymy for *frumentum*. Ceres is also associated with the concept of human fertility, through her connections with motherhood and weddings. All of these various fertility associations of the goddess are exploited in the political symbolism of the Empire to tie the goddess and her blessings to the person of the princeps.

Chapter 3

LIMINALITY

3.1 *Introduction*

The concept of liminality is closely associated with Ceres. The term "liminality" is derived from the Latin *limen*, "threshold," and concerns crossing a threshold or boundary from one state of being to another, e.g., an individual changing from being single to being married or a society changing from a state of peace to one of war. Such changes disturb social equilibrium, creating a crisis that affects both individuals in a society and the society as a whole. In many societies religious rituals are enacted to represent the crisis mimetically and to allay fears surrounding the transition to the new state. The anthropologist Van Gennep, in his classic study *The Rites of Passage*, identified three consecutive stages in such rituals: separation, transition, and incorporation.[1] The stage of separation involves the removal from everyday life of those who are to participate in the ritual. In the stage of transition, actions are carried out to establish a new set of social interactions. The final stage, that of incorporation, reintegrates those who have participated in the ritual into a new or rejuvenated social order. As we shall see, Ceres frequently has a role in this final stage of incorporation.

Chapple and Coon further refined Van Gennep's scheme by identifying two types of crises that necessitate the performance of liminal rituals to restore social equilibrium.[2] If the crisis is derived from the actions of a single individual, the ritual is called a "rite of passage," the term coined by Van Gennep. If the crisis, however, involves a disturbance of all the members of a group, then the ritual is termed a "rite of intensification." In the rite of passage, the focus is on integrating the individual into society after a change in his or her social status; the individual emerges from the ritual transformed and able to take up a new role in society. In the rite of intensification, the focus is on fortifying the members of a group to deal with a change in social activity or social structure; the members of the group emerge from the ritual strengthened in their ties to one another, and the society as a whole is rejuvenated. Rites of intensification are often periodic, repeated regularly each time a particular occurrence disturbs the equilibrium of a society—such as a change of season, which requires a shift in agricultural work. Rites of passage are generally nonperiodic and sometimes unique, performed only once in the lifetime of an individual—such as puberty ceremonies. Nevertheless, rites of passage too may be periodic, repeated each time an individual marries, for example, and rites of intensification may be nonperiodic, connected with a specific event, such as the establishment of a peace treaty.

The goddess Ceres is associated with both rites of passage and rites of intensification. For the individual, the goddess is connected with the rites surrounding death, birth, marriage, divorce, and initiation. For Roman society as a whole, Ceres is associated with the periodic rituals of agriculture and of the opening of the mundus, the passage between the world of the living and the world of the dead. The goddess also has ties to nonperiodic rituals surrounding the expiation of prodigies, the establishment of peace after war, the violation of the sacrosanctitas of the tribunes of the plebs, and the punishment for those who attempted to overthrow the Republic. In the rites of intensification, Ceres often operates as a normative force in restoring the social order after a challenge to its equilibrium has been made. This aspect of the goddess I call her "liminal/normative" role.

Ceres' liminal/normative role may go all the way back to her ancient Italic origins. In the Tablet of Agnone, two divinities named among those connected with Ceres (Kerrí) are Interstita (Anterstataí) and Legifera Intera (Líganakdíkeí Entraí).[3] The first is perhaps to be interpreted as "She Who Stands Between," the second as "She Who Bears the Laws Between." Caldarelli has argued that the first divinity was originally an attribute of Ceres that gives evidence of her normative aspect, her role of "tracing the just frontiers," and that this individual attribute later became a divinity in her own right, a companion of Ceres.[4] He provides comparative linguistic and anthropological evidence from Sanskrit sources for interpreting Anterstataí as referring to a divinity who serves to protect a boundary from an outside threat.

The second divinity, Legifera Intera, is certainly connected with an attribute of Ceres. Vergil refers to the goddess with this attribute (*Aen.* 4.58). Servius explains this passage of Vergil:

[Vergil says] "To Ceres Legifera," for she herself is said to have invented laws: for also her rites are called *thesmophoria*, that is, "bearing laws." But this is devised for the following reason—because before grain was discovered by Ceres, men used to wander here and there without law. This savagery was broken off when the use of grains was discovered, after laws were born from the division of the fields.

(Serv. on Verg. *Aen.* 4.58)

Servius' explanation connects Ceres' role in bringing laws to humankind with her discovery of grain and the invention of agriculture.[5] This accomplishment of the goddess is related to liminality in two ways: first, through the literal creation of a boundary in the "division of fields" (*divisio agrorum*) by which agriculture became possible, and secondly through the transition from savagery to civilization that the change from hunting and gathering to agriculture brought about.[6] Later in his explanation of this passage, Servius adds:

Some say that Ceres favors weddings, because she was the first to wed Jove, and she is in charge of the founding of cities, as Calvus teaches: "She taught the sacred laws and she joined the loving bodies in weddings and established the great cities": for thus also the city-state is enclosed by the furrow of the plow.

(Serv. on Verg. *Aen.* 4.58)

This explanation connects Ceres' role in establishing laws and the rites of marriage with her role in establishing cities. Her stablization of boundaries is not only practical, but also judicial, for she creates a norm of social behavior through the establishment of the laws that human society is to follow. If the Legifera Intera of the Agnone tablet is indeed to be interpreted as pointing to this liminal/normative aspect of Ceres, as I propose, then this aspect of the goddess derives from her native Italic origins.

In this chapter, we shall examine the connection of Ceres with both rites of passage and rites of intensification. We shall then explore the exploitation of her liminal/normative role in the political events at the beginning of the Late Republic connected with the death of Tiberius Gracchus.

3.2 Rites of Passage

3.2.1 DEATH

Ceres' connection with the rite of passage surrounding death are revealed in two rituals of Roman funerary custom: the sacrifice of the porca praesentanea and of the porca praecidanea. The lexicographer Festus explains the first:

The pig is called *praesentanea*, as Veranius says, that is sacrificed to Ceres for the sake of cleansing the family, because a certain part of this sacrifice is made in the presence of the dead person whose funerary rites are being held.

(Fest., s.v. praesentanea porca, 250 Müller)

A cleansing sacrifice was needed because the family was considered to be polluted by the death of a member.[7] Like the sacrifice of the porca praecidanea, the heir of the deceased probably performed this ritual as a condition of receiving his inheritance.[8] The ritual therefore is connected with the incorporation phase of this rite of passage. The sacrifice of the porca praesentanea was mandatory on the occasion of a death.[9] It was offered to Ceres, and at least a portion of it had to be performed in the presence of the corpse.[10]

Varro describes the related sacrifice of the porca praecidanea:

Praecidaneum is "that which must be cut down before." Varro, [in] On the Life of the Roman People, book 3, (says), "In case [one] is not buried, the porca praecidanea must be offered by the heir to Tellus and Ceres; otherwise the family is not pure."

(Varr. in Non. Marc., 163 Müller)

In contrast to that of the porca praesentanea, this sacrifice is conditional, not mandatory.[11] The heir offers this sacrifice only if the corpse has not been properly buried. The consequence of neglecting the proper expiatory ritual is to leave the family "impure," i.e., uncleansed of death's pollution, which the sacrifice of the porca praecidanea is meant to remedy. Varro notes that the sacrifice is made to both Ceres and Tellus. All other sources mentioning the deity to whom the porca praecidanea is dedicated name Ceres alone.[12] The weight of the ancient evidence makes the mention of Tellus by Varro untenable, and suggests that Ceres alone originally received the sacrifice.[13] Aulus Gellius reports that the sacrifice was conducted at a particular time of year, namely, before the harvest:

A pig was indeed called *praecidanea*, which it was the custom to sacrifice to Ceres for the sake of expiation before the new crops were gathered, either if any had not cleansed the family in mourning or otherwise had not seen to this matter as had been necessary.

(Gell. NA 4.6.8)

Gellius has perhaps confused two sacrifices of the porca praecidanea, one to be conducted at harvest time, the other whenever a fault in funerary ritual was discovered.[14] We have examined previously the sacrifice conducted at harvest time.[15] The sacrifice conducted when a fault was discovered in the funerary ritual is unlikely to have been postponed until the harvest, since the family would have been left impure until the ritual could be carried out.

Sacrificing the porca praesentanea or porca praecidanea has three meanings. First, both sacrifices provide a ritual cleansing, and their purpose is to rid the family of pollution caused by death. To purify themselves, the family underwent certain rituals culminating in the incorporation phase of the funerary ritual, which enabled them to resume ordinary life in the community. The rituals of the porca praesentanea and porca praecidanea, both dedicated to Ceres, belong to this phase of incorporation, which facilitated the transition from ritual pollution to ritual cleanliness, from death to life.

Secondly, the funerary sacrifice of a pig to Ceres has a particular legal and religious significance that Cicero discusses in his philosophical treatise *De Legibus*:

> And it is not necessary for me to discuss what end is made of mourning for a family, what type of sacrifice of castrated sheep is made to the Lar, in what matter the cut-out bone is concealed in the earth, and what laws are effected in the pig, at what time there begins to be a tomb and it is held in religious awe. . . . For those who have been buried are called "laid [to rest]." Nevertheless there is not a tomb for them before the due forms have been observed and the pig has been slaughtered. And what now commonly comes in use in all those buried, that they are called "interred," this was appropriate then for those upon whom earth was cast that covered them, and pontifical law confirms this custom. For before a clod of earth is cast on the bones, that place, where the body was cremated, has nothing of religious awe; when the clod of earth is cast and the body has been buried with them, not only is the place called a tomb but also then it embraces many religious laws.

> (Cic. *Leg.* 2.55–57)

Sacrificing the pig sanctifies the tomb and sets it off as a place held "in religious awe" (*religione*). This sacrifice enables the religious laws (*religiosa iura*) whereby the place of internment officially becomes a tomb. This is proved, Cicero states, by the fact that a place of cremation has no special religious significance until the funerary rites, including the sacrifice of a pig, are performed. These rites consecrate the place of burial, making it a sacred place set off from the profane world. They create a boundary between the world of the living and the world of the dead, a threshold associated with Ceres through the dedication to her of the funerary sacrifice of the pig.

Finally, the social significance of these rites of the porca praesentanea and porca praecidanea lies in their being carried out by the deceased's heir as part of the funerary ritual. Festus informs us that if the heir did not perform these required rituals properly, his life could be forfeit (Fest., s.v. *everriator*, 77 Müller). The heir performs these rites as a condition of receiving his inheritance, and his performance enabled the orderly transmission of property from one generation to the next.[16] In this way, the funerary sacrifices of the pigs also reveal Ceres' liminal/normative role in guarding the social order.

Ceres' connection with death and funerary ritual may perhaps be perceived in an artistic representation dated to the Trajanic period (fig. 19).[17] The goddess appears along with the deities Mercury, Proserpina, and Pluto in the marble relief from the architrave of the Tomb of the Haterii. Ceres is shown to the far right, holding a torch and stalks of wheat, then are Pluto with a staff, Proserpina with a bundle of fruit, and Mercury with his caduceus. The other three divinities are all associated with the world of the dead; Pluto and Proserpina are the rulers of the dead, and Mercury guides the souls to the underworld. The appearance of Ceres among these chthonic divinities suggests that she too could be linked to the underworld and the dead.[18]

3.2.2 BIRTH

Ceres may also be connected with the rite of passage for birth. I have already examined the goddess's association with motherhood, Ceres Mater, as she is called in both Roman cult and Latin literature.[19] Certain artistic representations associate her with Eileithyia, the goddess of childbirth, and suggest that she may have a role in this rite of passage. For example, on a cameo of imperial date, Ceres stands to the right holding wheat stalks in her hand; in the center of the composition is the seated Proserpina, who hands the newborn child Iacchus over to the standing Eileithyia on the left (fig. 18).[20] In other examples of imperial date Ceres is shown attending the birth of Dionysus or of Apollo and Diana.[21] Given her associations with other rites of passage, a connection with childbirth does not seem unlikely. It should also be noted that Ceres may be connected with an Italic divinity of the Peligni called Anaceta Ceria or Angitia Cerealis.[22] Scholars have suggested that this divinity may be identified with the Roman goddess Angerona, who was connected with childbirth. If so, this connection would suggest that the Italic Ceres may have had an association with birth.

3.2.3 MARRIAGE

The marriage ceremony also has associations with Ceres. Her companion in ancient Italic cult, the goddess Tellus, is certainly connected with this rite of passage, as seen in chapter 2.[23] Ceres, too, has a role in weddings. In explaining why Dido sacrifices to Ceres among other divinities before her marriage to Aeneas, the commentator Servius notes that "some say that Ceres favors weddings," and quotes the Late Republican poet Calvus as saying that the goddess "taught the sacred laws and joined the loving bodies in weddings" (on Verg. *Aen.* 4.58). This passage suggests that Ceres is implicated in the very foundation of wedding rites, establishing the social rules that lead to marriage. Varro mentions a rite in which the bride and groom sacrificed a pig at the beginning (initia) of the marriage (*Rust.* 2.4.9–10). The term "initia," I believe, points to the incorporation phase of the wedding rite, in which the bride and groom began their new lives together, now a married couple in the eyes of the community. Other evidence connects Ceres with the practice of throwing nuts in the wedding procession.[24] This ritual may be assigned to the transition phase of the wedding rite, as the bride and groom pass from the house of her parents, where the wedding was conducted, to their new home together.[25]

Finally, Festus reports:

> They were accustomed to carry the torch in weddings in honor of Ceres; the new bride was accustomed to be sprinkled with water, either so that she might come chaste and pure to her husband, or so that she might share fire and water with her husband.
>
> (Fest. s.v. *facem*, 87 Müller)

We will consider in chapter 5 the connection of the bride and Ceres with the concept of chastity. In the current context, Festus' interpretation of the torch as signaling a ritual sharing of fire and water (ignis et aquae communicatio) is significant. The groom offered the bride a torch and a vessel containing water once she had crossed the threshold of her new home.[26] As Treggiari notes, the elements of fire and water are basic to human life, and their ritual sharing has deep roots in the Roman ideas of home and of social incorporation.[27] An exiled man was to be denied fire and water by his fellow citizens as a symbol of their rejection of his role in the social group. Ovid indicates the significance of this ceremony in the wedding rite: by this ritual, he says, the bride is made into a wife (*Fast.* 4.792). This statement suggests that the ritual is to be read as part of the incorporation phase of the wedding ceremony, in which the bride assumes her new role in society. Thus again Ceres plays a part in the final phase of a rite of passage.

3.2.4 DIVORCE

In addition to her association with marriage, Ceres is connected with divorce, another rite of passage.[28] In his commentary on Vergil's *Aeneid*, Servius notes:

Some say that to diverse powers is consecrated the power of doing either well or badly, as weddings to Venus, divorce to Ceres.

(Serv. on Verg. *Aen.* 3.139)

Elsewhere he offers a mythological explanation for Ceres' connection with divorce in his commentary on Dido's sacrifice to Ceres Legifera and other divinities before her wedding to Aeneas:

Some say that those gods whom she commemorated are opposed to weddings, and that Ceres cursed weddings because of the rape of her daughter; or because she was repudiated as a wife by Jove, who preferred Juno. . . . For when we are about to do something, we supplicate before adverse gods, and thus we invoke propitious ones, as: "A black animal for winter, a white one for the happy west winds." Therefore, the bride-to-be supplicates before Ceres, because [the goddess] curses those about to be wed on account of the rape of her daughter.

(Serv. on Verg. *Aen.* 4.58)

Servius here provides a mythological explanation for a rite whose origin is not well known. Ceres' "opposition" to weddings and her association with divorce derive, I argue, from her liminal/normative role.

Evidence for this hypothesis is provided by a passage from the biographer Plutarch that relates a law attributed to the first king of Rome, Romulus, regarding divorce:

He [i.e., Romulus] established also certain laws, of which an excessive one provides that a wife may not leave her husband, but that the husband may cast out the wife for the poisoning of children, or the substitution of keys, and if she has committed adultery; and that if someone should send away his wife for other reasons, that a portion of his goods should be [the property] of his wife, and the other portion should be consecrated to Ceres [Demeter]; and that he who gives up [sells into slavery?] his wife should sacrifice [be sacrificed?] to the chthonic gods.

(Plut. *Vit. Rom.* 22.3)

Several aspects of this law are difficult to interpret. Plutarch calls the law "excessive" (σφοδρός), and its excessiveness apparently lay in the severity of its proscribed punishments.[29] The law provides that a husband may divorce his wife under specified conditions, but that a wife may not divorce her husband. In practice, this stipulation apparently applied only to marriages with *manus*, i.e., when the wife left her father's control and came under her husband's.[30]

The only acceptable grounds for divorce in archaic Rome, according to Plutarch, were the poisoning of children, the substitution of keys, and adultery. Adultery is self-evident, but the other two grounds are more difficult to under-

stand. The poisioning of children may refer to a stepmother poisoning her husband's children by an earlier marriage, or possibly not to literal poisoning at all
but to abortion.[31] The substitution of keys may refer to the wife obtaining a
fresh set of house keys to facilitate her adultery or to her securing a set of keys
to the wine cupboard, so that she might drink in secret, a forbidden pleasure
for Roman women in the regal period.[32] In any case, the phrase refers to the
wife's relationship to her husband's property. The law provides that if a man
divorces his wife for any other reason, his property should be confiscated, with
one portion to go to his wife, the other to Ceres, who oversees the divorce and
assures its propriety.

In the final provision of the law, the man giving up ($\dot{\alpha}\pi o\delta\acuteo\mu\epsilon\nu o\nu$) his wife
is to sacrifice/be sacrificed ($\theta\acute{\upsilon}\epsilon\sigma\theta\alpha\iota$) to the chthonic gods. I believe that the
participle "giving up" ($\dot{\alpha}\pi o\delta\acuteo\mu\epsilon\nu o\nu$) may be interpreted as "selling into slavery" and the infinitive "to sacrifice/be sacrificed" ($\theta\acute{\upsilon}\epsilon\sigma\theta\alpha\iota$) should be read as
"be sacrificed."[33] In this understanding, Romulus' law has three features: (1)
the three legitimate grounds for divorce, (2) the punishment for a husband who
unjustly repudiates his wife, and (3) the opposition of sale to simple repudiation. The most terrible punishment is then reserved for the greatest crime, the
selling of one's wife into slavery. For this crime the husband will be sacrificed
to the divinities of the underworld, among whom Ceres may be numbered, as
we have seen above.[34] Consecrating to Ceres the husband who attempts to sell
his wife suits Ceres' role as the deity who regulates legal divorce and whose
anger is roused by impious attempts at repudiation.

Ceres is therefore a goddess both of marriage and of divorce.[35] She is linked
to the rites of passage establishing the married state and those dissolving it. She
is, however, primarily connected with the stability of marriage in that divorce
is prescribed in very few circumstances. Ceres will let fewer out of marriage
than she lets into it. Her liminal function is normative and leads directly to the
stablity of marriage, of the family, and, by extension, of the state.

3.2.5 INITIATION

The rite of passage known as initiation is especially important to Ceres. Varro
says "those rituals (sacra) which are dedicated to Ceres are the ones chiefly
called 'initiations/beginnings' (initia)" (*Rust.* 3.1.5).[36] There are two types of
initiation ceremonies associated with the goddess: the initia Cereris and the
Eleusinian Mysteries.

The initia Cereris, the "initiations of Ceres," also known as the sacra Cereris, the "rites of Ceres," belong to the Greek cult of Ceres and Proserpina,
whose rituals and festivals were celebrated exclusively by women.[37] This cult

was related to the Greek Thesmophoric cult of Demeter and was imported from the Greek cities of Southern Italy to Rome by the third century B.C. Its mythological focus was the story of the rape of Proserpina and her return to her mother Demeter. This myth expressed the opposition between the two primary roles of women in ancient society: the young, sexually inexperienced maiden, and the mature, fertile mother. The ritual focus of the cult was on the themes of chastity and fertility, both human and agricultural. These ritual themes also symbolize the roles of women as maiden and mother. We will examine the significance of these rituals in detail in chapter 5. Here I shall simply note that through these rites, conducted by women and for women and focused on themes significant to them, the female worshippers of Ceres came to define and affirm the value of their identity as women in Roman society. The initia Cereris served to integrate Roman women into their society as a whole by proclaiming the importance of these women in producing and maintaining the fertility on which society depended. Ceres operates therefore in these initiation rites for women in her liminal/normative aspect.

The Eleusinian Mysteries were a very ancient initiatory rite conducted from at least the archaic period (seventh–sixth centuries B.C.) at Eleusis near Athens in Greece. These rituals were dedicated to the Greek goddess Demeter and to her daughter Persephone, to whom the Roman Ceres and Proserpina were assimilated at Rome by the third century B.C. In contrast to the rites of the Greek Thesmophoria and the Roman initia Cereris derived from it, the Eleusinian Mysteries were open to both men and women. By the time of the Late Republic, Romans were making the journey to Eleusis to be initiated into this ancient cult of the goddess—these Romans included the general Sulla, the orator Cicero, and Cicero's friend Atticus.[38] The cult grew in popularity under the Empire and was supported by many emperors: Augustus, Hadrian, Antoninus Pius, Commodus, Lucius Verus, M. Aurelius, Septimius Severus, and Gallienus were all initiated.[39] Indeed, literary sources inform us that Claudius tried to import the Eleusinian Mysteries to Rome (Suet. *Claud.* 25) and that Hadrian acually did so (Aur. Vict. *Caes.* 14).

Like the Thesmophoria and initia Cereris, the Eleusinian Mysteries focused on the myth of the Rape of Persephone. Scholars have attempted for decades with limited success to reconstruct what happened during the Mysteries, for the initiates in the cult swore an oath never to reveal any details of the rituals.[40] Although we may not be able to recover many of the details of the initiation rite, we do know of its significance to the Romans.[41] In his treatise on the ideal state, Cicero explains the appeal of these ancient mysteries as he speaks to his Greek interlocutor Atticus:

> For in my opinion your Athens seems not only to have produced many distinguished
> and divine things and to have brought them into the life of humankind, but also it has
> produced nothing better than those mysteries, in which we have been refined from a
> rustic and savage life to humanity and have been civilized, and as they are called
> *initia*, we have learned in truth the beginnings of life, and we have received not only
> with joy a method of living but even of dying with better hope.
>
> (Cic. *Leg.* 2.36)

Participation in the Mysteries thus offered to the initiates basic principles for living that made them more civilized human beings and also provided them with a hope for a better life after death. The civilizing influence of Ceres, which we have seen mentioned in other sources, is a function of her liminal/normative role. Ceres brings humankind over the threshold from savagery into civilization and establishes the laws through which society operates.

In Roman art there are many representations that point to the initiatory rituals of Ceres. From the Late Republic on the goddess is depicted holding a torch, riding in a chariot, or sitting on the mystic chest known as a *kiste*.[42] The torch has both a ritual and mythogical meaning. Ritually, torches were carried by the initiates of the mystery cult in the nocturnal ceremonies (Ov. *Fast.* 4.494). The torch suggests Ceres' mythological search for her daughter, for the story has it that the goddess lit torches in the fires of Mount Etna when she was combing the earth for her daughter (Ov. *Fast.* 4.490–494; *Met.* 5.441–443). The chariot in which the goddess rides also has a mythological meaning: when the goddess was unable to find her daughter in Sicily, the site of the Rape, she took to the heavens in her miraculous chariot drawn by two snakes (Ov. *Fast.* 4.497–498). The *kiste*, on the other hand, has a ritual significance: in it were placed the sacred objects, or sacra, of the mystery cult, which were carried in the procession from Athens to Eleusis.[43]

The Rape of Persephone, the myth that serves as a focal point for both the initia Cereris and the Eleusinian Mysteries, is represented frequently in sarcophagi of the second and third centuries A.D.[44] For example, in a sarcophagus relief dated to A.D. 220–230, Ceres appears to the left, holding two torches and standing in a chariot drawn by two snakes; to the right are Hades and Proserpina fleeing in a chariot drawn by four horses (fig. 21).[45] In other representations of the imperial period are portrayed scenes that seem to reflect details of the initiation at Eleusis.[46] For example, the initiation of Hercules into the Eleusinian Mysteries is portrayed in the famous Lovatelli urn, dated to the first half of the first century A.D. (fig. 20).[47] In the culminating scene Ceres appears to the left, seated on a *kiste* around which a snake is curled; she holds stalks of wheat in her right hand and a long torch in her left and wears a corona spicea on her head. Proserpina stands to the left and Iacchus in front. These representations signal the continuing interest in the initiatory rites of Ceres throughout the period of the Early Roman Empire and after. Indeed, we hear of a *mystes Cereris*, or initiate of Ceres, in an inscription dated to the fifth century A.D.[48] By this time the role of the goddess in the rite of passage known as initiation had been significant in the ancient world for over a millennium.

3.3 *Rites of Intensification*

3.3.1 AGRICULTURAL RITUALS

The rituals surrounding the various phases of agricultural work throughout the year are rites of intensification. These phases are tied to the change in the seasons, which requires the members of a society to alter their patterns of interaction to meet the needs of the changing environmental situation. As Chapple and Coon note, in the rites of intensification that accompany these changes, the ordered interaction of the members of the society is acted out, and this serves to reinforce or intensify their habitual relations.[49] Thus the performance of these rites leads to the reinvigoration of the ties on which the society depends.

As we saw in chapter 2, Ceres is connected with several agricultural rituals among the Romans, including both sowing and harvest ceremonies. These ceremonies mark important crises in the life of the agricultural community.[50] For example, the goddess is worshipped along with Tellus at the Feriae Sementivae, the festival of sowing held at the end of January. Ovid describes the rituals associated with this festival:

> Steward, give rest to the earth with the sowing completed; give rest to the men who tilled the earth. Let the district celebrate the festival: ritually purify the district, farmers, and give the yearly cakes to the hearths of the countryside. The mothers of crops, Tellus and Ceres, are pleased with their spelt, and with the entrails of a pregant sow.
> (Ov. *Fast.* 1.667–671)

The ritual calls for joint activity on the part of all the farmers: they must perform a lustration, or ritual purification of the fields, and offer spelt and a pregnant sow to the divinities associated with the festival, Tellus and Ceres. These rituals order the interaction of those responsible for the agricultural work. The result of the ritual is to strengthen the ties among these agricultural workers and thus to permit the work to continue over the long growing season ahead. The latter purpose is specifically addressed by Ovid, who offers a prayer to Ceres and Tellus on behalf of the farmers (*Fast.* 1. 675–694). In this prayer he asks for the help of the goddesses to make the seeds grow, to protect the tender shoots of the crops, to send rain to water them, and to protect them from birds, ants, mildew, darnel, and weeds. As a result of the protection of these divinities, the farmers will receive the rewards worthy of their cultivation (*Fast.* 1.678).

Vergil describes a similar rite conducted to Ceres at the time of the harvest:

> Among the first things, revere the gods and repeat the annual rites to great Ceres, worshipping on the joyful grasses near the very end of winter, then in the fair spring. Then the lambs are fat and the wines are the most pleasant, then sleep is sweet and the shadows are dense on the mountains. Let all your rural youth entreat Ceres; for her dilute the honeycombs with milk and mild wine, and three times let the auspicious victim go around the new crops, a victim that the entire chorus and companions accompany rejoicing, and let them call Ceres with a shout into the buildings; and let no one apply the sickle to the ripe grain before he, wreathed on his temples with an oak garland, has led unpracticed dances for Ceres and has sung songs.
>
> (Verg. *G.* 1.338–350)

Again we may note that all the workers, the rural youth, are to participate in the ritual, which includes a lustration and sacrifice to Ceres. The festival celebrates the harvest, the goddess who nourished it, and the workers who produced it. This annual ritual again unites the members of society and intensifies their ties to one another.

3.3.2 OPENING OF THE MUNDUS

Another periodic rite of intensification connected with Ceres is the opening of the *mundus* (literally "world"). The mundus was a monument in Rome whose opening was a state ritual, conducted on special occasions during which all public business was forbidden. This restriction was due to the belief that while the mundus was open, the spirits of the dead roamed the world, and so any business conducted then was ill-omened. Much controversy surrounds the mundus; its appearance, exact location, and origins are all open to debate.[51] Nevertheless, the literary evidence shows that the mundus represented a threshold between the world of the living and that of the dead, and that Ceres is the divinity associated with this liminal structure.

The evidence for the mundus comes from Festus and Macrobius, both scholars of the Early Empire. Festus links Ceres with the ritual of the opening of the mundus:[52]

> The mundus called "of Ceres" [is] that which is customarily opened three times a year: nine days before the Kalends of September [August 24], and three days before

the Nones of October [October 5], and six days before the Ides of November [November 8]. This is so called because the earth moves. [I.e., *mundus* is derived from *movere*, "to move."]

(Fest., s.v. *mundus*, 54 Müller)

Elsewhere, Festus quotes Cato, who provides further information about the ritual:

The name has been given to the mundus from that mundus which is above us, for its form is similar to it, as may be known from those who have entered into [the matter]. The elders decided that its lower part must be kept closed at all times, just as if it was consecrated to the Manes, except on those days which are written above [i.e., the three specified days for the opening], which days they judged ill-omened for the reason that at the time when those things that were secret and hidden belonging to the cult of the Manes are brought, so to speak, into the light and exposed, they did not want anything to be done at that time in the Republic. And so for those days they did not engage in battle with the enemy, nor was an army enrolled, nor was assembly held: nor was anything else taken care of in the republic except what extreme necessity urged.

(Fest., s.v. *mundus*, 142 Müller)

This passage points to the liminal significance of the opening of the mundus. During the period that the mundus lay open, the things that were hidden in the cult of the Manes, the spirits of the dead, were exposed to the light of the living. The ritual breaks down the barriers between the living and the dead, and the mundus itself represents a gateway between the underworld, where the dead dwell, and the world of the living. Macrobius states this idea clearly:

And when the mundus is open, it is a religious fault to undertake battle because it is dedicated as a thing sacred to Dis Pater (Pluto) and to Proserpina; and they thought it better for battle when the jaws of Pluto were closed. Whence also Varro writes thus: "When the *mundus* is open, it is as if the doorway of the sad and infernal gods is open: therefore it is ill-omened not only for battle to be initiated, but also to hold a levy for a military purpose, and for a soldier to set out, for a ship to sail, or to marry a wife for the sake of seeking children."

(Macrob. *Sat.* 1.16.16–18)

Here the mundus is associated with the rulers of the underworld, Pluto and Proserpina, the "sad and infernal gods" (tristes atque inferni dei). Ceres' connection with this ritual may well be related to her association with death and the divinities of the underworld examined above.[53] The mundus is a gateway (*ianua*) to these divinities, the "jaws of Pluto" (*fauces Plutonis*).

The significance of the opening of the mundus may be explained by comparing it to festivals of the dead, like the Roman Lemuria or the Greek Anthesteria, in which the spirits of the dead were thought to visit the world of the living.[54] Like the days when the mundus was open, the days on which these festivals were celebrated were considered ill-omened (*religiosi*), and no public business could be transacted on them. To the Greeks and Romans, the purpose of these festivals was to propitiate the dead by allowing them briefly to visit the world of the living; in this way, it was thought, they would remain content throughout the rest of the year and cause no trouble for the living. The rupturing of the boundary between the living and the dead in the end serves to reinforce that boundary.[55] The boundary itself was critical to the Roman religious system, which considered the dead imbued with supernatural power to aid or harm the living. The opening of the mundus is a rite of intensification for the Roman state in which the religious basis for beliefs about the afterlife and the cosmological scheme are reaffirmed, and the living Romans acknowledge their ties to one another and to those who have gone before them.

3.3.3 EXPIATION OF PRODIGIES

Prodigies are events that contradict the normal workings of nature, such as a rain of stones from heaven or the birth of a cow with two heads. The Romans considered such events as signs from the gods that something terrible had happened or was about to happen, and they believed that they needed to perform rituals to certain divinities to expiate or "procurate" (*procurare*) these supernatural occurrences. Prodigies often occur in association with events creating social stress, such as war or famine, and it is likely that explanations for these events were sought in the supernatural realm, leading to the identification of prodigies and the perceived need for their ritual expiation.[56] Ceres is frequently named among the divinities to whom the ritual expiation (*procuratio*) was directed. She is connected with this ritual, I believe, because of her association with the liminal rites of intensification.[57] The expiation of prodigies represents an example of such a rite, in that it unites the social group in the face of a disruption of both the natural and social order, strengthens their ties to one another through the performance of joint religious ceremonies, and thus restores equilibrium to the society.

Cicero directly connects Ceres with prodigies in the following passage from one of the Verrine orations:

> For often many prodigies declare her strength and divine power, often in difficult situations her prompt aid has been offered to many, so that this island [Sicily] seems not only loved by her, but even inhabited and guarded by her.

> (Cic. *Verr.* 2.4.197)

65

Here, the goddess is connected both with the production of prodigies, which Cicero says declare her power and divine presence, and also with the effect of their expiation, for she provides aid to those who seek it in the most difficult circumstances.

According to Roman tradition, Ceres' connection with prodigies dates back to the very beginnings of the Republic. After a terrible famine in Rome in 496 B.C., the dictator Aulus Postumius vowed a temple to Ceres, Liber, and Libera to propitiate these divinities.[58] Dionysius of Halicarnassus associates the prodigy of the famine with the need to provision the Roman army when it was about to face the Latins and the fear that the Romans would lose the upcoming battle with them (Dion. Hal. 6.17.3). The prodigy and its expiation therefore reflect both internal stress caused by the famine and external stress caused by the threat of the Latins. Ceres' connection with prodigies becomes common in the last three centuries of the Republic. In 217 B.C., Ceres is propitiated in a special ritual, called a *lectisternium*, which was held after a series of terrible prodigies (Livy 22.10.9).[59] Ceres appears in this rite in company with Mercury and the rest of the twelve great Olympian gods arranged in pairs. This event took place after the devastating defeat of the Romans by Hannibal in the Battle of Lake Trasimene.

Ceres is again connected with an expiatory rite in 206 B.C. that also may be associated with anxieties generated by the Second Punic War. The occasion of this rite was a number of supernatural occurrences, including a lightning strike on the Temple of Ceres, that were expiated by sacrifices and prayer conducted by the consuls (Livy 28.11.2–5). The divinities to whom the expiation was directed are not named in our sources, but it seems likely that Ceres would have been invoked, since her temple was involved in the prodigies. Several prodigies were recorded again in 191 B.C., and the expiatory rite was specifically directed to Ceres (Livy 36.37.4–5). The rite included the establishment of a special fast in honor of Ceres, the *ieiunium Cereris*, which was to be celebrated every five years, and a nine-day festival, the *novendiale sacrum*.[60] This event may be connected with the stress generated by the war being conducted by the Romans against Antiochus of Syria. Other prodigies and expiatory rites connected with Ceres took place in 182, 174, 133, 125, 104, 99, 92, 84, 42, and 32 B.C. and in A.D. 64. As the historical context shows, each of these events may pose a challenge to the social equilibrium, either external, such as war, or internal, such as social unrest.[61]

The female worshippers of the Greek cult of Ceres and Proserpina were often involved in these expiatory rites. The upper-class groups of the matronae, or married women, and the virgines, or maidens, both participated in the ritual,

offering gifts to two goddesses. The juxtaposition of these two female categories is characteristic of the Greek cult of Ceres as well as other "matronal"
cults.[62] Julius Obsequens offers an example in this description of the expiatory
rites of 99 B.C., recorded in his book on prodigies collected from earlier
sources:

> A growling from the underworld seemed to be born up to the sky and portended need
> and famine. The people offered a religious donation, the matronae a treasure, and the
> virgines gifts to Ceres and Proserpina. There was continual song by twenty-seven
> virgines. Two statues of cypress wood were set up to Juno Regina.
>
> (Obseq. *Prodig. Lib.* 46 [106])

The women, through their participation in these rites, signal their importance
to the community, strengthen their ties to one another, and reinvigorate society
as a whole. The participation of the women and the role of Ceres and Proserpina in the expiatory rite may be related to their associations with fertility. As
Gagé has noted, the power of the fecundity of the female is often invoked as
one of the principal remedies when society is threatened, especially if the threat
is to the food supply or to the lives of children.[63] Ceres often appears along with
other divinities, such as Juno Regina and Apollo, in the rites of intensification
that take place in association with prodigies.[64]

3.3.4 ESTABLISHMENT OF PEACE

Ceres is also tied to the rite of intensification that takes place when peace is
established after war. The end of war creates a disequilibrium in the social
order that is resolved through the rituals that establish peace. Ceres' association
with the ritual establishing of peace may be inferred from a passage from Varro
that we have already examined in another context:[65]

> The Greek name for the pig is ὖς, once called θῦς from the verb θύειν, that is "to
> sacrifice"; for it seems that at the beginning of making sacrifices they first took the
> victim from the swine family. There are traces of this in these facts: that pigs are
> sacrificed at the initial rites of Ceres; that at the rites that initiate peace, when a treaty
> is made, a pig is killed; and that at the beginning of the marriage rites of ancient kings
> and eminent personages in Etruria, the bride and groom, in the ceremonies which
> united them, first sacrificed a pig. The ancient Latins, too, as well as the Greeks living
> in Italy, seem to have had the same custom. . . .
>
> (Varr. *Rust.* 2.4.9—Loeb trans.)

Varro associates the sacrifice of the pig with three types of rituals connected
with initia, or beginnings: the initiation rites of Ceres (initia Cereris), the rites

initiating peace (initia pacis), and the rites initiating weddings (initio nuptia-rum). The pig was a customary sacrifice to Ceres, as we have seen in the rituals of the porca praecidanea and porca praesentanea.[66] The initiation rites and the marriage rituals that Varro mentions are also rites of passage associated with Ceres. It therefore seems very likely that the sacrifice of the pig at the initiation of peace was also dedicated to her.

Both literary and artistic sources from the Augustan period and later make clear Ceres' close connection with the concept of peace. Tibullus gives Pax, the personified figure of peace, the attributes of Ceres:

> Meanwhile let Pax tend our fields. Bright Pax first led under the curved yoke the cows to plow the fields. Pax nourished the vine plants and stored the grape juice so that pure wine might flow for the son from the father's jar. In peace shall shine the hoe and plowshare, but decay masters the sad arms of the harsh soldier in the darkness. . . . Then come to us, nourishing Pax, and hold the wheat stalk in your hand, and let fruits pour forth from your shining bosom.
>
> (Tib. 1.10.45–50, 67–68)

Pax, like Ceres, tends the fields, supervises the plowing animals, and nourishes the crops. She has the stalks of wheat and fruits that are attributes of Ceres. The connection between these two divinities is suggested by the appearance of Ceres in a famous relief from the Ara Pacis Augustae (fig. 11), as we shall see in chapter 6. Two coin types also provide evidence for the close association between Ceres and Pax. On the reverse of an *as* from the short-lived reign of Galba (A.D. 68–69) appears a seated divinity holding two wheat stalks (or a wheat stalk and a poppy) in her right hand, the symbols of Ceres. In her left hand, however, she holds a caduceus, the symbol of Pax; the legend reads CERES AUGUSTA (fig. 31).[67] On the reverse of an aureus dated to the same period of the Civil Wars, a goddess appears standing left, holding a caduceus in her right hand and wheat stalks and a poppy in her left; the legend reads PAX (fig. 32).[68] The commonality of the attributes suggests an identification of the two goddesses.[69] Ovid explains the relationship between these two divinities and their connection with the princeps Augustus:

> Wars long occupied humankind; the sword was more suitable than the plowshare, and the plowing bull yielded to the war-horse. Then the hoes used to lie idle, the mattocks were turned into javelins, and from the weight of the rake the helmet was made. Thanks to the gods and to your house! Bound in chains, for a long time now wars lie under your foot. Let the cow come under the yoke, let the seed come under the plowed earth. Peace nourishes Ceres, Ceres is the nursling of Peace.
>
> (Ov. *Fast.* 1.697–704)

Peace is brought to the Romans through the actions of Augustus and his family; this peace produces the fertility personified by the goddess Ceres. Ceres is therefore connected with the return to peace that Augustus brought to the Roman Empire. The goddess here again operates in her liminal/normative role.

3.3.5 VIOLATION OF TRIBUNICIAN SACROSANCTITAS

The liminal/normative role of Ceres in rites of intensification is also apparent in her connection with the law punishing those who violated the sacrosanctitas, or inviolability, of a tribune of the plebs.[70] Sacrosanctitas protected the tribunes from attack by patrician magistrates, and its recognition was a critical step in the struggle of the plebs to gain political power from the patricians. The violation of sacrosanctitas threatened the role of the plebs in the state and rendered the relationship between patricians and plebeians insecure. The law punishing those who attacked a tribune reinforced the social ties that bound both plebeians and patricians into Roman society as a whole. The law is associated with a religious ritual in which those who committed this crime were to be executed for the benefit of Ceres.

Dionysius of Halicarnassus records the details of the ritual in his account of the law on sacrosanctitas, which he attributes to the First Secession, traditionally dated to 494 B.C.:

> Let no one compel a tribune of the plebs to do anything against his will, as if he were one of the many; let no one whip him or order another to whip him; let no one kill him or order another to kill him. If anyone should do any of these forbidden things, let him be accursed, and his goods be sacred to Ceres, and let the person who kills one who has done these things be cleansed of murder.
>
> (Dion. Hal. 6.89.3)

According to Dionysius, the one who violated the sacrosanctitas of a tribune was to be made accursed (ἐξάγιστος) and to suffer the consecration of his goods to Ceres (τὰ χρήματα αὐτοῦ Δήμετρος ἱερά). Moreover, the person who killed him was to be made ritually pure of murder (φόνου καθαρός). The latter provision marks the malefactor as a homo sacer, as Festus indicates:

> But a homo sacer is he whom the people have convicted on account of his wrongdoing, and it is not ritually correct to sacrifice him, but he who kills him is not condemned for murder.
>
> (Fest., s.v. sacer mons, 424 Lindsay)

The term "sacer" corresponds to the word ἐξάγιστος from the passage of Dionysius. The person who commits the crime is to be "accursed" or "consecrated"; he is to suffer "consecration of his head," or *consecratio capitis*, that is, execution. Dionysius does not name the divinity who is to receive the *consecratio capitis*. Ceres may be implied, however, since she is specifically named as the recipient of the consecration of the goods, or *consecratio bonorum*. A specific deity was generally named or implied in consecrations of this sort.[71]

Moreover, we know that Ceres received *consecratio capitis* in another law mentioned by Pliny, a scholar of the first century A.D., which dealt with damage to the harvest:

> It was a capital crime in the Twelve Tables for an adult to tread upon or to cut secretly at night a crop obtained by the plow. They ordered that [the malefactor] be hanged and put to death for Ceres in a more severe way than for a man convicted of homicide; a youth was to be beaten or either [a penalty of] the damage or double [the damage] was to be assessed, according to the judgement of the praetor.
>
> (Pliny *HN* 18.3.13)

According to this law, any adult who damaged the harvest was "to be killed for Ceres" (*Cereri necari*). This phrase suggests a *consecratio capitis* dedicated to the goddess. In any case, Ceres is clearly associated with the punishment of consecration prescribed by the law on sacrosanctitas.

Livy also connects Ceres with the law on violation of tribunician sacrosanctitas, which he associates with the Valerio-Horatian Laws of 449 B.C. He records the law as follows:

> Whoever harmed a tribune or aedile of the plebs or the decemviral judges should have his head vowed to Jupiter and his goods should be sold at the Temple of Ceres, Liber, and Libera.
>
> (Livy 3.55.7)

Although *consecratio bonorum* to Ceres is not specified in this law, it is suggested by the mention of the sale of the goods of the offender at the temple of the triadic cult of the goddess, in which she was worshipped along with Liber and Libera. The *consecratio capitis*, however, is specified as going to Jupiter. As Le Bonniec has noted, Livy's version of the law may be later than that in Dionysius and may represent the attempt to extend to the Roman state as a whole an oath taken originally by the plebs alone to defend its tribunes.[72] It is perhaps for this reason that Jupiter, protector of the Roman state, has been added as a recipient of the *consecratio* along with Ceres, protectress of the plebeians. In Livy's version, too, Ceres is associated with the punishment of the violator of the law on tribunician sacrosanctitas. Ceres operates here in a rite of intensification that fortifies the ties of plebeians to one another and to Roman society as a whole, and thus strengthens the political and social structure of that society.

3.3.6 ATTEMPTED TYRANNY

Ceres is associated with another law similar to the one punishing the violator of the sacrosancititas of the tribune. The crime this law punished was the attempt to overthrow the Republic and to establish a tyranny.[73] Such an act threatened the entire political structure of Roman society. Again, the religious ritual of *consecratio* is invoked in the law, pointing to a rite of intensification that unites society after a threat of violent political change.

The similarites of the law against attempted tyranny with that on tribunician sacrosanctitas suggest that Ceres was once again the divinity who had to be appeased for its violation. According to tradition, the law on attempted tyranny was proposed by the consul P. Valerius Publicola in 509 B.C., at the time of the establishment of the Roman Republic. Livy characterizes this law as:

> [The one] concerning . . . consecrating the person, along with the goods, of the person who had entertained plans of seizing royal power.
>
> (Livy 2.8.2)

Plutarch further describes the provisions of this law, as written by Publicola:

> For he wrote a law providing to kill without trial the person wishing to be a tyrant, and he established that the slayer be cleansed of murder, if he should furnish arguments for refutation of the crime.
>
> (Plut. *Vit. Publ.* 12.1)

The law on attempted tyranny, like the one on violation of sacrosanctitas, provides for the consecration of the goods and person of the malefactor. As in Dionysius' version of the law on sacrosanctitas, the slayer of the attempted tyrant is to be "cleansed of murder" (φόνου καθαρός). This provision indicates that the malefactor is to be named a homo sacer, as in the case of the law on sacrosanctitas. Neither version of the law on attempted tyranny names the divinity who is to receive the *consecratio bonorum* and *consecratio capitis*. However, given the close similarities to the provisions regarding the violation of sacrosanctitas, I suggest that in this case too the consecration was dedicated to Ceres and possibly Jupiter as well.

Support for the connection of Ceres with the punishment for violation of the law on tyranny is provided by the story of the downfall of the consul Spurius

Cassius in 486–485 B.C.[74] According to our sources for this story, during his consulship Spurius Cassius had proposed an agrarian reform law that was intended to benefit the Roman plebs and the Latins.[75] He also had proposed another bill, in which the plebs were to be compensated for recent expenses in obtaining grain. After his term of office ended, Spurius was accused of using these proposals to buy plebeian support for his own excessive political ambition. According to Dionysius (8.69.3), pride in his earlier achievements had caused him to "acquire a desire for monarchical power" (μοναρχικῆς ἐξουσίας ἐλάμβανε πόθον). According to Livy (2.41.5), Spurius' co-consul, Proculus Verginius, warned the plebs that Spurius was "making a road to royal power" (regno viam fieri). When the latter proposed to compensate the plebeians for their grain expenses, they recognized this as an "obvious bribe for royal power" (praesentem mercedem regni) (Livy 2.41.9–10). The result was that Spurius was accused of "striving to seize royal power" (de occupando regno molientem) (Cic. *Rep.* 2.35.60). This phrase recalls Livy's version (2.8.2) of the law on attempted tyranny, which punished "whoever had entertained plans of seizing royal power" (qui regni occupandi consilia inisset), and suggests that Spurius was accused of violating this law. By its provisions, we would expect that he would be punished with *consecratio bonorum* and *consecratio capitis*. This is exactly what happened. Moreover, the sources indicate that the goddess Ceres was a recipient of the consecration.

Although the specifics of Spurius' punishment differ in our various sources, that punishment always in some way involves Ceres.[76] According to one version, his father had Spurius beaten and killed, and consecrated his property to Ceres (Livy 2.41.10); from the proceeds of this consecrated property a statue was made and dedicated to her.[77] In this instance, the goods of Spurius clearly were consecrated to the goddess. The *consecratio capitis* may also have been dedicated to her, since no other divinity is named, and the manner of execution accords with that prescribed in another law we have already examined, the one on damage to the harvest (Pliny *HN* 18.3.13).[78] In this law, the adult offender was to be hanged and killed for Ceres (suspensumque Cereri necari), while the juvenile offender was to be beaten (*verberari).* In this version of the punishment of Spurius, his father beat him (*verberasse*) and then killed him (*necasse*).[79]

In another version of Spurius' punishment, the quaestors executed him on behalf of the state by casting him from the Tarpeian Rock; they confiscated his goods and dedicated them, at least in part, to Ceres.[80] Again, the *consecratio bonorum* was to Ceres, even if the *consecratio capitis* was probably to Jupiter, with whose cult the Tarpeian Rock was closely associated.[81] Moreover, we know that those who had violated the sacrosanctitas of a tribune were executed by being thrown from this precipice.[82] As we have seen, according to Livy's version of the law dealing with this crime, the person of the offender was sacred to Jupiter. It therefore seems likely that this version of the punishment of Spurius indicates that his person was consecrated to Jupiter. It may be that in similar fashion to the development of the law on sacrosanctitas, the original version of the law on attempted tyranny named Ceres alone as the recipient of both *consecratio bonorum* and *consecratio capitis*. This version is reflected in the story that Spurius' father killed his son and dedicated his goods to Ceres. In a later version the state took over the father's role, and so the divinity who was the protector of the state as a whole, Jupiter, was added as the recipient of the *consecratio capitis*. In any case, Spurius was punished for violating the law on attempted tyranny, and his story indicates that Ceres was the divinity who had to be placated for this crime.

Ceres thus served as a guardian of the law on attempted tyranny as well as the law on violation of sacrosanctitas. She operates in both these laws in her liminal/normative aspect as she restores the social status quo after a challenge has been made to it. The *consecratio capitis* and *consecratio bonorum* to Ceres represent rites of intensification dedicated to the goddess, in that they unify Roman society in the face of internal threats to its stability.

3.4 *Ceres and the Death of Tiberius Gracchus*

Ceres' liminal/normative role was exploited for the purposes of political propaganda during the Gracchan crisis at the beginning of the Late Republic. The goddess's connection with the laws on sacrosanctitas and attempted tyranny were used by the Senate to discredit the political reformer Tiberius Gracchus and ultimately the latter law was used to justify his murder as a form of *consecratio capitis*.[83]

In the following passage Cicero indicates the connection of Ceres with the events surrounding the death of Tiberius:

And so among our fathers in that terrible and difficult time for the Republic, when, with Tiberius Gracchus killed, fear of great dangers was indicated by prodigies, in the consulship of Publius Mucius and Lucius Calpurnius, there was a consultation of the Sibylline Books, from which it was found that it was necessary to placate the most ancient Ceres. Then priests of the Roman people from the most distinguished decemviral college—even though there was in our city a most beautiful and magnificient temple of Ceres—nevertheless set out for Henna. For so great was the authority and antiquity of that cult, that when they went there they seemed to set out not for the temple of Ceres, but for Ceres herself.

(Cic. Verr. 2.4.108)

The delegation to Ceres of Henna after the death of Gracchus is also described briefly by Valerius Maximus:

> Although they had a very beautiful temple of her [i.e., of Ceres] in the city, when they were warned in the Gracchan disturbances by the Sibylline Books that they should placate the most ancient Ceres, they sent the *quindecimviri* to propitiate her at Henna, since her rites were believed to have originated there.

(Val. Max. 1.1.1)

I believe that the delegation to Ceres served to validate the view that Tiberius Gracchus had transgressed the laws that protected the equilibrium of the social and political order, the laws on tribunician sacrosanctitas and attempted tyranny, and hence was subject to the punishment they prescribed, consecration of his goods and person.[84] When prodigies were reported in the tumult following the death of Tiberius, the Senate ordered the consultation of the Sibylline Books and manipulated the instructions found there to produce the desired result. Senatorial control over this form of divination has been well established.[85] It is therefore not surprising that these instructions could be manipulated to suit political purposes.[86] In this instance, the decision of the Senate was that the Ceres of Henna had to be placated. By sending the delegation to Ceres, the Senate signaled that she had been offended by the actions of Tiberius and had to be appeased for his violation of the laws that were in her charge. The cult of the goddess at Henna was selected because its great antiquity and authority added symbolic weight to this action, and because this cult did not have the potentially inflammatory political associations of the cult of Ceres at Rome. The mission to Ceres at Henna thus represents part of a program by Tiberius' senatorial opponents to discredit him and to justify his murder as a legal form of execution.

Our evidence for the events surrounding the death of Tiberius Gracchus comes primarily from two literary sources of the second century A.D., Appian's history of the Civil Wars (*B.Civ.* 1.1.9–1.2.17) and Plutarch's biography of Tiberius Gracchus (*Vit. Ti. Gracch.* 9–20). These sources provide ample evidence for the strategy of the campaign against Tiberius. It focused on two charges: first, that Tiberius was attempting to overthrow the government and become a tyrant; and second, that he had violated the sacrosanctitas of his colleague in the tribunate, Octavius, when he had him removed from office. Plutarch (9.3) informs us that when Tiberius first proposed his land distribution bill, the lobby of the rich alleged that he was acting "for the confusion of the state" (ἐπὶ συηχύσει τῆς πολιτείας), and that he was "stirring up all things" (πάντα πράγματα κινοῦντος).

According to Appian (1.1.13), when Tiberius convinced the assembly to remove Octavius from office in order to permit the bill to be passed, those who had opposed it intimated that he should be punished for "having outraged the sacred and inviolable office" (ἀρχήν τε ὑβρίσαντα ἱερὰν καὶ ἄσυλον), that is, for violating tribunician sacrosanctitas. The accusation that Tiberius had violated the sacrosanctitas of Octavius is given further weight by Plutarch (12.4), who reports that Tiberius ordered one of his freedmen physically to drag Octavius from the speaker's platform. This accusation may have been intended to counter the charge that Tiberius had made against Octavius, namely that since the latter was blocking a measure designed to benefit the plebs, he was in effect no longer a tribune of the plebs (App. 1.1.12).

As Plutarch reports (14.2–6), the opponents of Tiberius formalized their accusations against him at the Senate meeting deliberating Tiberius' proposal to appropriate the legacy of Attalus of Pergamum for the land commission. First the senator Pompeius reported that the Pergamene envoy had given the diadem and purple robes of the king to Tiberius, "as the one about to become king in Rome" (ὡς μέλλοντι βασιλεύειν ἐν Ῥώμῃ). The alleged incident had a clear propagandistic effect, by associating Tiberius with the trappings of monarchy and therefore suggesting that this was what he was trying to achieve. Another senator, Quintus Metellus, then accused Tiberius of surrounding himself with a group of the most needy and reckless men—conduct befitting a man who would become tyrant. Finally, Titus Annius proposed a formal judicial proceeding against Tiberius for violating the sacrosanctitas of Octavius. Tiberius was reportedly so taken aback at Annius' attack that he said nothing in response. His silence suggests that the charges were finding their mark. Further evidence of their success is provided by the loss of support Tiberius reportedly experienced after this meeting. Plutarch (15.1) attributes this loss to the people's displeasure at Tiberius' violation of the tribunate: "For it was thought that the great and honorable dignity of the tribunes, so carefully guarded up to that time, had been insulted and destroyed" (μέγα γάρ τι καὶ καλὸν ἐδόκει τὸ τῶν δημάρχον ἀξίωμα μέχρι τῆς ἡμέρας ἐκείνης διατετηρημένον ἀνηρῆσθαι καὶ καθυβρίσθαι). For this reason Tiberius went on the defensive. He made a speech attempting to justify his actions and decided to stand for office for a second consecutive term to prevent his prosecution (Plut. 15.1–16.1).

In connection with this election, the campaign against Tiberius reached its climax. The precipitating event was a signal made by Tiberius at the meeting of the plebeian assembly to elect the new tribunes. Tiberius touched his head to indicate to his friends that he was in danger. This signal was misinterpreted, either accidentally or deliberately, by his opponents at the assembly, who ran to the Senate to report that he was "asking for a crown" (αἰτεῖν διάδημα) (Plut. 19.2). Upon hearing this report, the Pontifex Maximus, Scipio Nasica, demanded that the consul "come to the aid of the state and destroy the tyrant" (τῇ πόλει βοηθεῖν καὶ καταλύειν τὸν τύραννον) (Plut. 19.3). Nasica put forth this demand, I believe, because as Pontifex Maximus, he was held responsible for seeing that proper religious forms were observed in official state rituals. He would be the one to oversee the *consecratio capitis* of the attempted tyrant. Nasica called on the consul, P. Mucius Scaevola, to carry out this demand, since as the chief magistrate of the state the consul was responsible for its safety. The actions reported here are very similar to those Cicero reports for *consecratio bonorum*, in which a pontifex and a magistrate act together to carry out consecration.[87] When the appropriate magistrate, Scaevola, refused to carry out the demand of the Pontifex, the latter took it upon himself to perform the consecration as the law demanded. So, according to Plutarch (19.3), Nasica sprang to his feet and cried out to the senators, "Since then the consul betrays the state, those wishing to come to the aid of the laws, follow me" (ἐπεὶ τοίνυν . . . προδίδωσιν ὁ ἄρχων τὴν πόλιν, οἱ βουλόμενοι τοῖς νόμοις βοηθεῖν ἀκολουθεῖτε). The "laws" (νόμοι) to which Nasica referred were the laws on attempted tyranny and violation of sacrosanctitas. He urged the senators to help put their provisions into effect, that is, to carry out *consecratio*.

The actual killing of Tiberius corresponds in certain important ways to a *consecratio capitis*. First, both Appian (1.2.16) and Plutarch (19.4) report that as Nasica marched out of the Senate on his way to kill Tiberius, he covered his head with his toga.[88] Earl has suggested that this action was intended to indicate that the Pontifex Maximus was proceeding to a sacrifice, whose victim was to be Tiberius.[89] The draping of the toga over the head, *capite velato*, was part of the dress adopted for certain ritual acts by the Romans. I agree that Nasica's action did signify a ritual act on his part, but that act was not a sacrifice. By committing the crime of attempting to seize royal power, Tiberius became a homo sacer, and as such could not be sacrificed, as the entry from Festus (s.v. *sacer mons*, 424 Lindsay) that we have examined previously indicates.[90] Rather, Nasica's action signified that he was performing a *consecratio*, as Badian has suggested.[91] Similarly, the magistrate who performs *consecratio bonorum* does so *capite velato*.[92]

The method by which Tiberius and his followers were killed also suggests a *consecratio capitis*. Plutarch (19.6) reports that Tiberius was killed with the wooden leg of a bench. Similarly, his supporters were killed by blows from sticks or stones (Plut. 19.6) or driven to their death from the precipice of the Capitoline (App. 1.2.16). Plutarch (19.6) emphasizes the fact that none of them was killed by the sword (σιδήρῳ δὲ οὐδείς). The word used here for sword, σίδηρος, means literally "iron." Iron was excluded in Roman sacrificial ritual and so Plutarch's emphasis on its absence at the killing of Tiberius may indicate that the killing was a ritual act.[93] Moreover, the precipice mentioned by Appian was probably the Tarpeian Rock. From this rock, as we have seen, violators of the laws on sacrosanctitas and attempted tyranny were cast. The killing of the supporter of Tiberius in this manner suggests that they too were suffering *consecratio capitis*. The refusal to bury Tiberius and his supporters, which Plutarch (20.3) disapprovingly mentions, may also be a consequence of the consecration.[94] By the act of *consecratio capitis*, the malefactors became sacer and hence the property of the divinity to whom they had been consecrated. Their spirits therefore could not be handed over to the spirits of the underworld through the normal funerary rites.[95]

Following the death of Tiberius, his opponents backed away from the charge that he had violated the law on sacrosanctitas by deposing Octavius. They were in no position to accuse Tiberius of this crime, since they had committed it themselves by killing him.[96] However, the allegation that Tiberius had been attempting to seize royal power continued to be spread.[97] Presumably, it was on this basis that Scaevola after the fact defended the actions of Nasica. Cicero (*Dom.* 91) informs us that Scaevola, after the murder of Tiberius, not only defended the deed of Scipio with many senatorial decrees, but even honored it.

The inquisition conducted against Tiberius' supporters by the consuls of the following year probably also was based on the charge of attempted tyranny.[98] Plutarch (20.3–4) reports that in the course of this inquisition some of the supporters were banished, others were put to death, and one was executed in what appears to be a ritual slaughter, by placing him in a cage with vipers and serpents. Soon after the inquisition, however, the rising tide of negative popular opinion regarding these acts forced the Senate to try to conciliate the people. The Senate therefore ceased its opposition to the work of the land commission, proposed that the people should elect a new land commissioner in place of

Tiberius, and sent Nasica away from Rome (Plut. 21.1–3). The issue, however, refused to die. In 131 B.C., C. Papirius Carbo proposed a bill to legalize immediate reelection to the tribunate.[99] Scipio Aemilianus spoke against the bill and was interrogated by Carbo.[100] Reportedly, when Scipio was asked what he thought about the killing of Tiberius, he replied, "If he had the intention of seizing the republic, he was killed in accordance with the law" (si is occupandae reipublicae animum habuisset, iure caesum) (Vell. Pat. 2.4.4). The wording used here recalls Livy's version (2.8.2) of the law on attempted tyranny, which punished "whoever had entertained plans of seizing royal power" (qui regni occupandi consilia inisset). Clearly, Scipio linked Tiberius' death with the punishment for attempted tyranny.[101] His answer to Carbo makes sense only on the assumption that the connection was widely understood, even if it were not generally accepted. In fact Scipio's response provoked a popular outcry against him.[102]

The mission to Ceres at Henna, which soon followed the death of Tiberius, must be understood in this wider context. Presumably, murmurings had already begun that the killing of Tiberius had been unjust. The mission was designed to counter these rumors and validate further the view that Tiberius had committed the crime for which *consecratio bonorum* and *consecratio capitis* were the prescribed punishment. It is possible that the *sacerdotes* made some offering from his property as an actual *consecratio bonorum* to Ceres. No evidence for this, however, exists in our sources. More likely, the continued power of the Gracchi and their supporters prevented any confiscation of Tiberius' goods. Indeed, the prodigies that occurred after Tiberius' death may have been interpreted by some as Ceres' anger for not having received the *consecratio bonorum*.

In any case, the Senate decided to send a delegation to propitiate the goddess. The mission was sent to the cult of Ceres at Henna for two reasons. First, as the most ancient cult of the goddess, it had the most auctoritas in the eyes of the Romans.[103] The symbolic gesture of the Senate was lent more authority and dignity by attaching it to this cult. Secondly, the cult of Ceres at Henna had no associations with plebeian rebellion, as did the one at Rome,[104] so the Senate could safely appeal to this goddess as a higher authority, without inflammatory political overtones. By sending the mission to Ceres at Henna, the Senate propitiated her as the divinity who had been offended by Tiberius' actions and therefore signaled that he had been justly punished for his violation of the laws.

In the events surrounding the death of Tiberius Gracchus we thus see a clear example of the political use of Ceres' liminal/normative aspect. The goddess serves in this incident as the protectress of the social and political equilibrium of the Roman state, which had been disrupted by Tiberius' actions. The Senate's mission to Henna represented an attempt to restore that equilibrium and reinforce the status quo in Roman society.

3.5 Conclusion

The concept of liminality is closely associated with Ceres. Under this aspect, she presides over both rites of passage connected with the individual and rites of intensification connected to society as a whole. As a divinity of the rites of passage, she is associated by the Romans with death, birth, marriage, divorce, and initiation. In her role as a goddess of rites of intensification, Ceres is associated with the periodic rituals of agriculture and of the opening of the mundus, the passage between the world of the living and the world of the dead.

The goddess is also connected with nonperiodic rituals surrounding the expiation of prodigies, the establishment of peace after war, the violation of the sacrosanctitas of the tribunes of the plebs, and the punishment for those who attempted to overthrow the Republic. In these nonperiodic rites of intensification, Ceres operates as a normative force in restoring the social order after a challenge to the equilibrium was made. This aspect of the goddess I have called her "liminal/normative" role. At the beginning of the Late Republic, the Senate made use of Ceres' liminal/normative role in order to assuage the crisis following the death of Tiberius Gracchus.

Chapter 4

THE·PLEBS

4.1 *Introduction*

At Rome Ceres is closely associated with the social class of the plebeians, or plebs. This class existed in opposition to the class of the patricii, or patricians, from at least the time of the Early Republic. The origins of the distinctions between the two classes are obscure, although scholars have proposed an ethnic, economic, or political basis.[1] The conflict between the two classes was overtly manifested during the Early Republic, with the plebeians struggling to gain political and social equality with the patricians in the so-called Conflict of the Orders. This struggle ended in the early third century B.C., when the plebeians for the most part had gained their goals. By this time certain plebeian families had become part of the ruling class at Rome. The social distinctions between patricians and plebeians remained significant, however, for some time. The term "plebeian" gradually came to be applied to those of the lower social and economic group, the "urban mob" of Rome. During the Late Republic the ruling class of the city competed for the political support of these plebeians in their struggles for power. Under the Empire the princeps also courted the support and loyalty of the plebs.

The origin of Ceres' association with the plebs is tied to the foundation of the Temple of Ceres, Liber, and Libera.[2] As we have seen, this temple was established traditionally in 494/3 B.C., near the very beginning of the Republic. During the Early Republic the building became the nucleus of the plebeian political organization in its struggle under the patricians, and the plebeian magistrates were closely associated with both the temple and the triadic cult associated with it. The cult became the focal point for the development of the class consciousness of the plebs during the Early and Middle Republic. The temple was destroyed by fire during the Late Republic, and Augustus undertook its restoration, which was completed by Tiberius (Tac. *Ann.* 2.49). The new temple was still standing in the fourth century A.D. (*Not. Reg.* XI).

In this chapter, I shall examine the evidence for the association of Ceres with the plebs. First, I shall consider the plebeian associations of the Temple of Ceres, Liber, and Libera and explore the connections of the plebeian magistrates, the tribunes and aediles of the plebs, with the cult associated with this temple. Then, I shall look at Ceres' involvement with the development of plebeian class consciousness through the opposition of the plebeian cult of the goddess to the patrician cults of Jupiter, Juno, and Minerva, and of Cybele. Finally, I will consider the use of Ceres as a symbol of the plebs in Roman political propaganda of the Late Republic.

4.2 The Temple of Ceres, Liber, and Libera

4.2.1 LOCATION

The very location of the Temple of Ceres, Liber, and Libera may provide evidence for its links to the plebs. As we have seen, scholars have often located this temple on the slopes of the Aventine Hill, which was the preeminently plebeian district of Rome (fig. 1).[3] Although no archaeological evidence for this temple has been found, it must be remembered that the area has not been fully excavated. The location of the temple may be reconstructed from literary evidence. Vitruvius (3.3.5), Pliny (*HN* 35.154), and Tacitus (*Ann.* 2.49) all report that the temple was located "near the Circus Maximus." The Circus was in the valley between the Palatine and Aventine Hills, so if the Temple of Ceres were located on the Aventine, facing north (toward the Palatine), it would indeed be near the Circus Maximus. Moreover, the temple is noted in other sources to be near two others whose Aventine location is well established. According to Tacitus (*Ann.* 2.49), Tiberius rebuilt the Temple of Ceres and in the same place the Temple of Flora. The latter has been located on the north slope of the Aventine, at the beginning of the Clivus Publicus.[4] Livy (40.2.1–2) relates that during a terrible storm, a door blew off the Temple of Luna on the Aventine (*in Aventino*) and plastered itself against the back wall of the Temple of Ceres. These passages all point to the location on the Aventine of the latter temple as well.

The best evidence, however, for the Aventine location of the Temple of Ceres is provided by Dionysius of Halicarnassus:

Cassius, the other consul, having been left in Rome, in the meantime dedicated the Temple of Ceres, Liber, and Libera, which is after the turning points (ἐπὶ τοῖς τέρμασι) of the greatest of the hippodromes (= the Circus Maximus), lying above the starting posts themselves (ὑπὲρ αὐτὰς τὰς ... ἀφέσεις).

(Dion. Hal. 6.94.3)

The significance of this passage has not been fully appreciated. The phrases ἐπὶ τοῖς τέρμασι and ὑπὲρ αὐτὰς τὰς ... ἀφέσεις, I argue, define the location of the temple exactly. The *termata* (τέρμασι) are the goals around which horses and chariots had to turn at races, located in Roman circuses at the ends of the *spina*, or the central divider on the long axis of the track. In the Circus Maximus the *spina* ran east-west. In this passage, then, the term *termata*, plural here being used for the singular, should apply to one end of the *spina*, probably the westernmost one, as this was the final turn before the end of the race, and *terma* also means "end, culmination." The phrase ἐπὶ τοῖς τέρμασι defines the location of the temple in relation to the *spina*; it is located after or behind its western end. This sets its location along an east-west axis. The ἀφέσεις are the starting points for a race, in Latin the *carceres*, located at the western end of the Circus Maximus. The phrase ὑπὲρ αὐτὰς τὰς... ἀφέσεις defines the location of the temple as "over (or beyond) the *carceres*." This defines its location on a north-south axis. The Temple of Ceres may therefore be placed exactly: west of the western end of the spina and south of the *carceres*, that is, in line with the western end of the Circus Maximus on the northern slope of the Aventine Hill.

The Aventine is often named by ancient sources as the refuge for the plebeians when they withdrew from the state to enforce their political demands in the First and Second Secessions.[5] Furthermore, the *Lex Icilia de Aventino publicando* in 456 B.C. provided that the hill be given over to the plebs for settlement.[6] If, as seems likely, the Temple of Ceres was located on this hill, then it would share its plebeian associations.

4.2.2 THE TREASURY OF THE PLEBS

Direct evidence also links the plebs with the Temple of Ceres, Liber, and Libera. First, the temple probably served as the treasury of the plebs. In chapter 3, we noted three instances in which confiscated goods were sold to benefit the goddess: in cases of unjustified divorce, of violation of a tribune's sacrosanctitas, and of attempted tyranny.[7] In the second instance the goods were even sold at the temple itself.[8] Furthermore, out of the fines they had collected, the plebeian aediles customarily made votive offerings to the goddess in her temple.[9] These facts suggest that the income generated from fines and from the consecration of goods, *consecratio bonorum*, was stored in the Temple of Ceres. Similarly, the Temple of Saturn served as the public treasury, and the use of temples as treasuries was common at Rome.[10]

4.2.3 THE *ASYLUM CERERIS*

The Temple of Ceres, Liber, and Libera may also have been a place of sanctuary for the plebs. Varro notes:

> Those who were lacking in wealth and fled (*confugissent*) to the asylum of Ceres (*asylum Cereris*) were given bread.
>
> (Varro, quoted in Non., 63 Lindsay)

The phrase *asylum Cereris* requires interpretation. First, *Cereris*, "of Ceres," by itself is a common locution for the Temple of Ceres, Liber, and Libera (aedes Cereris Liberi Liberaeque).[11] At issue, then, is the meaning of *asylum*. If *asylum* here means "a place of relaxation or recuperation, a retreat,"[12] then it refers to the temple as a place of retreat for the poor from their problems of subsistence. If, however, the term designates here "a place affording sanctuary for criminals, etc., a refuge, asylum,"[13] then the temple is to be understood as a place of legal sanctuary, perhaps for plebeians threatened by the sanctions of patrician magistrates.[14] Plebeians confronted by these magistrates or their agents could flee to temporary refuge there while appealing to the tribunes of the plebs for aid against these magistrates. The tribunes had the right to obstruct the prosecution of any plebeian by a patrician magistrate (the *ius auxilii*). The use of *confugissent* tends to support the latter interpretation. *Confugere* ("to flee") most often means "to flee for refuge or safety (to), to flee (to a person or god) for protection," and is often used in connection with altars or statues of the gods, or later of the emperors, which provided the right of sanctuary to those who touched them.[15] In antiquity temples were often considered to provide sanctuary from any compulsion, so it would not be unprecedented if the Temple of Ceres provided asylum for plebeians seeking sanctuary from plebeian magistrates.[16]

4.2.4 THE *GRAIN SUPPLY*

The passage from Varro cited above also suggests that a free distribution of bread or the grain with which to make it was made at the temple. This type of distribution was called a frumentatio. A fragment from Lucilius (200 Marx) also indicates a connection between Ceres and the distribution of bread: "Nourishing Ceres is failing and the plebs do not have bread" (deficit alma

Ceres, nec plebs pane potitur). This passage suggests a connection among the goddess, the plebs, and grain, that may have arisen from the practice of distributing grain at her temple. Some scholars believe that the annona, the grain supply of the city of Rome, was also administered from the Temple of Ceres, Liber, and Libera, but the evidence is sketchy.[17]

4.2.5 THE ARCHIVES OF THE PLEBS

Finally, the decrees of the Roman Senate (the senatus consulta) and of the Concilium Plebis, or Council of the Plebs, (the plebiscita), seem to have been stored in this temple. Livy provides evidence for the storage of the senatus consulta in the Temple of Ceres:

> It was also established by these same consuls [i.e., Lucius Valerius and Marcus Horatius] that the senatus consulta be brought into the Temple of Ceres to the aediles of the plebs. These decrees before used to be suppressed and altered on the authority of the consuls.
>
> (Livy 3.55.13)

Livy's date for this arrangement has been challenged because the period of the Valerio-Horatian Laws (449 B.C.) may be too early for the transfer of the Senate's archives to the control of the plebs.[18] The provision itself, however, should reflect an actual transfer of responsibility at some period, perhaps that of the *leges Hortensiae* in 287 B.C.[19] In any case, Livy here implies that the senatus consulta were moved to the Temple of Ceres to protect the plebs from arbitrary changes in these decrees by the patrician consuls. Similarly, the plebiscita seem to have been stored in the Temple of Ceres under the care of the aediles, as the following passage from the imperial jurist Pomponius reveals:

> They established that there be two of the plebs who were in charge of the temple (*aedibus*) in which the plebs placed all their decisions. These (magistrates) were furthermore called "aediles."
>
> (Pompon. *Dig.* 1.2.2.21)

Pomponius does not name the temple in which the plebiscita were stored.[20] Since we know from Livy, however, that the senatus consulta were stored in the Temple of Ceres, it seems logical to assume that Pomponius means this temple. A purely plebeian function should have antedated its use as a senatorial depository, and the similarity of the plebeian practice would also have justified its added responsiblity for senatus consulta. The Temple of Ceres was then the repository for the decrees affecting the plebs, and their officers, the plebeian aediles, acted as guardians of these decrees. The Temple of Ceres seems to have served the plebs in a variety of ways: as grain distribution center, as treasury, as place of sanctuary, and as record house. These functions illustrate the close connection between the plebs and the goddess.

4.3 Plebeian Magistrates and Ceres

4.3.1 THE TRIBUNES OF THE PLEBS

From its origins the office of the tribune of the plebs was protected by Ceres. As we have seen in chapter 3, according to the law (*lex sacrata*) promulgated during the First Secession of the plebs, anyone who violated the person of a tribune was to be put to death and his goods sold at the Temple of Ceres (Dion. Hal. 6.89.3).[21] The sacrosanctitas that this law establishes reinforced the power of the tribunes. Sacrosanctitas originally was guaranteed by the oath of the plebeians, who swore to defend the tribunes by physical force if necessary against arrest or intimidation by patrician magistrates. The oath was taken in the name of Ceres, who guarded this basic privilege of the tribunate.[22]

From the power that the privilege of sacrosanctitas granted the tribunate were derived the other essential powers of that office: the *ius auxilii*, the "right of aid," i.e., the right to protect plebeians from patrician magistrates; and the *ius intercessionis*, the "right of intercession," i.e., the right of impeding action by any magistrate.[23] With the assumption of these rights and the sacrosanctitas that backed them, the tribunate became one of the most powerful offices in the Roman state, rivaling the power of the consulate (even though the tribunate technically only served the plebs, not the whole state).[24] The tribunate played a significant role in establishing plebeian rights during the fifth and fourth centuries B.C.

4.3.2 THE AEDILES OF THE PLEBS

The plebeian aediles may even owe their title to Ceres, since *aedilis* may well be derived from *aedes Cereris*, the Temple of Ceres.[25] The etymological dictionaries agree on its derivation from *aedes*, "temple," as *civilis*, "civil," from *civis*, "citizen." [26] The ancient sources, moreover, connect acting aediles with the *aedes Cereris* in particular: "that the decrees of the senate be given over to the aediles of the plebs (*aediles plebis*) in the Temple of Ceres (*aedes Cereris*)" (Livy 3.55.13).[27] Furthermore, the Caesar's creation of an *aedilis Cerealis* (Dio 43.51.3) has an archaizing ring and may reflect either the original title of the aedileship or else its original historical associations.[28] If this etymology is correct, then the original function of the aediles was probably to oversee the Temple of Ceres itself, and only gradually was their power extended into other areas.

As we have seen, the political duties of the aedileship show close affinities to the cult of the goddess whose temple seems to have been their headquarters. Here were stored the archives of plebiscita and senatus consulta over which they had charge; here too was the treasury of the plebs under their jurisdiction; from this temple the aediles may well have administered the grain supply (annona) and the distributions of grain (frumentationes) to the plebs. Indeed, Rickman has argued that the three primary duties of the aediles (cura urbis, cura annonae, cura ludorum sollemnium) were derived from their superintendence of the temple and cult of Ceres.[29] The *cura urbis*, "care of the city," referred to the maintenance of the public buildings and streets of Rome. This duty may have been an extension of the aediles' responsibility for the Temple of Ceres. The *cura annonae*, "care of the grain supply," then grew directly out of this overall care for the city's physical plan and may also reflect Ceres' role as goddess of the grain. Finally, the *cura ludorum solemnium*, "care of the sacred games," was probably derived from the aediles' administration of the games of Ceres, the ludi Ceriales.[30]

The aediles of the plebs had other religious duties and seem to have served occasionally as priests of Ceres.[31] They managed a number of festivals associated with the goddess, like the lectisternium celebrating the foundation day (*dies natalis*) of the Temple of Tellus, the lectisternium for the *dies natalis* of the Temple of Ceres, and the ludi Ceriales. The Christian writer Arnobius reports on the lectisternium for the Temple of Tellus:

> The lectisternium of Ceres will be on the next Ides. For the gods have beds, and so that they can sleep on softer beds, the impression of the cushions is lifted up and it is raised. It is the [Dies] Natalis of Tellus.
>
> (Arnob. *Adv. Nat.* 7.32)

The Roman calendar also refers to a lectisternium of Ceres and Tellus, a ritual celebrated by the aediles at the Temple of Tellus in the district of Carenae:[32]

> To Tellus and Ceres in Carenae. The aediles . . . also make the lectisternium from the beds . . . for which the contractor is responsible.
>
> (*CIL* 1², p. 336)

Scholars generally agree that both texts refer to the same festival.[33] This ritual took place at the Temple of Tellus on its foundation day, the Ides (13th) of

December, and was dedicated to Ceres and presumably to Tellus.[34] The aediles, who managed this lectisternium, therefore officiated as priests of Tellus and Ceres during the ceremony.

A similar ritual dedicated to Ceres was performed at the temple of the triad. Cornificius Longus relates: "For these [gods] indeed at [the Temple] of Ceres beds are laid out to renew the memory" (ipsis vero ad Cereris memoriae novandae gratia lectus sternuntur).[35] The phrase "to renew the memory" (memoriae novandae gratia) probably indicates the celebration of the foundation day of the Temple of Ceres, Liber, and Libera.[36] If so, this lectisternium exactly parallels the one performed by the aediles at the Temple of Tellus on its foundation day. It seems reasonable therefore to assume that the aediles also performed this ritual and again functioned as priests of the goddess.

The aediles were also in charge of the ludi Ceriales, which included the ludi scaenici and the ludi Circenses as well.[37] The ludi scaenici were a festival of theatrical performances dedicated to Ceres and celebrated from the twelfth through the eighteenth of April. In the early first century B.C. C. Memmius issued denarii with the legend MEMMIUS AED. CERIALIA PREIMUS FECIT, "Memmius the aedile was the first to celebrate the Cerialia" (fig. 34a).[38] This legend should refer to the establishment of the ludi scaenici of the Cerialia by C. Memmius c. 175 B.C.[39] Tacitus alludes to the ludi scaenici when he mentions that the celebration of the ludi Ceriales in the theater at Rome was scarcely interrupted by news of Otho's death in A.D. 69 (*Hist.* 2.55.1).[40]

The ludi Circenses on April 19, the very day of the Cerialia, included horse races in the Circus Maximus, as Ovid mentions (*Fast.* 4.679–680). Dio Cassius, a historian of the early third century A.D., shows that the aediles managed the games when he relates how they once supplanted the customary horse races with combat games (47.40.6). This information is given along with other unprecedented occurrences taken later as bad omens. The aediles committed a ritual fault by substituting gladitorial combats for the customary horse races, and the natural implication is that the aediles regularly conducted the games. Livy is even clearer on this point when he notes that after the elected aediles of the plebs had to abdicate due to a fault in the election proceedings, the dictator and the *magister equitum* celebrated the ludi Ceriales by senatorial decree (Livy 30.39.8). A senatus consultum was necessary on this occasion to transfer the normal function of one magistrate to another, and this decree was promulgated precisely because managing the Cerialia was a regular duty of the plebeian aediles.

Cicero shows the political significance of this duty when he enumerates the responsiblities that he is about to assume as an aedile:

Now I have been elected aedile; I take account of what I have received from the Roman people. I must celebrate with the greatest care and reverence the most holy games of Ceres, Liber, and Libera. I must reconcile mother Flora to the Roman people and plebs by the fame of the games. I must celebrate the most ancient games, which were the first called "Roman," to Jupiter, Juno, and Minerva with the greatest dignity and religious scruple. To me is entrusted the administration of sacred buildings; to me is entrusted the protection of the whole city.

(Cic *Verr.* 2.5.36)

Responsibility for the games of Ceres comes first in Cicero's list, and its position indicates its importance among the aedile's duties. Managing such games became a critical tool in winning popular support when an aedile later ran for higher office. Aediles who produced lavish games gained considerable public approval.[41]

It is important, however, not to lose sight of the fact that all ludi served religious as well as political ends. Cicero acknowledges this religious significance by calling the games of Ceres "most holy" (*sanctissimos*) and by noting that he must direct them "with the greatest care and reverence" (maxima cum cura et caerimonia, where *caerimonia* means "reverence for the gods as shown by acts of worship"[42]). Similarly, Cicero remarks that he must perform other games in honor of Jupiter, Juno, and Minerva "with the greatest dignity and religious scruple" (cum dignitate maxima et religione). Most importantly, however, he emphasizes the religious purpose of the ludi Florales, and states that as aedile he is charged with "reconciling mother Flora to the people and plebs of Rome" (Floram matrem populo plebique Romanae . . . placandam). The religious purpose of the ludi Ceriales similarly involved making Ceres favorably disposed to the Romans, and these games may also have had a magical function in assuring the production of a good harvest.[43] The aediles of the plebs were thus performing a religious ritual in honor of the goddess, but at its inception the ritual may have been designed specifically to assure a good harvest by means of magic.

The fines levied by the plebeian aediles were frequently presented as gifts to the goddess, and this practice also has priestly overtones. Livy notes three important instances from 296, 210, and 197 B.C., respectively:[44]

And likewise games were held and golden *paterae* placed at the temple of Ceres by the plebeian aediles L. Aelius Paetus and C. Fulvius Curvus with the money from fines that they had collected from those convicted of [illegally] using public pasture.

(Livy 10.23.13)

The aediles of the plebs, Q. Catius and L. Porcius Licinus, offered bronze statues at the temple of Ceres with money from fines and celebrated games that were magnificently equipped for the means of the age.

(Livy 27.6.19)

The (ludi) Plebei were repeated seven times; M'. Acilius Glabrio and C. Laelius celebrated these games, and with the money from fines they erected three bronze statues of Ceres, Liber, and Libera.

(Livy 33.25.3)

In each instance the fines imposed and collected by the aediles were dedicated to Ceres: either by being deposited in her temple or by being spent for statues. In all other known cases the revenue was spent by the aediles for religious purposes, at least in part; if not dedicated to Ceres herself, then it was given to another plebeian divinity, like Flora or Faunus.[45]

Spending fines for religious ends was the special prerogative of the aediles, and the legal term for imposing fines to be spent in this manner was *in sacrum iudicare*.[46] This expression may be contrasted with the term *multum inrogare*, which applies to fines to be deposited in the public treasury.[47] Mommsen suggested that the right of the aediles *in sacrum iudicare* was derived from the ancient practice of *consecratio bonorum*, in which the goods of a malefactor were consecrated to a particular deity.[48] In collecting fines to be dedicated to Ceres, therefore, the aediles performed the same act as priests who consecrated goods to a divinity.

We have already noted three instances in which *consecratio bonorum* was dedicated to Ceres, i.e., in cases of unjustified divorce, of violation of the sacrosanctitas of a tribune, and for attempted tyranny.[49] For violation of sacrosanctitas, the goods of the malefactor were specifically to be sold at the Temple of Ceres.[50] Latte suggested that the aediles conducted this sale and therefore acted again as agents of the goddess.[51] The aediles of the plebs seem to have both served as the agents of Ceres in collecting fines and spent those fines on gifts to the goddess.

4.4 Ceres and Plebeian Social Consciousness

The evidence thus indicates a close association between the plebs and the cult of Ceres, Liber, and Libera. In addition this cult was the nucleus for developing a plebeian social consciousness. The goddess Ceres became an integrative symbol for the plebs as a social order distinct from the patricians. Later on her cult also continued to express the ongoing opposition between plebeians and patricians.

4.4.1 THE FIRST SECESSION OF THE PLEBS AND THE CULT OF CERES

The connection of the cult of Ceres, Liber, and Libera with plebeian social consciousness seems to date back to the Early Republic. According to Dionysius of Halicarnassus (6.17.2–4; 6.94.3), the dictator Aulus Postumius vowed a temple to Demeter, Dionysus, and Kore (probably the Greek translation of Ceres, Liber, and Libera) during a famine before the Battle of Lake Regillus in 496 B.C.; the consul Spurius Cassius then dedicated the temple in 493 B.C.[52] The latter date marks the establishment of the cult, and is the same date given by both Dionysius (6.89–90) and Livy (2.31–33) for the first plebeian secession and the official recognition of the tribunes of the plebs. This synchronism, whether historically accurate or not, reflects the close association in the mind of later Romans between the foundation of this cult and the political organization of the plebs.

If the synchronism is historical, the special association of the plebs with the cult would coincide with the origin of the plebs as a social order. Le Bonniec has suggested that this cult belonged to the plebeians even before the establishment of the Roman Republic.[53] The official "foundation" of the cult of Ceres, Liber, and Libera by Aulus Postumius would then represent its recognition by the patricians and assimilation into the official religion. Such recognition was politically expedient, if not imperative, since the military cooperation of the plebeians was required for the war with the Latins.

If, however, as I believe, the synchronism of the cult's foundation with the plebeian political organization is false, then the literary tradition of the synchronism indicates a tendency to push the date of plebeian institutions as far back as possible and to make them rival patrician institutions in this regard.[54] The political action of the plebeians during the First Secession was made parallel to the patrician organization at the establishment of the Republic a few years before.

4.4.2 THE CAPITOLINE CULT OF JUPITER, JUNO, AND MINERVA

The foundation of the plebeian cult of Ceres, Liber, and Libera paralleled that of the patrician cult of Jupiter, Juno, and Minerva. The political organization of the plebs and the foundation of the plebeian cult were synchronized to the very beginning of the Republic. This synchronization enabled the plebs to affirm its own legitimacy by making its foundation as an *ordo* parallel to that of the patricians. This usage provided the religious justification and approval for the establishment of the new social group.

The very nature of the cult and the location of its temple solidified the plebs as a social class distinct from, and opposed to, the patriciate. The plebeian cult of Ceres, Liber, and Libera and the patrician one of Jupiter, Juno, and Minerva were both triadic and dedicated to two female and one male deity.[55] The plebeian cult, however, had at its center the female divinity, Ceres, whereas the patrician cult was centered on the male Jupiter. As Le Bonniec states, the plebeian cult was the "copy and antithesis" of the patrician cult.[56]

The location of two temples further illustrates the opposition of the cults. The Temple of Jupiter Optimus Maximus, Juno Regina, and Minerva was located on the Capitoline Hill; the Temple of Ceres, Liber, and Libera was most likely located on another hill, the preeminently plebeian Aventine (fig. 1).[57] The patrician triad had a temple situated within the pomerium, or sacred boundary of Rome, whereas the plebeian triad was housed outside of the pomerium.[58] A number of religious and political factors may have contributed to the extrapomerial status of the Temple of Ceres, Liber, and Libera. First, since Ceres had been assimilated to a foreign goddess, the Greek Demeter, her worship might have been excluded from the sacred boundary of the city.[59] Secondly, because the temple belonged in any event to the plebeians, the patricians may have distinguished its status from that of their own established cults.[60] Third, from the plebeian side, the revolutionary plebeian social and political organization associated with the temple may have required a temple outside the pomerium in order to preserve its own independence from the patrician state.[61] Finally, the liminal associations of the goddess may have pointed to an extrapomerial status. For whatever reason, there is clear opposition between the Temple of Jupiter, Juno, and Minerva located intra pomerium and the Temple of Ceres, Liber, and Libera extra pomerium, and this carefully delineated opposition further attests the formation of plebeian social consciousness. Thus, inasmuch as the plebeians were united by the cult of the triad, they felt for the first time that they were able to establish a community conscious of its own strength and of the possibility of resisting patrician power.[62]

4.4.3 THE CULT OF THE MAGNA MATER

The cult of Ceres, Liber, and Libera continued to distinguish plebeian ideals from patrician, as illustrated by the antagonism between it and the cult of Magna Mater at Rome. The cult of Magna Mater, the Greek Cybele, was always closely associated with the patricians.[63] Patrician senators imported this cult to Rome from Pessinus in Asia Minor in 204 B.C., and they also chose a man from one of the most distinguished patrician families, Publius Cornelius Scipio, as the "best man," vir optimus, to welcome this cult into the city.[64] Matrons of Rome's great patrician families personally escorted the image of the goddess from Ostia to Rome.[65] On the road to Rome, the image was miraculously rescued by Claudia Quinta, a member of the patrician clan of the Claudii, noted for its antiquity and the purity of its noble descent.[66] Finally, when the Temple of Magna Mater on the Palatine was completed in 191 B.C., games were established to honor the goddess at which the the patrician senators received special privileges.[67]

The opposition between the patrician and plebeian cults is manifest in the rituals of Magna Mater, which express symbolically the opposition between patricians and plebeians.[68] The games of Magna Mater, the ludi Megalenses, immediately preceded the ludi Ceriales in April.[69] The ludi Megalenses, moreover, were celebrated by the curule aediles, who originated as patrician officers and were still drawn, even if no longer exclusively, from the patricians.[70] The ludi Ceriales, in contrast, were celebrated by the plebeian aediles.[71] More significantly, the festival of Magna Mater, the Megalensia, opened with banquets among the patrician families of Rome; the festival of Ceres, the Cerialia, opened with banquets among the plebeian families.[72] Even if we cannot prove which cult began these practices, there cannot be any doubt that the fact of assimilation in cult practices reflects the sense of rivalry and opposition that imitation may confer. Aulus Gellius notes this opposition in discussing the reciprocal invitations (*mutitationes*) to these banquets:

> Afterward there was an inquiry of this nature, for what reason the patricians were accustomed to invite one another to the Megalensia, the plebeians to the Cerealia.
> (Gell. *N.A.* 18.2.11)

Moreover, the very location of the Temple of Magna Mater indicates an opposition of her cult to that of Ceres. The Temple of Magna Mater was located on the Palatine Hill, a predominantly patrician district (fig. 1).[73] The Temple of Ceres, Liber, and Libera faced it from the predominantly plebeian area of the Aventine Hill.[74] The Temple of Magna Mater was located within the pomerium, while that of Ceres was outside this sacred boundary.[75] This is especially significant, since the dedication of this temple to a foreign goddess normally required that it be located outside the pomerium.[76] This exception may well indicate patrician influence. According to Graillot, the two cults of the Magna Mater and of Ceres represented the two elements of the city, just as their two temples faced one another.[77] The opposition of the two cults thus expresses deliberately and symbolically the opposition between patricians and plebeians. The establishment of the cult of Magna Mater represents the creation of a new symbol to express patrician social consciousness in opposition to a symbol of plebeian social consciousness, the cult of Ceres, Liber, and Libera.

The political situation at Rome toward the end of the third century B.C. may explain why the new patrician symbol was created then. The war with Hannibal was dragging on, and the Romans had already suffered several humiliating defeats at the hands of the Carthaginian general. Patrician prestige suffered in turn because the great patrician families had supplied much of the military and political leadership during these years. These families made likely supporters for introducing the new cult of Magna Mater in order to reassert and to revive their waning prestige. This revitalization came from equating Magna Mater and the patriciate with divine patronage for reviving the Roman spirit. In this way the patricians claimed responsibility for the new spirit in the city.

The vaunted Trojan ancestry of the patricians could have justified their role in introducing into Rome the ancient cult of this goddess associated with the Troad. Magna Mater had a long association with Troy and with Rome's Trojan ancestors.[78] Dardanus, progenitor of the Trojan race, is called the first to have received her rites (Clem. Al. *Cohort. ad gentes* 2). One of his sons allegedly built the Metroon, her shrine on Mount Ida, the mountain sacred to her (Dion. Hal. 1.61). The father of the Romans, the Trojan prince Aeneas, sought refuge on Mount Ida after Troy fell, and he built a fleet from pines sacred to her (Dion. Hal. 1.4.7).[79] The Romans claimed the image of Magna Mater based on their Trojan ancestry, as Herodian, a historian of the third century A.D., reports about the Roman embassy sent to obtain the image:[80]

> Sending then ambassadors to Phrygia, they asked for the statue; and they obtained it easily, putting forward as argument their kinship and recounting to them their descent from Aeneas the Phrygian.
>
> (Herodian 1.11.3)

It was precisely this Trojan ancestry that patrician families emphasized. Many of these families sought Trojan ancestors in their past, as did the Julii, Fabii, Furii, Volteii, Plaetorii, and Metelli.[81] Varro published a work, entitled *De familiis Troianis*, detailing various patrician claims to Trojan descent (Serv. on *Aen.* 5.704.). This work, published in the first century B.C., apparently drew on a long tradition.[82] By claiming Trojan descent, patrician families increased

their prestige both directly and indirectly. Direct descent from the heroic Trojans and indirect ties therefore to the new goddess both enhanced patrician
ideology and perhaps led to reasserting their claims of social preeminence
as well.

This effect was encouraged by also associating Magna Mater with the rea-
wakening of Rome and Roman power. The importation of her cult was allegedly responsible for bringing victory to the Romans. Livy reports that the
Sibylline Books ordered the importation of this cult to assure victory over
Hannibal:

> At that time, a sudden religious scruple had invaded the state because of an oracle
> which had been found in the Sibylline Books, that had been consulted because of the
> rather frequent showers of stones from the sky in that year. [The oracle predicted that]
> whenever a foreign enemy should bring war to the land of Italy, he would be able to
> be driven from Italy and conquered, if the Idaean mother were to be brought from
> Pessinus to Rome. . . . And so that they might more quickly be masters of the victory
> foreshadowed in the divine utterances, omens, and oracles, there was deliberation and
> discussion [in the Senate] as to what the plan of action was for transporting the god-
> dess to Rome.
>
> (Livy 29.10.4–8)

The association between Magna Mater and victory over Hannibal was reinforced by installing her image in the Temple of Victory on the Palatine until
her own temple could be built.[83] By assuming responsiblity for the cult, the
patricians took credit for the victory. Magna Mater, Roman victory, and the
patricians were now firmly joined together in a single conception. Herodian
specifies that the enhancement of Roman power and prestige motivated bringing this cult to Rome in the first place:

> When the state of the Romans had grown, they say that an oracle announced to them
> that their rule would remain and grow greater if they brought to themselves the god-
> dess of Pessinus.
>
> (Herodian 1.11.3)

Roman tradition long held that Magna Mater had presided over a renewal
and extension of Roman power. In this context, the date chosen to establish her
cult seems especially significant. The year 204 B.C. also marked the fifth *saeculum* ("age," or roughly "century") of the city's existence since 754 B.C. (110
x 5 = 550), and this synchronism may be deliberate.[84] The beginning of the
new age is marked by the importation of a new cult; this cult renews the power

of Rome at the start of the new *saeculum*. The connection between the cult of the Magna Mater and the new *saeculum* may perhaps be recognized in the following verses from Ovid's account of the introduction of the cult to Rome:

> Afterward, when Rome, powerful in resources, already had seen five ages and lifted her head after the world had been entirely subdued, the priest contemplated the fateful words of the Euboean song. They say these were of such a sort when they had been contemplated: "The Mother is absent: I order, Roman, that you seek the Mother. When she comes, she must be received by a chaste hand."
>
> (Ov. *Fast.* 4.255–260)

The new cult of Magna Mater symbolized the rebirth of Rome and Roman power, while patrician endorsement of the cult also implied their responsibility for the city's consequent revitalization. This revival was immediate: Pliny reports that the year Cybele arrived in Rome, the grain harvest was better than it had been in a decade (*HN* 18.16). The association of the goddess with grain is especially significant. It suggests that she was taking over some of the functions of the plebeian goddess Ceres.[85]

A new festival of Ceres, the *ieiunium Cereris*, may have marked a response on behalf of the plebs to the new patrician cult and its sweeping claims.[86] Livy reports the establishment of this festival in 191 B.C.:

> When, in accordance with a decree of the Senate, the *decemviri* had consulted the Sibylline Books regarding the cause of these prodigies, they announced that a fast was to be instituted for Ceres, and to be enacted every fifth year, and that there be nine days of prayer and one of supplication, and that they supplicate with their heads garlanded, and that the consul Publius Cornelius sacrifice to those gods and with those victims that the *decemviri* ordered.
>
> (Livy 36.37.4–5)

Anomalies in the institution of the festival point to its importance. First, the ancient sources give no other example in which a general fast is inaugurated to expiate prodigies. Secondly, an expiatory rite generally is not repeated periodically, while this festival was held every five years.[87] The unusual importance attached to the festival may be due to its political significance. The festival was inaugurated in the same year as the dedication of the new temple of Magna Mater on the Palatine. The coincidence of dates is not accidental. If Ceres had taken offence at the honors given to the Magna Mater, then she would be appeased by the institution of a public fast. The quinquennial celebration of this festival represents a permanent enrichment of the plebeian cult. This effect was brought about by the actions of the decemviri, who were controlled by the

Senate. The institution of the *ieiunium Cereris* thus may well represent a compensatory gesture by the Senate to the plebeians and their patron goddess in the face of the new patrician cult of the Magna Mater.

4.5 *Ceres, the Plebs, and Political Propaganda*

The antagonism between the cult of Ceres and that of Magna Mater thus further linked Ceres and the plebs. This association was firmly entrenched by the second century B.C., when the *ieiunium Cereris* was introduced. During the Late Republic and less commonly under the Empire, this association was exploited by various individuals and political factions for political propaganda. This symbolic use of Ceres is most visible in numismatic evidence, for the coin types represented an important medium for the dissemination of propaganda in the Roman world.[88]

Le Bonniec has argued that the symbol of Ceres on coins produced during Late Republic appealed to the sympathies of the plebs and garnered their support for the issuing authority.[89] Now, to be sure, the interpretation of coins is notoriously difficult, and I do not agree with Le Bonniec that every instance of Ceres on the coins of this period necessarily represents an appeal to the plebs.[90] Nevertheless, Le Bonniec's hypothesis does help to interpret certain coin types in their political context.

A denarius issued c. 102 B.C. by Lucius Cassius Caeicianus bears on the obverse a head of Ceres with the legend CAEICIANI (fig. 33a) and on the reverse a yoke of oxen with the legend L. CASSI (fig. 33b).[91] This coin type may refer to the Temple of Ceres, Liber, and Libera, founded in 494/3 B.C. by Spurius Cassius, who was of the same clan (gens) as the moneyer. The bust of Ceres refers to the temple, known in many sources simply as the *aedes Cereris*.[92] The yoke of oxen suggests Ceres as the goddess of agricultural fertility. The coin therefore refers to the glorious exploits of the ancestor of the moneyer in founding the temple. The reference to the temple appeals to the plebs, who considered Ceres their protector. The clan of the Cassii was plebeian and L. Cassius Caeicianus could well make an appeal to the plebs for their political support by reminding them of his family's historical role in the plebeian cause under Ceres' patronage.[93]

Another coin from 56 B.C. bearing the image of Ceres may also have appeal to the plebs. The coin, a denarius issued by Gaius Memmius, bears on its obverse a laureate head of Quirinus with the legends QUIRINUS and C. MEMMI C. F. (fig. 34a); on its reverse appears Ceres, seated with a torch in her left hand, grain ears in her right, a snake in front of her, and the legend MEMMIUS AED. CERIALIA PREIMUS FECIT, "Memmius the aedile first celebrated the Cerialia" (fig. 34b).[94] The legend refers to the founding of the Cerialia by Memmius' ancestor, or more properly to the founding of the games of that ancient festival, the ludi Ceriales. As we have seen, the Cerialia was an especially plebeian festival, and the plebs issued *mutitationes*, mutual invitations, to it. Moreover, the games of this festival, the ludi Ceriales, were celebrated by the aediles of the plebs. The *gens Memmia*, to which this moneyer belonged, was a plebeian family.[95] Like L. Cassius Caeicianus, C. Memmius might well make an appeal to the plebs for political support based on his family's role in the cult of their patron goddess.[96]

Another appeal to the plebs is seen in a denarius issued c. 86 B.C. by Marcus Fannius and Lucius Critonius.[97] This coin bears on the obverse a head of Ceres with the legend AED. PL. (aediles plebis, "aediles of the plebs") (fig. 4a); on the reverse appear two male figures seated on a bench, side by side with a wheat stalk on the right and with the legends M. FAN. L. CRI. and P. A. (*publico argento*, "from public money") (fig. 4b). The wheat stalk and the legend *publico argento* indicate that this type refers to a public distribution of grain to the plebs by the two aediles.[98] The aediles probably administered these grain distributions to the poor, the frumentationes, from their headquarters at the Temple of Ceres, Liber, and Libera.[99] On one level, therefore, this coin refers to Ceres as the goddess of grain and the grain supply. It is an attempt by the plebeian aediles to advertise their functions in relation to the grain supply.[100] The association of the legend AED. PL. with the bust of Ceres on the obverse, however, indicates more. By placing their title next to the image of the goddess, the issuers of the coin emphatically identified their magistracy, an office of the plebs, with the goddess Ceres, the protectress of the plebs. On another level, therefore, this coin appeals to the sympathies of the plebs by referring to the close association of the issuers with their tutelary deity. The two levels of meaning in this coin type are not unrelated. The grain distributions to which the coin refers were a special concern of the plebs.[101] On the coin of M. Fannius and L. Critonius, therefore, Ceres appears both as the patroness of the plebeian aediles, hence of grain distributions to the plebs and as tutelary deity of that social class.

The image of Ceres became especially significant in the 40s B.C. when it appears on nine coin types between 48 and 42 B.C. The popularity of the type during this tumultuous period may perhaps be explained as an attempt by various political factions to obtain plebeian support. By placing the goddess on coins, the issuers proclaimed their allegiance to the political values she embodied, foremost among which was the survival of the plebs and their libertas, liberty.

Ceres appears on the coins of Caesar and his supporters in three instances. Two denarius types of Gaius Vibius Pansa issued c. 48 B.C. bear an image of the goddess. The first shows on the obverse the head of Liber with an ivy wreath and the legend PANSA (fig. 35a); on the reverse is Ceres walking with a torch in either hand and a plow before her with the legend C. VIBIUS C. F. C. N. (fig. 35b).[102] The second type has the same obverse and a reverse with Ceres in a *biga* of snakes holding a torch in her left hand with the legend C. VIBIUS C. F. C. N. (fig. 5).[103] Pansa, a Caesarian, had been tribune of the plebs in 51 B.C., and was to serve as consul with Hirtius in 43 B.C.[104] These coins may appeal to the plebs through their connection with the political slogan of libertas.[105] This slogan was used by those who wished to appeal to the masses for their political support; in the Late Republic, these were the Populares.[106] The divinity Liber on the obverse of these coins was closely connected with the concept of libertas and was often used by the Populares, including those of Caesar's faction, to appeal to the plebeians.[107] The appeal to plebeian liberty is made more secure by another coin of Pansa that depicts the personified Libertas.[108]

As we saw in chapter 1, Caesar himself is the issuing authority for another coin with the image of Ceres on the reverse (fig. 6).[109] The form of the legend on the obverse of this coin, a denarius, indicates that it was struck on behalf of Julius Caesar by an underling in 46 B.C., and that it was a special issue given out free in honor of a public celebration.[110] In this case, it seems likely that the occasion was Caesar's victory over the Pompeians at Thapsus in Africa on April 6, 46 B.C.[111] Ceres appears on this coin as protectress of the plebs, with whose support Caesar had founded his dictatorship.[112] The date of the coins supports this view. If the coin was issued soon after the Battle of Thapsus, as is likely, then it could have been timed to coincide with the ludi Ceriales and the Cerialia held on April 12–19, a festival highly symbolic for the plebs. Caesar therefore would have been honoring Ceres as the goddess of the plebs, whose support he was seeking with the issue.

In 43–42 B.C. Ceres appears on the coinage of both the tyrannicides and the triumvirs, who thus lay claim simultaneously to the patronage of the goddess of the plebs. From the camp of the tyrannicides appear two types issued under the authority of Brutus. On the first, issued on both an aureus and a denarius, the obverse shows a bust of Ceres, crowned with grain (fig. 36a) and the legends L. SESTI and PRO Q.; the reverse bears a tripod, axe, and *simpulum*, and the legend Q. CAEPIO BRUTUS PRO COS. (fig. 36b).[113] The second type, on a quinarius, has a similar obverse (fig. 37a) and a reverse of Victory bearing a palm branch in her left hand and a wreath in her right and the legend Q. CAEPIO BRUTUS PRO COS. (fig. 37b).[114] Although Crawford has identified the deity represented on the obverse of these coins as Libertas,the presence of the corona spicea indicates that it is Ceres.[115] L. Sestius served as proquaestor to Brutus during his expedition to Thrace.[116] Ceres appears on these coins as the patroness of libertas, a concept that the tyrannicides widely exploited in justifying Caesar's death.[117] The personified Libertas appears on several coins struck under the authority of Brutus.[118] The appearance of Ceres on the coins of Brutus attempted to coopt the goddess and the libertas she protected. In so doing the tyrannicides bid for plebeian support.

The Second Triumvirate also used Ceres in its numismatic propaganda. The goddess appears on three aureus coin types issued by L. Mussidius Longus, moneyer of a college supportive of the triumvirs. On the obverse of all three types appears the head of Ceres (e.g., fig. 38a); on the reverse a wreath of wheat stalks with the legend L. MUSSIDIUS LONGUS or L. MUSSIDI LONGI. (fig. 38b).[119] These coins may be dated to between 43 and 41 B.C.[120] Le Bonniec argues that with these types the moneyer reclaimed for the triumvirs the goddess of the plebs.[121]

The goddess also turns up on two coin types of Octavian/Augustus. On a denarius dated to 42 B.C. and issued by the moneyer P. Clodius appears the head of Octavian on the obverse with the legend CAESAR III VIR R. P. C. (fig. 39a); on the reverse is a goddess holding what appears to be a stalk of wheat in her right hand and a sceptre in her left, with the legend P. CLODIUS M.F. (fig. 39b).[122] Clodius was a member of the same college of moneyers associated with the triumvirs as L. Mussidius Longus. If indeed the object in the right hand of the female figure on the coin is wheat, then she may be identified as Ceres, here claimed for the triumvir Octavian.[123] On an aureus dated to A.D. 13–14 and issued at the imperial mint at Lugdunum appears on the obverse the head of Augustus with the legend CAESAR AUGUSTUS DIVI F. PATER PATRIAE (fig. 40a); on the reverse is a goddess seated on a chair, holding a sceptre in her right hand and possibly a bundle of wheat stalks in her left with the legend PONTIF. MAXIM. (fig. 40b).[124] Again, if the object held by the figure is indeed wheat, then she may be identified as Ceres. The type is repeated under Tiberius, and a similar Claudian type is especially interesting.[125] On the latter, a dupondius issued century A.D. 41–50, the head of the deified Augustus appears on the obverse (fig. 41a), while on the reverse appears a seated female figure holding stalks of wheat in her right hand and a long torch in her left with the legend DIVA AUGUSTA (fig. 41b). Here, the figure may be identified as Au-

gustus' wife Livia, assimilated to the goddess Ceres after her death and consecration. The Augustan types may indicate that the princeps was appealing to
the plebs for their political support.

Other evidence also points to Augustus' interest in the plebs and their goddess Ceres. Augustus began the restoration of the Temple of Ceres, Liber, and
Libera during his principate (Tac. *Ann.* 2.49). As we have seen, this temple was
closely connected with the plebs, and Augustus may well have undertaken this
restoration with the benefits of plebeian support in mind. As I shall argue in
chapter 6, an important relief of the Ara Pacis Augustae, dedicated in 9 B.C.,
represents Ceres (fig. 11). The altar was erected at the order of the Roman
Senate, who wished to commemorate Augustus' return from the provinces.
Ceres appears here at the rear entrance of the altar, opposite the scenes with
Aeneas and Romulus and Remus on the front. Both Aeneas and Romulus may
be connected with the patricians: Romulus founded the order of the patricians,
and Aeneas was the father of the Julian clan, a patrician gens. The plebeian
goddess Ceres may then appear on the altar in opposition to the patricians Aeneas and Romulus.[126] Since the foundation of the cult of Ceres, Liber, and Libera is traditionally connected with the establishment of the Republic, the appearance of the goddess on the altar honors plebeian participation in the very
origin of the Roman state.[127]

It is difficult to identify specific examples of the use of Ceres' image under
the Empire to appeal to the plebs. The goddess certainly does appear frequently
in imperial coinage, but scholars have usually interpreted this as a reference to
her association with the grain supply.[128] Her appearance may also be connected
with the practice of identifying women of the imperial family with Ceres,
which I shall examine in chapter 5 and appendix 2. It is generally thought that
the plebeian associations of the goddess became less important as the constitution of the Republic gave way to that of the Empire and the old political
rivalries were transformed.[129] To be sure, we know that the Temple of Ceres,
Liber, and Libera continued in use under the Empire, as did the celebration of
her festival, the Cerialia.[130] We must not assume that simply because the plebeian associations of the temple and festival are little mentioned in this period,
they had died out. One piece of evidence suggests a continued linkage among
Ceres, the plebs, and the princeps. On the obverse of a coin of Nerva dated to
A.D. 97 appears the laureate head of the princeps (fig. 23a); on the reverse is a
modius filled with wheat stalks and a poppy with the legend PLEBEI URBANAE
FRUMENTO, "with the grain having been established for the urban plebs"
(fig. 23b).[131] The legend indicates Nerva's concern for the grain supply of the

plebs, while the symbols used suggest a connection with Ceres as a grain goddess, and perhaps also as a goddess of the plebs. The coin type suggests that connection between Ceres and the plebs is now mediated through the person of the princeps.[132]

4.6 Conclusion

The specifically plebeian and political associations of Ceres, as we have seen, had their roots in the very establishment of the plebs as a social class. The relationship between Ceres and the plebs during the Republic is indicated by the development of associations between the temple of the goddess and the plebs and of the connections between the plebeian magistrates and Ceres. In the late third century B.C., the importation of the cult of Magna Mater indicates the continued significance of the cult of the goddess as a focus for plebeian social consciousness. The association of Ceres with the plebs remained an important aspect of the goddess at least until the end of the first century B.C. With the principate of Augustus, the significance of this association was transformed in the new social order of the Empire. During the Early Roman Empire, the goddess was associated with the princeps, and her associations with fertility, women, and the plebs were mediated through him and through his family.

Chapter 5

WOMEN

5.1 *Introduction*

T he connection of Ceres with Roman women is most evident in the cult of the goddess and her daughter, Proserpina, which was introduced to Rome during the Middle Republic.[1] Women alone officiated at and participated in the rituals and festivals of this cult. Moreover, the myth and ritual of the cult focused on themes especially significant to women. As we shall see, the cult of Ceres and Proserpina was particularly related to Roman women of the upper class and served to reinforce their social roles. Ceres herself became identified with the ideal Roman woman and the virtues of chastity and motherhood promoted for women of the upper class by the ruling male elite. The official encouragement of these virtues served to buttress the traditional patriarchal structure of Roman society. The paradigmatic nature of Ceres was exploited in Roman political propaganda under the Empire, when the female relatives of the princeps were identified with the goddess. In this chapter, I will explore the significance of the cult of Ceres and Proserpina, analyze the connection of Ceres to the virtues of Roman womanhood, and survey the use of this association in imperial political propaganda through the identification of women of the imperial family with Ceres.

5.2 *The Cult of Ceres and Proserpina*

5.2.1 ORIGINS

The evidence indicates that the Roman cult of Ceres and Proserpina had a Greek origin and was related to the Thesmophoric cult of the goddess Demeter. Cicero identifies the origins of the cult in his speech on behalf of L. Cornelius Balbus:

> Jurors, our forefathers wished the sacra Cereris to be performed with the greatest religious scrupulousness and reverence; these, since they were brought over from

Greece, were both taken care of always by Greek priestesses and were named altogether Greek. But although they selected from Greece that woman, who was to show and conduct that Greek rite, nevertheless they wanted her to perform the rites as a citizen on behalf of citizens, so that she might pray to the immortal gods with a foreign and external knowledge, but with a domestic and civil intention. I see that these priestesses generally were either from Naples or Velia, without a doubt [women] of federated cities.

(Cic. *Balb.* 55)

According to Cicero, the rites of the Roman cult of Ceres, the *sacra Cereris*, were "brought over from Greece" (adsumpta de Graecia).[2] The word "Graecia" could refer either to Greece proper or to Magna Graecia, the Greek cities in Southern Italy. Cicero suggests the latter, since he goes on to tell us that the priestesses of this cult came from Naples or Velia. Southern Italy, particularly Campania, was a region particularly devoted to the worship of Demeter Thesmophoros and her daughter, Persephone. As Peterson has shown, this cult had its center at Cumae, whence it spread to Naples and the other cities of Southern Italy.[3] The Greek cult of Demeter Thesmophoros was particularly associated with women.[4] Its primary festival was the Thesmophoria, in which women alone participated, and the officiants of this cult were exclusively female. As we shall see, the Roman cult of Ceres and Proserpina shared the close relationship to women of its Greek model.

5.2.2 OFFICIANTS AND PARTICIPANTS

As in the Greek cult, the chief officiant of the cult of Ceres and Proserpina was a woman. The female leadership of this cult contrasts with other Roman cults of Ceres, in which the goddess was served by male personnel. In the ancient Italic cult of Ceres, the chief officiant was the male flamen Cerialis.[5] The triadic cult of Ceres, Liber, and Libera was served by the male aediles of the plebs.[6] By contrast, the *sacerdos Cereris* or *Cerealis*, the officiant of the cult of Ceres and Proserpina, was female.[7] Numerous inscriptions from various sites in Italy name women who are identified as the *sacerdos Cereris* or *Cerealis*.[8] No men are ever named as holding this office.[9]

The female nature of the priesthood of this cult is further supported by the passage from the *Pro Balbo* cited above. In this passage, Cicero refers to the officiants of the cult with exclusively feminine adjectives (Graecas and Neapolitanas). Moreover, he specifically identifies "that woman, who was to show and conduct that Greek rite" (illam, quae Graecum illud sacrum monstraret et faceret). According to Cicero, the rites were always celebrated by Greek priestesses (per Graecas curata sunt semper sacerdotes). This implies the exclusive right of women to hold the priesthood.

In a passage from another oration, Cicero tells us that at Catena in Sicily the officiants of the cult of Ceres and Proserpina in Sicily (sacerdotes Cereris atque illius fani antistae) were "older women respected for their noble birth and character" (maiores natu probatae ac nobiles mulieres) (*Verr.* 2.4.99). The passage indicates the class as well as the gender of the officiants of the cult. Like the one at Catena, the priesthood of Ceres at Rome also was almost certainly exclusively held by women of the upper class.

The importance the Romans assigned to this female priesthood is indicated by its designation as a public office. In inscriptions, the officiant of the cult of Ceres and Proserpina may be further specified as a "public priestess of Ceres for the Roman people and citizens" (sacerdos Cereris publica populo Romano Quiritibus).[10] The term "publica" defines the priestess as operating pro bono publico or, as Cicero has it in the passage we have been examining, "for the citizens" (*pro civibus*). Those rites that were performed by a public priestess, the publica sacra, were conducted at public expense on behalf of the people, as Festus informs us (s.v. *publica sacra*, 244 Müller). Pomeroy has noted that the priestesses of Ceres and Proserpina were the only women, besides the Vestal Virgins, who had the prestige of administering a public cult and of expending public funds.[11] By serving as officiants of this cult, therefore, these upper-class women gained an important public status. Plutarch shows his awareness of the importance of the public priesthood of Ceres when he states that it was the greatest honor to which a Roman matrona could aspire (*De mul. vir.* 26).

The participants in the cult of Ceres and Proserpina, like its officiants, were probably also exclusively female. Again, this exclusivity serves to contrast this cult with the other Roman cults of Ceres, in which both men and women participated. The proposition that only women participated in the rituals and festivals of the cult of Ceres and Proserpina is supported by literary evidence. In the *Laws*, his philosophical treatise on the ideal state, Cicero discusses the cultic practices of women:

> Let there not be nocturnal sacrifices by women, except those which are made on behalf of the people according to proper form; nor let one initiate anyone [any woman], except as is customary to Ceres in the Greek ritual.
>
> (Cic. *Leg.* 2.21)

The mention of the rite of the Greek cult of Ceres (Cereri Graeco sacro) in this context suggests that the initiates of this cult were exclusively female. This conclusion is supported by another passage from the *Laws*, in which Cicero elaborates on his proposal:

> I return therefore to our laws. In these laws indeed it must be made inviolable most carefully that the clear light [of day] guard the reputation of women in the eyes of the many, and that they be initiated with that rite to Ceres with which they are initiated at Rome.
>
> (Cic. *Leg.* 2.36–37)

Here again Cicero refers specifically to women in connection with the initiation rites of Ceres and suggests that only they were permitted to participate in these rituals.[12] This conclusion is supported by another passage from Cicero. In his description of the cult of Ceres at Catena in Sicily, the orator notes:[13]

> Entrance into this shrine is not [permitted] for men; the rites were accustomed to be performed by women and maidens (mulieres ac virgines).
>
> (Cic. *Verr.* 2.4.99.)

Literary references to the chief festival of the cult, the sacrum anniversarium Cereris, provide further evidence for exclusively female participation in the activities of the cult and also point to the upper-class origins of these participants. This "annual rite of Ceres" refers to the festival of the goddess that the Augustan historian Livy notes was interrupted as a result of the disastrous Battle of Cannae in 216 B.C.:

> Then also private disasters were made common among the houses and mourning so filled the entire city that the yearly rite of Ceres (sacrum anniversarium Cereris) was interrupted, because it is not religiously correct for those in mourning to celebrate it, and at that time there was no matrona having no part in grief. And so, lest for this reason other public or private rites also be neglected, by decree of the Senate, mourning was limited to thirty days.
>
> (Livy 22.56.4–5)

Elsewhere, Livy returns to this incident:

> Because the sacrificium Cereris had been interrupted when all the matronae were in mourning the Senate ordered that mourning be limited to thirty days.
>
> (Livy 34.6.15)

In this passage, part of the festival, the "sacrifice of Ceres" (sacrificium Cereris), is made to stand for the whole, the sacrum anniversarium. In both passages Livy names the participants in the mourning and hence in the festival as the Roman matronae.[14] The term "matrona" generally refers to an upper-class married woman. Its use by Livy indicates that those who participated in this festival of the cult of Ceres and Proserpina were women of this social class.[15]

5.2.3 MYTH AND RITUAL

As the membership of this cult indicates its association with upper-class women, so too do its myth and ritual. The central myth of the cult focuses on the relationship between two female divinities: Ceres and Proserpina. Festus connects this myth with the annual festival of Ceres:

> The Greek festive rites of Ceres were brought over from Greece, [rites] that the ma-
> tronae celebrated on account of the finding of Proserpina. Since there were no ma-
> tronae to celebrate the rites because of the slaughter at Cannae and the large number
> of mourners, it was decreed that mourning not last more than one hundred days.
>
> (Fest., s.v. *Graeca sacra*, 97 Müller)

Festus notes that the festival of Ceres, which he calls the "Greek festive rites of Ceres" (Graeca sacra festa Cereris), was celebrated "on account of the finding of Proserpina" (ob inventionem Proserpinae). His association of this festival with the mourning of the matronae after the Battle of Cannae indicates that this is the same festival as Livy's sacrum anniversarium Cereris, although Festus gives a different limit to mourning imposed by the Senate, one hundred instead of thirty days. Moreover, the mention of the matronae again suggests that the women participating were of the upper class. Festus' explanation for the festival directly links these rites to the Greek myth of Demeter and Persephone. The myth, known from a variety of sources, tells of the rape of Persephone by the god of the underworld, the search of Demeter for her daughter, and Persephone's return to her mother.[16]

Further support for the association of this myth with the Roman cult of the two goddesses is provided by Servius' commentary on Vergil:

> When Ceres sought through all the earth with lit torches for Proserpina, who had
> been seized by Dis Pater, she called her with shouts where three or four roads meet;
> from this it has endured in her rites that on certain days a lamentation is raised at the
> crossroads everywhere by the matronae, just as in [the rite] of Isis.
>
> (Serv. on Verg. *Aen.* 4.609)

Servius notes that the matronae performed a ritual cry in memory of the cries Ceres made when she searched for her daughter. The involvement of the matronae suggests the sacrum anniversarium Cereris and would also justify Festus' understanding of the mythical *aition* behind that festival.

Similarly, the myth of Demeter and Persephone served as the *aition* for the Greek Thesmophoria.[17] According to our sources for this festival, the first day, called Anodos, or "Ascending," included the ritual casting of pigs into pits sacred to Demeter and Persephone. This ritual reportedly commemorated the fall of Eubouleus and his pigs into the earth when it opened to receive Hades and his captured bride, Persephone. The second day, called Nesteia, or "Fasting," included a period of mourning, in which the women sat on the ground and fasted all day. This mourning ritually reenacted Demeter's grief for her lost daughter. The final day, Kalligeneia, or "Fair Birth," was a day of celebration with sacrifices and a feast to celebrate Persephone's return to her mother.

These rituals show an interesting correspondence to those of the sacrum anniversarium Cereris. The ritual mourning of the matronae at the crossroads mentioned by Servius corresponds to the second day of the Thesmophoria.[18] The third day of the festival may correspond to Plutarch's mention of a sacrifice and procession during the sacrum anniversarium Cereris (*Vit. Fab. Max.* 18.1–2). Given the evidence for the association of the myth of Ceres and Proserpina with the Roman sacrum anniversarium and the similarities of this festival to the Thesmophoria, we may identify the ritual reenactment of the myth of the two goddesses as the central focus of the Roman festival as well.

This myth is represented frequently in Roman art of the Late Republic and Empire.[19] Thus on a Late Republican coin Ceres is shown holding a torch and riding in her serpent chariot as she flies through the heavens in search of her daughter (fig. 5).[20] In a sarcophagus of the third century A.D., Ceres appears to the left, holding two torches and standing in a chariot drawn by two snakes; to the right are Hades and Proserpina, fleeing in a chariot drawn by four horses (fig. 21).[21]

The symbolic significance of the myth of Ceres and Proserpina to which these representations allude lies in its definition and affirmation of the roles of upper-class women in Roman society. As Zeitlin has noted, the myth underlying the festival of the Thesmophoria expresses the opposition and dynamic tension between two primary roles of women: the mature, fertile mother, symbolized by Demeter; and the young, sexually inexperienced girl, symbolized by Persephone.[22] The myth presents the necessary divergence between the lives of mother and daughter but promises the reconciliation of these two roles through the eventual reunification of the two symbolic figures. Through this myth these two roles can be seen as a continuum in which mother and daughter are but two facets of a single human figure, a woman.

Evidence suggests that the Roman cult of Ceres and Proserpina also focused on these two roles of women. We have seen that the participants in this cult were the matronae of Rome, whom we have noted were women of the upper class in Roman society. The term "matronae" may embrace both married and unmarried women, especially in a religious context. Gagé has proposed that, as in other cults of the Roman matronae, the female participants in the cult of Ceres and Proserpina included two categories of women: married women, or matronae proper, and unmarried women, or virgines.[23] The participation of both groups of women in the cult is supported by Cicero's mention of both "women" (mulieres) and "maidens" (virgines) in the rites conducted at the shrine of Ceres at Catena, in the passage which we examined above (*Verr.* 2.4.99), and by the following passage from Valerius Maximus:

> By so much [was] the Senate of our state more reverent toward the gods, which decreed after the disaster at Cannae that the matronae not extend their mourning beyond the thirtieth day, so that the sacra Cereris could be celebrated by them; because with virtually the greater part of the Roman forces lying dead on that cursed and hard ground, no one's household gods were inexperienced in sorrow. And so the mothers and daughters, and wives and sisters, of those recently killed, with their tears wiped off and their emblems of mourning set aside, were compelled to put on white robes and to offer incense on the altars.
>
> (Val. Max. 1.1.15)

He names the participants in the festival of Ceres as all the female relatives of those slain in the Battle of Cannae, their "mothers and daughters and wives and sisters" (matres ac filiae coniugesque et sorores). This suggests that both older, married women and younger, presumably unmarried, women participated in this festival. The two categories of matron and maiden correspond to the mythic roles of the two goddesses. Through their reenactment of the central myth of the cult these women define the parameters of their roles in Roman society.

The relationship between these two categories of women is also expressed in Roman art. Images of Ceres and Proserpina together in Roman art suggest the close relationship of mother and daughter, as in a sardonyx cameo dated to the first century A.D. (fig. 24).[24] In the foreground appears the bust of Ceres, veiled and crowned with wheat; in the background is the bust of Proserpina with a diadem. Bieber has noted that the statue types of the Large Herculaneum Woman and the Small Herculaneum Woman were used to represent contemporary women in the guise of Ceres and Proserpina, respectively.[25] These types appear on Roman imperial sarcophagi and funerary stelae, where the Large represents the wife of the deceased, and the Small his daughter.[26] For example, in a relief from Athens dated to the late Antonine period, the Large Herculaneum Woman type is used for the older woman to the left, the mother, and the Small Herculaneum Woman type for the younger woman to the right, her daughter (fig. 26).[27] Ceres and Proserpina therefore represent, respectively, the married matron and the unmarried maiden, two basic social categories for Roman women of the upper class.

Two themes emphasized in the sacrum anniversarium Cereris, chastity and fertility, express on a ritual level what the story of Ceres and Proserpina expresses mythically—the nature of these women's roles in Roman society.[28] In Ovid's series of love poems, the *Amores*, the poet refers to a festival of Ceres that he connects with ritual chastity:

> The yearly time of the rite of Ceres has come; my girl sleeps alone in an empty bed. Golden Ceres, crowned on your fine hair with wheat stalks, why do you limit our happiness with your rites? You, goddess, people everywhere call generous, nor does any [goddess] less begrudge human blessings. Before, neither did the hairy farmers parch the grain, nor was the word "threshing floor" known on earth, but the oaks, the first oracles, bore the acorn; this and the grass of the tender turf were food. Ceres first taught the seed to swell in the fields and cut with the sickle its colored tops; she first compelled the bulls to bend their necks to the yoke, and she turned the ancient earth with the curved plow. Does anyone believe that she rejoices in the tears of lovers and that she is worshipped well in torments and by lying in bed alone? Although she loves fertile fields, nevertheless she is not so countrified as to have a breast empty of love. . . . [The story of Iasion and Ceres, lines 19–42, is here omitted.] . . . Because lying alone had been sad for you, golden goddess, am I compelled to bear now this in your rites? Why should I be sad when your daughter has been found and rules over a kingdom of a lesser share than Juno? A festal day calls for Venus, and songs, and unmixed wine; these gifts are fit to bring to the gods, our masters.
>
> (Ov. *Am.* 3.10.1–18 and 43–48)

Ovid calls this festival "the yearly time of the rite of Ceres" (annua Cerealis tempora sacri), which seems to be a poetic expansion of sacrum anniversarium Cereris. Again the occasion is associated with finding Ceres' daughter, Proserpina: "when your daughter has been found" (line 45). The daughter is Proserpina, and Ovid's words recall the "finding of Proserpina" that Festus assigned to the festival interrupted by the Battle of Cannae. All these connections indicate that Ovid's festival is the sacrum anniversarium Cereris.[29] Ovid laments the ritual chastity that characterizes this festival: he notes that his mistress must sleep alone in her empty bed (line 2). The poet returns to this theme twice: "Does anyone believe that she rejoices in the tears of lovers and that she is worshipped well in torments and by lying in bed alone?" (lines 15–16); and again, "Because lying alone was sad for you, golden goddess, am I compelled to bear now this in your rites?" (lines 43–44). Ovid illuminates one aspect of this imposed chastity (lines 45–46): as Ceres slept alone in her grief for the loss of her daughter, so the worshippers of the goddess commemorate her grief and loneliness through their chastity.

In the Thesmophoria, women were also required to remain chaste during the festival and for several days beforehand.[30] In addition, during the festival itself they used the *agnus castus* plant to reduce sexual desire and to aid in maintaining chastity (Pliny *HN* 24.59). According to Zeitlin, the chastity required for the Thesmophoria symbolizes the natural or preliminary chastity of the daughter Persephone, as well as the forced sexual abstinence of her mourning mother.[31] If we may presume the same applies to the Roman festival, then the ritual chastity imposed by that festival serves to express responses to sexuality and to define sexual identity among the female participants.

The social class of those participants is especially important in this context. The chastity of women of the upper class was an important factor in the status quo of patriarchal Roman society. The men who were the leaders in that society needed to be sure that their wives and daughters remained chaste, so the social ties that those women embodied remained under their control. In this context, an emphasis on chastity in a cult sanctioned for women of this class seems readily explicable. As we have seen, the emphasis on chastity in the cult of Ceres and Proserpina contrasts with the promiscuity associated with the cult of the Bacchanalia by the Romans, and helps explain why the Roman state encouraged the former, but suppressed the latter.[32]

The ritual chastity of the Greek and Roman festivals of the Thesmophoria and sacrum anniversarium Cereris has its opposite, or, perhaps better, correlate in ritual fertility. The close connection between these two concepts is indicated by a passage from Propertius.

Ancient Lanuvium is under the protection of a long-lived serpent. Here an hour of so rare delay is not wasted for you. Where a sacred descent is snatched away by a blind cleft, where penetrates (Maiden, beware every such road) the offering of the hungry snake, when he demands his yearly nourishment and from the lowest region of the earth he twists his hissings. The girls who are sent down to such rites turn pale when their hand is trusted with fear to the mouth of the snake. He seizes the tidbits brought by the maiden; the very food baskets tremble in the hands of the maiden. If they have been chaste, they return to the embrace of their parents, and the farmers cry, "It will be a fertile year."

(Prop. 4.8.3–14)

Propertius describes here an ancient ritual of Lanuvium in which maidens fed a terrible snake. He signals the significance of this ritual in the final lines of the passage, when he connects the chastity of the maidens with the fertility of the growing season. Fertility and chastity are two sides of the same coin, two aspects of being female.[33] These ritual themes are correlates of one another, just as the two social roles of women, the matron and the maiden, are correlates. These roles are symbolized on the mythic level by the story of Ceres and Proserpina, and on the ritual level by fertility and chastity.

Ritual emphasis on fertility is seen in both the Greek Thesmophoria and the Roman sacrum anniversarium Cereris. At the Thesmophoria, our sources report, symbols of human fertility, such as models of phalluses, were employed, and the female participants of this engaged in ritual obscenity, *aischrologia*. Both of these rituals, Burkert has noted, were intended to promote fertility among humans and crops.[34] The Roman festival also employed symbols of fertility, exclusively agricultural ones according to our sources, which may however be incomplete.[35] As Ovid reports in the passage cited above from the *Amores*, the goddess worshipped in the festival wore a corona spicea, or crown of wheat stalks (Ov. *Am.* 3.10.3). As we saw in chapter 2, this crown symbolizes Ceres' role in the production of crops, especially grain, and hence in agricultural fertility.[36] She wears it in numerous representations in Roman art.[37] The stalks of wheat associated with Ceres are also mentioned in the following passage from Ovid's *Metamorphoses*:

> The pious mothers were celebrating that annual festival of Ceres at which, having veiled their bodies with white clothing, they give as first-fruit offerings wheat stalks in garlands, and for nine nights they consider love and the touch of men among forbidden things. In that crowd was Cenchreis, the wife of the king, and she was taking part in the secret rites.
>
> (Ov. *Met.* 10.431–436)

Ovid here is ostensibly referring to another festival of the goddess, the "annual festival of Ceres" (festa annua Cereris), celebrated in Cyprus. However, many of the elements of this festival suggest its roots in the Roman sacrum anniversarium, including the exclusive participation of women, the "pious mothers" (piae matres), and the requirement of ritual chastity.[38] At this festival the women offered stalks of wheat in garlands as first fruits to the goddess (primitias frugum dant spicia serta suarum). First-fruit offerings were made to agricultural deities, and Ceres received them as the protectress of the fertility of the fields.[39] By participating in the festival of Ceres, her female worshippers reinforced the presence of fertility in the goddess, in crops, and in themselves.

112

Fertility is identified as the responsibility of these women and hence as an element of their identity.

Again we must consider the social class of these women in determining the significance of this ritual theme. By the Late Republic, the lack of fertility among women of the upper class had become problematic. There were not enough sons of patrician families to fill the priesthoods that required those of this social class, and the military as well was suffering from a dearth of upper-class men to fill leadership roles. The seriousness of the problem is indicated by Augustus' attempt to solve it through his laws on marriage and children.[40] The princeps tried to encourage men and women of the upper class to marry, have a large number of children, and remain wedded. His attempts at social engineering seem to have been largely unsuccessful, however, and the problem continued into the Early Empire. In this context, the emphasis on fertility in the cult of Ceres and Proserpina takes on special significance. The upper-class women who participated in this cult were encouraged to assume responsibility for the fertility of the Roman state and to produce the results of their own fertility, their sons and daughters, for the needs of Rome.

The rituals and festivals of the cult of Ceres and Proserpina thus served as rites of intensification, in that they strengthened the social ties that bound upper-class women to one another and to Roman society as a whole. Through this cult, these women set themselves apart from men, affirming themselves and their role in society. As Burkert states for the Thesmophoria, it was through this festival that the women demonstrated "their independence, their responsibility, and their importance for the fertility of the community and the land. The . . . festival emphasizes the creation of solidarity in the role of the woman."[41] This affirmation of the importance of women in Roman society, however, ultimately served to reinforce the rule of men. The Roman cult of the two goddesses encouraged the control of the sexuality of these women for the benefit of the ruling male elite. It therefore operated to maintain the status quo of sexual politics in ancient Rome and served to support the patriarchal basis of Roman society.

5.3 Female Virtues

Through the association of her cult with women and the issues of female identity, the goddess Ceres herself became identified with the Roman matronae and with the ideals of conduct that they were expected to uphold. These ideals were chastity and motherhood, which the Romans praised as the primary virtues of these upper-class women. Again, the intent was to encourage these women to practice these virtues and therefore to support the patriarchal foundation of Roman society.

5.3.1 CHASTITY

Chastity, or castitas, was central to the Roman ideal of womanhood. The Latin term "castitas" in fact has a wider application than the English "chastity," which applies only to sexual purity or virginity. In contrast, castitas applies to purity in general.[42] It may be used to mean ritual purity, as in "pure priests" (*casti sacerdotes*), to refer to morality or ethics, as in "pure from blame" (*a culpa castus*), or to signify sexual purity, as in "chaste maiden" (*casta virgo*). In the latter sense it can apply either to virginity or sexual abstinence, or more broadly to proper sexual conduct, as in "born from a chaste parent" (*ex casta parente natus*).

Castitas is often named as a chief virtue of women in Roman funerary epitaphs.[43] For example, the virtues of the woman Amymone are enumerated in the following epitaph:

> Here lies Amymone, daughter of Marcus, the best and most beautiful woman, a worker of wool, pious, modest, discreet, *casta*, a homebody.
>
> (*CE* 237)

The term *casta* used here probably applies to moral, or, more specifically, sexual purity. In epitaphs the woman who is *casta* is often also *univira*, a "one-man woman," one who has married for life and never remarried, not even after divorce or widowhood, as in the following example:

> Veratia held the flower of her lifetime so chastely that no joy of dishonor seized her. For content with one tried husband she lived; a woman worthy of good things endured the other things done to her.
>
> (*CE* 968)

The phrase "content with one tried husband" (coniuge uno probato) indicates that the woman was an *univira* and the context suggests that this was one of her greatest virtues. The *univirae* were considered the greatest exemplars of castitas: their purity was so renowned that only they were permitted to sacrifice at the shrine of Pudicitia or to function as *pronubae* at a wedding.[44]

The virtue of castitas is prominent in depictions of women in Latin literature as well as in epigraphy. As Williams has pointed out, Vergil's depiction of Dido, an *univira* who abandons the memory of her dead husband and subsequently commits suicide, illustrates the perils in Roman eyes of abandoning marital exclusivity.[45] As Dido is the paradigm of the woman who abandons castitas, the matron Lucretia is the exemplar of those who uphold the ideal.[46] In his recital of the tale of Lucretia set at the end of the regal period, Livy emphasizes her chastity. According to his story (Livy 1.57–59), the Etruscan prince Sextus Tarquinius sees Lucretia in the house of her husband, and "her chastity along with her beauty once looked upon inflames him" (cum forma spectata castitas incitat). After he steals back to the house at night to rape her, she kills herself, "so that an unchaste woman might never live through the example of Lucretia" (nec ulla deinde inpudica Lucretiae exemplo vivet). Later her kinsman Brutus takes up the knife she had used, and, "on the blood most chaste until wronged by a prince" (castissimum ante regiam iniuriam sanguinem), he swears to depose the Etruscan king of Rome, Tarquin. The outrage against Lucretia's chastity, in Livy's view, precipitated the fall of Tarquin and the establishment of the Roman Republic. The story was popular throughout the history of Latin literature, further indicating the importance the Romans placed on the virtue of female chastity, at least for women of the upper class.[47] Both Lucretia and Dido are women of this class, and it is among these women that the virtue of chastity was particularly encouraged.

Like Lucretia, Ceres exemplified castitas to the Romans. We have already noted that sexual chastity was an important part of the annual festival honoring the goddess. Moreover, we learn from the Christian writer Tertullian that the priestesses of Ceres in North Africa had to lead a life of complete sexual abstinence like the Vestal Virgins did (Ad uxor., 1.6 Oehler). Although this restriction is mentioned only in connection with the North African cult of the Cereres, it may well have applied to the Roman one as well.[48]

Ceres' association with both sexual and ritual castitas is supported by literary evidence. The satirist Juvenal notes the lack of women of old-fashioned morals in Rome of the late first century A.D.:

> And what [of the fact that] a wife of ancient morals is sought by him? O doctors, puncture his veins a bit! The extravagant notions of men! Fall forward and worship the Tarpeian threshold and sacrifice a gilded heir to Juno if a matron of chaste head befalls you. Few indeed are the women worthy to touch the fillets of Ceres, whose father does not fear their kisses.
>
> (Juv. 6.45–51)

The fillets of Ceres to which Juvenal refers are either those which decorated the cult statue of the goddess and which only her worshippers were allowed to touch, or those the women wore in the procession of the sacrum anniversarium

Cereris. In either case, they are symbolic of the ritual castitas associated with the goddess, and only those women who were themselves sexually chaste could touch them.

Rituals conducted for Ceres also reveal an emphasis on castitas. Ovid says that even small sacrifices are pleasing to Ceres, so long as they are *casta* (parva bonae Cereri, sint modo casta, placent) (*Fast.* 4.411–412). Festus connects the wedding torch carried in honor of Ceres with the chastity of the bride:

> They were accustomed to carry the torch in weddings in honor of Ceres; the new bride was accustomed to be sprinkled with water, either so that she might come chaste and pure to her husband, or so that she might share fire and water with her husband.
>
> (Fest., s.v. *facem*, 87 Müller)

Statius names the goddess herself *casta Ceres* with all the ritual, moral, and sexual purity implied by that epithet (*Silv.* 4.311). Ceres thus exemplifies the virtue of chastity deeply ingrained in the Roman concept of the ideal woman.

The chastity associated with Ceres has a number of meanings. First, as we noted above, its celebration in the festival dedicated to the goddess serves to indicate proper responses to sexuality and to define sexual identity among women of the upper class. Chastity also may be associated with Ceres in her liminal capacity. Ceres guards boundaries, which are symbolized in the female body by chastity.[49] These boundaries have an economic, political, and social significance.[50] Economically, as we have seen, the Romans connected chastity with the agricultural fertility on which Roman society depended. Politically, chastity symbolizes the physical integrity of the city; the chastity of its women kept the city pure and thus protected it from invaders. Socially, this virtue represents the integrity of the marriage bond among members of the upper class, on which the social structure of Rome depended. The chastity connected with Ceres may be compared to that associated with Vesta. The Vestal Virgins symbolized the integrity of the state through the chastity of their bodies.[51] For this reason, the violation of a Vestal's chastity was considered to be an attack on the state itself, punishable by a horrible death. Through her identification with the concept of chastity, Ceres embodied the value of this virtue to upper-class Roman women for the benefit of the state as a whole.

5.3.2 MOTHERHOOD

Ceres is emblematic of another essential virtue of women, motherhood. The Romans highly valued the concept of the mother.[52] Linguistically, the Latin word *materies*, the "substance of which something is composed," is derived from the Latin for "mother."[53] The term "mother" hence refers to what is primary and essential for existence. The importance the Romans accorded women in their role as mothers is indicated by ancient legends that supposedly date back to the very foundations of the city.[54] Aeneas' mother Venus guided him from Troy to Italy and helped him in his battle against Turnus. Romulus and Remus traced their claim to kingship through their mother to their maternal grandfather and their claim to divine lineage to their mother's union with the god Mars. The Sabine women appealed to their Sabine fathers and Roman husbands to stop fighting, since they would bear the common descendants of those very fathers and husbands.

The immense respect accorded to mothers is perhaps best illustrated by the story of the upper-class woman Cornelia, mother of Tiberius and Gaius Gracchus, who became the standard by which later Roman women were measured. In his biography of Tiberius Gracchus (1.2), Plutarch praises her discretion as a matrona, her affection as a mother, and her constancy and nobility as a widow. Seneca speaks of her bravery (*Helv.* 16), Cicero of her eloquence (*Brut.* 58.211), and Tacitus of her piety, modesty, and devotion to maternal duty (*Dial.* 28). Even Juvenal, in his satire on women, must praise Cornelia for her great virtues, although he finds fault with her for her pride (6.166–169). The greatest of her virtues in Roman eyes was her pride in her role as a mother and her success in that role. Valerius Maximus (4.4) relates that when a Campanian matron showed off her jewels to Cornelia, the latter presented her children and said, "These are my jewels." According to Seneca, when Cornelia's friends wept in her presence for her losses and cursed Fortune, she forbade them to make any indictment against fortune, since "it was Fortune who had made the Gracchi her sons" (*Helv.* 16). Her success as a mother is indicated by Plutarch's statement that she brought up the two Gracchi with such care that they seemed to owe their virtue to nurture more than to nature (*Vit. Ti. Gracch.* 1.2). Cornelia herself was said to desire recognition for her role as a mother. Plutarch tells us that she encouraged her sons to succeed in the political arena by telling them that she wished to be known not as the mother-in-law of Scipio, but as the mother of the Gracchi (*Vit. Ti. Gracch.* 8.6). Indeed, the Romans came to identify her with her maternal role. Again according to Plutarch, the inscription on her statue erected by the Roman people read "Cornelia, Mother of the Gracchi" (*Vit. Ti. Gracch.* 4.3).

As Cornelia was the paradigm of the human mother, Ceres was the exemplum of the divine. I have already examined Ceres' role in motherhood in chapter 2 and will summarize the important points here.[55] The goddess's cult title, at least from the Augustan period on, is Mater, as in the altar of Ceres Mater and Ops Augusta. Latin poets of the Empire also use the term "mater" to refer to the goddess. Arnobius (*Adv. Nat.* 2.73) implies that the epithet "Mater" belonged to the goddess in her Greek cult, which he calls "the Greek rites of Ceres Mater" (Graeca sacra Cereris matris). This cult, as we have seen, honored Ceres and Proserpina. On one level, then, the title "Mater" refers to Ceres as the divine mother of the maiden Proserpina. She is the mater dolorosa whose loss of and search for her daughter are told and retold throughout classical literature.

The association of Ceres with Demeter suggests another meaning, too. Demeter is given a variey of epithets linking her with children, including *kourotrophos*, "Child-Nourishing." She is the mother or foster mother of a variety of children in mythology and is frequently represented holding a child in Greek art. The Roman Ceres, too, is sometimes portrayed nourishing a young child, as in Lucretius' line "but if she is swollen and big-breasted, she is Ceres with Iacchus at her breast" (*RN* 4.1168). Demeter's role as Kourotrophos foreshadows Ceres' paradigmatic Roman role as Mater.

As her role in agricultural fertility indicates, Ceres is the mother not only of children but also of crops. An inscription calls her "mother of the fields" (*mater agrorum*) (*CIL* 11.3196), and Ovid refers to Ceres and Tellus together as the "mothers of crops" (*frugum matres*) (*Fast.* 1.671). Here the epithet "Mater" refers to the ancient Italic cult of Ceres, in which she was worshipped together with Tellus or Tella Mater,[56] as is illustrated by the following pun from Varro:

> Not without cause were they accustomed to call the same earth Mother (matrem) and Ceres.
>
> (*Rust.* 3.1.4)

Ceres was thus the Divine Mother of the Divine Maiden, the nourishing mother of children, and the mother of crops. In her being, she united the various aspects of motherhood and female fertility. Ovid expresses her essential unity in the following lines from the *Metamorphoses* (5.489–490): "O Progenitress of the maiden sought throughout the world and Progenitress of crops" (o toto quaesitae virginis orbe et frugum genetrix). As I shall argue in chapter 6, this image of Ceres as mother of children and crops is presented visually in the famous relief from the Ara Pacis Augustae (fig. 11).

To the Romans, then, Ceres was a symbol of motherhood and fertility as well as castitas, an emblem of these particular elements in female identity. These concepts were virtues that the ruling male elite of Roman society particularly encouraged among upper-class women.

5.4 Ceres and Women of the Imperial Family

The influence of Ceres on female identity was exploited widely in the political propaganda of the Empire. The wives, mothers, daughters, and sisters of the princeps or his designated heir were identified with the goddess in inscriptions, coins, sculptures, and gems dating from the Augustan period to that of Septimius Severus. The goddess served as the symbol of the ideal woman and the virtues of chastity and motherhood, particularly associated with women of the upper class. By their association with her, these women also became identified with these concepts and linked them to the imperial household and the princeps himself. In the remainder of this chapter, I will examine the connection between female members of the imperial household and Ceres and consider the significance of this connection in imperial propaganda. The point is this: the overt propagandistic use of this connection shows the general power of the symbolism of Ceres for the ordinary Roman and in addition indicates how strongly the underlying religious ideology of this symbolism could and did affect Roman daily life. Appendix 2 presents a catalog of all the identifications of women of the imperial family with Ceres that I have collected in my research. Here I present my conclusions based on this evidence.

Two types of identification of historical persons with Ceres may be distinguished: association and assimilation.[57] Association represents the indirect identification of a woman with the goddess. For example, Faustina the Elder, the wife of Antoninus Pius, is represented on the obverse of a coin struck by an imperial mint during the reign of her husband (fig. 42a), while the goddess Ceres is portrayed on its reverse, holding her torch and a sceptre (fig. 42b).[58] This type of identification may identify a woman's patroness as Ceres without implying that she had been directly identified with the goddess. The association of women of the imperial family with Ceres is common in all periods and media, and is especially prevalent in state coinage from the Trajanic period to the Severan age.[59]

The other type of identification, assimilation, is more rare. In this direct form of identification with the goddess, the woman assumes her attributes or titles. For example, Livia, the wife of Augustus, appears on a cameo wearing the corona spicea of Ceres (fig. 10).[60] This representation suggests that she had in some sense become the goddess herself and hence was accorded her symbol of agricultural fertility. Another example is provided by the numerous inscriptions that name women of the imperial family as "the new Ceres" or "the new Demeter." [61]

Sometimes it is difficult to distinguish between association and assimilation, as in the so-called Ceres-type sculpture.[62] This type shows a woman in a singular stance and drapery style, often holding symbols of Ceres, such as poppies, stalks of wheat, or torches. Bieber has suggested that this type was developed in the Hellenistic period to represent the goddess herself or her priestess.[63] The type was used during the second century A.D. for several women of the imperial family. For example, a statue whose portrait feature identify her as Faustina the Elder, wife of Antoninus Pius, holds a torch in her right hand and a bundle of wheat stalks and poppies in her left (fig. 25).[64] The portrayal of a woman in this guise may indicate that she was a devotee or priestess of Ceres, and hence associate her with the goddess; it may signal her direct assimilation to Ceres; or it may simply indicate that she was identified with the ideal type of the mother, symbolized by Ceres.[65]

In general direct assimilation to the goddess occurs only under two circumstances: when the woman represented is no longer living, or when the medium of representation is unofficial. After the death of a woman and her consecration as a *diva*, her assimilation to Ceres was not uncommon, even in official media such as state coinage. For example, in a coin issued after her death during the reign of Claudius, his mother, Antonia Minor, appears on the obverse, wearing the corona spicea of Ceres; the legend reads ANTONIA AUGUSTA (fig. 27).[66] The assimilation of living women to Ceres in official media, however, is quite rare. It occurs only in state coinage only for Agrippina the Younger, the wife of Claudius, and for Sabina, the wife of Hadrian. For example, Agrippina the Younger wears the wheat crown of Ceres in a coin issued by Claudius before her death, and this is the earliest extant example for the direct and official assimilation to Ceres of a living member of the imperial family (fig. 43).[67] The distinction is not surprising, since the Romans considered the dead to belong to the supernatural, or divine sphere, while the living remained in the natural or human sphere. The representation of a deceased woman in the guise of Ceres would therefore have been acceptable to Roman sensibilities, and hence could be promoted in official media.

In unofficial media, such as local coinage or private works of art, this distinction did not necessarily hold. Coins produced by local mints in various cities of the Empire frequently show the living wife of the princeps with the attributes of Ceres, as in the reverse of a coin of Alexandria, which shows

Messalina, the wife of Claudius, holding the wheat stalks of Ceres (fig. 44).[68] Similarly, local communities might honor such a woman with an inscription naming her as the "New Demeter," as the people of Ephesus and Aphrodisias honored Livia.[69] Private individuals, too, might commission or purchase a work of art, such as a sculpture or gemstone, with a portrait of a woman of the family of the princeps as Ceres. For example, a woman of the imperial household is represented in a cameo with her two children wearing the wheat stalk and poppy crown of Ceres (fig. 45),[70] in an image that recalls the figure on the Ara Pacis relief (fig. 11). Vollenweider has identified this woman as Livilla, the wife of Drusus Minor.[71] These examples of assimilation do not represent official propaganda, since they were not dictated by the princeps or produced by the imperial administration. However, they may reflect such propaganda inasmuch as they indicate how the concept of identification with Ceres was accepted and internalized by the inhabitants of the Empire.[72]

We must now consider the significance of these practices. I have suggested above that women of the imperial family were identified with Ceres as the symbol both of the ideal woman and of her virtues of castitas, motherhood, and female fertility. This identification served, I argue, a variety of propagandistic purposes.

First, it suggested that the human and agricultural fertility that the goddess symbolized was attached to the princeps and hence could be assured by him for the Empire as a whole.[73] Such assurance was significant in an economy that depended so heavily on agriculture, especially the growing and importation of grain. Ceres was the protectress of the grain, and by associating himself with her the princeps implied that he could assure the supply of grain for the people of the Empire.

Second, since the mechanism of this association operated through women, the identification also brought to mind Ceres' close relationship to the ideal woman and her virtues of chastity and motherhood. In this way the princeps supported the female virtues associated with the goddess and suggested that these virtues were exemplified in the women of his family. The identification thus promoted a moral revival in Roman society by example from above.[74] The same purpose also underlies, for example, Augustus' encouragement of Roman women to bear more children and his punishment of his own daughter and granddaughter for sexual misconduct. The princeps recognized the practical implications of motherhood and chastity and attempted to embody these virtues paradigmatically in the imperial household in the same way that Ceres embodied them on a symbolic level.

The identification with Ceres also bolstered imperial dynastic propaganda.[75]

The wife and mother of the princeps became or was thought of as Ceres Mater, the mother goddess. The primary role of the princeps' wife was to bear him a son and to continue the imperial line.[76] By producing an heir she augmented and revitalized the Domus Augustea, and also provided a living symbol for the continuity of the Empire.[77] She therefore symbolized her own dynastic functions as well as the idealized function of all Roman women. In this capacity her position and image were appropriately propagandized by her husband.[78] Moreover, in time her son, the imperial heir, could use his own mother to symbolize and to assert his political legitimacy as princeps. For this reason, I suggest, the titles Mater Augusti and Mater Caesaris were used to characterize the women of the imperial household. Livia, Agrippina the Younger, Domitia Longina, Faustina the Younger, and Julia Domna all received these titles in inscriptions and on imperial coinage.[79]

Finally, Ceres Mater symbolized the very legitimacy of the prestige or authority (auctoritas) of the princeps and, by extension, the more limited auctoritas of his wife. Just as the princeps was pater patriae, father of his country, so his wife was mater patriae, its mother.[80] These roles gave them the auctoritas of the paterfamilias, the male head of the household, and the materfamilias, the female head of the household, over the peoples of the Empire. The Senate initially voted the title "mater patriae" to Livia after Augustus' death.[81] Although Tiberius officially rejected the Senate's recommendation, Dio Cassius informs us that at the time of Livia's death many members of the Senate nevertheless called her by this title:

> Moreover they also voted an arch to her, [a thing] which [had been voted] to no other woman, because she had saved not a few of them, and because she had raised the children of many [of them] and had helped many in paying for dowries for their daughters, on account of which some were even calling her Mater Patriae [Mother of the Country].
>
> (Dio Cass. 58.2.3)

Some senators apparently felt very strongly that Livia had been a mother to their families, and they therefore called her mater patriae to express their gratitude and affection. Livia actually bore this title on a coin from Leptis in Africa Proconsularis,[82] and she was called genetrix orbis, "progenitress of the (Roman) world," on coins from Aispalis (Romula) and on an inscription from Anticaria, both in Hispania Baetica.[83] This second title approximates mater patriae but it has a somewhat more general, less political connotation.[84]

The image of the wife of the princeps as a mother figure for the Empire served official propaganda chiefly in the second and third centuries A.D.

The title mater castrorum, "mother of the camp," characterized Faustina the Younger and Julia Domna in official coinage and inscriptions that identified these women as mother figures for the Roman armies.[85] In inscriptions Julia Domna also received the titles genetrix orbis terrae, "progenitor of the (Roman) world," and mater castrorum et senatus et patriae, "mother of the camp and the senate and the country."[86] The identification of the wife of the princeps as mother of the Empire in its many aspects idealized and extended the concept of a mother's authority over her own children; it also suggested that she be granted the same loyalty and love that children give their mother. The assimilation of these women to Ceres Mater fostered the same idea. Their images in the guise of Ceres became a major integrative symbol, or series of symbols, for the Roman Empire, which served to unify the peoples of the Empire as symbolic children of the princeps and his wife. The ideology of Ceres therefore helped to put the control of the princeps over his Empire on a powerful symbolic basis.

5.5 Conclusion

Ceres is thus closely tied to Roman women as a social group. This relationship is most evident in the rituals and myths of the cult of the goddess and her daughter Persephone. The participants in this cult of the goddess were the matronae and virgines, married and unmarried women of the upper class. Through the connection of her cult with these women, Ceres herself became a symbol of Roman womanhood and a model for the conduct of upper-class women in society. She was particularly associated with the female virtues of chastity and motherhood encouraged in women of this social class. This encouragement had the effect of strengthening the patriarchal basis of Roman society. Under the Empire, the ideological associations of the goddess were exploited by identifying women of the imperial family with Ceres. Through that identification the iconography of Ceres legitimized the most prominent women in Roman society as symbols of prosperity, female virtues, and the unity and continuity of the Empire.

Chapter 6

CERES·IN·THE·ARA PACIS·AUGUSTAE

6.1 Introduction

As we have seen in the previous chapters, the Romans connected Ceres with two concepts, fertility and liminality, and with two social categories, women and the plebs. So far we have considered these four aspects of Ceres separately, as different facets of her character. In order to illustrate how these various aspects of Ceres are interrelated, I propose to examine in this chapter one image of the goddess that combines all four of the ideological associations we have examined. This image appears in an important state monument of the Augustan period, the Ara Pacis Augustae, or Altar of Augustan Peace.

The Senate vowed the Ara Pacis in 13 B.C. in honor of Augustus' return to Rome from his successful campaigns in Spain and Gaul, and it was dedicated in 9 B.C. (*Res Gestae* 12). The altar celebrates the return of peace to the Roman world through the agency of the princeps, a theme that is reflected in its elaborate decorative program.[1] The altar itself is surrounded by a precinct wall that has sculptural decoration on both the interior and exterior faces. The interior face of the wall is an imitation in stone of a temporary altar precinct: a wooden fence in the lower zone; and garlands, *paterae* (libation dishes), and *bucrania* (skulls of sacrificial bulls) in the upper. The exterior face of the wall has an elaborate floral frieze in the lower zone; in the upper on the north and south sides are long processional reliefs and on the corners of the east and west sides are four relief panels.

The figure of Ceres, I argue, appears in the restored relief panel located at the southeast corner of the monument (fig. 11).[2] This panel, discovered in 1568, has been recognized as one of the most significant reliefs of this monument.[3] A scholarly controversy has long raged over its interpretation. In the center of the relief appears a veiled female figure, crowned with a wreath of wheat and poppies. She is dressed in a long, thin dress, which is slipping off her right shoulder, and wears a heavier robe pulled up over her head as a veil. Her hair is piled on her head, except for two strands that flow down onto her shoulders. She sits on a rocky throne and holds in her lap two children and several different types of fruit, including grapes, pomegranates, and nuts. One of the children in her lap offers her a round fruit, possibly a pomegranate or apple. Behind her and to the viewer's right grow wheat, poppies, and several other types of flowers. At her feet are a grazing sheep and a reclining cow. Further to the viewer's right appears a seminude female figure with drapery billowing over her head. She is seated upon a *ketos*, or sea monster, which rises up out of turbulent waves. She seems also to wear a crown, which, however, is badly abraded. To the viewer's left appears another seminude female figure with billowing drapery and a crown of reeds. She is riding a large water bird, either a goose or a swan. Beside her grows a tall reed plant, and beneath her appear a number of different plants, an overturned water jug from which a stream of water flows, and a small water bird, probably a crane.

Several theories have already been proposed for the interpretation of this relief. The central figure has been identified as Tellus, Italia, Venus, Rhea Silvia, and Pax, or a combination of several of these.[4] The two side figures have been identified as: spirits or Aurae (breezes) of land and sea, air and water, or fresh and salt water; an Aura and a Nereid; nymphs; a nymph and a Nereid; a Muse and a sea divinity; the celestial and marine aspects of Venus; and the Horae.[5] Valid criticisms have been made of each of these identifications.[6] The continuing controversy indicates that an entirely acceptable interpretation of the relief has yet to be found.

Through a detailed reexamination of the iconography of the Ara Pacis relief, I have arrived at a new interpretation of its figures. I propose that the various motifs in the relief point to the identification of its central figure as Ceres and of the two subsidiary figures as nymphs, one of fresh water and the other of salt water.[7] With the identification of the nymphs in the relief comes a recognition of their symbolic importance in Roman myth, cult, and art, and of their associations with the central figure of Ceres.

The identification of Ceres in this relief of the Ara Pacis indicates the importance of her ideological associations for the interpretation of this particular panel, the sculptural decoration of the altar as a whole, and the propagandistic message of the monument. Ceres' connections with fertility and liminality explain the iconography of the panel in question. The goddess' association with these two concepts as well as her connections with women and the plebs serve to unite this panel with the other reliefs in the overall decorative scheme of the Ara Pacis in a carefully designed pattern of iconographic cross-references. Ceres' liminal/normative role, in particular her association with the establishment of peace after war, reinforces the propagandistic message of the altar, the celebration of the peace restored to the Roman world by Augustus after the terrible wars of the Late Republic. This pivotal image of Ceres thus includes all the aspects of the goddess that I have identified and shows how these associations operate in the context of an important monument in the history of Roman art.

6.2 The Central Figure of the Ara Pacis Relief

Let us consider first the evidence for the identification of the central figure of the Ara Pacis relief as Ceres. As we have noted previously, the iconography of this divinity in Roman art is largely borrowed from her Greek counterpart, Demeter.[8] Farnell has described the Demeter type in Greek art as follows: "[The goddess] is given usually the veil and maturer forms proper to maternity, and the countenance is marked with emotion and the impress of experience."[9] This description closely resembles the central figure of the Ara Pacis relief. The description of Demeter in literary sources also reveals parallels with the Ara Pacis figure. This literary image of the goddess remained practically unchanged throughout antiquity.[10] The goddess is called queenly (*anassa, potnia, polypotnia, hagne, semne*) and is often shown as a figure seated upon a throne and wearing a crown (*eustephane, kallistephanos*). Demeter is also described as solemn (*agelastos*), characterizing her grief and anger at the loss of her daughter, and she generally wears the veil (*kredemnon* or *kalyptra*) as a sign of her grief. Her flowing hair is emphasized, which is as yellow (*xanthe*) as the grain that is her gift to humankind. The goddess is viewed as both generous and benevolent, for she provides the gift of fruits of the field for humankind (*aglaokarpos, aglaodoros, horephoros, polyphorbe*). This general literary description of Demeter points to some of her important attributes: the crown, throne, veil, grain, and fruits. The central figure of the Ara Pacis relief has all of these attributes, as well as others closely associated with Demeter/Ceres. These attributes generally relate to the goddess' connection with the concept of fertility.

The crown that the Ara Pacis figure wears is composed of wheat stalks and poppy capsules (fig. 46).[11] The wheat points to its identification as the corona spicea, which is, as we have seen, a primary attribute of Demeter/Ceres.[12] She wears this crown on both Greek and Roman coin types.[13] On Greek types, a legend is sometimes added to identify the goddess directly, but she never is so identified on the Roman types, suggesting that the crown alone was sufficient to identify Ceres to the Romans.[14] In the Roman period, the crown frequently appears on the head of the goddess in other media as well, such as gems and sculpture, and during the Empire it may also include the poppy capsules like those visible in the crown of the Ara Pacis figure.[15] In Latin literature also Ceres is frequently described with the corona spicea.[16]

The wheat stalks and poppy capsules of the crown are prominent in the group of plants that grow to the right of the figure (fig. 47). These two plants are specifically associated with Demeter/Ceres in Greek and Roman literature, religion, and art. In chapter 2 we examined the Roman goddess's close relationship with grain. Demeter, too, was connected with grain, both in literature from Homer onward and in religious rites.[17] Her epithets of Megalartos (Abundant in Bread) and Sito (Related to Grain) also indicate this association.[18] Grain, particularly wheat, is a characteristic attribute of Demeter/Ceres in both Greek and Roman art, where she is often represented wearing the wheat-stalk crown, holding stalks of wheat, or having wheat at her side.[19]

The poppy capsules shown growing among the wheat stalks also point to an identification with Demeter/Ceres. The poppy seems to have been associated with the goddess from the earliest times. A Mycenaean divinity who holds poppies or wears a crown with poppy capsules has been identified as Demeter.[20] The association continued down to the Roman period; Vergil (*G.* 1.212) calls the flower "the poppy of Ceres," *Cereale papaver.* The poppy capsules on the Ara Pacis relief are those of the opium poppy, *papaver somniferum*, which was particularly associated with Demeter.[21] The capsule of the poppy was regularly dedicated to the goddess.[22] The symbolic associations of the poppy capsule are connected with various aspects of Demeter/Ceres: the innumerable seeds of the capsule suggest the fertility she produces; these seeds were also raised as a cereal crop, and hence are connected with her role as the goddess of grain; the opium that the plant produces connects it with sleep and death, and hence refers to her liminal aspect.[23] The goddess frequently is represented in classical art holding the wheat sheaf in one hand and poppy capsules in the other.[24] In literature as well these plants are given as attributes of the goddess, as by the Hellenistic poet Theocritus (7.157), who describes a statue of Demeter as "holding wheat stalks and poppies in either hand" (δράγματα καὶ μάκωνας ἐν ἀμφοτέραισιν ἔχοισα).[25]

The other flowers appearing in this group of plants may also be connected with the goddess, although their identification is uncertain. The large central flower seems to be a poppy. The one immediately to the left of this may belong to the iris family, while the one further to the left may be a narcissus. If these identifications are correct, then the relief is not true to life, for the flowers represented would not normally have been in bloom at the same time.[26] Thus the collection signals the fantastic quality of the image represented, as do the other vegetal motifs on the Ara Pacis (e.g., the floral scroll and garland frieze), which we shall examine in detail later in this chapter. These types are among the flowers that Persephone was gathering when she was raped by Hades on the miraculous plain of Enna, where flowers bloomed the year round.[27] The narcissus in particular had a special significance for Demeter and Persephone.[28] In the *Homeric Hymn to Demeter* (8–18), when Persephone plucked the miraculous narcissus, the earth opened and Hades appeared to carry her away. Whatever the specific species represented in the relief may be, we know that flowers in general played an important role in the cult of Demeter at a variety of sites, including Eleusis, Hipponium, Hermione, and Sardis, often in connection with the myth of Persephone's flower gathering.[29] Flowers may therefore appear appropriately with Demeter and Persephone, as in their temple at Megalopolis, where Pausanias (8.31.2), a Greek travel writer of the second century A.D., tells us that Persephone's companions Artemis and Athena were represented with flower baskets on their heads. In Roman art as well, Ceres is associated with flowers. For example, in an image we have already examined, the goddess, wearing a veil and *kalathos*, emerges from a floral scroll in a relief dated to the Augustan period (fig. 29).[30]

Another significant attribute of the Ara Pacis figure is the rocky throne on which she is seated. The hieratically seated figure is one of the most common types of Demeter/Ceres.[31] According to Pausanias the statues of Demeter that were to be counted among the most ancient represented the seated goddess (Paus. 2.13.5, 5.17.3). The seat may be a throne, a *kiste* (round basket), a rock, or the earth itself.[32] The rocky seat is sometimes identified as the *agelastos petros*, or "Mirthless Stone," on which the goddess sat when she first came to Eleusis after her daughter had been taken from her.[33] On the other hand, the goddess is also found seated upon a rock in contexts that do not seem to refer to the Eleusinian myth. So, for example, Pausanias (8.42.4) informs us that the original cult statue of Demeter Melaina at Phigaleia in the Peloponnese showed the goddess seated on a rock. In this instance, the rock may symbolize Demeter's connection with the earth, as in the ancient etymology for her name: De-meter = Ge-meter, the Earth Mother.[34] Ceres too is closely associated with the earth, as in Varro's remark (*Rust*. 3.1.4): "Not without cause was the same earth called both Mother and Ceres" (nec sine causa terram eandem appellabant matrem et Cererem). In classical art Demeter/Ceres' association with the earth is expressed in a different manner from that of the earth goddess Ge/Tellus. The latter divinity is generally shown rising up out of the earth or reclining upon it, as befits a personification of the earth itself.[35] As the figure on the Ara Pacis, however, Demeter/Ceres is shown seated upon the earth or a rock, indicating her association rather than identification with this element.

The details of the drapery of the Ara Pacis figure also point to an identification with Demeter/Ceres. The outer garment of this figure is a heavy robe pulled over her head as a veil. The association of the veil with the Ara Pacis figure contradicts both the Tellus and Italia identifications: Tellus is consistently represented bareheaded, and Italia is either shown with a helmet or bareheaded.[36] In Greek and Roman art and literature, however, Demeter/Ceres is frequently represented with the veil.[37] It is generally interpreted as a symbol of the mourning that the goddess experienced at the rape of her daughter. The undergarment of the Ara Pacis figure is a thin dress that is slipping off her right shoulder. Galinsky compared this drapery arrangement with similar representations of Aphrodite/Venus.[38] However, parallels may also be adduced to representations of Ceres, such as the bust of the goddess from Aricgia we have already examined (fig. 2).[39] This bust, identified as Ceres by the corona spicea, shows a female figure wearing a garment slipping off her right shoulder.[40] The emphasis on the breast in this representation suggests fertility and nurture, an appropriate reference for Demeter/Ceres.

The fruit that appears in the lap of the Ara Pacis figure may also be associated with this divinity (fig. 48). The Greeks gave Demeter the epithet Karpophoros (Bearer of Fruit), while the Romans called Ceres Frugifera (Bearer of Fruit) and Mater Frugum (Mother of Fruits).[41] Indeed, as we have seen, the Romans derived her very name from the bearing of fruits: "She, because she bears fruits, [is called] Ceres" (quae quod gerit fruges, Ceres) (Varr. *Ling.* 5.64). Moreover, the specific type of fruits portrayed on the Ara Pacis relief are closely associated with Demeter/Ceres: pomegranates, grapes, and nuts.

Pomegranates are an important attribute of the goddess, perhaps in reference to the myth of her daughter, Persephone.[42] According to the myth, Persephone ate several seeds of a pomegranate when she was in the underworld, and so had to spend the same number of months in the land of the dead.[43] In votive statuettes from the sanctuary of Demeter Malophoros at Selinus in Sicily, the goddess often holds a pomegranate (fig. 49),[44] and terracotta imitations of this fruit were also found at the sanctuary.[45] Indeed, the epithet of Malophoros may connect her with pomegranates, if indeed it refers to μῆλον, meaning "apple," or, by extension, "any tree-born fruit."[46] Like the poppy capsule, the pomegranate with its many seeds was a symbol of fertility and hence appropriate to Demeter/Ceres.[47]

The other fruits in the lap of the Ara Pacis figure may also allude to this divinity. Grapes are the attribute of Ceres' cult companion, the god Liber/Bacchus.[48] The nuts shown among the fruits are another symbol of fertility. Nuts were thrown at Roman wedding ceremonies, as rice is today.[49] At the Cerialia, nuts were thrown to the onlookers of the procession.[50] The fruits associated with the Ara Pacis figure may thus be interpreted as referring to Demeter/Ceres as a goddess of agricultural fertility.

The children represented in the lap of this figure point to the role of Demeter/Ceres in human fertility, as the mother or nurse of children.[51] As we have seen, in both Greek and Roman cult the goddess was worshipped as the nurturer of children: Demeter Kourotrophos and Ceres Mater. In Greek and Latin literature, she is the mother or foster mother of a variety of children, including Persephone/Proserpina, Iacchus, and Triptolemus. We have previously noted Lucretius' portrait of Ceres as a mother, nursing the child Iacchus at her breast (*RN* 4.1168). In Greek art Demeter is often represented as a Kourotrophos type, with a child in her lap. For example, in a statuette from the Malophoros sanctuary at Selinus, the goddess holds in her lap a child who stretches a hand to her breast in a gesture remarkably reminiscent of the figure in the Ara Pacis relief (fig. 50).[52]

The number of the children in the relief may be significant. Two children are also held by a nursing female figure in votive figurines from central and southern Italy and Sicily, as in an example from the Sicilian site of Megara Hyblaea (fig. 51).[53] This type appears to be native Italic rather than Greek, since the theme of motherhood and especially of the nursing mother is uncommon in Greek art.[54] Perhaps the Italic model influenced the presentation of the goddess on the Ara Pacis relief. A mythological explanation for the two children may come from Cicero: "Those born from Ceres are called Liber and Libera" (Cerere nati nominati sunt Liber et Libera) (*Nat. D.* 2.62). According to Saint Augustine, Liber was connected with male fertility, and Libera with female:

Let him preside in the name of Liber over the seed of men, and in the name of Libera over that of women.

(Aug. *Civ. D.* 4.11)

The gender of the children in the relief is indeterminate, perhaps deliberately so to allow for more than one level of meaning.[55] Their significance, I believe, lies in their number, not their gender. The two children on the Ara Pacis may be meant to suggest, at least on one level, Ceres' children Liber and Libera, and hence to refer to their connections with human fertility.

Finally, the cow and sheep represented at the feet of the central figure are also related to Demeter/Ceres. Numerous terracotta votive statuettes were discovered in the sanctuary of Demeter at Lycosura in the Peloponnese, including those representing draped female figures with the head of a cow or a sheep.[56] These animals may be associated with the goddess as protectress of agricultural work and animal husbandry. Varro calls the bull "this companion of humankind in agricultural work and servant of Ceres" (hic socius hominum in rustico opere et Cereris minister) (*Rust.* 2.5.3).[57] According to myth, Ceres was the first to domesticate cattle for plowing.[58] In a gem carving the goddess appears riding on a bull and carrying poppies, stalks of wheat, and a torch.[59] The enthroned goddess with a cow and a calf in front of her represented on the west side of the Harpy Monument from Xanthus in Lycia has also been recognized as Demeter.[60] In Greek cult Demeter could receive cattle as an offering.[61] Pausanias (2.35.6–8) notes that at her sanctuary on Mount Pron at Hermion in the Peloponnese, cattle were regularly sacrificed to Demeter. In the Dedicatory Epigrams, Demeter and Hera are invoked as the objects of heifer-sacrifice, and in one case Demeter is offered clay models of heifers.[62] Cattle bones have been found in sanctuaries of Demeter at Knidos and Knossos.[63]

The sheep is also connected with the goddess in myth and ritual. Pausanias (2.3.4) refers to a story involving Hermes and a ram that was told in connection with the mysteries of Demeter. Although Pausanias does not relate the story, it may be connected with another told by one of the early Christian fathers, Clement of Alexandria (*Protr.* 2.13). The male divinity in this version was not Hermes, but Zeus, who raped Demeter, and then in repentance tore off the testicles of a ram and threw them into her lap, claiming that they were his own. This myth may be an *aition* for a fertility ritual dedicated to Demeter that involved rams.[64] Although sheep were rarely offered to Demeter in Greek cult, we hear of them as a sacrifice to Ceres in Roman sources.[65] Vergil (*G.* 1.338–350) reports an agricultural rite held in the spring for Ceres, in which a sheep was led around the crops three times before its sacrifice. In the *Aeneid* (4.56–59), Dido and Anna sacrifice sheep to Ceres and several other divinities before Dido's wedding to Aeneas. Moreover, some scholars believe that Demeter's cultic epithet of Malophoros means "Bearer of Sheep" (where μᾶλον is equivalent to μῆλον, "sheep").[66] This seems to be how Pausanias understood the epithet, for he reports that the goddess was given this epithet by "those who first reared sheep in this land" (τοὺς πρώτους πρόβατα ἐν τῇ γῇ θρέψαντας). (Paus. 1.44.3). In his *Hymn to Demeter*, the Hellenistic poet Callimachus places both cattle and sheep under the protection of the goddess:

> Hail goddess and save this city in harmony and in prosperity, and bring all crops in abundance in the fields! Nourish the cattle, bring the flocks, bring the wheat stalk, bring harvest! And nourish peace, so that he who has sown may reap. Be gracious to me, thrice-prayed for, wide-ruling queen of goddesses!
>
> (Callim. *Cer.* 134–138)

The cow and sheep on the Ara Pacis relief therefore reflect the role of Demeter/ Ceres as goddess of fertility and patroness of the agricultural and pastoral work that that fertility requires.

Based on the iconographical associations of the various motifs displayed in association with the central figure of the Ara Pacis relief, I argue that this figure must be understood primarily as the goddess Demeter/Ceres. Some of the attributes associated with this figure belong almost exclusively to Ceres, such as the corona spicea, wheat stalks, and poppy capsules. These attributes point to the goddess's connections with agricultural fertility, particularly with the growth and cultivation of grain. Although a few instances may be found in which these attributes are represented with another divinity, the overwhelming majority of them point to Demeter/Ceres.

Other attributes of the central figure are closely connected to this goddess, although they may also be related to other divinities. The arrangement of her drapery is also connected with Aphrodite/Venus, and the fruits, children, and animals with Ge/Tellus.[67] These attributes also allude to fertility, although their reference is extended beyond the fertility of plants to that of animals and humans. The fact that these attributes may be assigned to a variety of goddesses may simply be due to the similarity in the iconography of all female fertility divinities. On the other hand, this allusive richness may reflect a deliberate attempt to syncretize, to connect Ceres with these specific divinities. Significantly, both Venus and Tellus have important cultic connections with Ceres in Roman religion.[68] The multivalent attributes of the central figure in the Ara Pacis relief may be intended to recall the cultic associations of Ceres with these other divinities, to connect her with them, and to call upon their powers as well as her own in guarding the fertility of Italy. This view would allow for a polysemantic interpretation of the relief, as several scholars have proposed.[69] The Ara Pacis figure would then be interpreted as Ceres on the primary level, but also suggest secondary references to Venus and Tellus.

In any case, Ceres' close association with fertility, both agricultural and human, and her virtual identification with grain explain the iconography of the central figure of the Ara Pacis relief. As we shall see, other associations of this divinity help to elucidate the relationship of the side figures of the relief to this central figure and lead to a comprehensive interpretation of the relief as a whole.

6.3 The Side Figures of the Ara Pacis Relief

Although some scholars have treated the side figures of the Ara Pacis relief as mere "space-fillers" with little intrinsic connection to the central figure, Galinsky has argued rightly that they are essential to its composition and interpretation.[70] I propose that these figures be interpreted as water nymphs, the one on the right, a nymph of the sea, or Nereid, the one on the left, a nymph of springs and fountains, or Naiad.[71]

The most common identification of these figures is as Aurae, or breezes.[72] As De Grummond has shown, however, this identification rests on a thin foundation.[73] Iconographically, the figures are identified as Aurae by the drapery billowing over their heads, called *velificatio*. The Aurae are connected with the *velificatio* motif through a description that Pliny the Elder (*HN* 36.29) made of a group of sculptures in the Portico of Octavia at Rome: "two Aurae making sails with their clothing," (duae Aurae velificantes sua veste). Other representations of Aurae represented with *velificatio* provide artistic parallels.[74] The connection is then made to the figures on the Ara Pacis relief, and often the following passage from Horace's *Carmen Saeculare* is cited in this connection:

> Let Tellus, fertile in crops and herds, present Ceres with a crown of wheat stalks; let the healthy waters and breezes of Jupiter nourish the offspring.
>
> (Hor. *Carm. Saec.* 29–32)

Based on this passage, Tellus is taken as the central figure of the relief and the Aurae as the side figures. Tellus, it is argued, wears the corona spicea, holds offspring and fruits in her lap, and has at her feet representatives of the herds. The Aurae of Jupiter may be recognized at the side of the goddess by their billowing drapery.

This argument has many problems. First, *velificatio* is not exclusively associated with Aurae. Many other divinities and semidivinities are shown with this motif.[75] In addition, *velificatio* is only one of a number of attributes associated with the two side figures of the Ara Pacis relief. Among the other attributes are the mounts they ride, the crowns they wear, and the creatures and plants represented below them. Any interpretation of the side figures must take these other attributes into account. Finally, the passage from Horace has been misused. The poet says that Tellus (i.e., the earth itself) presents the goddess Ceres with a corona spicea. Horace thus attributes the crown to Ceres, not Tellus, as indeed we would expect given the close connection in art of this attribute with the former. The identification of the side figures of the Ara Pacis relief as Aurae may therefore be rejected.

Identifying these figures as a sea nymph and a freshwater nymph avoids the problems of the Aura identification. As we shall see, this identification accounts for the various attributes associated with these figures in the relief. Moreover, this interpretation of the figures points to their significance for the understanding of the relief as a whole. In both Greek and Roman myth and cult, the nymphs play an important role.[76] In Italy, the cult of the nymphs may be traced back to the sixth century B.C. It gained in importance during the time of Caesar and Augustus and spread rapidly through the Empire during the Early Empire. The somewhat colorless Aurae have no such significance in Roman religion. Also, the nymphs have important associations with the goddess Demeter/Ceres in myth, cult, and art. Their association with this divinity on the Ara Pacis relief may be interpreted on several different levels.

The attributes of the figure on the right side of the relief support her identification as a Nereid. She rides on a sea dragon, or *ketos*, who emerges from the waves of the sea.[77] This animal has the essential characteristics of the *ketos*: the canine head and large erect ears, open denticulated jaw, and scaly serpentine body. The figure most frequently represented riding the *ketos* is a Nereid. The motif of the Nereid on the *ketos* became especially popular in Greek art and was appropriated by the Romans for their depictions of the band of sea divinities, or sea *thiasos*.[78] Pliny the Elder (*HN* 36.26) describes Nereids "sitting upon dolphins, or *ketoi*, or hippocamps" (supra delphinos aut cete aut hippocampos sedentes). In his description of the creatures of the sea portrayed on the doors of the Palace of the Sun God, Ovid mentions Dores, the wife of Nereus, and her daughters, the Nereids,

> some of whom are seen to swim; some, sitting on a rock, to dry their green hair; some to be carried on a fish.
>
> (Ov. *Met.* 2.11–13)

The Nereids "carried on a fish" are equivalent to the figure on the Ara Pacis relief riding the *ketos*.

The other attributes of this figure may also be connected with Nereids. The figure wears a crown, the details of which have been badly abraded.[79] Perhaps this crown represented seaweed and other plants of the sea. In the passage quoted above, Ovid describes the Nereids with green hair, perhaps a reference to seaweed in their hair. Like the figure in the Ara Pacis relief, Nereids were frequently shown as nude or seminude and were often depicted with the billowing veils of the *velificatio* motif.[80] The closest parallel to the Ara Pacis figure is found on the carved mantle of the cult statue from the sanctuary of Demeter at Lycosura in the Peloponnese (fig. 52).[81] In this representation a Nereid with a billowing veil rides upon a *ketos*. This iconographic correspondence suggests that the right side figure of the Ara Pacis relief is to be interpreted as a Nereid, or sea nymph.

The attributes of the left side figure of the relief suggest its interpretation as a Naiad. The Naiads are nymphs of fountains, rivers, pools, and lakes, that is, of fresh water (Ov. *Met.* 2.238 and 14.326–332). The figure rides upon a large water bird, either a goose or a swan, which rises from a marsh. The identity of the bird is difficult to determine, since its neck has been restored. Both birds, however, are closely associated with freshwater divinities. The coins of the Greek city of Katania in Sicily show the river god Symaethus with a goose.[82] The goose is connected with the nymph Herkyna in a story related by Pausanias (9.39.2). Indeed, the goose is a natural attribute of the nymph, who rules over the waters on which the bird lives.[83] For the same reason, the swan too is an appropriate attribute for the nymph. This bird is closely connected with rivers, ponds, and marshes in classical literature.[84] Swans are also depicted with nymphs in classical art. Perhaps the closest parallel to the figure on the Ara Pacis is provided by the didrachmas of the Greek city of Kamarina in Sicily, dated to 415–405 B.C. (fig. 53).[85] These coins show a seminude female figure riding on a swan; the figure has her drapery billowing up behind her in the *velificatio* motif. This figure was interpreted as an Aura by Rizzo, who was followed by many scholars.[86] Westermark and Jenkins have shown, however, that she represents the nymph Kamarina, personification of the lake near the ancient city, who is addressed by the classical Greek poet Pindar (*Ol.* 5.2–4) as the "daughter of Okeanos."[87] The close iconographic correspondence suggests that the Ara Pacis figure is also to be interpreted as a freshwater nymph.

The marshy scene represented beneath the figure on the Ara Pacis contains other details that may be associated with nymphs. Primary among these is the overturned urn from which emerges a stream of water. The urn is a common attribute of nymphs in classical art.[88] The stream emerging from the urn on the relief may symbolize the water source over which the nymph rules. The reed plants growing around the urn, as well as the large reed that grows beside the nymph on the relief and the reed crown she wears, are all indicative of the type of plants that grow around freshwater sources and are therefore symbolic of the realm of the nymph. The small bird that appears on top of the urn in the relief is also a water bird, and therefore subject to the rule of the nymph.

This bird may have an additional meaning, however. It may be identified as a crane, which was connected with the time of sowing grain and was a herald of the rains that were necessary after the sowing if the grain was to sprout.[89] Its association with rain again connects the bird with the nymphs.[90] Its connection with the sowing of grain, however, also associates the crane with Demeter/ Ceres. Indeed, the crane was considered in antiquity to be the herald of Demeter (Porph. *Abst.* 3.5). This interpretation of the crane provides a direct connection between the side figures of the relief, the nymphs, and its central figure, the goddess Demeter/Ceres.

An association of Demeter/Ceres and the nymphs is not surprising, for the two have links in Greek and Roman myth and religion. Piccaluga has done a thorough study of the connection of Demeter/Ceres with water and water divinities, both of the sea and and of fresh water.[91] In the various versions of the Rape of Persephone in classical literature, for example, water divinities play an important role. The companions of Persephone before her rape are identified variously as the Oceanids, Naiads, and nymphs, or the Sirens, daughters of the river god Acheloos.[92] In other myths and legends, Demeter is connected with a variety of beings associated with water, including Nereids and nymphs, as well as Poseidon, Okeanos, Pelasgos, Tantalos, Keleos, Kychreos, the Danaids, and the Sirens.[93] For example, according to one of the Greek Orphic hymns the Nereids were the first to introduce the mysteries of her daughter, Persephone (*Hymn. Orph.* 24.10–12). Various classical authors inform us that Demeter received sacrifice and prayers together with the nymphs.[94] This literary evidence is supported by archaeological finds. The cult sites of Demeter were generally near water, either salt or fresh, and special arrangements were made at many of these sites for the use of water in the rituals of the goddess.[95] Her worship at many sites is frequently combined with that of the local water divinities, and Demeter herself may bear cultic epithets that connect her with water nymphs.[96] In Roman cult as well, Ceres was linked with the nymphs. A marble puteal from Ostia dated to A.D. 197 bears a dedicatory inscription to Ceres as the goddess of grain and to the nymphs (*CIL* XIV.2). In Greek art Demeter is shown with the nymphs in several representations, such as in an Attic votive relief dedicated to the nymphs and depicting Demeter, Persephone, and a local hero in the lower register, and Hermes, the nymphs, and Pan in the upper (fig. 54).[97] These mythic and cultic connections indicate the close relationship between the goddess Demeter/Ceres and the nymphs.

This relationship, as expressed visually in the Ara Pacis relief, bears a variety of meanings. First, the nymphs are symbolic of the nutritive powers of the goddess, her role as a goddess of fertility. Nymphs are also goddesses of vegetative growth and fertility, for they are connected with rain, which makes the plants grow.[98] Eustathius in his commentary on Homer's *Odyssey* (1.14, p. 1384, 35) calls them the goddesses through whom the fruit comes to ripeness, and in the Greek Orphic hymns they are given the epithets of Aglaokarpoi (Those with Beautiful Fruit) (*Hymn. Orph.* 51.12) and Karpophoroi (Bearers of Fruit) (*Hymn. Orph.* 51.4).[99] The nymphs are also divinities of spring and are associated with flowers and gardens.[100] Their connection with fertility and the growth of vegetation explains their association with Demeter. According to a scholion on Pindar (*Pyth.* 4.106a), no sanctuary of Demeter would be honored without the nymphs, for they were the first to make known the fruits of the field.[101] Antipater of Thessalonica (*Anth. Pal.* 9.418), a Greek epigrammatist from the Augustan period, says that the nymphs grind the grain by the command of Demeter.[102] Because of the nymphs' close connection with the growth of vegetation and hence the nourishment of human beings, they received sacrifices and prayers along with Demeter during a time of famine (schol. Pind. *Ol.* 13.74).[103]

Like Demeter/Ceres, the nymphs extended their role as divinities of fertility not only to crops but also to animals and human beings. According to Eustathius (*Od.* 14.435, p. 1765, 64), the nymphs provided food for the herds, and they were connected in myth and cult with other divinities associated with the herds, including Faunus, Pan, and Apollo.[104] In myth, nymphs frequently served as nurses of children, e.g., of Dionysus, Hermaphroditus, and Jupiter.[105] In art and literature, the nymphs were represented as nurses of children, *kourotrophoi*.[106] As we have seen, the vegetation, animals, and children that the nymphs nurture all appear as attributes of the central figure of Demeter/Ceres on the Ara Pacis relief. On one level, then, the nymphs of the relief symbolize the nurture that the goddess provides.

The nymphs and their attributes point toward another level of interpretation as well; these attributes may also be interpreted as signs of weather phenomena. The swelling sea on the right side of the relief is a signal of approaching wind and storm.[107] The water birds (swan/goose and crane) represented on the left side of the relief are connected with rain. As we have already noted, the crane is the herald of the winter rains.[108] The flight of water birds from the marsh or their sportive play in its waters are signs of approaching storm.[109] The windblown cloaks of the nymphs also indicate the approach of stormy weather. The rains that these iconographic details suggest are necessary for the growth of the crops, but may also do damage if they are too heavy. The storm suggested by the nymphs and their attributes is countered by the calm presence of the goddess in the center. The peaceful attitude of the animals, the undisturbed growth of the plants around her, and the cheerful play of the children in her lap all counteract the implicit threat of the storm. In her role as a protectress of agricultural fertility, Ceres guards the crops against the storm.[110] In the *Georgics*, Vergil instructs the farmer to guard against the storms that destroy crops by worshipping the gods, especially Ceres:

> Among the first things, revere the gods and repeat the annual rites to great Ceres, worshipping on the joyful grasses near the very end of winter, now in the fair spring.
> (Verg. *G.* 1.338–340)

The central figure of the relief is Ceres, who protects the farmers and the crops from the storm signaled by the attributes of the two nymphs represented at the sides of the relief.

On yet another level, the two nymphs, beings of fresh water and the sea, point to the goddess's connections with the two different kinds of water, as Piccaluga has defined them: "useful" water (*acqua utile*), that is, fresh water to be used for watering plants, for fertilization; and "nonuseful" water (*acqua non utile*), that is, sea water, or water as an element, a power of nature.[111] "Useful" water is associated with Demeter/Ceres as an agricultural divinity who controls the fertility of plants. "Nonuseful" water is tied to her role as one of the supernatural beings who gave form to the cosmos at its time of origin through manipulating the elements of nature. In this association, the goddess operates as a liminal divinity who helped to bring about the transition from chaos to order at the very beginning of the universe.

Finally, the two nymphs of the relief point to the dual origin of Rome itself: her foreign origin through the Trojan prince Aeneas, and her native Italic origin through the twins Romulus and Remus. The Nereid symbolizes the foreign origin of Rome. In Latin literature sea nymphs are generally given Greek names and are considered foreign to native Italic beliefs.[112] In Vergil's *Aeneid* (5.823–826), Aeneas is accompanied by Greek sea divinities as he leaves Sicily and sets out for his destiny in Italy, including the sea nymphs Thetis, Melite, Panopea, Nesaea, Spio, Thalia, and Cymodoce. When his ships, built from the timbers of the trees of Trojan Mount Ida, are threatened by the native Italian Turnus and the Rutuli, they turn into sea nymphs (*Aen.* 9.107–122).

One of these nymphs later protects Aeneas by warning him of Turnus' attack on the Trojan camp, and she too has a Greek name: Cymodocea (*Aen.* 10.225). These foreign sea nymphs may be contrasted with the native Italic stream and fountain nymphs.[113] The latter have Latin names and ancient Italic cults and are connected with the early history of Rome, such as Juturna, Egeria, Carmentis, and the Camenae.[114] Vergil (*Aen.* 8.314) and Ovid (*Met.* 6.329–330) call these nymphs the "native gods," *indigenae dei*. In the *Aeneid* (8.314–320), Evander tells Aeneas that the nymphs were among the first inhabitants of Rome before even Saturn arrived. Aeneas himself prays to the nymphs, among other divinities, as the native spirits in whose protection the land of Italy lies on three critical occasions: upon his landing in Italy (*Aen.* 7.135–140), before receiving the omen of the sow (*Aen.* 8.71–78), and before his single combat with Turnus (*Aen.* 12.176–186).

Ceres appropriately serves as the mediator between these symbols of Rome's dual origin. As we have seen, Ceres was both a native Italic divinity and a foreign Greek one. The native Italic cult of Ceres was very ancient and linked the goddess to the worship of Tellus.[115] The Greek cult of Ceres assimilated her to the goddess Demeter and was imported from the Greek cities of Southern Italy.[116] As the central figure of the relief, Ceres mediates between the foreign origin of Rome, represented in the sea nymph and the city's native origin, symbolized by the freshwater nymph. She serves here again liminally, as a divinity connected with the transition from the primitive villages of Italy to the city-state of Rome. She is associated with the very origins of the city, the initia of Rome. This association of the goddess fits in with her connection to other types of initia, discussed in chapter 3, and, as we shall see, also connects the Ceres panel with the two relief panels on the other side of the altar.

The nymphs of the Ara Pacis relief therefore carry a variety of meanings. On one level, they symbolize the nutritive powers inherent in the water that is their domain and hence link them to the fertility associated with Ceres. The nymphs also signal the possible destructive effects of rain and storm, which are counteracted by Ceres in her role as protectress of agricultural fertility. Through their distinction into freshwater and sea divinities, they refer to Ceres' control of both the fertilizing and elemental qualities of water, deriving from the goddess's associations with fertility and liminality. Finally, the nymphs symbolize the dual origin of Rome, which is connected with Ceres' liminal role as a goddess of initia. The various ideological associations of Ceres serve to link the figures of the relief together and to express a remarkably complex set of meanings for the relief as a whole. As we shall see, these associations also help to connect this particular panel with the other reliefs of the Ara Pacis.

6.4 *The Ceres Panel and the Relief Program of the Ara Pacis*

The identification of Ceres in this panel of the Ara Pacis has significant implications for the interpretation of the sculptural program of the Ara Pacis as a whole. As several scholars have noted, the reliefs of the altar must be read as an integrated program, for they complement and contrast with one another.[117] The Ceres panel has important associations with the other three relief panels at the corners of the exterior precinct wall, the processional friezes on the long sides of the exterior wall, the garland frieze on the interior precinct wall, and the floral scroll on the lower level of the exterior wall. These associations operate through references to the concepts and social categories connected with Ceres: her roles as a goddess of fertility and liminality and as patroness of women and the plebs.

The Aeneas and Lupercal panels at the opposite side of the altar from the Ceres panel are closely connected with it in theme and symbols. The basic theme of these two panels is the dual origin of Rome: her foreign origin from the Trojan Aeneas, and her native origin from the twins Romulus and Remus.[118] This theme is implicit in the Ceres panel through the representation of the two types of nymphs and is connected to Ceres' role as a liminal divinity associated with initia. Although the Lupercal panel on the northwest survives only in fragments, scholars have deduced that it represented the twins Romulus and Remus nursed by the wolf as they were discovered by the god Mars on the marshy banks of the river Tiber.[119] The scene recalls the marsh represented below the freshwater nymph in the Ceres panel. The twins themselves suggest the two children in the lap of the goddess and her role in human fertility.[120]

The Aeneas panel on the southwest is also closely linked with the Ceres relief.[121] In this panel, Aeneas prepares to sacrifice a large sow, and he is accompanied by two attendants and the hero's adult son, Iulus-Ascanius. The figure of Aeneas himself suggests an association with the sea nymph of the Ceres relief, since the hero was saved by the sea nymphs who had been transformed from his ships.[122] This association reinforces the interpretation of the sea nymph as being symbolic of the foreign origin of Rome. The sow in the Aeneas panel is another link with the Ceres relief. The sacrifice of a female pig is a common offering to the goddess in both Greek and Roman religion.[123] As we have seen, in Roman cult such a sacrifice was conducted in agricultural and funerary rituals dedicated to the goddess and at the Cerialia, her annual festival.[124] This is not to say, however, that the sow in the Aeneas panel is being offered to Ceres directly. I agree with those who argue that the recipients of the sacrifice in the panel are the Penates, who are represented in the small temple in the upper left corner of the relief.[125]

The occasion for this sacrifice, however, merits further discussion. Some argue that the scene on the panel represents Aeneas' sacrifice of the sow of Lavinium upon his landing in Italy, here offered to the Penates, as in the version of Dionysius of Halicarnassus (1.57.1), rather than to Juno Maxima as in the *Aeneid* (8.81–85).[126] However, the literary tradition also indicates that the sacrifice of the sow by Aeneas was followed by an annual sacrifice of a pig to the Penates of Lavinium.[127] The scene on the Aeneas panel may well represent this annual sacrifice.

The choice of the sacrificial victim has special significance. As we have previously noted, Varro associates the sacrifice of a pig with "beginnings" (initia) in general:

> For it seems that at the beginning of making sacrifices they first took the victim from the swine family. There are traces of this in these facts: that pigs are sacrificed at the initial rites of Ceres that at the rites that initiate peace, when a treaty is made, a pig is killed; and that at the beginning of the marriage rites of ancient kings and eminent personages in Etruria, the bride and groom, in the ceremonies which united them, first sacrificed a pig. The ancient Latins, too, as well as the Greeks living in Italy, seem to have had the same custom . . .
>
> (Varr. *Rust.* 2.4.9—Loeb trans.)

I propose that the sacrifice of the pig to the Penates primarily commemorates the establishment of peace between the Trojans and the Latins, and thus is related to Varro's initia pacis.[128] The theme is very appropriate for the Ara Pacis and relates to Ceres' role in liminal rites of intensification.[129] The sacrifice, however, also recalls the initia of weddings and may thus commemorate Aeneas' wedding to Lavinia. In this instance, it would refer indirectly to the marriage legislation that Augustus promoted and would connect the Aeneas panel with the processional panels of the Ara Pacis, in which women and children significantly appear.[130] This interpretation of the sacrifice also connects the Aeneas panel with the role of Ceres in the rite of passage of marriage.[131] The sacrifice of the pig may be related to the third type of initia to which Varro refers, the initia Cereris, or initiation rites of Ceres, and hence associate the panel with this other rite of passage connected with the goddess.[132] Finally, we may relate this sacrifice to one conducted by consuls at various points of transition in their office: on entering into their duties, and at their departure and return from a province. The common purpose of these sacrifices seems to have been an oath ceremony in which the Penates were honored and the sacrifice of a pig was performed.[133] Perhaps the sacrifice of the pig on the Ara Pacis is connected with Augustus' return from the provinces of Spain and Gaul, the occasion for which the altar was vowed by the Senate. The sacrifice would then relate to yet another type of initium, the reinauguration of Augustus' rule in Rome. As we have noted previously, Varro states elsewhere that the ceremonies known as initia are especially connected with Ceres (*Rust.* 3.1.5). Ceres is a goddess closely connected with "beginnings," and the sacrifice of the pig in the Aeneas panel recalls a variety of such initia.[134]

The goddess's connection with initia also points to another level of meaning linking the Ceres panel with its counterparts on the other side of the altar. The Aeneas and Lupercal panels both refer to the role of patricians in the founding of Rome. Aeneas was the father of Iulus-Ascanius, the founder of the patrician clan of the Julii, and the ancestor of the twins Romulus and Remus, who established the city of Rome. Romulus, as the first king of the city, created the *ordo*, or social class, of the patricians (Livy 1.8.7). The goddess Ceres on the eastern side of the altar is closely tied to another initium in the history of the city, the establishment of the plebeian organization at the very beginnings of the Roman Republic. As we have seen, the dedication of the Temple of Ceres, Liber, and Libera took place traditionally on the same date assigned to the First Secession of the Plebs, in 494/3 B.C., soon after the establishment of the Republic in 509 B.C.[135] The First Secession marks the beginning of the Conflict of the Orders, the power struggle between patricians and plebeians. During the Early Republic, the Temple of Ceres, Liber, and Libera became the nucleus of the plebeian struggle to obtain social recognition and political power. As we saw in chapter 4, Ceres herself was closely tied to the plebeians as their patron goddess.

I propose that the goddess appears on the eastern side of the Ara Pacis to honor plebeian contributions in the origins of the Roman state and that she is deliberately contrasted with Romulus and Aeneas, who appear on its western side to honor the patrician role in the origins of the city. Although the political conflict between the patricians and plebeians had ended long before the Augustan period, significant social and religious distinctions between the two orders continued for quite some time.[136] A reference to both patrician and plebeian pride in the early history of Rome would be entirely appropriate in a monument intended to celebrate the new era of peace brought to all Roman citizens by the princeps Augustus.

The Ceres panel is also deliberately contrasted with its counterpart on the eastern side of the altar, the Roma panel to the north. Only a small fragment of the latter panel survives. This fragment shows the upper thigh of a female figure seated upon a pile of weapons. Scholars generally reconstruct the panel on the basis of iconographic comparison as representing Roma, the personification of the city, accompanied by two other figures, possibly Honos and Virtus, the embodiments of Honor and Virtue. The composition of the Ceres and Roma panels is therefore quite similar: an enthroned female divinity accompanied on either side by two other figures.[137] In the manner of representation of the two central figures, however, the two reliefs are clearly contrasted: Roma is a warrior, enthroned on a pile of weapons, while Ceres is a nurturer of plants, children, and animals, enthroned on the earth, which is her element.[138]

The contrast points to other differences between the two divinities: Roma is the protective goddess of the city of Rome, while Ceres is preeminently a goddess of the countryside.[139] Roma has little religious significance, with no temple, altar, or cult in Rome itself during the Augustan period (although such a cult did exist in the provinces), while Ceres is an ancient divinity with a venerable temple and three separate cults.[140] Roma, indeed, seems more a personification than a divinity: she represents the power and might of the Roman people.[141] In the Ara Pacis relief, she symbolizes the power that has produced the peace the altar celebrates: "peace produced on land and sea through victories" (pax terra marique parta victoriis).[142] But peace is not merely the absence of war; it is also the benefits that accrue to humankind in a peaceful state. Ceres represents the other aspect of peace, the blessings of fertility that it nurtures: as Ovid says, "Peace nourishes Ceres, [and] Ceres is the nursling of Peace" (Pax Cererem nutrit, pacis alumna Ceres) (*Fast.* 1.704). Ceres' connection with peace, as we have seen, is related to her liminal role, and she presides over the transition from a time of war to one of peace.[143] The peace that Roma represents is produced by war, the work of the Roman soldier. The peace Ceres represents permits agriculture, the work of the Roman farmer. The two contrasting divinities of the rear entrance to the Ara Pacis symbolize these two aspects of peace.[144]

The contrast between Roma and Ceres implied in the sculptural program of the Ara Pacis is made explicit in the *Hymn to Roma* written by the female poet Melinno (*Anthl. Lyr. Graec.* Diehl II², 315–316).[145] The hymn begins (1–2) with an invocation to Roma, "daughter of Ares, warlike Lady who wears the golden girdle" (Θυγάτηρ ῎Αρηος / χρυσεομίτρα δαίφρων ἄν-ασσα). As on the Ara Pacis relief, so in the hymn the goddess Roma is preeminently a warrior. At the end of the hymn, Roma is deliberately contrasted with Demeter:

> For indeed you alone from all produce the bravest strong spearmen, just as if you produced the blooming fruit of Demeter from the fields.
>
> (Melinno, *Hymn to Roma* 17–20)

Melinno here contrasts the stern Amazonian Roma, who gives birth to full-grown warriors, and the nurturing Demeter/Ceres, who produces young crops. On the Ara Pacis relief panels, these divinities appear as pendants to one another, symbolizing the might of the Roman people and the divinity who protects and nourishes them.[146]

The Ceres panel also has significant associations with the processional frieze of the Ara Pacis. In the south frieze, which depicts Augustus and members of his family along with a variety of magistrates and priests, one figure (S-31) has been identified on the basis of portraiture comparison as Augustus' wife, Livia (fig. 55).[147] This figure has been compared to the central figure of the Ceres panel.[148] The attitude and expression of these two veiled and crowned figures are remarkably alike. The association of Livia in the south processional frieze with Ceres in the southeast panel parallels the identification of Augustus in the south frieze with Aeneas in the southwest panel. As we have seen, there is considerable other evidence for the identification of Livia with the goddess Ceres.[149] For example, in an image examined previously (fig. 10), the portrait features of Livia may be recognized in a gem assimilating her to Ceres.[150] The veil and the corona spicea with poppies that she wears here make this image very similar to the central figure of the Ceres panel. The identification of Ceres and Livia in other sources makes it likely that the similarity of their representations in the Ara Pacis is deliberate and reflects an attempt to associate the two. This identification arises out of Ceres' connection with the social category of women, and we have seen in chapter 2 how her association with female members of the imperial family continued throughout the period of the Early Empire.

If, on one level, the central figure of the Ceres panel is meant to recall Livia, then it would seem likely that the children this figure holds in her lap are meant to suggest the adoptive children of Augustus and Livia, probably Gaius and Lucius Caesar.[151] These children may also be represented in the processional frieze of the Ara Pacis, suggesting another connection between this frieze and the Ceres panel.[152] The children of the Ceres panel are polysemantic: symbolizing the role of Ceres in human fertility, referring indirectly to the twins Romulus and Remus of the Lupercal panel, and suggesting also an identification with the children of Augustus' family.

The identification of the children of the relief with the children of the imperial family may be supported by a later parallel. On an agate cameo, a woman
of the imperial family appears wearing a crown of wheat stalks and poppies
and holding two children in the fold of her drapery (fig. 45).[153] Vollenweider
has suggested that this gem was commissioned at the birth of twins to Livilla,
the granddaughter of Livia and wife of Drusus Minor, the son of Tiberius.[154]
The image is remarkably similar to the Ceres panel of the Ara Pacis and, I
suggest, was modeled on it. The Ceres panel thus connects Augustus and his
family with the peace and fertility that his rule was to produce, as symbolized
by the goddess Ceres.

The garland and floral scroll reliefs of the Ara Pacis also exhibit associations
with the Ceres panel through their references to the concepts of fertility and
liminality connected with the goddess. These reliefs have an ideological significance, not merely a decorative function.[155] On one level they symbolize the
fertility that the peace imposed by Augustus has returned to the land of Italy.
The garlands decorating the inner wall of the altar precinct contain fruits of
various seasons, including pomegranates, wheat stalks, apples, and nuts. These
plants are represented in the Ceres panel and are connected with the goddess's
role in agricultural fertility. A statue of Ceres or her priestess from Carthage
holds a garland of fruits quite similar to those represented on the Ara Pacis.[156]
The garlands are appropriate offerings to the divinity who is named Bearer of
Fruits (Karpophoros or Frugifer) and Bearer of the Seasons (Horephoros).[157]

The floral scroll frieze on the bottom of the exterior precinct walls of the
altar also contains plants in wild profusion. The abundant growth of vegetation
may be connected with Ceres as the power that causes plants to grow.[158] One
of the antecedents to the floral scroll on the Ara Pacis may be the vegetal scrolls
of South Italian vases.[159] These vases often show a female divinity rising up out
of a plant or the earth itself. The divinity may be identified, at least in some
cases, as Demeter/Ceres.[160] So, on an architectural relief from the Augustan
period we have already examined, Ceres, wearing a veil and a *kalathos*, rises
up out of a floral scroll (fig. 29).[161] As the goddess of agricultural fertility, Ceres
is appropriately associated with the floral scroll and garland friezes symbolizing the abundant harvests of the Augustan Age.

These friezes, however, also have another meaning. The fruits and plants
represented in these reliefs do not represent actual growing vegetation. Their
variety is as unnatural as their profusion, for they represent plants that grow in
different seasons. These reliefs also refer to the Golden Age, the *saeculum
aureum*, an important theme of the Augustan period.[162] The Golden Age was
an era in the mythical past when the world was at peace and all the needs

and wants of humankind were supplied effortlessly. A return to that mythical period of happiness was earnestly desired and indeed anticipated by those who had survived the troubles of the Late Republic. Augustus seized on that feeling of anticipation and proclaimed the return of the Golden Age in 17 B.C. with the celebration of the ludi Saeculares. As we have seen in the passage from Horace's *Carmen Saeculare* quoted above (*Carm. Saec.* 29–30), Ceres was named among the divinities whose blessings were sought on that occasion. Ceres appears in this context as a divinity of abundant fertility, an important element of the new Golden Age.

Ceres' role in agricultural labor supports her association with the Golden Age as represented in the reliefs of the Ara Pacis. As Galinsky recently noted, this new Golden Age of the Ara Pacis is not the idyllic existence envisioned by Vergil at the beginning of the *Fourth Eclogue* (18–25), in which the earth pours forth its bounty without tillage, and all dangers are removed.[163] Rather, it is a world in which humankind must continue to labor and to confront danger, or as Vergil says (*Ecl.* 4.32–33): "to try ocean with ships, to encircle towns with walls, to cut furrows into the earth." The divinity who supervises such work, in particular the work of the farmer, is Ceres, as Vergil indicates in the first poem of the *Georgics*:

> Much, moreover, does he please his fields, who breaks the lifeless clods with rakes and draws the wicker harrows, and golden Ceres does not look down upon him in vain from high Olympus.
>
> (Verg. *G.* 1.94–96)

A link between Ceres and labor is also indicated later in this poem:

> Persistent labor and pressing need in harsh matters have conquered all things. Ceres first established that mortals turn the earth with iron, when now acorns and wild strawberries of the sacred forest were failing and Dodona neglected to ensure nourishment.
>
> (Verg. *G.* 1.145–149)

The role of the goddess in agricultural labor is suggested in the Ara Pacis by the appearance of the farm animals, the cow and sheep, in the Ceres panel. The goddess is an appropriate symbol for the new Golden Age represented on the Ara Pacis, an era of blessings for man, to be sure, but blessings produced by his own hard work.

Ceres has other important connections to the return of the Golden Age. According to Manilius (*Astr.* 2.442), the constellation of Virgo belonged to Ceres:

spicifera est Virgo Cereris.[164] Virgo, as other scholars have noted, is closely connected with the Golden Age.[165] She may be identified with the Parthenos who bears the gleaming wheat sheaf, described by the Hellenistic poet Aratus (*Phaen.* 96–136). The Parthenos ruled on earth during the Golden Age but fled in the Bronze Age to dwell in the heavens. In another passage from Manilius, the Maiden is identified with the mythological heroine Erigone and associated with Augustus and the new Golden Age he brings to Rome:

> As she rises, Erigone, who ruled the previous ages with justice and fled away when they slipped back, allots the high ranks through the greatest power and she will give a governor of the laws and of the sacred code, one tending with purity to the holy temples of the gods.
>
> (Manil. *Astr.* 4.542–546)

The "governor of the laws and of the sacred code" is Augustus, and his actions are supervised by the Maiden, who herself is ruled by Ceres.[166] The wheat imagery in the Ceres panel implicitly suggests a connection with the Maiden, Virgo *spicifera*.[167] This astrological interpretation is supported by the place of the Ara Pacis in the larger program of the Campus Martius. The Augustan building program in this area included the Horologium Augusti, a gigantic sundial displaying not only the hours of the day but the seasons and constellations as well.[168] The construction of the Horologium indicates the importance attributed to astrology by Augustus himself, and the publication of Manilius' *Astronomica* further indicates the interest in astrology in this period.[169] A reference to the astrological connections of Ceres in the Ara Pacis panel is highly probable in this context.

Furthermore, the Return of the Maiden that signals the start of the Golden Age suggests the annual return of Persephone/Proserpina, also called the Maiden (Kore), to her mother Demeter/Ceres. This annual event is the mythological *aition* for the return of fertility to the land with the change of seasons. In her liminal capacity Ceres is the appropriate divinity to supervise this transition.[170] In Ovid's description of the return of Proserpina to her mother, the Augustan poet emphasizes Ceres' reaction and its effect on the fertility of the land:

> Only then did Ceres recover her expression and her spirit and she put the wheat-sheaf garland on her hair: and a great harvest was produced in the fallow fields and the threshing floor scarcely received the heaped-up wealth.
>
> (Ov. *Fast.* 4.615–618)

The mention of Ceres' donning the corona spicea suggests the image of the goddess in the Ara Pacis relief, as well as Horace's line regarding Ceres from the *Carmen Saeculare* commemorating the opening of the new Golden Age (*Carm. Saec.* 29). The imagery of the beginning of the annual season of planting and growth is closely related to that of the beginning of the new Golden Age, and Ceres is the divinity associated with both types of initia.

The theme of the return of fertility, moreover, directly links the princeps Augustus with Ceres and hence connects the goddess to the political message of the Ara Pacis. In the fifth poem of Book 4 of Horace's *Odes*, the anticipated return of Augustus to Rome is tied to the return of fertility to the land under the protection of Ceres:

The fatherland yearns for Caesar. [For when he is here] the cow in safety roams through the fields, Ceres and nourishing Prosperity nurture the fields, the ships fly over the pacified sea.

(Hor. *Carm.* 4.5.16–19)

The promise of fertility is fulfilled in the fifteenth poem of the book (4.15.4–5): "your era, Caesar, / has brought back abundant fruits to the fields" (tua, Caesar, aetas / fruges et agris rettulit uberes). Book 4 of the *Odes* may be dated to 13 B.C., when Augustus returned from the provinces, and when the Senate vowed the construction of the Ara Pacis in thanksgiving.[171] In the Ara Pacis, I suggest, the abundant plants and fruits of the Ceres panel and of the garland and floral scroll friezes may also be connected with the return of Augustus to Rome. Augustus' return to the city, like Proserpina's return to Ceres, represents a new beginning and fertile reinvigoration of the land.[172] Ceres' connection with the revitalized fertility associated both with the annual growing season and with the new Golden Age links her with the political message of the Ara Pacis, the celebration of Augustus' return and with it the return of peace and fertility to the Roman world.

6.5 Ceres and the Political Message of the Ara Pacis

Ceres, then, is a central symbol in the iconography of the Ara Pacis as a whole and is highly appropriate for its political message. Peace, in particular Pax Augusta, the peace engendered and maintained by Augustus, is the central theme of the altar. As we have seen, the concept of peace is closely tied to the

goddess Ceres in her liminal/normative role.[173] In the work of the Augustan
poet Tibullus, Pax is given the duties and attributes of Ceres:

> Meanwhile let Pax tend our fields. Bright Pax first led under the curved yoke the
> cows to plow the fields. Pax nourished the vine plants and stored the grape juice so
> that pure wine might flow for the son from the father's jar. In peace shall shine the
> hoe and plowshare, but decay masters the sad arms of the harsh soldier in the
> darkness. . . . Then come to us, nourishing Pax, and hold the wheat stalk in your hand,
> and let fruits pour forth from your shining bosom.
>
> (Tib. 1.10.45–50, 67–68)

Pax, like Ceres, tends the fields, supervises the plowing animals, and nourishes
the crops. She also has the wheat stalks and fruits that are the attributes of
Ceres.

The similarity of this passage on the goddess Pax to two from Ovid's *Fasti*
on the goddess Ceres is striking. In the first book of the *Fasti*, Ovid ties both
Ceres and Pax to Augustus:

> Wars long occupied humankind; the sword was more suitable than the plowshare,
> and the plowing bull yielded to the war-horse. Then the hoes used to lie idle, the
> mattocks were turned into javelins, and from the weight of the rake the helmet was
> made. Thanks to the gods and to your house! Bound in chains, for a long time now
> wars lie under your foot. Let the cow come under the yoke, let the seed come under
> the plowed earth. Peace nourishes Ceres, Ceres is the nursling of Peace.
>
> (Ov. *Fast.* 1.697–704)

This passage closely connects Ceres with the transition from the violence that
characterized the period of the Civil Wars to the peace that the rule of Augustus
brought to the Roman world. The divinities whom Ovid thanks are Ceres and
Pax; the house to whom he owes his gratitude is that of Augustus. The association among Ceres, Pax, and Augustus is made even more explicit in a passage
from Book 4 of the *Fasti*:

> Ceres was the first to change the acorn for a more useful food when humankind had
> been called to better sustenance. She compelled the bulls to offer their necks to the
> yoke: then for the first time did the exposed earth see the sun. Bronze was of value,
> the mass of steel lay hidden: alas! it should have been hidden forever! Ceres is joyful
> in peace, and pray, you farmers, for perpetual peace and a peace-making leader.
>
> (Ov. *Fast.* 4.401–408)

The "peace-making leader" is, of course, Augustus, who has brought peace to
Italy and thus enabled fertility, provided and nurtured by the goddess Ceres, to

return to the land. These associations of Ceres help to reinforce the political message of the altar, that the princeps Augustus provides the blessings of peace to Rome and her citizens with the benevolent aid of the gods.

6.6 Conclusion

The goddess Ceres was frequently used in Roman political propaganda of the imperial period as an important symbol tied to the princeps and linking him in turn to her connections with the concepts of fertility and liminality and her associations with the social groups of women and the plebs. These connections are expressed most clearly in the monument examined in this chapter, the Ara Pacis Augustae. Ceres, Mother of Children and of Crops, Patroness of the Plebs and of Women, Foster Child of Peace, is a pivotal image of this important monument. Her appearance in the southeastern panel helps to tie together the decorative program of the altar through explicit and implicit links to its other reliefs. The liminal/normative role of this goddess, her association with the reestablishment of peace, supports the primary message of the altar as a whole, the celebration of the peace Augustus had restored to the Roman world. This study of the Ceres panel of the Ara Pacis has shown that the ideological associations of the goddess are a critical element in our understanding of this important monument and its role in Roman political propaganda.

These associations of Ceres represent her essence in the Roman mind. Through examining the concepts and categories that the Romans connected with Ceres in this book, I have revealed one example of the way in which Roman divinities were "constructed" and how they reflected the social and political concerns of the period in which they were worshipped and had meaning. I hope that this study will suggest the wonderful complexity and diversity that the entire pantheon of female divinities represented in antiquity.

ORIGINAL·TEXT·OF
TRANSLATED·PASSAGES

Inscriptions

CE 237

hic sita est Amymone Marci optima et pulcherrima,
lanifica pia pudica frugi casta domiseda.

CE 968

seic florem aetatis tenuit Veratia caste
    nulla ut perciperet gaudia dedecoris.
coniuge namque uno vixit probato
    cetera digna bonis femina facta tulit.

CIL 1², p. 336

Tellu[ri et Cere]ri in Carenis. Aedi[les . . .] et lectisternium e lec[tis . . . faciunt,
quos] manceps praestat.

Literary Sources

Arnob. *Adv. Nat.* 7.32

Lectisternium Cereris erit Idibus proximis. Habent enim dii lectos atque, ut
stratis possint mollioribus incubare, pulvinorum tollitur atque excitatur inpres-
sio. Telluris natalis est.

Aug. *Civ. D.* 4.11

. . . ipse praesit nomine Liberi virorum seminibus et nomine Liberae
feminarum. . . .

Aug. *Civ. D.* 4.11

Ipse (deus) in aethere sit Iuppiter . . . Liber in vineis, Ceres in frumentis . . .

Callim. *Cer.* 134–138

χαῖρε θεὰ καὶ τάνδε σάω πόλιν ἔν θ' ὁμονοίᾳ
ἔν τ' εὐηπελίᾳ, φέρε δ' ἀγρόθι νόστιμα πάντα·
φέρβε βόας, φέρε μᾶλα, φέρε στάχυν, οἶσε θερισμόν,
φέρβε καὶ εἰράναν, ἵν' ὃς ἄροσε τῆνος ἀμάσῃ.
ἵλαθί μοι τρίλλιστε μέγα κρείοισα θεάων.

Cato *Agr.* 134

Priusquam messim facies, porcam praecidaneam hoc modo fieri oportet. Cereri porca praecidanea porco femina, priusquam hasce fruges condas, far, triticum, hordeum, fabam, semen rapicium.

Cic. *Balb.* 55

Sacra Cereris, iudices, summa maiores nostri religione confici caerimoniaque voluerunt; quae cum essent adsumpta de Graecia, et per Graecas curata sunt semper sacerdotes et Graeca omnino nominata. Sed cum illam, quae Graecum illud sacrum monstraret et faceret, ex Graecia deligerent, tamen sacra pro civibus civem facere voluerunt, ut deos immortales scientia peregrina et externa, mente domestica et civili precaretur. Has sacerdotes video fere aut Neapolitanas aut Velienses fuisse, foederatarum sine dubio civitatum.

Cic. *Leg.* 2.21

Nocturna mulierum sacrificia ne sunto praeter olla, quae pro populo rite fient; neve quem initianto, nisi ut adsolet Cereri Graeco sacro.

Cic. *Leg.* 2.36–37

M: . . . nam mihi cum multa eximia divinaque videntur Athenae tuae peperisse atque in vitam hominum attulisse, tum nihil melius illis mysteriis, quibus ex agresti immanique vita exculti ad humanitatem et mitigati sumus, initiaque, ut appellantur, ita re vera principia vitae cognovimus, neque solum cum laetitia vivendi rationem accepimus, sed etiam cum spe meliore moriendi. . . . Ad nostra igitur revertor. Quibus profecto diligentissime sanciendum est, ut mulierum famam multorum oculis lux clara custodiat, initienturque eo ritu Cereri quo Romae initiantur.

Cic. *Leg.* 2.55–57

Neque necesse est edisseri a nobis, quae finis funestae familiae, quod genus sacrificii Lari vervecibus fiat, quem ad modum os resectum terra obtegatur, quaeque in porca contracta iura sint, quo tempore incipiat sepulchrum esse et religione teneatur. . . . Nam siti dicuntur ii, qui conditi sunt. Nec tamen eorum ante sepulchrum est, quam iusta facta et porcus caesus est. Et quod nunc communiter in omnibus sepultis venit usu, ut humati dicantur, id erat proprium tum in iis, quos humus iniecta contexerat, eumque morem ius pontificale confirmat. Nam priusquam in ossa iniecta gleba est, locus ille, ubi crematum est corpus, nihil habet religionis; iniecta gleba tum et illis humatus est, et sepulchrum vocatur, ac tum denique multa religiosa iura conplectitur.

Cic. Nat. D. 3.52
Iam si est Ceres a gerendo—ita enim dicebas—, terra ipsa dea est (et ita habetur; quae enim alia Tellus?).

Cic. Verr. 2.4.99
. . . Aditus enim in id sacrarium non est viris; sacra per mulieres ac virgines confici solent. . . . Postridie sacerdotes Cereris atque illius fani antistitae, maiores natu probatae ac nobiles mulieres, rem ad magistratus suos deferunt.

Cic. Verr. 2.4.102
An minime mirum quae sacra per summam castimoniam virginum ac mulierum fiant. . . .

Cic. Verr. 2.4.107
Etenim multa saepe prodigia vim eius numenque declarant, multis saepe in difficillimis rebus praesens auxilium eius oblatum est, ut haec insula ab ea non solum diligi, sed etiam incoli custodirique videatur.

Cic. Verr. 2.4.108
Itaque apud patres nostros atroci ac difficili rei publicae tempore, cum Tiberio Graccho occiso magnorum periculorum metus ex ostentis portenderetur, P. Mucio L. Calpurnio consulibus, aditum est ad libros Sibyllinos; ex quibus inventum est Cererem antiquissimam placari oportere. Tum ex amplissimo collegio decemvirali sacerdotes populi Romani, cum esset in urbe nostra Cereris pulcherrimum et magnificentissimum templum, tamen usque Hennam profecti sunt. Tanta erat enim auctoritas et vetustas illius religionis ut, cum illuc irent, non ad aedem Cereris sed ad ipsam Cererem proficisci viderentur.

Cic. Verr. 2.5.36
Nunc sum designatus aedilis; habeo rationem quid a populo Romano acceperim; mihi ludos sanctissimos maxima cum cura et caerimonia Cereri Libero Liberaeque faciundos, mihi Floram matrem populo plebique Romanae ludorum celebritate placandam, mihi ludos antiquissimos, qui primi Romani appellati sunt, cum dignitate maxima et religione Iovi Iunoni Minervaeque esse faciundos, mihi sacrarum aedium procurationem, mihi totam urbem tuendam esse commissam. . . .

Dio Cass. 47.40.6

. . . καὶ οἱ ἀγορανόμοι τοῦ πλήθους ὁπλομαχίας ἀγῶνας ἀντὶ τῆς ἱπποδρομίας τῇ Δήμητρι ἐπετέλεσαν.

Dio Cass. 58.2.3

καὶ προσέτι καὶ ἁψῖδα αὐτῇ, ὃ μηδεμιᾷ ἄλλῃ γυναικί, ἐψηφίσαντο, ὅτι τε οὐκ ὀλίγους σφῶν ἐσεσώκει, καὶ ὅτι παῖδας πολλῶν ἐτετρόφει κόρας τε πολλοῖς συνεξεδεδώκει, ἀφ᾽ οὗ γε καὶ μητέρα αὐτὴν τῆς πατρίδος τινὲς ἐπωνόμαζον.

Dion. Hal. 6.89.3

Δήμαρχον ἄκοντα, ὥσπερ ἕνα τῶν πολλῶν, μηδεὶς μηδὲν ἀναγκαζέτω δρᾶν, μηδὲ μαστιγούτω μηδ᾽ ἐπιταττέτω μαστιγοῦν ἑτέρῳ μηδ᾽ ἀπο-κτιννύτω μηδ᾽ ἀποκτείνειν κελευέτω. ἐάν δέ τις τῶν ἀπηγορευμένων τι ποιήσῃ, ἐξάγιστος ἔστω, καὶ τὰ χρήματα αὐτοῦ Δήμητρος ἱερά, καὶ ὁ κτείνας τινὰ τῶν ταῦτ᾽ εἰργασμένων φόνου καθαρὸς ἔστω.

Dion. Hal. 6.94.3

Κάσσιος δ᾽ ὁ ἕτερος τῶν ὑπάτων ὁ καταλειφθεὶς ἐν τῇ Ῥώμῃ τὸν νεὼν τῆς τε Δήμητρος καὶ Διονύσου καὶ Κόρης ἐν τῷ μεταξὺ χρόνῳ καθιέρω-σεν, ὅς ἐστιν ἐπὶ τοῖς τέρμασι τοῦ μεγίστου τῶν ἱπποδρόμων ὑπὲρ αὐτὰς ἱδρυμένος τὰς ἀφέσεις . . .

Fest., s.v. cocum, 58 Müller

Naevius "cocus" inquit "edit Neptunum Venerem Cererem." Significat per Cererem panem, per Neptunum pisces, per Venerem olera.

Fest., s.v. facem, 87 Müller

Facem in nuptiis in honorem Cereris praeferebant, aqua aspergebatur nova nupta, sive ut casta puraque ad virum veniret, sive ut ignem atque aquam cum viro communicaret.

Fest., s.v. Graeca sacra, 97 Müller

Graeca sacra festa Cereris ex Graecia translata, quae ob inventionem Proser-pinae matronae colebant. Quae sacra, dum non essent matronae quae facerent propter cladem Cannensem et frequentiam lugentium, institutum est ne am-plius centum diebus lugeretur.

Fest., s.v. mundus, 54 Müller

Cereris qui mundus appellatur qui ter in anno solet patere: [IX] Kal. Sept. et III Non. Octobr. et [VI] Id. Novemb. Qui vel omni dictus est quod terra movetur.

Fest., s.v. *mundus*, 142 Müller

"Mundo nomen impositum est ab eo mundo, qui supra nos est: forma enim eius est, ut ex his qui intravere cognoscere potuit adsimilis illae." eius inferiorem partem veluti consecratam Dis Manibus clausam omni tempore, nisi his diebus qui supra scripti sunt, maiores censuerunt habendam, quos dies etiam religiosos iudicaverunt ea de causa quod quo tempore ea, quae occulta et abdita ea religionis Deorum Manium essent, veluti in lucem quandam adducerentur, et patefierent, nihil eo tempore in rep. geri voluerunt. itaque per eos dies non cum hoste manus conserebant: non exercitus scribebatur; non comitia habebantur: non aliud quicquam in rep. nisi quod ultima necessitas admonebat, administrabatur.

Fest., s.v. *praesentanea porca*, 250 Müller

Praesen\<tanea\> porca dicitur, ut ait Veranius, quae familiae purgandae causa Cereri immolatur, quod pars quaedam eius sacrifici fit in conspectu mortui eius cuius funus institutur.

Fest., s.v. *sacer mons*, 424 Lindsay

At homo sacer is est, quem populus iudicavit ob maleficium; neque fas est eum immolari, sed, qui occidit, parricidii non damnatur. . . .

Fest., s.v. *sacrima*, 319 Müller

Sacrima appellabant mustum, quod Libero sacrificabant pro vineis et vasis et ipso vino conservandis; sicut praemetium de spicis, quas primum messuissent, sacrificabant Cereri.

Fest., s.v. *Sementivae*, 337 Müller

Sementivae feriae fuerant institutae quasi ex his fruges grandescere possint.

Gell. *N.A.* 4.6.8

Porca etiam praecidanea appellata, quam piaculi gratia ante fruges novas captas immolare Cereri mos fuit, si qui familiam funestam aut non purgaverant aut aliter eam rem quam oportuerat procuraverant.

Gell. *N.A.* 18.2.11

Postea quaestio istaec fuit, quam ob causam patricii Megalensibus mutitare soliti sint, plebes Cerealibus.

Herodian 1.11.3

ἐπεὶ δὲ Ῥωμαίων ηὔξετο τὰ πράγματα, φασὶν αὐτοῖς χρησθῆναι μενεῖν τε τὴν ἀρχὴν καὶ ἐς μέγα προχωρήσειν, εἰ τὴν Πεσσινουντίαν θεὸν με-

ταγάγοιεν ὡς αὑτούς. πέμψαντες δὴ πρέσβεις ἐς Φρύγας τὸ ἄγαλμα
ἥτουν· ἔτυχον δὲ ῥᾳδίως συγγένειαν προβαλλόμενοι καὶ τὴν ἀπ'
Αἰνείου τοῦ Φρυγὸς ἐς αὑτοὺς διαδοχὴν καταλέγοντες.

Hor. *Carm.* 4.5.16–19
quaerit patria Caesarem.
tutus bos etenim rura perambulat.
nutrit rura Ceres almaque Faustitas,
pacatum volitant per mare navitae . . .

Hor. *Carm. Saec.* 29–32
fertilis frugum pecorisque Tellus
spicea donet Cererem corona;
nutriant fetus et aquae salubres
et Jovis aurae.

Juv. 6.45–51
quid quod et antiquis uxor de moribus illi
quaeritur? o medici, nimiam pertundite venam.
delicias hominis! Tarpeium limen adora
pronus et auratam Iunoni caede iuvencam,
si tibi contigerit capitis matrona pudici.
paucae adeo Cereris vittas contigere dignae,
quarum non timeat pater oscula . . .

Livy 2.8.2
. . . de . . . sacrandoque cum bonis capite eius, qui regni occupandi consilia
inisset . . .

Livy 3.55.7–8
. . . qui tribunis plebis, aedilibus, iudicibus, decemviris nocuisset, eius caput
Iovi sacrum esset, familia ad aedem Cereris, Liberi Liberaeque venum iret.

Livy 3.55.13
Institutum etiam ab iisdem consulibus, ut senatus consulta in aedem Cereris
ad aediles plebis deferrentur, quas antea arbitrio consulum supprimebantur
vitiabanturque.

Livy 10.23.13
Et ab aedilibus plebeiis L. Aelio Paeto et C. Fulvio Curvo ex multaticia item
pecunia, quam exegerunt pecuariis damnatis, ludi facti pateraeque aureae ad
Cereris positae.

Livy 22.56.4–5

Tum privatae quoque per domos clades volgatae sunt, adeoque totam urbem opplevit luctus, ut sacrum anniversarium Cereris intermissum sit, quia nec lugentibus id facere est fas, nec ulla in illa tempestate matrona expers luctus fuerat. Itaque ne ob eandem causam alia quoque sacra publica aut privata desererentur, senatus consulto diebus triginta luctus est finitus.

Livy 27.6.19

Aediles plebei Q. Catius et L. Porcius Licinus ex multaticio argento signa aenea ad Cereris dedere, et ludos pro temporis eius copia magnifice apparatos fecerunt.

Livy 29.10.4–8

Civitatem eo tempore repens religio invaserat invento carmine in libris Sibyllinis propter crebrius eo anno de caelo lapidatum inspectis, quandoque hostis alienigena terrae Italiae bellum intulisset, eum pelli Italia vincique posse, si mater Idaea a Pessinunte Romam advecta foret. . . . Itaque quo maturius fatis ominibus oraculisque portendentis sese victoriae compotes fierent, id cogitare atque agitare, quae ratio transportandae Romam deae esset.

Livy 30.39.8

P. Aelius Tubero et L. Laetorius aediles plebis vitio creati magistratu se abdicaverunt. . . . Cerialia ludos dictator et magister equitum ex senatus consulto fecerunt.

Livy 33.25.3

(Ludi) Plebei septiens instaurati; M'. Acilius Glabrio et C. Laelius eos ludos fecerunt; et de argento multaticio tria signa aenea, Cererem Liberumque et Liberam, posuerunt.

Livy 34.6.15

. . . quia Cereris sacrificium lugentibus omnibus matronis intermissum erat, senatus finiri luctum triginta diebus iussit.

Livy 36.37.4–5

Eorum prodigiorum causa libros Sibyllinos ex senatus consulto decemviri cum adissent, renuntiaverunt ieiunium instituendum Cereri esse, et id quinto quoque anno servandum; et ut novemdiale sacrum fieret et unum diem supplicatio esset; coronati supplicarent; et consul P. Cornelius, quibus diis quibusque hostiis edidissent decemviri, sacrificaret.

Macrob. *Sat.* 1.16.16–18

... et cum Mundus patet, nefas est proelium sumere... quod sacrum Diti patri et Proserpinae dicatum est: meliusque occlusa Plutonis fauce eundum ad proelium putaverunt. Unde et Varro ita scribit: "Mundus cum patet, deorum tristium atque infernum quasi ianua patet: propterea non modo proelium committi, verum etiam dilectum rei militaris causa habere, ac militem proficisci, navem solvere, uxorem liberum quaerendorum causa ducere, religiosum est."

Manil. *Astr.* 4.542–546

Erigone surgens, quae rexit saecula prisca
iustitia rursusque eadem labentia fugit,
alta per imperium tribuit fastigia summum,
rectoremque dabit legum iurisque sacrati
sancta pudicitia divorum templa colentem.

Melinno, *Hymn to Roma* 17–20

ἦ γὰρ ἐκ πάντων σὺ μόνα κρατίστους
ἄνδρας αἰχματὰς μεγάλους λοχεύεις
εὔσταχυν Δάματρος ὅπως ἀνεῖσα
καρπὸν ἀπ' ἀγρῶν.

Obseq. *Prodig. Lib.* 46 (106)

Fremitus ab inferno ad caelum ferri visus inopiam famemque portendit. Populus stipem, matronae thesaurum et virgines dona Cereri et Proserpinae tulerunt. Per virgines viginti septem cantitatum. Signa cupressea duo Iunoni Reginae posita.

Ov. *Am.* 3.10.1–18 and 43–48

Annua venerunt Cerealis tempora sacri;
    secubat in vacuo sola puella toro.
flava Ceres, tenues spicis redimita capillos,
    cur inhibes sacris commoda nostra tuis?
te, dea, munificam gentes ubiquaque loquuntur,
    nec minus humanis invidet ulla bonis.
ante nec hirsuti torrebant farra coloni,
    nec notum terris area nomen erat,
sed glandem quercus, oracula prima, ferebant;
    haec erat et teneri caespitis herba cibus.
prima Ceres docuit turgescere semen in agris
    falce coloratas subsecuitque comas;

prima iugis tauros supponere colla coegit,
    et veterem curvo dente revellit humum.
hanc quisquam lacrimis laetari credit amantum
    et bene tormentis secubituque coli?
nec tamen est, quamvis agros amet illa feraces,
    rustica hic viduum pectus amoris habet.
Story of Ceres and Iasion: lines 19–42
Quod tibi secubitus tristes, dea flava, fuissent,
    hoc cogor sacris nunc ego ferre tuis?
cur ego sim tristis, cum sit tibi nata reperta
    regnaque quam Iuno sorte minore regat?
festa dies Veneremque vocat cantusque merumque;
    haec decet ad dominos munera ferre deos.

    Ov. *Fast.* 1.666–684
vilice, da requiem terrae semente peracta;
    da requiem, terram qui coluere, viris.
pagus agat festum: pagum lustrate, coloni,
    et date paganis annua liba focis.
placentur frugum matres, Tellusque Ceresque,
    farre suo gravidae visceribusque suis.
officium commune Ceres et Terra tuentur:
    haec praebet causam frugibus, illa locum.
consortes operis, per quas correcta vetustas
    quernaque glans victa est utiliore cibo,
frugibus immensis avidos satiate colonos,
    ut capiant cultus praemia digna sui.
vos date perpetuos teneris sementibus auctus,
    nec nova per gelidas herba sit usta nives.
cum serimus, caelum ventis aperite serenis;
    cum latet, aetheria spargite semen aqua.
neve graves cultis Cerialia rura, cavete,
    agmine laesuro depopulentur aves.

    Ov. *Fast.* 1.697–704
bella diu tenuere viros: erat aptior ensis
    vomere, cedebat taurus arator equo:
sarcula cessabant, versique in pila ligones,
    factaque de rastri pondere cassis erat.

gratia dis domuique tuae; religata catenis
  iampridem vestro sub pede bella iacent.
sub iuga bos veniat, sub terras semen aratas.
  Pax Cererem nutrit, Pacis alumna Ceres.

Ov. *Fast.* 2.519–520
farra tamen veteres iaciebant, farra metebant,
  primitias Cereri farra resecta dabant.

Ov. *Fast.* 4.255–260
post, ut Roma potens opibus iam saecula quinque
  vidit et edomito sustulit orbe caput,
carminis Euboici fatalia verba sacerdos
  inspicit; inspectum tale fuisse ferunt:
"mater abest: matrem iubeo, Romane, requiras
  cum veniet, casta est accipienda manu."

Ov. *Fast.* 4.401–412
prima Ceres homine ad meliora alimenta vocato
  mutavit glandes utiliore cibo.
illa iugo tauros collum praebere coegit:
  tum primum soles eruta vidit humus.
aes erat in pretio, chalybeia massa latebat:
  eheu! perpetuo debuit illa tegi!
Pace Ceres laeta est; et vos orate, coloni,
  perpetuam pacem pacificumque ducem.

Ov. *Fast.* 4.547–551
abstinet alma Ceres somnique papavera causas
  dat tibi cum tepido lacte bibenda, puer.
noctis erat medium placidique silentia somni:
  Triptolemum gremio sustulit illa suo
terque manu permulsit eum. . . .

Ov. *Fast.* 4.615–618
tum demum voltumque Ceres animumque recepit
  imposuitque suae spicea serta comae;
largaque provenit cessatis messis in arvis
  et vix congestas area cepit opes.

Ov. *Met.* 2.11–13
Doridaque et natas, quarum pars nare videtur,
pars in mole sedens viridis siccare capillos
pisce vehi quaedam. . . .

Ov. *Met.* 3.437–438
non illum Cereris, non illum cura quietis
        abstrahere inde potest. . . .

Ov. *Met.* 5.642–647
. . . geminos dea fertilis angues
curribus admovit frenisque coercuit ora
et medium caeli terraeque per aera vecta est
atque levem currum Tritonida misit in urbem
Triptolemo partimque rudi data semina iussit
spargere humo, partim post tempora longa recultae.

Ov. *Met.* 10.431–436
festa piae Cereris celebrabant annua matres
illa, quibus nivea velatae corpora veste
primitias frugum dant spicea serta suarum
perque novem noctes venerem tactusque viriles
in vetitis numerant: turba Cenchreis in illa
regis adest coniunx arcanaque sacra frequentat.

Pliny *HN* 18.2.8
. . . ne degustabant quidem novas fruges aut vina antequam sacerdotes primitias
libassent.

Pliny *HN* 18.3.13
Frugem quidem aratro quaesitam furtim noctu pavisse ac secuisse puberi XII
Tabulis capital erat, suspensumque Cereri necari iubebant gravius quam in
homicidio convictum, impubem praetoris arbitratu verberari noxiamve dupli-
onemve decerni.

Plut. *Vit. Publ.* 12.1
ἔγραψε γὰρ νόμον ἄνευ κρίσεως κτεῖναι διδόντα τόν βουλόμενον τυρ-
αννεῖν· κτείναντα δὲ φόνου καθαρὸν ἐποίησεν, εἰ παράσχοιτο τοῦ
ἀδικήματος τοὺς ἐλέγχους.

Plut. *Vit. Rom.* 22.3
Ἔθηκε δὲ καὶ νόμους τινὰς, ὧν σφοδρὸς μέν ἐστιν ὁ γυναικὶ μὴ διδοὺς
ἀπολείπειν ἄνδρα, γυναῖκα δὲ διδοὺς ἐκβάλλειν ἐπὶ φαρμακείᾳ τέκνων

ἢ κλειδῶν ὑποβολῇ καί μοιχευθεῖσαν· εἰ δ' ἄλλως τις ἀποπέμψαιτο, τῆς οὐσίας αὐτοῦ τὸ μὲν τῆς γυναικὸς εἶναι, τὸ δὲ τῆς Δήμητρος ἱερὸν κελεύων· τὸν δ' ἀποδόμενον γυναῖκα θύεσθαι χθονίοις θεοῖς.

Pompon. *Dig.* 1.2.2.21

. . . ut essent qui aedibus praeessent, in quibus omnia scita sua plebs deferebat, duos ex plebe constituerunt, qui etiam aediles appelati sunt.

Prop. 4.8.3–14

Lanuvium annosi vetus est tutela draconis:
  hic tibi tam rarae non perit hora morae;
qua sacer abripitur caeco descensus hiatu
  qua penetrat (virgo, tale iter omne cave!)
ieiuni serpentis honos, cum pabula poscit
  annua et ex ima sibila torquet humo.
talia demissae pallent ad sacra puellae,
  cum temere anguino creditur ore manus.
ille sibi admotas a virgine corripit escas:
  virginis in palmis ipsa canistra tremunt.
si fuerint castae, redeunt in colla parentum,
  clamantque agricolae "Fertilis annus erit."

Serv. on Verg. *Aen.* 3.139

Quidam dicunt, diversis numinibus vel bene vel male faciendi potestatem dicatam, ut Veneri coniugia, Cereri divortia. . . .

Serv. on Verg. *Aen.* 4.58

LEGIFERAE CERERI leges enim ipsa dicitur invenisse: nam et sacra ipsius thesmophoria vocantur, [id est legumlatio.] sed hoc ideo fingitur, quia ante inventum frumentum a Cerere passim homines sine lege vagabantur: quae feritas interrupta est invento usu frumentorum, postquam ex agrorum divisione nata sunt iura. . . . Alii dicunt, hos deos quos commemoravit nuptiis esse contrarios, Cererem quia propter raptum filiae nuptias exsecratur; vel ex quo Iovi nupta praelata Iunone repudiata est. . . . Alii dicunt favere nuptiis Cererem, quod prima nupserit Iovi et condendis urbibus praesit, ut Calvus docet: Et leges sanctas docuit, et cara iugavit corpora conubiis et magnas condidit urbes: nam ideo et aratri sulco clauditur civitas. . . . Nam facturi aliquid, ante adversos placamus deos: et sic propitios invocamus: ut: "Nigram hiemi pecudem, Zephyris felicibus albam." Ergo modo nuptura placat ante Cererem: quae propter raptum filiae nupturas exsecratur.

Serv. on Verg. *Aen.* 4.166

Quidam . . . Tellurem praesse nuptiis tradunt; nam et in auspiciis nuptiarum invocatur: Cui etiam virgines, vel cum ire ad domum mariti coeperint, vel iam ibi positae diversis nominibus vel ritu sacrificant.

Serv. on Verg. *Aen.* 4.609

Proserpinam raptam a Dite patre Ceres cum incensis faculis per orbem terrarum requireret, per trivia eam vel quadrivia vocabat clamoribus, unde permansit in eius sacris, ut certis diebus per compita a matronis exerceatur ululatus, sicut in Isidis sacris. . . .

Tib. 1.10.45–50, 67–68

interea pax arva colat. pax candida primum
     duxit araturos sub iuga curva boves;
pax aluit vites et sucos condidit uvae,
     funderet ut nato testa paterna merum;
pace bidens vomerque nitent, at tristia duri
     militis in tenebris occupat arma situs.
. . .
at nobis, Pax alma, veni spicamque teneto,
     profluat et pomis candidus ante sinus.

Val. Max. 1.1.1

Cuius cum in urbe pulcherrimum templum haberent, Gracchano tumultu moniti Sibyllinis libris ut vetustissimam Cererem placarent, Hennam, quoniam sacra eius inde orta credebantur, XVviros ad eam propitiandam miserunt.

Val. Max. 1.1.15

Quanto nostrae civitatis senatus venerabilior in deos, qui post Cannensem cladem decrevit, ne matronae ultra tricesimum diem luctus suos extenderent, uti ab his sacra Cereris peragi possent, quia maiore paene Romanarum virium parte in execrabili ac duro solo iacente nullius penates maeroris expertes erant. Itaque matres ac filiae coniugesque et sorores nuper interfectorum abstersis lacrimis depositisque doloris insignibus candidam induere vestem et aris tura dare coactae sunt.

Varr. in Non., 63 Lindsay

. . . qui ope indigerent et ad asylum Cereris confugissent panis daretur

Varr. in Non., 240 Lindsay

Praecidaneum est praecidendum. Varro de Vita Populi Romani, lib. III: "Quod humatus non sit, heredi porca praecidanea suscipienda Telluri et Cereri; aliter familia non pura est.

Varr. Ling. 6.26

Sementivae Feriae dies is qui a pontificibus dictus, appellatus a semente, quod sationis causa susceptae.

Varr. Rust. 2.4.9–10

Sus graece dicitur ὗς, olim θῦς dictus ab illo verbo quod dicunt θύειν, quod est immolare. Ab suillo enim pecore immolandi initium primum sumptum videtur, cuius vestigia, quod initiis Cereris porci immolantur, et quod initiis pacis, foedus cum feritur, porcus occiditur, et quod nuptiarum initio antiqui reges ac sublimes viri in Etruria in coniunctione nuptiali nova nupta et novus maritus primum porcum immolant. Prisci quoque Latini, etiam Graeci in Italia idem factitasse videntur. Nam et nostrae mulieres, maxime nutrices, naturam qua feminae sunt in virginibus appellant porcum, et Graecae *choeron*, significantes esse dignum insigne nuptiarum.

Varr. Rust. 3.1.4–5

Nec sine causa terram eandem appellabant matrem et Cererem, et qui eam colerent, piam et utilem agere vitam credebant atque eos solos reliquos esse ex stirpe Saturni regis. Cui consentaneum est, quod initia vocantur potissimum ea quae Cereri fiunt sacra.

Verg. Aen. 1.177–179

tum Cererem corruptam undis Cerealiaque arma
expediunt fessi rerum, frugesque receptas
et torrere parant flammis et frangere saxo.

Verg. Aen. 4.56–59

principio delubra adeunt pacemque per aras
exquirunt; mactant lectas de more bidentis
legiferae Cereri Phoeboque patrique Lyaeo,
Iunoni ante omnis cui vincla iugalia curae.

Verg. Ecl. 4.32–33

quae temptare Thetim ratibus, quae cingere muris
oppida, quae iubeant telluri infindere sulcos.

Verg. *G.* 1.24–31

tuque adeo, quem mox quae sint habitura deorum
concilia, incertum est, urbisne invisere, Caesar,
terrarumque velis curam et te maximus orbis
auctorem frugum tempestatumque potentem
accipiat, cingens materna tempora myrto,
an deus immensi venias maris ac tua nautae
numina sola colant, tibi serviat ultima Thule
teque sibi generum Tethys emat omnibus undis

Verg. *G.* 1.94–96

multum adeo, rastris glaebas qui frangit inertes
vimineasque trahit crates, iuvat arva, neque illum
flava Ceres alto nequiquam spectat Olympo.

Verg. *G.* 1.145–149

. . . labor omnia vicit
inprobus, et duris urgens in rebus egestas.
prima Ceres ferro mortales vertere terram
instituit, cum iam glandes atque arbuta sacrae
deficerent silvae et victum Dodona negaret.

Verg. *G.* 1.338–350

In primis venerare deos atque annua magnae
sacra refer Cereri laetis operatus in herbis
extremae sub casum hiemis, iam vere sereno.
Tum pingues agni et molissima vina,
tum somni dulces densaeque in montibus umbrae.
Cuncta tibi Cererem pubes agrestis adoret;
quoi tu lacte favos et miti dilue Baccho,
terque novas circum felix est hostia fruges,
omnis quam chorus et socii comitentur ovantes
et Cererem clamore vocent in tecta; neque ante
falcem maturis quisquam supponat aristis,
quam Cereri torta redimitus tempora quercu
det motus incompositos et carmina dicat.

Appendix 2

WOMEN·OF
THE·IMPERIAL·FAMILY
IDENTIFIED·WITH·CERES

This catalog is intended in general to be representative, not comprehensive. I have checked through a wide variety of sources, including inscriptions, coins, gems, and sculpture, to find evidence for the identification of women of the imperial family with Ceres. A number of earlier studies proved particularly useful for this search, including: De Angeli (1988); Wrede (1981); Temporini (1978); Bieber (1977); Kruse (1968/1975); Grether (1946); Scott (1936); and Riewald (1912). Since imperial state coinage is especially significant for my arguments, I conducted a comprehensive search of all volumes of Mattingly and Sydenham's catalog of Roman imperial coinage (*RIC*) for numismatic evidence connecting women of the imperial family with Ceres. A summary of my conclusions based on the evidence presented in this catalog is given in sec. 5.4.

The catalog is arranged chronologically by the names of the women identified with Ceres, from Livia to Julia Domna. I found no evidence for the identification of women of the imperial family with Ceres in official media (e.g., state coinage) after Julia Domna, so I have concluded the catalog with this woman, the wife of the emperor Septimius Severus. The evidence for identification of each woman with Ceres is presented in the following order: inscriptions, coins (local and state), gems, and sculpture. I have included references to previous publications that provide additional information and photographs. In addition, I have provided references to figures in this book that illustrate the evidence cited.

1. *Livia*
Wife of Augustus; mother of Tiberius

1.1. Inscription from the island of Gaulos (Gozo, Malta) dedicated by a local priestess to "Ceres Julia Augusta, wife of the deified Augustus, mother of Ti-

berius Caesar Augustus" (CERERI IULIAE AUGUSTAE DIVI AUGUSTI MATRI TI.
CAESARIS AUGUSTI).

Riewald (1912) nr. 58; *CIL* 10.7501; *ILS* 121.

1.2 Inscription from Lampsacus dedicated by the local *gerousia* to "Julia Augusta Hestia, the New Demeter" (Ἰουλίαν Σεβαστὴν νέαν Δήμητρα).

Riewald (1912) nr. 76; *CIG* 2.3642; *IGR* 4.180.

For the identification of this Julia Augusta as Livia, see Riewald (1912) 305;
Temporini (1978) 74; Grether (1946) 241. Cf. Scott (1936) 51, who identifies
the woman as Julia Titi.

1.3 Inscription from Aphrodisias dedicated by the priests "of the goddess,
Julia, the New Demeter" (Θεᾶς Ἰουλίας νέας Δήμητρος).

Riewald (1912) nr. 57; *CIG* 2.2815.

For the identification of this Julia as Livia, see Riewald (1912) 305; Temporini (1978) 74; Grether (1946) 241. Another possible identification is Julia
Domna.

1.4 Inscription from Ephesos dedicated to Livia as "Demeter the Bearer of
Fruit" (Δήμητηρ Καρποφόρος).

SEG 4.515; Temporini (1978) 74.

1.5 Inscription recording the dedication by Augustus of the Altar of Ceres
Mater and Ops Augusta in Rome on August 10, A.D. 7.

CIL 1², pp. 240 and 324.

For the association of Livia and Ceres implied by the inscription, see Platner-
Ashby (1929) 110; Wissowa (1912) 204; Grether (1946) 226.

1.6 Inscription from an Italian town recording offerings to Ceres Augusta
(CERERI AUGUST.).

CIL 11.3196; Grether (1946) 239.

Grether has argued that this inscription, dated to A.D. 18, indicates an assimilation of Livia (here called Augusta) to Ceres. However, the epithet Augusta may simply have associated Ceres with the imperial house in general, not
identified her with Livia.

On coins the epithet Augusta was frequently applied to Ceres and other deities or personifications such as Pax, Concordia, and Salus. In these cases no
direct identification with a particular member of the imperial family seems to
have been intended and the reference seems rather to have been to the power
of the princeps himself. The contemporaneous use of the related epithet Augusti, "of Augustus," for such deities or personifications supports this objection to Grether's argument. Sutherland (1951) 133 has interpreted the epithet

Augusti as "implicit in the princeps" and the epithet Augusta as "inalienable from the princeps."

1.7 Local coin of Pergamon showing Livia holding wheat stalks.
   Riewald (1912) nr. 59; *BMC Mysia* 140 nrs. 250–251; Grether (1946) 232.

1.8 Local coin of Trallis showing Livia holding wheat stalks and poppies.
   BMC Lydia 344 nrs. 114–120; Temporini (1978) 74.
   Cf. Grether (1946) 231, who identifies this type as Livia in the guise of Hekate.

1.9 Local coin of Sardis showing Livia holding wheat stalks.
   BMC Lydia 250–251 nrs. 98–101; Temporini (1978) 74.

1.10 Local coin of Panormus showing Livia with the corona spicea.
   BMC Sicily 125 nr. 43; Grether (1946) 227 n. 24.

1.11 Official state coin of Augustus possibly showing Livia with the attributes of Ceres, issued during her lifetime (fig. 40b).
   RIC 1²:56.219; *BMCRE* Augustus 544; De Angeli (1988) nr. 178.
   On the reverse of this coin, minted at Lugdunum, appears a seated female figure holding a sceptre and possibly wheat stalks. The portrait features of the female figure, although rather indistinct, have been identified as those of Livia. The type is very similar to one from the reign of Tiberius (1.12 below) and to one from Claudius' rule (1.13 below) which, moreover, bears the legend DIVA AUGUSTA, i.e., the deified Livia. Since the Claudian type definitely indicates direct assimilation of Livia to Ceres, some scholars argue that this is also true of the Augustan type. So Mattingly (1923) 1:91; Grether (1946) 227; Rickman (1980) 260; Chirassi-Colombo (1981) 427.
   Cf., however, Pollini (1990) 350, who argues that a positive identification of Livia in the guise of a goddess cannot be made, because of the small size of the facial features, the generalized nature of the hairstyle, and the absence of a legend making any claim of divine association.
   The relationship between the Augustan and Claudian types is perhaps better explained by assuming that Claudius adapted an earlier type of Ceres for the now deified Livia, in which case Livia was directly assimilated to Ceres on official coinage only after her death and consecration.

1.12 Official state coin of Tiberius possibly showing Livia with the attributes of Ceres, issued during her lifetime.
   RIC 1²:95.25–29.
   See nr. 1.11 above.

1.13 Official state coin of Claudius showing Livia with the attributes of Ceres, issued after her death and consecration (fig. 41b).

RIC 1²:128.101; *BMCRE* Augustus 544; De Angeli (1988) nr. 179, pl. 610. Livia is identified here by the inscription DIVA AUGUSTA. See nr. 1.11 above.

1.14 Grand Camée de France, showing Livia, seated next to Tiberius, wearing the wheat stalk and poppy crown, and holding wheat and poppies.

Paris, Cabinet des Méd.; De Angeli (1988) nr. 174, pl. 610; Richter (1971) 105; Vollenweider (1966) 117, pl. 73.6; Grether (1946) 243; Furtwängler (1900) 2:208, 296, pl. 9.

1.15 Sardonyx fragment in Rome showing Livia with the wheat stalk and poppy crown.

Vollenweider (1966) 68, 117, pl. 73.7; Righetti (1955) 46, nr. 121, pl. 12.2.

1.16 Cameo in the Leningrad Hermitage showing Livia with the corona spicea.

Hermitage 154; De Angeli (1988) nr. 173, pl. 609.

1.17 Onyx cameo in the Vienna Kunsthistorisches Museum showing Livia holding wheat stalks and poppies.

Richter (1971) 101–102, nr. 486; Bieber (1968) 12; Eichler and Kris (1927) 57, pl. 5.9.

1.18 Cameo from Florence showing Livia with the wheat stalk and poppy crown (fig. 10).

Florence, Mus. Arch. 26; De Angeli (1988) nr. 172, pl. 609; Vollenweider (1966) 68–69, pl. 76.4.

1.19 Onyx cameo from Florence showing Tiberius and Livia, who wears the wheat stalk and poppy crown.

Florence, Mus. Arch. 177; Vollenweider (1966) 118, pl. 76.3.

1.20 Cameo from Paris of a family group, including Tiberius, Germanicus, and Livia, who holds poppies and wheat stalks.

Paris, Cabinet des Méd.; Grether (1946) 243; Curtius (1934) 119–156; Furtwängler (1900) 2, pl. 56.

1.21 Sardonyx in the British Museum showing Livia with the corona spicea of Ceres.

Walters (1926) nr. 1976.

1.22 Onyx cameo in the British Museum showing Livia seated on a throne above a cornucopia, surrounded by various fruits and wheat.

Walters (1926) nr. 3580.

1.23 Head and statue in Copenhagen of Livia wearing the corona spicea and holding wheat stalks.
Glyptotek Ny Carlsberg nrs. 351 and 618; Gross (1962) 118, pls. 26–29.

1.24 Head in Bonn of Livia with the corona spicea.
Bonn, Rhein. Landesmus.; De Angeli (1988) nr. 185.

1.25 Head in Leningrad of Livia with the corona spicea.
Leningrad, Hermitage A 116; De Angeli (1988) nr. 186, pl. 611.

1.26 Head in Copenhagen of Livia with the wheat stalk and poppy crown.
Copenhagen, Glyptothek 1631; De Angeli (1988) nr. 187, pl. 611.

2. Antonia Minor
Mother of Claudius and Germanicus

2.1 Local coin of Alexandria showing Antonia Minor with the corona spicea.
BMC Alexandria 9.65–67; Polaschek (1973) 17; Trillmich (1971) 196; Vogt (1924) 1:24.

2.2 Official state coins of Claudius showing Antonia Minor with the corona spicea, issued after her death and consecration (fig. 27).
RIC 1²:124.65–68, 125.75, 126.80–81; *BMCRE* Claudius 109; De Angeli (1988) nr. 180, pl. 610.

2.3 Amethyst intaglio showing Antonia Minor holding a cornucopia filled with fruit, wheat stalks and poppies.
Paris, Cabinet des Méd.; Richter (1971) 509.
The portrait bust has also been identified as Livia; see Furtwängler (1900) pl. 61.36. For portrait identification of Antonia Minor, see Erhard (1978).

2.4 Statue in the Louvre of Antonia Minor in the Ceres type without attributes.
Bieber (1977) 171; Charbonneaux (1963) 152–153, nr. 1228.

3. Livilla
Daughter of Antonia Minor; sister of Claudius and Germanicus

3.1 Agate cameo from Berlin possibly showing Livilla with the wheat stalk and poppy crown (fig. 45).
Berlin, Staatliche Museen, inv. FG 11096; Vollenweider (1966) 73–74, pl. 84.2; Furtwängler (1900) 249, pl. 52.9.

The woman holds two children in the fold of her drapery, whom Vollenweider identifies as Livilla's twins. The identification of the woman as Livilla is uncertain, since there are no securely identified portraits of her.

4. Agrippina the Elder
Wife of Germanicus; mother of Caligula

4.1 Inscription honoring Agrippina the Elder as the Aeolian Karpophoros (Αἰολὶς Καρποφόρος) from Mytilene on Lesbos.
   IGR 4.74–75; *IG* 12.2.212–213.
   The epithet Karpophoros assimilates Agrippina the Elder to Demeter/Ceres.

4.2 Local coin of Philadelphia Neokaisareia showing Agrippina the Elder holding a cornucopia and wheat stalks.
   Riewald (1912) nr. 61; Imhoof-Blumer (1897) 119, nr. 21.

4.3 Colossal head from Cos, possibly belonging to a cult statue of Demeter and bearing the portrait features of Agrippina the Elder.
   IGR 4.1062; Price (1984) 183; Vermeule (1968) 193; *Annuario* 33–34 (1955–1956) 124, nr. 142.

5. Drusilla
Daughter of Agrippina the Elder; sister of Caligula

5.1 Local coin of Smyrna showing Drusilla with the attributes of Ceres.
   Riewald (1912) 68; *Zeitschrift für Numismatik* 18 (1892) 5.

6. Agrippina the Younger
Sister of Caligula; daughter of Agrippina the Elder; wife of Claudius; mother of Nero

6.1 Inscription from Thermae honoring Agrippina the Younger as the Aeolian Karpophoros (Αἰολὶς Καρποφόρος).
   IGR 4.22; *IG* 12.2.208; Temporini (1978) 75.
   The epithet Karpophoros assimilates Agrippina the Younger to Demeter/Ceres.

6.2 Inscription from Mytilene honoring Agrippina the Younger as the Aeolian Karpophoros (Αἰολὶς Καρποφόρος).

IGR 4.81, 4.100; *IG* 12.2.211, 12.2.258; Temporini (1978) 75.

The epithet Karpophoros assimilates Agrippina the Younger to Demeter/ Ceres.

6.3 Local coin from Acmoniae showing Agrippina the Younger with wheat stalks and a poppy at her breast.

Riewald (1912) nr. 66; *BMC* Phrygia 9 nr. 35.

6.4 Local coin from Cymarum showing Agrippina the Younger with the corona spicea.

Riewald (1912) nr. 64; *BMC* Troas, Aeolis, and Lesbos 118 nr. 130.

6.5 Local coin from Magnesia ad Sipylum showing Agrippina the Younger holding wheat stalks and a torch.

Riewald (1912) nr. 63; Imhoof-Blumer (1897) 89, nr. 4.

6.6 Local coin from Aninetus showing Agrippina the Younger with the corona spicea.

Riewald (1912) nr. 62; Imhoof-Blumer (1897) 23, nr. 7.

6.7 Local coin from Alexandria showing Agrippina the Younger with the corona spicea.

Riewald (1912) nr. 65; *BMC* Alexandria 14 nrs. 108–111.

6.8 Official state coins of Claudius showing Agrippina the Younger with the corona spicea, issued during her lifetime (fig. 43).

RIC 1²:134.92; *BMCRE* Claudius 72.

These coins provide the earliest extant evidence for the direct and official assimilation to Ceres of a living imperial family member.

6.9 Double cornucopia cameo in Vienna showing a family group including Agrippina the Younger wearing the corona spicea.

Kunsthistorisches Museum 9a63; De Angeli (1988) nr. 175, pl. 610; Ober-leitner (1985) 55, figs. 37–38; Richter (1971) 516, pl. 9.19; Eichler/Kris (1927) 61–62, nr. 19, pl. 9; Furtwängler (1900) 3.321, fig. 164.

7. Messalina
Wife of Claudius

7.1 Local coin from Alexandria showing Messalina holding wheat stalks (fig. 44).

BMC Alexandria 9 nr. 69, 10 nrs. 70–76; Riewald (1912) nr. 69.

7.2 Engraved vase from Braunschweig showing Messalina as Ceres and Claudius as Triptolemus.
Furtwängler (1900) 3, 338–339, figs. 185–188.

7.3 Sardonyx cameo from Paris showing Messalina as Ceres and Claudius as Triptolemus.
De Angeli (1988) nr. 176, pl. 610; Furtwängler (1900) 3, 320.

7.4 Sardonyx cameo from Den Haag with a family group including Messalina holding wheat stalks and poppies.
Furtwängler (1900) 2, 304–305, pl. 66.1.

8. Julia Titi
Daughter of Titus

8.1 Official state coin of Titus, showing a bust of Julia on the obverse and Ceres on the reverse, issued during Julia's lifetime.
RIC 2:139 nrs. 177–177a.
This type associates the daughter of the princeps with the goddess, by placing their images on opposite sides of the same coin type. So Scott (1936) 49–50; Rickman (1980) 262.

8.2 Official state coin of Domitian, showing Julia with wheat stalks and a sceptre, seated in a car drawn by two elephants, issued after her death and consecration.
RIC 2:181.219–220; Scott (1936) 77.
Scott has recognized here the image of the deified Julia, assimilated to the goddess Ceres and carried in the *pompa circensis*. Cf. nrs. 10.1 and 13.4 below.

8.3 Statue in the Vatican of Julia, possibly in the guise of Ceres.
Museo Vaticano, Braccio Nuovo 108; Helbig (1963) 1, 342, nr. 447; Hausmann (1966) 57, 118.
The type has also been identified as Julia in the guise of Juno.

9. Domitia Longina
Wife of Domitian

9.1 Local coins of Alexandria showing Domitia Longina wearing the corona spicea and holding a basket containing wheat and poppies.
Scott (1936) 85; Vogt (1924) 1.48, 2.18.

9.2 Local coin of Bageis showing Domitia Longina holding wheat stalks and a sceptre.
    Riewald (1912) nr. 70; Imhoof-Blumer (1897) 47, nr. 3; Scott (1936) 85.

9.3 Local coin of Smyrna showing Domitia Longina with veil and a cornucopia.
    BMC Ionia 273 nr. 305, pl. 29.1; Scott (1936) 84.
    The identification with Demeter/Ceres is uncertain, since neither wheat nor poppies are present.

9.4 Local coin of Trallis with Domitia Longina on the obverse and Ceres on the reverse.
    BMC Lydia 346 nr. 135.
    This coin type indirectly associates the wife of the princeps with the goddess.

9.5 Local coin of Alexandria showing Domitia Longina as Euthenia enthroned with a standing Demeter/Ceres at her side.
    Scott (1936) 85; Vogt (1924) 1.53, 2.20.
    This coin type indirectly associates the wife of the princeps with Ceres.

9.6 Official state coin of Domitian possibly showing Domitia Longina with the corona spicea, issued during her lifetime.
    RIC 2:188.276a–b.
    The identification of the female as Domitia is uncertain. See Scott (1936) 85.

9.6 Official state coin of Domitian with the bust of Domitia Longina on the obverse and Ceres on the reverse, issued during Domitia's lifetime.
    RIC 2:209.443; Scott (1936) 73.

10. *Marciana*
Sister of Trajan; mother of Matidia; grandmother of Sabina

10.1 Official state coin of Trajan showing Marciana with wheat stalks and a sceptre, seated in a car drawn by two elephants, issued after her death and consecration.
    De Angeli (1988) nr. 182.
    The image recalls nr. 8.2 above, with Julia Titi, and like this example probably associates the deified woman with the image of the goddess carried in the *pompa circensis*. Cf. also nr. 13.4 below.

10.2 Statue in the Munich Glyptothek showing Marciana in the Ceres type with the attributes of the goddess.

Munich Glyptothek 377; De Angeli (1988) nr. 188; Wrede (1981) 214–215, nr. 60; Bieber (1977) 165, 171–172.
This statue is sometimes identified as Matidia (so De Angeli).

11. Matidia
Daughter of Marciana; niece of Trajan

11.1 Statue from Aphrodisias showing Matidia in the Ceres type with the attributes of the goddess.
Istanbul Archaeological Museum 2269; Wrede (1981) 214; Bieber (1977) 165, 172; Bieber (1968) 13; Kruse (1968/1975) 233–234, nr. A2.

12. Sabina
Daughter of Matidia; grandniece of Trajan; wife of Hadrian

12.1 Inscription from Herakleia honoring Sabina as "the new Demeter" (νέα Δημήτηρ).
IGR 1.785; Temporini (1978) 75.

12.2 Inscription from Megara honoring Sabina as the "New Demeter" (νέα Δημήτηρ).
Riewald (1912) nr. 71; IG 7.73.

12.3 Inscription from Tchelidjik honoring Sabina as "Demeter the Bearer of Fruit" (Δημήτηρ Καρποφόρος).
IGR 3.17; Temporini (1978) 75.

12.4 Inscription from Athens honoring Sabina as "the Bearer of Fruit" (Καρποφόρος).
Riewald (1912) nr. 72; IG 3.12.
The epithet Karpophoros identifies Sabina with Demeter/Ceres.

12.5 Official state coins of Hadrian showing Sabina with the corona spicea, issued during Sabina's lifetime.
RIC 2:387.401c; 477.1025c, 1029c, 1032c, 1033c; 478.1037c–e, 1038d–e; De Angeli (1988) nr. 181.

12.6 Official state coins of Hadrian showing Sabina with the corona spicea, issued after her death and consecration.
RIC 2:390.418b, 420b, 421, 422; 479.1051b, 1052.

12.7 Official state coins of Hadrian with Sabina on the obverse and Ceres on the reverse, issued during her lifetime.

    RIC 2:388.409, 411a–b; 389.416; 475.1019; 476.1023.

12.8 Statue from Ostia showing Sabina in the Ceres type with the attributes of the goddess.

    Ostia Museum 1242; Wrede (1981) 214, 239; Bieber (1968) 7, 16, fig. 17; Kruse (1968/1975) 238–239, nr. A11.

12.9 Statue from Ostia showing Sabina in the Ceres type with the attributes of the goddess.

    Ostia Museum 25; De Angeli (1988) nr. 189, pl. 611; Wrede (1981) 214; Bieber (1977) 165, 171; Bieber (1968) 19; Kruse (1968/75) 239–240, nr. A12.

12.10 Statue from Bulla Regia showing Sabina in the Ceres type.

    Tunis, Mus. du Bardo, C1015; Kruse (1968/1975) 351–353, 488, nr. D49.

13. *Faustina the Elder*
Wife of Antoninus Pius

13.1 Funerary inscription from Rome honoring Faustina the Elder as "the new Demeter" (νέη Δηώ).

    Riewald (1912) nr. 75; *IG* 4.1389; Kaibel (1878) 1046.

13.2 Local coin from Apameia showing Faustina the Elder with the attributes of Ceres.

    Riewald (1912) nr. 73; Imhoof-Blumer (1890) 653.

13.3 Offical state coins of Antoninus Pius showing Faustina the Elder on the obverse and Ceres on the reverse, issued during her lifetime.

    RIC 3:159.1084, 160.1085; *BMCRE* Antoninus Pius 1124.

13.4 Official state coins of Antoninus Pius showing Faustina the Elder holding wheat stalks and a torch, seated in a cart drawn by two elephants, issued after her death and consecration.

    RIC 3:73.390 a-b, 164.1139; De Angeli (1988) nr. 183.

    The image recalls nr. 8.2 above, with Julia Titi, and like this example probably associates the deified woman with the image of the goddess carried in the *pompa circensis*. Cf. also nr. 10.1 above.

13.5 Official state coins of Antoninus Pius showing Faustina the Elder on the obverse and Ceres on the reverse, issued after her death and consecration (figs. 42a–b).

RIC 3:70.356, 357a–b; 71.358–362; 72.378–379, 382a; 73.382b; 75.403, 404a–b; 161.1099–1101; 162.1116–1118; 163.1119–1122, 1128; 166.1154; 167.1169–1176; 168.1185–1186.

13.6 Statue from Timghad showing Faustina the Elder in the Ceres type without attributes.
Wrede (1981) 214; Kruse (1968/1975) 256–257, nr. A41.

13.7 Statue from Campana, now in the Louvre, possibly showing Faustina the Elder in the Ceres type (fig. 25).
Paris Louvre MA 1139; De Angeli (1988) nr. 190, pl. 611; Kruse (1968/1975) 242, 466, nr. A16; Bieber (1977) 166, fig. 738.
Kruse rejects the identification as Faustina the Elder on the basis of the hairstyle. The figure may be Sabina.

13.8 Sarcophagus from Ostia showing Ceres in a cart, holding stalks of wheat, followed by Proserpina with a torch; the head of Ceres is a portrait of the deceased that shows characteristics related to Faustina the Elder.
Ostia Mus. 1101; De Angeli (1988) nr. 184, pl. 611.

14. *Faustina the Younger*
Daughter of Antoninus Pius and Faustina the Elder; wife of Marcus Aurelius; mother of Commodus

14.1 Official state coin of Antoninus Pius showing Faustina the Younger on the obverse and Ceres on the reverse, issued during Faustina's lifetime.
RIC 3:92.493.

14.2 Official state coins of Marcus Aurelius showing Faustina the Younger on the obverse and Ceres on the reverse, issued during Faustina's lifetime.
RIC 3:268.668–669; 344.1619–1624.

14.3 Sardonyx from Paris possibly showing Faustina the Younger wearing the wheat stalk and poppy crown.
Paris, Cab. des Méd.; De Angeli (1988) nr. 177, pl. 610.
De Angeli (1988) 906 suggests that the figure may be Julia, the daughter of Augustus, rather than Faustina the Younger.

14.4 Statue from Timghad showing Faustina the Younger in the Ceres type without attributes.
Wrede (1981) 214; Kruse (1968/1975) 255–256, nr. A40.

15. Lucilla

Daughter of Marcus Aurelius and Faustina the Younger; wife of Lucius Verus

15.1 Official state coins of Marcus Aurelius showing Lucilla on the obverse and Ceres on the reverse, issued during Lucilla's lifetime.
RIC 3:352.1728–1729.

15.2 Statue from Madauros showing Lucilla in the Ceres type with the attributes of the goddess.
Guelma Mus. des Ant. M396; Wrede (1981) 214; Kruse (1968/1975) 251, nr. A34.

15.3 Statue from Bulla Regia showing Lucilla in the Ceres type with the attributes of the goddess.
Tunis, Mus. du Bardo; Wrede (1981) 214; Kruse (1968/1975) 253, nr. A37.

16. Bruttia Crispina

Wife of Commodus

16.1 Official state coin of Commodus showing Bruttia Crispina on the obverse and Ceres on the reverse, issued during Bruttia Crispina's lifetime.
RIC 3:398.276–277; 442.674.

16.2 Statue from Bulla Regia of Bruttia Crispina in the Ceres type with the attributes of the goddess.
Tunis, Mus. du Bardo; Kruse (1968/1975) 254, nr. A38.

17. Julia Domna

Wife of Septimius Severus

17.1 Official state coins of Septimius Severus showing Julia Domna on the obverse and Ceres on the reverse, issued during Julia Domna's lifetime.
RIC 4(1): 166.546; 175.616a-618; 177.636; 179.650; 208.848–849; 210.870; 311.596.

17.2 Statue from Ostia showing Julia Domna in the Ceres type with the attributes of the goddess.
Ostia Mus. 21; De Angeli (1988) nr. 191; Bieber (1977) 166, 172; Kruse (1968/1975) 258–259, nr. A45.

NOTES

The abbreviations used in this book follow the conventions listed in the *American Journal of Archaeology*, volume 95 (1991), pages 1–16.

"Preface"

1. On the problems of the various approaches to Goddess religion, see also Frymer-Kensky (1992) vii–ix; Townsend (1990) 180–204.

2. See, e.g., Gadon (1989); Eisler (1987); Starhawk (1979); Stone (1976).

3. See, e.g., Gadon (1989); Bolen (1985); Downing (1984); Whitmont (1982).

4. See especially: Altheim (1931) 108–129; Wissowa (1912) 191ff., 297ff.; Wissowa (1899a) cols. 1970–1979; Pestalozza (1897).

5. Le Bonniec (1958). Le Bonniec provides a comprehensive bibliography of the early scholarship on pp. 474–485.

6. For recent scholarship on Ceres, see Simon (1990) 43–50, 265–266.

7. Crawford (1974); Mattingly and Sydenham (1923–1981).

8. De Angeli (1988).

1. "Historical Overview"

1. Vetter (1953) 241. See also Simon (1990) 43 (with photograph and bibliography); Radke (1965) 180. The inscription may go on to name Liber and to connect him with wine, but the reading here is highly controversial.

2. Dumézil (1966) 374–375; Ernout and Meillet (1959–1960), s.v. *cerus*; Walde and Hofmann (1938), s.v. *Ceres*.

3. On the ritual hymn of the Salian priests, see Varr. *Ling.* 7.26. On Cerus, see Schilling (1991a) 121; Dumézil (1966) 375; Radke (1965), s.v. *Cerus*, 91–92. Cf. also *CIL* 1², 445 = 11.6708, 6.

4. On the Osco-Umbrians, see Pallottino (1991) 47–48.

5. Vetter (1953) 147. See also Bianchi (1978) 222; Devoto (1967) 179–197; Salmon (1967) 157–162; Radke (1965); De Angeli (1988). The divinities listed in the tablet are: Evklúi Patereí (Euclus Pater = Liber Pater); Kerrí (Ceres); Futreí Kerríiaí (Filia

Cereris = Daughter of Ceres); Anterstataí (Interstita = She Who Stands Between); Ammaí Kerríiaí (Nutrix Cerealis = Nurse of Ceres); Diumpaís Kerríiaís (Lymphi Cereales = Nymphs of Ceres); Líganakdíkeí Entraí (Legifera Intera = She Who Bears Laws Between?); Anafríss Kerríiúís (Imbres Cereales = Rain Showers of Ceres); Maatúís Kerríiúís (Mati Cereales = Dew Dispensers of Ceres?); Diúveí Verehasiúí (Jupiter Vergarius); Hereklúí Kerríiúí (Hercules Cerealis = Hercules of Ceres); Diúveí Regatureí (Jupiter Rigator = Jupiter the Irrigator?); Patanaí Piístíaí (Panda Pinsitrix = She Who Opens Up?); Deívaí Genetaí (Diva Genita = Divine Progenitress); Pernaí Kerríiaí (Perna Cerealis); and Fluusaí Kerríiaí (Flora Cerealis).

6. For Ceres' connections with human fertility, see sec. 2.3.

7. For Ceres' connections with agricultural fertility, see sec. 2.2.

8. For Liber and Ceres, see Le Bonniec (1958) 296–304, with literary references. For Hercules and Ceres, see Macrob. *Sat.* 3.11.10; Bayet (1926) 357ff. and 390–392. For Jupiter and Ceres, see Cato, *Agr.* 134; Livy 3.55.6–7; Le Bonniec (1958) 148–157, 345–347. For Flora and Ceres, see schol. in Juv. 6.249; Dumézil (1966) 270; Le Bonniec (1958) 195–202. Some argue that the Daughter of Ceres (Futreí Kerríiaí = Filia Cerealis) is to be understood as Proserpina, also associated with Ceres in a Roman cult borrowed from Magna Graecia. This identification is not certain, however: see Bianchi (1978) 208.

9. Vetter (1953) 6. Vetter (1953) 37–45 cites Huschke's interpretation of the Keri named in this inscription as Κηρί, the Greek goddess Kore, or Persephone, Queen of the Underworld.

10. For the mundus Cereris, see sec. 3.3.2; for the funerary rituals of the porca praesentanea and porca praecidanea, see sec. 3.2.1.

11. Vetter (1953) 218. For the connection of the divinity named here with human fertility, see Bianchi (1978) 209.

12. Vetter (1953) 204–208, 211. For the association of this divinity with Angerona, see Bianchi (1978) 213, 227. For an alternate interpretation of the phrase *anaceta cerialis*, see Pocetti (1985), (1982), (1980). Pocetti proposes that the phrase is actually a title, *sacerdos Cereris*.

13. Vetter (1953) 213. Cf. Vetter (1953) 204, connecting Anaceta Ceria with the *aisis sato*, possibly *diis satuum*, or "the gods of sowing." See Pocetti (1980) 509–516. For the interpretation of the Cereres, see Bianchi (1978) 222–223.

14. Cf. the North African cult of the Cereres, dated to the Late Republic and Empire. See sec. 1.5.

15. On the priesthood of Ceres and Venus, see Colonna (1953) 216–217; Chirassi-Colombo (1981) 426; and Spaeth (1994) 77 and nn. 93–95.

16. Vetter (1953) 239. See also Bianchi (1978) 210–211; Dumézil (1966) 244–245; Poultney (1959).

17. Dumézil (1966) 244–245.

18. For Ceres as an Etruscan divinity, see Arn. *Adv. Nat.* 3.40; Mart. Cap. *Nupt. Philol.* 1.41. For the possible identification of Ceres with the Etruscan goddess

Ethausva, see Pfiffig (1975) 307. For the identification of Ceres/Demeter with the Etrus-can goddess Vei at the Cannicella sanctuary at Orvieto and the sanctuary at Gravisca, see Edlund (1987) 70, 76–77.

19. Gantz (1971) 1–22 and pls. 1–12. See also Phillips (1993) 43 and figs. 52–54; Edlund (1987) 91; and Pfiffig (1975) 34–36 and fig. 2.

20. For these problems, see Pfiffig (1975) 36.

21. For Ceres' association with poppy capsules and pomegranates, see sec. 6.2.

22. On Ceres and Proserpina, see sec. 1.4 and 5.2.

23. For the problem of Etruscan triads of divinities, see Banti (1943).

24. *CIL* 1², p. 283ff. On the dating of the pre-Julian calendar, see Michels (1967) 119–144 and 207–220. Michels discusses the possibility of a later date for this calen-dar, in the decemviral period (c. 450 B.C.), but notes that many of the festivals named in it probably predated the foundation of Rome itself.

25. For the flamen Cerialis, see *CIL* 11.5028; Fabius Pictor in Serv. on *G.* 1.21. Varro (*Ling.* 7.45) does not specifically name the flamen Cerialis among those offices created by Numa. However, since the other flamines were created in the early regal period, the creation of the flamen Cerialis probably also belongs to this era. See Le Bonniec (1958) 342–343.

26. The other festivals are the Fordicidia (April 15), Parilia (April 21), and Robigalia (April 25). On the cycle, see Schilling (1991*b*) 93 and Torelli (1984) 85–95.

27. For the Cerialia see Ov. *Fast.* 4.679–712 and sec. 2.2.1.

28. On the archaic agrarian cults of the Vallis Murcia, see Le Bonniec (1958) 185–193.

29. On these agricultural rituals in general, see sec. 2.2 and 3.3.1. The references for these specific rituals are: Cato *Agr.* 134 (porca praecidanea); Fest., s.v. *sacrima*, 319 Müller (first-fruit offering); Tib. 2.1.2–4; Verg. *G* 1.345–347 (Ambarvalia); Ov. *Fast.* 1.666–684 (Feriae Sementivae); *CIL* 1², pp. 336–337 (feast day of Ceres and Tellus).

30. Le Bonniec (1958) 48–107.

31. Wissowa (1899*b*).

32. Fest., s.v. *mundus*, 54 and 142 Müller. On the mundus Cereris, see sec. 3.3.2.

33. On this issue, see Coarelli (1983) 208–226; Chirassi-Colombo (1981) 418–420; Verzar (1976–1977) 378–398; Rykwert (1976) 129–132; Le Bonniec (1958) 175–184, with references to earlier scholarship.

34. For the law on divorce, see sec. 3.2.4.

35. For Ceres' association with marriage, see sec. 3.2.3.

36. For the dating to the regal period of Ceres' association with marriage, see Le Bonniec (1958) 77–88. Le Bonniec is followed by the later scholarship on Ceres; see, e.g., De Angeli (1988) 893.

37. On the sacrifices of the porca praecidanea and porca praesentanea, see sec. 3.2.1.

38. Le Bonniec (1958) 91–107, again followed by later scholarship.

39. On the problem of the origins of the distinctions between the patricians and the plebeians, see Mitchell (1990) 1–30.

40. On the Temple of Ceres, Liber, and Libera, see sec. 4.2.

41. On the connections of the plebeian magistrates and Ceres, see sec. 4.3.

42. On Ceres' connection with plebeian social consciousness, see sec. 4.4.

43. For the historical problems, see Sordi (1983) 135; Ridley (1968) 552–553; Alföldi (1963) 92–100; and Le Bonniec (1958) 213–242.

44. Simon (1990) 45; Nash (1968) 1:227; Le Bonniec (1958) 266–277; Van Berchem (1935) 91–95; Giovenale (1927) 352–371. See sec. 2.2.2.

45. Richardson (1992) 80; Coarelli (1988) 66–70; Platner-Ashby (1929) 110; Merlin (1906) 93–95. See sec. 4.2.1.

46. Both proposed locations for the temple are outside the pomerium. For the Aventine location, see Merlin (1906) 53–68. For the Forum Boarium location, see Le Bonniec (1958) 232, n. 3. On the pomerium in general, see Gell. 13.14.4–7; Platner-Ashby (1929) 392–396; Antaya (1980) 184–189; Richardson (1992) 293–296. On the exclusion of foreign cults from the area enclosed by the pomerium, see Strab. 5.232; Serv. on *Aen.* 1.292; Vitruv. 1.7.1; and Schilling (1949) 27–33.

47. As we have seen, the name of Ceres herself is found in the calendar in capital letters. The names of Liber and Libera are added below in smaller letters, signaling the later date of their association with the festival. See *CIL* 1², pp. 210, 213, 224, 235, 283ff. On the issue of the interpretation of the large versus the smaller letters in the calendar, see Michels (1967) 119–140, 207–220. See also her replica of a Republican calendar (pl. 4) with the entry for *a.d. XII Kal. Mai.* For the association of Liber and Libera with Ceres in the ludi conducted for the festival of the Cerialia, see Cic. *Verr.* 2.5.36 and Le Bonniec (1958) 312–341.

48. For a survey of various proposals for the origin of the triad, see Le Bonniec (1958) 279–292.

49. Le Bonniec (1958) 292–305.

50. For the relationship of Liber and Libera, see Dumézil (1966) 377–378. On the etymological pairs of divinities, see Radke (1987) 218–226.

51. Varro in Aug. *Civ. D.* 6.9, 7.21; cf. also 3.16, 4.11.

52. Varro in Aug. *Civ. D.* 7.21. See also Radke (1965) 175–176.

53. Simon (1990) 47–48; De Angeli (1988) 898 nr. 76, and 906–907.

54. Bloch (1954) 211; Bruhl (1953) 19.

55. Alföldi (1963) 98.

56. Le Bonniec (1958) 243–247; Wissowa (1899a) col. 1975.

57. For the law on sacrosanctitas, see sec. 3.3.5.

58. For the law on attempted tyranny, see sec. 3.3.4.

59. Livy 2.41.1–12; Dion. Hal. 8.77–79; Cic. *Rep.* 2.35.60; Val. Max. 6.3.16.

60. Chirassi-Colombo (1984) 747.

61. De Angeli (1988) 893; Dumézil (1966) 379–380; Le Bonniec (1958) 379–380. See sec. 2.2.2 and 4.2.4.

62. Other examples of representations of Ceres from this early period include the

following: De Angeli (1988) nr. 3—gem with head of Ceres crowned with wheat; nr. 24—terracotta sculpture of head of Ceres, veiled and crowned with wheat; nr. 108—terracotta statue of enthroned Ceres, wearing a veil, a diadem with two stalks of wheat, and a snake bracelet, and holding a stalk of wheat (from Ariccia); nr. 110—terracotta statue of enthroned Ceres (?) (from Ariccia).

63. Terracotta bust of Ceres from Ariccia: Rome, Mus. Naz. 112375; De Angeli (1988) nr. 23. On the finds from Ariccia, see also Zevi-Gallina (1973) 321–327, pls. 62–69; Borda (1950) 765–770; and Paribeni (1930) 370–380.

64. On the coins from Lucera, see De Angeli (1988) nr. 12; *RRC* 97.9, 16, 23 (pl. 18); 99.2a–c; cf. 82.1 (pl. 15) on a similar coin of this period, possibly from Sicily. On the coins from Capua, see De Angeli (1988) nr. 11.

65. For Demeter with the corona spicea on Greek coins, see Beschi (1988) nrs. 162–173, 176–186, 188.

66. For the earrings, see Paribeni (1930) 375. For the protome shape, see Paribeni (1930) 379.

67. Le Bonniec (1958) 390–395 dates the cult to between 249 and 216 B.C. On this cult, see sec. 5.2.

68. On the female virtues of chastity and motherhood, see sec. 5.3.

69. On the religious innovations of the late third and early second centuries B.C., see Schilling (1991c) 72–73. On the cults of Venus Erycina and Cybele, see Stehle (1989) 143–164. On the Bacchanalia, see Gallini (1970) and Bruhl (1953) 47–69.

70. Chirassi-Colombo (1979) 51 and (1981) 421.

71. Other sources also associate the interruption of the festival of the Greek cult of Ceres with the Senate's adoption of a limit to mourning, but with important differences from the account of Valerius Maximus. Livy (22.56.4–5 and 34.6.15) says that the festival was interrupted after the Battle of Cannae, and that after this the Senate decreed that mourning be limited, so that no other public or private rites might ever be neglected. Festus (s.v. *Graeca sacra*, 97 Müller) implies that the rites were actually cancelled after Cannae, and so the Senate decreed a limit to mourning. The sources also differ in the number of days to which the Senate limited mourning: thirty days according to Livy and Valerius Maximus; one hundred days according to Festus.

72. Holst-Warhaft (1992) 98–126.

73. On the ritual of the lectisternium, see Schilling (1991c) 74–75. The first lectisternium had only three pairs of divinities, among whom Ceres was not included. Ceres later had an annual lectisternium of her own on December 13: Arnob. *Adv. Nat.* 7.32; cf. *CIL* 1², p. 336 and Cornificius Longus, frag. of *De etymis deorum* in Funaioli (1961) 1.475.

74. *CIL* 1², p. 331. On this festival, see Vidman (1978) 87–95 and sec. 4.4.3.

75. The *ieiunium Cereris* is perhaps to be identified with the *castus Cereris* cited by Festus (s.v. *minuitur populo luctus*, 154 Müller). See Le Bonniec (1958) 400–404. For the *castus Cereris*, cf. *CIL* 1², p. 973.

76. 182 B.C. (Livy 40.2.1–3); 174 B.C. (Livy 41.28.2); 133 B.C. (Cic. *Verr.* 2.4.108); 125 B.C. (Phlegon *Mir.* 10, in *FrGrH* 2B, p. 257, nr. 36); 104 B.C. (Obseq. *Prodig. Lib.* 43.103); 99 B.C. (Obseq. *Prodig. Lib.* 46.106); 92 B.C. (Obseq. *Prodig. Lib.* 53.113); 84 B.C. (App. *BCiv.* 1.78.359); 42 B.C. (Dio Cass. 47.40.5–6); 32 B.C. (Dio Cass. 50.8.1); A.D. 64 (Tac. *Ann.* 15.44.2).

77. Le Bonniec (1958) 448–449.

78. Livy 10.23.13; 27.6.19; 27.36.9; 33.25.3.

79. On the ludi scaenici, see Le Bonniec (1958) 320–323. For Memmius, cf. also *RRC* 427.2; *BMCRR* Rome 3940.

80. For the *nuptiae Orci*, see Le Bonniec (1958) 438–446.

81. Ceres and the earth: Cic. *Nat. D.* 1.39–40, 2.71, 3.64; Varr. *Ling.* 5.64. Ceres and agricultural work: Varr. *Rust.* 2.5.3–4, 3.1.5. Ceres and crops/grain/bread: Lucr. *RN* 2.655–656, 5.14–15; Cic. *Verr.* 2.4.108, 114; 5.99, 188; *De Or.* 3.167; *Nat. D.* 2.60, 3.41, 52, 62; Varr. *Rust.* 1.1.5; *Ling.* 5.64; Catull. 63.36; Varr. *Sat. Men.* 251.

82. Denarius of L. Cassius Caecicianus, dated to 102 B.C. (fig. 33): *RRC* 321.1; *BMCRR* Rome 1725; Le Bonniec (1958) 370–371. Denarius serratus of C. Marius Capito, dated to 81 B.C.: *RRC* 378.1a; *BMCRR* Rome 2853; and Le Bonniec (1958) 372–373.

83. Ceres with corona spicea: denarius of Q. Cornificius (fig. 3): *RRC* 509.5; *BMCRR* Africa 27. Denarius of M. Fannius and L. Critonius (fig. 4a): *RRC* 351.1; *BMCRR* Rome 2463. Denarius of Julius Caesar (fig. 6a): *RRC* 467.1a; *BMCRR* Africa 21. Denarius of L. Cassius Caecicianus (fig. 33a): *RRC* 321.1; *BMCRR* Rome 1725. Aureus of Q. Caepio Brutus and L. Sestius (fig. 36a): *RRC* 502.2; *BMCRR* East 41. Quinarius of Q. Caepio Brutus (fig. 37a): *RRC* 502.3; *BMCRR* East 46. Aureus of L. Mussidius Longus (fig. 38a): *RRC* 494.44a; *BMCRR* Rome 4233. The goddess also appears with the corona spicea on a relief on a gold disk and on two gems dated to this period: De Angeli (1988) nrs. 10, 29, 30. Ceres with wheat and barley grains: denarius of L. Furius Brocchius, dated to 63 B.C.: *RRC* 414.1; *BMCRR* Rome 3896; Le Bonniec (1958) 374–375. Ceres holding stalks of wheat: denarius of P. Clodius (fig. 39a): *RRC* 494.19; *BMCRR* Rome 4282. Crawford (1974) 1:502–509 believes that the standing figure holds a branch and identifies her as Pietas. Le Bonniec (1958) 378 thinks that the object is a wheat stalk and identifies her as Ceres. Cf. also the stucco relief from the Villa Farnesina showing two Ceres figures as Karyatids, both holding stalks of wheat: De Angeli (1988) nr. 40.

84. Bronze denarius, Africa: *RRC* 509.5; *BMCRR* Africa 27; De Angeli (1988) nr. 20: Crawford (1974) 1:519 identifies the figure as Tanit. For the Ceres identification, cf. also Vollenweider (1966) 97, pl. 17.4; 110, pl. 52.4; and Le Bonniec (1958) 376, 576–577.

85. Aureus of L. Plaetorius Cestianus, dated to 43–42 B.C.: *RRC* 508.1. Crawford (1974) 1:518 argues that the object on the head of the goddess is a *polos*, and suggests that the divinity is Artemis. Le Bonniec (1958) 377 argues that it is a *modius* and the figure is Ceres.

86. Denarius of M. Fannius and L. Critonius, dated to 86 B.C.: *RRC* 351.1; *BMCRR* Rome 2463; Le Bonniec (1958) 372.

87. Alfödi (1956) 93. Cf. Rickman (1980) 259, who states that in the Late Republic there was no consistent attempt to depict concern for the grain supply in the state coinage.

88. On the cult of the Cereres, see Gascou (1987) 95–128; Pugliese-Caratelli (1981) 367–382; Gesztelyi (1972) 75–84; Toutain (1967) 346–354; Barbieri (1961) 30–33; Charles-Picard (1954) 87–88, 98; Carcopino (1942) 13–37; and Spaeth (1994) 99–100.

89. See sec. 2.3.2, 3.2.3, 3.2.5, and 3.3.4 for further discussion of this passage from Varro.

90. On Ceres' association with the liminal rite of initiation, see sec. 3.2.5.

91. Bayet (1951) 5–32, 341–366; and (1950) 297–302. See also the following examples. Ceres with torches: Triens of Q. Titius, dated to 90 B.C.: *RRC* 341.6; *BMCRR* Rome 2237; Le Bonniec (1958) 371. Denarius of C. Vibius Pansa, dated to 90 B.C.: *RRC* 342.3a–b; *BMCRR* Rome 2242, 2238; Le Bonniec (1958) 371. Denarius of C. Memmius, dated to 56 B.C. (fig. 34b): *RRC* 427.2, *BMCRR* Rome 3940, Le Bonniec (1958) 320–321. Ceres with snake-drawn chariot: Denarius of M. Volteius, dated to 78 B.C.: De Angeli (1988) nr. 81; *RRC* 385.3; *BMCRR* Rome 3160; Le Bonniec (1958) 373.

92. *RRC* 449.3a; *BMCRR* Rome 3973; De Angeli (1988) no. 80.

93. See sec. 5.2.1.

94. For Ceres' association with prodigies, see sec. 3.3.3; for her connection with the law on attempted tyranny, see sec. 3.3.6; for her role in the events surrounding the death of Tiberius Gracchus, see sec. 3.4.

95. Le Bonniec (1958) 370–378.

96. *RRC* 467.1a; *BMCRR* Africa 21. For the interpretation of this coin presented here, see Le Bonniec (1958) 375–376.

97. See sec. 4.5.

98. For further discussion of these passages from Cicero, see sec. 5.2.

99. Cic. *Verr.* 2.4.106–107, 111.

100. Cic. *Verr.* 2.4.99, 102, 112; 2.5.187.

101. For Ceres' connection with chastity, see sec. 5.3.1.

102. Ceres and earth/fields: Hor. *Carm. Saec.* 29–32; *Carm.* 4.517–519; Ov. *Fast.* 1.671–674; Manil. *Astr.* 2.19–22. Ceres and farming/farmers/those who dwell in the country: Verg. *Ecl.* 5.78–79; *G.* 1.94–99, 147–149, 160–168, 338–350; Ov. *Am.* 3.2.53; *Met.* 5.341–344, 474–486, 8.273–277; *Fast.* 1.695–704, 4.401–412, 559–560; *Pont.* 2.9.29–30. Ceres and crops/grain: Tib. 1.1.15–15, 2.1.3–4; Verg. *G.* 1.5–92.513–518; Hor. *Carm. Saec.* 29–32; Ov. *Am.* 3.10.1–18; *Met.* 5.341–344, 5.474–486, 489–490, 642–647; 8.273–277, 780–781; 10.431–435; *Fast.* 1.349–352, 671–674; 2.519–520; 4.615–620; 6.469–470; Manil. *Astr.* 2.442, 4.733–736; Germ. *Astr.* 4.1–4; Festus, s.v. *sacrima*, 319 Müller. (Note: I include Festus as an Au-

gustan source because his writings, dated to the second century A.D., represent a summary of the work of an Augustan Age author, Verrius Flaccus.) Ceres and bread/food: Verg. *Aen.* 8.179–181; Ov. *Fast.* 10.73–74.

103. *Fecunda*: Manil. *Astr.* 2.21. *Fertilis*: Ov. *Met.* 5.642. *Flava*: Verg. *G.* 1.96; Tib. 1.1.15; Ov. *Am.* 3.10.3. *Frugifera*: Germ. *Arat.* 38. *Genetrix frugum*: Ov. *Met.* 5.490. *Potens frugum*: Ov. *Am.* 3.10.35. *Rubicunda*: Verg. *G.* 1.297.

104. Ceres = "grain": Verg. *G.* 1.29–30, 2.227–229; *Aen.* 1.177–179; Hor. *Carm.* 3.24.11–13; *Sat.* 2.2.123–125; Ov. *Am.* 1.1.9–10, 2.16.7, 3.7.31; *Ars Am.* 1.401; *Met.* 8.290–292, 11.112–113; *Fast.* 4.645–666, 917–919, 931–932, 6.381–383, 389–392; Manil. *Astr.* 2.658, 3.152, 629, 664–665. Ceres = "bread": Verg. *Aen.* 1.701–702, 7.112–113; Ov. *Fast.* 2.537–540, 3.665–666; Manil. *Astr.* 4.250–251, 5.279–284; Grattius 397–398; Fest., s.v. *cocum*, 58 Müller.

105. Rome, Mus. Naz. 121313: De Angeli (1988) nr. 7. From the vicinity of Cinecittà. Cf. also De Angeli (1988) nrs. 5, 6, 8, 9.

106. Cf. Simon (1990) 49 and n. 40, 266, who interprets these reliefs as Ceres Ultrix, the avenging goddess equivalent to Demeter Erinys, and suggests that they were used for funerary monuments to protect the sleep of the dead.

107. Ceres with corona spicea: wall painting from Pompeii, dated to the early Augustan period, showing a standing Ceres crowned with wheat: De Angeli (1988) nr. 158. Ceres holding wheat stalks: aureus from the imperial mint at Lugdunum, dated to between A.D. 11 and 13, and showing on the reverse a seated female figure (Livia as Ceres?) holding stalks of wheat in her left hand and a long sceptre in her right: fig. 40b.

108. Ceres in wedding ceremonies: Verg. *Aen.* 4.56–59; Fest., s.v. *facem*, 87 Müller. Dedication of the Altar of Ceres Mater and Ops Augusta: *CIL* 1², p. 244 = 9.4192; 1², p. 240 = 6.2298; 1², p. 248 = 10.6638.

109. Ceres and funerary rites: Fest., s.v. *praesentanea porca*, 250 Müller. Ceres and the mundus: Fest., s.v. *mundus*, 54 and 142 Müller. Ceres and prodigies: Livy 22.10.9, 20.9; 28.11.4; 36.37.4–5; 40.2.1–3; 41.28.2. Ceres and the law on attempted tyranny: Livy 2.41.10; Dion. Hal. 8.79.3. Ceres and the Eleusinian Mysteries: Ov. *Met.* 5.341–571; *Fast.* 4.417–620.

110. Copenhagen, Ny Carlsburg Glyptothek 1480: De Angeli (1988) nr. 48. Cf. also De Angeli (1988) nr. 158: Wall painting with Ceres standing, crowned with wheat, and holding a long torch.

111. For the Roman knowledge of the procession in this period, see Hor. *Sat.* 2.8.10–15. On the *ciste*, see Mau (1899) col. 2592; Jahn (1869) 326–331; Kanta (1979) 12, 102–104.

112. Livy 3.55.7, 13; 10.23.13; 27.6.19, 36.9; 33.25.3. Dion. Hal. 6.17.2–4, 89.3.

113. Le Bonniec (1958) 378. See sec. 4.5.

114. Cf. also Fest., s.v. *Graeca sacra*, 97 Müller.

115. Ov. *Met.* 5.341–571; *Fast.* 4.417–620.

116. Simon (1990) 49.

117. *Alma*: Verg. *G.* 1.7; Ov. *Met.* 5.572, *Fast.* 4.547. *Genetrix*: Ov. *Met.* 5.490.

Mater: Verg. *G.* 1.163; Ov. *Met.* 5.509, 567, 6.118; *Fast.* 1.671, 4.447. Cf. also the altar of Ceres Mater and Ops Augusta: *CIL* 1², p. 244 = 9.4192; 1², p. 240 = 6.2298; 1², p. 248 = 10.6638.

118. Chirassi-Colombo (1981) 422–423.

119. Chirassi-Colombo (1981) 422–423; Le Bonniec (1958) 458–462.

120. On Ceres' association with the princeps and his family, see sec. 2.4 and 5.4 and appendix 2.

121. Ellul (1973) 71–77. On the application of Ellul's categories to the Roman world, see Evans (1992) 1–4.

122. Consecration of the altar of Ceres Mater and Ops Augusta by Augustus in A.D. 7: *CIL* 1², p. 244 = 9.4192; 1², p. 240 = 6.2298; 1², p. 248 = 10.6638. Augustus' initiation into the Eleusinian Mysteries in 31 B.C. or 19 B.C. (date problematic): Suet. *Aug.* 93; Dio Cass. 51.4.1, 54.9.10. Augustus' restoration of the Temple of Ceres, Liber, and Libera: Tac. *Ann.* 2.49.

123. Vat. Mus. inv. 715. The significance of the crown has been variously interpreted. Chirassi-Colombo (1981) 423–425 argues that it refers to Augustus' revival of the ancient agricultural cult of the Arval Brethren. Alföldi (1979) 582–583 connects the bust with Augustus' initiation into the Eleusinian Mysteries.

124. Other gem types of Livia as Ceres: De Angeli (1988) nr. 173 (first half of first century A.D.), 174 (first half of first century A.D.). Coin types of Livia as Ceres: De Angeli (1988) nrs. 178 (Augustan: A.D. 11–13), 179 (Claudian: A.D. 41–42).

125. Florence, Mus. Arch. 26, De Angeli (1988) nr. 172. See also Vollenweider (1966) 69, 118, pl. 76.4.

126. See sec. 5.4 and appendix 2.

127. On Ceres' connection with peace and its significance for Augustan political propaganda, see sec. 3.3.4 and 6.5.

128. Cf. also Tib. 1.10.45–50, 67–68; Hor. *Carm.* 4.5.16–19.

129. Ceres and fields/countryside: Petron. *Sat.* 135.8; Pliny *HN* 3.60 (Campania); Sil. *Pun.* 12.375 (Sicily), 14.130; Stat. *Silv.* 4.3.11–12; Pliny *Ep.* 39.1; Juv. 4.319; Florus 1.11. Ceres and country-dwellers: Sil. *Pun.* 13.535–536. Ceres and farming: Val. Flacc. *Argo.* 1.69–70; Hyg. *Fab.* 277.4; Luc. Ampel. 9.11. Ceres and crops: Pliny *HN* 18.3.13; Quint. *Inst.* 3.7.8; Gell. *N.A.* 4.6.8; Apul. *Met.* 6.2, 11.2. Ceres and grain: Calp. 4.122–123; Pliny *HN* 7.191; Stat. *Silv.* 5.3.226; Hyg. *Fab.* 259, 274.19. Ceres and food/bread: Val. Flacc. *Argo.* 2.69–70, 4.532; Stat. *Silv.* 1.4.31–32, 4.2.32–35.

130. Ceres = "grain": Sen. *Phaed.* 968–971, *Herc. Fur.* 62, *Oed.* 49–51, *Phoen.* 219–220, 370–373, *Med.* 759–761; Luc. 3.347–348, 4.93–96, 9.854–858; Val. Flacc. *Argo.* 1.577–578, 3.5; Sil. *Pun.* 1.211–214, 237–238, 9.204–205, 11.265–266; Stat. *Theb.* 1.522–524; Mart. 3.58.6–7. Ceres = "bread/food": Sen. *Phaed.* 373–374; Luc. 4.381, 7.329–331; Val. Flacc. *Argo.* 1.253–254, 5.215–216; Mart. 13.47; Sil. *Pun.* 17.194–195; Stat. *Achil.* 2.101–102; Quint. *Inst.* 8.6.23, 24.

131. *Flava*: Luc. 4.412. *Frugifer*: Sen. *Phoen.* 219. *Larga*: Luc. 3.347.

132. Paris, Bibliothèque Nationale: De Angeli (1988) nr. 75.

133. Naples, Mus. Naz. 9457: from Pompeii, Casa del Naviglio (VI.10.11). De Angeli (1988) nr. 84.

134. De Angeli (1988) nrs. 153−156a−b (coins of Nero, Domitian, Nerva, Trajan, and Hadrian).

135. Bronze sestertius minted at Rome. *RIC* 1²: 161.136; *BMCRE* Claudius 137; De Angeli (1988) nr. 153.

136. De Angeli (1988) nrs. 136−144.

137. London, British Museum inv. nr. 1306: De Angeli (1988) nr. 139.

138. *CIL* 2.5028 = Dessau 1447.

139. Serv. on Verg. *G.* 1.21. See sec. 1.2.

140. *CIL* 14.2 (Ostia): corpora mensorum adiutorum nauticariorum et acceptorum; *CIL* 14.409 (Ostia): mensores frumentarii; *CIL* 3.3835 (Emona in Pannonia): frumentarius of the *legio* XV; *CIL* 3.10511 (Aquincum): collegium Cereris; *CIL* 9.1545 (Beneventum): horrearius.

141. For the link among Ceres, agricultural fertility, and the ruling princeps, see sec. 2.4.

142. *RIC* 1²: 127.94; *BMCRE* Claudius 137; De Angeli (1988) nr. 94.

143. De Angeli (1988) 907; Chirassi-Colombo (1981) 424; Rickman (1980) 257; Beaujeu (1955) 306, 326.

144. *RIC* 1²: 275.131, 277.166; *BMCRE* Vitellius 47; De Angeli (1988) nr. 157.

145. Alföldi (1979) 581−585, pls. 27.2−4, 38.1−2,4. Alföldi interprets the wheat crown as referring to the Arval Brethren for Antoninus Pius, Marcus Aurelius, and Lucius Verus; and to the Eleusinian Mysteries for Hadrian.

146. Ceres at the birth of Dionysus: De Angeli (1988) 149−150. Ceres at the birth of Apollo and Diana: De Angeli (1988) 151.

147. Sardonyx, Paris, Bibliothèque Nationale. De Angeli (1988) nr. 149.

148. Vatican 10.018, from the Via Labicana. De Angeli (1988) nr. 165. Cf. also De Angeli (1988) nr. 152: Ceres with Hermes; De Angeli (1988) nrs. 126−135: Ceres at the Rape of Proserpina, with Hades/Pluto and Proserpina.

149. Eleusinian Mysteries: Sen. *Herc. Fur.* 845−847; Stat. *Silv.* 4.8.50−51; Juv. 5.15.140−142; Suet. *Aug.* 93., *Claud.* 25; Ap. *Met.* 6.2, 11.5; Hyg. *Fab.* 147.5. Rape: Columella *Rust.* 10.1.1.268−274; Luc. 6.739−742; Stat. *Theb.* 4.122−123, 12.270−274; Hyg. *Fab.* 141.1, 146, 147.1, 251.1.

150. De Angeli (1988) nrs. 145−148.

151. Marble cinerary urn from Rome near the Porta Maggiore. First half of the first century A.D. Rome, Mus. Naz. 11301. De Angeli (1988) nr. 145.

152. De Angeli (1988) nrs. 126−134. Cf. also nr. 135: an ivory relief depicting the Rape of Proserpina, dated to the imperial period.

153. Aachen, Münster G3. De Angeli (1988) nr. 133.

154. For references, see Alföldi (1979) 585−606.

155. Laws that established civilization: Pliny *HN* 7.191; Ap. *Met.* 11.2. Law on attempted tyranny: Pliny *HN* 34.15. Expiation of prodigies: Tac. *Ann.* 15.44.

156. On the law on attempted tyranny, see: Livy 2.1.9, 82; Plut. *Vit. Publ.* 12.1; and sec. 3.3.6.

157. Concordia—*RIC* 1²:211.91 (Civil Wars), 241.149–153 (Galba). Fides Publica—*RIC* 2:185.244, 192.291a–b, 298, 195.325, 332, 197.348, 198.352, 199.366, 200.370 (Domitian); 256.176, 299.740, 741 (Trajan); 368.241–241a, 427.668, 437.758, 442.809 (Hadrian). For Ceres as Fides Publica, see also De Angeli (1988) nrs. 111–122. Pax—*RIC* 1²:212.114 (Civil Wars), 239.129 (Galba); *RIC* 2:45.258 (Vespasian), 214.142 (Galba: posthumous), 402.514 (Hadrian). Salus—*RIC* 2:158.41 (Domitian); 223.9, 224.20, 225.33 (Nerva).

158. For examples with Fides Publica as legend, see *RIC* 2:16.14, 21.55, 34.167, 41n, 60.376, 61.382, 73.486n, 89n, 100.731 (Vespasian); 130.125, 134n (Titus).

159. *RIC* 1²:206.34; *BMCRE* Galba 6.

160. Temple of Ceres, Liber, and Libera: Cornificius Longus, frag. of *De etymis deorum* in Funaioli (1961) 1.475; Pliny *HN* 35.24, 99, 154; Tac. *Ann.* 2.49; Pompon. *Dig.* 1.2.2.21.

161. Juv. 14.262–64; Gell. *N.A.* 18.2.11; Dio Cass. 47.40.6.

162. Ceres and Dionysus in the Eleusinian cult: De Angeli (1988) nrs. 144–147. Cf. also Ceres attending the birth of Dionysus: De Angeli (1988) nrs. 149–150. Ceres and Liber as country divinities: De Angeli (1988) nr. 166. Cf. also Ceres, Liber, and Hercules on a triple marble herm: De Angeli (1988) nr. 169.

163. Sestertius dated to A.D. 97, *RIC* 2:229.89, 230.103; *BMCRE* Nerva 115. Cf. also Rickman (1980) 264.

164. Juv. 6.50–51, 9.22–26. *CIL* 6.2181, 10.6640. See Chirassi-Columbo (1981) 426; Colonna (1953) 216–217.

165. Cf. also Stat. *Silv.* 4.3.11: casta Ceres.

166. Literary sources: Columella *Rust.* 10.1.1.268–274; Luc. 6.739–742; Stat. *Theb.* 4.122–123, 12.270–274; Hyg. *Fab.* 141.1, 146, 147.1, 251.1. Artistic sources: De Angeli (1988) nrs. 126–135.

167. Gems: De Angeli (1988) nrs. 123, 125. Coins: De Angeli (1988) nr. 124.

168. Paris, Bibliothèque Nationale: De Angeli (1988) 123.

169. Ceres type: Bieber (1977) 163–167. Herculaneum Woman types: Bieber (1977) 163–167. For the Ceres type, see also De Angeli (1988) 907–908; Wrede (1981) 21–27, 213–219; Kruse (1968/1975) *passim*, esp. 3–4 and 14.

170. Cf. also Stat. *Silv.* 5.1.231–233.

171. Paris, Louvre MA 1139: De Angeli (1988) 190.

172. Bieber (1977) 157.

173. Relief inserted into the small Metropolis at Athens. Bieber (1977) 154, fig. 718.

174. De Angeli (1988) 907–908 associates practice with Eleusinian cult; Bieber (1977) 165 interprets the Ceres type as representing a "priestess of Demeter."

175. Wrede (1981) 112 suggests interpretation of the Ceres type as "the *sanctitas* and *pietas* of a *mater familias.*"

176. See, e.g., De Angeli (1988) nrs. 175 (Agrippina the Younger), 176 (Messalina),

177 (Faustina the Younger), 180 (Antonia Minor), 181 (Sabina), 182 (Marciana), 183 (Faustina the Elder), 184 (Faustina the Elder), 188 (Matidia), 189 (Sabina), 190 (Faustina the Elder), 191 (Julia Domna). There is evidence also for Livilla, Agrippina the Elder, Julia Titi, Domitia Longina, Lucilla, and Bruttia Crispina. See sec. 5.4 and appendix 2.

177. *BMCRE* Claudius 109, pl. 33.19; De Angeli (1988) nr. 180.

178. *RIC* 4(1): 166.546, 175.616a−618; 177.636, 179.650, 208.848−849, 210.870, 311.596.

179. *RIC* 5(1): 213.24.

180. Temple of Ceres in Rome: Not. Reg. XI, Platner-Ashby (1929) 110, Richardson (1992) 81. *Mystes Cereris*: *EE* 4.866. Cf. also *CIL* 6.1779, 1780.

181. Servius on Verg. *Aen.* 1.171, 177, 179, 306, 323, 430, 686, 701, 724; 2.325, 713, 714; 3.118, 139, 689, 707; 4.56, 58, 99, 402, 462, 511, 609; 6.273, 402, 484, 603; 7.377; 8.181; *Ecl.* 3.26, 5.79; *G.* 1.5, 7, 19, 21, 39, 78, 96, 147, 163, 165, 212, 344, 347, 348, 378; 2.229, 380, 498; 3.7, 122. See also Arn. *Adv. Nat.* 2.73, 7.32.

182. Berger (1985) 37−76.

183. Berger (1985) 89−104. Cf. also Bieber (1977) 167, who mentions a miniature of the ninth century depicting Mary in the Ceres type, holding ears of wheat in her hand. Bieber (1977) 155−157 also notes the use of the Large Herculaneum Woman type in Christian sarcophagi for Mary or for Ecclesia, the personification of the Church.

184. Paris, Bibliothèque Nationale: Berger (1985) fig. 57.

185. Warner (1983) 276.

186. Ceres type: Bieber (1977) 167. Large Herculaneum Woman type: Bieber (1977) 155−157. Bieber notes that the latter type was also used in the Late Empire for Ecclesia.

187. Bieber (1977) 167.

2. *"Fertility"*

1. So, too: Cic. *Nat. D.* 2.26.67, 3.20.52, 24.62; Firm. Mat. *Err. prof. rel.* 17.3.

2. So, too, Goetz, *Corpus Gloss. Lat.* 5.550.26; Isid. *Etym.* 8.11.59.

3. On the etymology of "Ceres" see: Dumézil (1966) 374−375; Ernout and Meillet (1959−1960), s.v. *cerus*; Walde and Hofmann (1938), s.v. *Ceres*.

4. On Cerus, see *CIL* 1², p. 145; Schilling (1991) 121; Dumézil (1966) 375; Radke (1965), s.v. *Cerus*, 91−92. On the Tablet of Agnone, see Vetter (1953) 147; Bianchi (1978) 222; Devoto (1967) 179−197, Salmon (1967) 157−162, Radke (1965), s.v. *Cerrai*, 90. See also sec. 1.1.

5. On Ceres in the regal period, see sec. 1.2.

6. *CIL* 1², pp. 283ff. On the dating of this calendar, see Michels (1967) 119−144 and 207−220.

7. For the flamen Cerialis, see sec. 1.2.

8. Vetter (1953) 241. On this inscription, see sec. 1.1.

9. For more on the Feriae Sementivae, see Le Bonniec (1958) 56–65; Bayet (1950) 172–206.

10. So Frazer (1929) 2:255. Frazer provides comparative anthropological evidence. Although Frazer has often been criticized for his methodology, much of what he has to say remains interesting and is often pertinent to this study.

11. On the sacrum Cereale, see Le Bonniec (1958) 67–77; Bayet (1950) 202–205.

12. For the interpretation of these names, see Chirassi-Colombo (1981) 405.

13. On the liminal significance of the agricultural rituals dedicated to Ceres, see sec. 3.3.1.

14. For more on the porca praecidanea, see Le Bonniec (1958) 93–107, 148–157; Chirassi-Colombo (1981) 418; Wissowa (1899a) cols. 1970–1972. Also see the discussion in sec. 3.2.1.

15. Lustration: Tib. 2.1.2–4; Verg. G. 1.345–347. Harvest festival: Verg. G. 1.349–350. First-fruit offering: Ov. Fast. 2.519–522; Fest., s.v. sacrima, 319 Müller.

16. On the Cerialia, see Le Bonniec (1958) 108–140; Bayet (1951) 5–32, 341–366; Wissowa (1899b) cols. 1980–1981. On the entire cycle, see Schilling (1991) 93 and Torelli (1984) 85–95.

17. Frazer (1929) 4:331–332 proposed that the fox represents all vermin and is destroyed symbolically in an apotropaic rite to protect the farm and its fields. Wissowa (1899b) cols. 1980–1981 took the redness of the fox and of the fire as a symbol for blight, which is homeopathically driven away from the crops. Reinach (1912) 4:158–159 suggested that the fire represented the heat of the sun, which was magically driven away from the crops.

18. Bayet (1951) 20–24; Le Bonniec (1958) 121–122; Köves-Zulauf (1986) 62–65.

19. I interpret fruges to mean "crops" in general, unless some clue that grain is meant is provided in the context. Ceres and crops: Lucr. RN 2.655–656, 5.14–15; Cic. Verr. 2.4.108, 114, 5.188; Nat. D. 3.52, 62; Ov. Met. 5.341–344, 474–486, 489–490; Fast. 1.671–674; Manil. Astr. 4.733–736; Germ. Astr. 4.1–4; Pliny HN 18.3.13; Quint. Inst. 3.7.8; Gell. N.A. 4.6.8; Apul. Met. 6.2, 11.2. Ceres and farming/farmers/those who dwell in the country: Varr. Rust. 2.5.3–4, 3.1.5; Verg. Ecl. 5.78–79; G. 1.94–99, 147–149, 160–168, 338–350; Ov. Am. 3.2.53; Met. 5.341–344, 474–486, 8.273–277; Fast. 1.695–704, 4.401–412, 559–560; Pont. 2.9.29–30; Sil. Pun. 13.535–536; Val. Flacc. Argo. 1.69–70; Hyg. Fab. 277.4; Luc. Ampel. 9.11.

20. Ceres and fields/countryside: Petron. Sat. 135.8; Pliny HN 3.60 (Campania); Sil. Pun. 12.375 (Sicily), 14.130; Stat. Silv. 4.3.11–12; Pliny Ep. 39.1; Juv. 4.319; Florus 1.11. Ceres and the earth: Cic. Nat. D. 1.39–40, 2.71, 3.52, 3.64; Varr. Ling. 5.64.; Hor. Carm. Saec. 29–32; Carm. 4.517–519; Ov. Fast. 1.671–674; Manil. Astr. 2.19–22.

21. Fecunda: Manil. Astr. 2.21. Fertilis: Ov. Met. 5.642. Frugifera: Germ. Arat. 38; Sen. Phoen. 219. Genetrix frugum: Ov. Met. 5.490. Larga: Luc. 3.347. Potens frugum: Ov. Am. 3.10.35.

22. De Angeli (1988) nrs. 5–9.

23. Roma, Mus. Naz. 121313, Augustan period: De Angeli (1988) nr. 7.

24. Cophenhagen, Glyptotek Ny Carlsberg, inv. 1719, Augustan period: De Angeli (1988) nr. 8.

25. Cf. Simon (1990) 49 and 266, n. 40, who interprets these reliefs as representing Ceres Ultrix and suggests that they were used for funerary monuments to protect the sleep of the dead.

26. Ceres and grain: Cic. *Verr.* 5.99, 188; *Nat. D.* 2.60, 3.41; Varr. *Rust.* 1.1.5; Tib. 1.1.15 – 16, 2.1.3 – 4; Verg. *G.* 1.5 – 9, 2.513 – 518; Hor. *Carm. Saec.* 29 – 32; Ov. *Am.* 3.10.1 – 18; *Met.* 5.642 – 647, 8.273 – 277, 780 – 781, 10.431 – 436; *Fast.* 1.349 – 352, 2.519 – 521, 4.615 – 620, 6.469 – 470; Manil. *Astr.* 2.442; Fest., s.v. *sacrima*, 319 Müller; Calp. 4.122 – 123; Pliny *HN* 7.191; Stat. *Silv.* 5.3.226; Hyg. *Fab.* 259, 274.19.

27. Vetter (1953) 241. On this inscription, see sec. 1.1.

28. For Ceres' discovery of grain and invention of agriculture, see also Cic. *Verr.* 2.4.106, 108; 2.5.187 – 188. Cicero sets the discovery of grain in Sicily and says that Ceres gave the gift first to the Sicilians, and only later to the Athenians. I have suggested in sec. 1.6 that the transference of the story from Sicily to Athens reflects the growing influence of the Eleusinian cult of Demeter/Ceres on the Romans of the Augustan period.

29. For the story of Triptolemus, see also: Apollod. *Bibl.* 1.5.2; Paus. 1.14.1 – 3, 7.18.2 – 3; Ov. *Fast.* 4.559 – 560; Hyg. *Fab.* 147.

30. De Angeli (1988) nrs. 136 – 144.

31. Sardonyx, London, British Museum inv. nr. 1306: De Angeli (1988) nr. 139. On this gem, see also sec. 1.7.

32. Of the 191 representations of Ceres cited in De Angeli (1988), the goddess is represented with wheat in 125, that is, c. 65 percent of them. On the connection of wheat stalks with Ceres, see Wolters (1930) 284 – 301; Muthmann (1982) 68.

33. Figs. 7 – 8, 11 – 16, 18 – 20, 25, 31, 34b, 40b, 41b, 44.

34. Ceres wears the corona spicea in 47 of the 191 representations cited in De Angeli (1988), that is, in c. 25 percent of these representations.

35. See, e.g., figs. 2 – 6, 10 – 11, 13, 20, 24, 27, 33a, 36a, 37a, 38a, 43, 45.

36. Cf. also Tib. 2.1.4; Hor. *Carm. Saec.* 29 – 30; Ov. *Am.* 3.10.3., *Fast.* 4.615 – 616.

37. *Flava*: Verg. *G.* 1.96; Tib. 1.1.15, Ov. *Met.* 6.118, Luc. 4.412. *Rubicunda*: Verg. *G.* 1.297.

38. Goetz, *Corpus Gloss. Lat.* 4, 317 no. 39.

39. Ceres = "grain": Verg. *G.* 1.29 – 30, 2.227 – 229; *Aen.* 1.177 – 179; Hor. *Carm.* 3.24.11 – 13; *Sat.* 2.2.123 – 125; Ov. *Am.* 1.1.9 – 10, 2.16.7, 3.7.31; *Ars Am.* 1.401; *Met.* 8.290 – 292, 11.112 – 113; *Fast.* 4.645 – 666, 4.917 – 919, 4.931 – 932, 6.381 – 383, 389 – 392; Manil. *Astr.* 2.658, 3.152, 629, 3.664 – 365; Sen. *Phaed.* 968 – 971; *Herc. Fur.* 62; *Oed.* 49 – 51; *Phoen.* 219 – 220, 370 – 373; *Med.* 759 – 761; Luc. 3.347 – 348, 4.93 – 96, 9.854 – 858; Val. Flacc. *Argo.* 1.577 – 578, 3.5; Sil. *Pun.* 1.211 – 214, 237 – 238, 9.204 – 205, 11.265 – 266; Stat. *Theb.* 1.522 – 524; Mart. 3.58.6 – 7.

40. For Ceres = "bread/food": Verg. *Aen.* 1.701 – 702, 7.112 – 113; Ov. *Fast.* 2.537 –

540, 3.665–666; Manil. *Astr.* 4.250–251, 5.279–284; Grattius 397–398; Sen. *Phaed.* 373–374; Luc. 4.381, 7.329–331; Val. Flacc. *Argo.* 1.253–254, 5.215–216; Mart. 13.47; Sil. *Pun.* 17.194–195; Stat. *Achil.* 2.101–102; Quint. *Inst.* 8.6.23, 8.6.24.

41. Frazer (1929) 2:425–426.

42. So Le Bonniec (1958) 160–163. See also Frazer (1929) 2:424–425.

43. Pseudo-Acron. *In Horat. Sermon.* 1, prologue. For the flamen Cerialis as the officiant, see Le Bonniec (1958) 161. However, cf. the passage from Pliny quoted above that mentions a *sacerdos* in connection with the rite (*HN* 18.2.8).

44. Cf. Varr. in *de vita pop Rom. ad Atticum*: 50.1 in Funaioli (1961) 253, no. 201.

45. On the Temple of Ceres as an asylum, see sec. 4.2.3.

46. *CIL* 14.2 (Ostia): corpora mensorum adiutorum nauticariorum et acceptorum; *CIL* 14.409 (Ostia): mensores frumentarii; *CIL* 3.3835 (Emona in Pannonia): frumentarius of the *legio* XV; *CIL* 3.10511 (Aquincum): collegium Cereris; *CIL* 9.1545 (Beneventum): horrearius.

47. For the following argument, see Simon (1990) 45; Nash (1968) 227; Le Bonniec (1958) 266–277; Van Berchem (1935) 91–95; Giovenale (1927) 352–371.

48. Cic. *Leg.* 3.3.7. Under Julius Caesar a special aedile, the aedilis Cerealis, was designated for this purpose (Dio Cass. 43.51.3). Under Augustus an imperial official, the praefectus annonae, was assigned the function (Dio Cass. 60.24.3; Suet. *Claud.* 24.2). For a discussion of these officials, see Rickman (1980) 34–35, 59.

49. *CIL* 6.1151, 31856.

50. Rickman (1980) 81.

51. For the Aventine location, see Richardson (1992) 80; Coarelli (1988) 66–70; Platner-Ashby (1929) 110; Merlin (1906) 93–95. See also sec. 4.2.1.

52. On the assimilation of Ceres and Liber to Greek divinities, see sec. 1.3.

53. See Preston (1982) 330–331.

54. Preston (1982) 330.

55. *CIL* 1² pp. 240 and 324; 9.4192. On the altar of Ceres Mater and Ops Augusta, see also Pouthier (1981) 285–293. On Ceres Mater, cf. also *CIL* 3.6096; 8.9020; 10.7501.

56. Verg. *G.* 1.163; Ov. *Met.* 5.509, 567, 6.118; *Fast.* 1.671, 4.447; Claud. *Rapt. Pros.* 1.178. Cf. also Ceres as Mater Frugum: Ov. *Fast.* 1.671; *Met.* 6.118.

57. *Alma*: Verg. *G.* 1.7; Ov. *Met.* 5.572; *Fast.* 4.547. *Genetrix*: Ov. *Met.* 5.490.

58. Cf. also Arn. *Adv. Nat.* 3.10; 6.25.

59. Munro (1928) 2:278.

60. On these epithets, see T. Price (1978) 190, with references.

61. See T. Price (1978) 117–120, with references.

62. For Demeter and Persephone, see Beschi (1988) 889, and nrs. 245–246, 258–259, 288–292, 300–303. For Demeter and the young male child, see p. 891, and nrs. 389, 397, 402–404, 407–409.

63. For the various sites in Greece and Asia Minor see Price (1978): 88 (Knossos); 106–114 (Athens); 117–120 (Eleusis); 153–154 (Kos); 159–160 (Halikarnassos); 160

(Knidos). For sites in Magna Graecia and Sicily, see Zuntz (1971) 110−114. Price (28−29, 129−130, 154−156, 181−186) also discusses the *kourotrophos* types from these sites, which she does not always identify as Demeter. On the Demeter Kourotrophos type, see also Beschi (1988) 844, 889, 891 and nrs. 300−302.

64. Vetter (1953) 147. On the tablet from Agnone, see also sec. 1.1.

65. Vetter (1953) 204−208, 211. See also sec. 1.1.

66. Ceres at the Rape of Proserpina: De Angeli (1988) nrs. 126−135; cf. also nrs. 123−125 (Ceres and Proserpina alone) and nrs. 142−144 (Ceres, Proserpina, and Triptolemus).

67. Aachen, Münster G3: De Angeli (1988) nr. 133.

68. Ceres and Triptolemus: De Angeli (1988) nrs. 136−144. Ceres and Iacchus: De Angeli (1988) nrs. 145−149.

69. London, British Museum inv. nr. 1306: De Angeli (1988) nr. 139. See sec. 1.7.

70. Marble cinerary urn from Rome near the Porta Maggiore. First half of the 1st century A.D. Rome, Mus. Naz. 11301: De Angeli (1988) nr. 145.

71. Ceres at the birth of Dionysus: De Angeli (1988) nrs. 149−150. Ceres at the birth of Apollo and Diana: De Angeli (1988) nr. 151.

72. Sardonyx cameo, Paris, Bibliothèque Nationale: De Angeli (1988) nr. 149.

73. Ceres' role in weddings is also related to her connection with rites of passage. Ceres' liminal function also explains her connection with divorce, over which many scholars have puzzled: how can a goddess of weddings also be connected with divorce? See Le Bonniec (1958) 83−88 for a discussion of other solutions to this problem. For a full discussion of Ceres' connection with divorce and marriage as rites of passage, see sec. 3.2.3 and 3.2.4.

74. Pomeroy (1975) 214.

75. See Le Bonniec (1958) 78, n. 2, for references.

76. For more on the connections between Ceres and Tellus, see Le Bonniec (1958) 48−107.

77. Feriae Sementivae: Ov. *Fast.* 1.657−696. Festival on Dec. 13: *CIL* 1², pp. 336−337.

78. Cf. also Hor. *Carm.* 4.517−519; Manil. *Astr.* 2.19−22.

79. Cf. also Cic. *Nat. D.* 1.39−40, 2.71, 3.52, 3.64; Varr. *Ling.* 5.64.

80. Le Bonniec (1958) 78.

81. See also Rossbach (1853) 302−304.

82. Le Bonniec (1958) 82, n. 11, notes that the source is probably Varro.

83. Rossbach (1853) 347−349.

84. Le Bonniec (1958) 82, 114−115. The evidence is a poorly preserved fragment of the Augustan grammarian Sinnius Capito; for the text, see Funaioli (1961) 463, no. 16.

85. E.g., the porca praecidanea and the porca praesentanea (see sec. 3.2.1). See also Sabbatucci (1957) 54.

86. Ceres may also be connected with the peace treaty; see sec. 3.3.4.

87. So Le Bonniec (1958) 82.

88. So Rossbach (1853) 347 – 349.

89. So Sabbatucci (1957) 54.

90. Florence, Mus. Arch. 26: De Angeli (1988) nr. 172. See also Vollenweider (1966) 69, 118 pl. 76.4.

91. Paris, Louvre MA 1139: De Angeli (1988) 190.

92. *BMCRE* Claudius 109 pl. 33.19; De Angeli (1988) nr. 180.

93. The titles Mater Augusti (mother of the Augustus) and Mater Caesaris (Mother of the Caesar) were used to characterize the women of the imperial household in their role as the producer of the heir to the throne. See Temporini (1978) 44. The title Mater Patriae (Mother of the Country) was given unofficially to Livia (Tac. *Ann.* 1.14.1; Dio Cass. 57.12.4, 58.2.3). In the second and third centuries A.D., the title Mater Castrorum (Mother of the Army Camps) was used for Faustina the Younger and Julia Domna; the latter also received the titles Genetrix Orbis Terrae (Progenitress of the Roman World) and Mater Castrorum et Senatus et Patriae (Mother of the Camp and of the Senate and of the Country). See sec. 5.4 and appendix 2.

94. Vat. Mus. inv. 715. The significance of the crown has been variously interpreted. Chirassi-Colombo (1981) 423 – 425 argues that it refers to Augustus' revival of the ancient agricultural cult of the Arval Brethren. Alföldi (1979) 582 – 583 connects the bust with Augustus' initiation into the Eleusinian Mysteries. Also portrayed with the corona spicea are the emperors Antoninus Pius, Marcus Aurelius, Lucius Verus, and Hadrian. See Alföldi (1979) 581 – 585, pls. 27.2 – 4, 38.1 – 2, 4. Alföldi interprets the wheat crown as referring to the Arval Brethren for Antoninus Pius, Marcus Aurelius, and Lucius Verus; and to the Eleusinian Mysteries for Hadrian.

95. *RIC* 1²: 127.94; *BMCRE* Claudius 137 pl. 35.1; De Angeli (1988) nr. 94.

96. So De Angeli (1988) 907; Chirassi-Colombo (1981) 424; Rickman (1980) 257; Beaujeu (1955) 306, 326.

97. *RIC* 1²: 161, 136; *BMCRE* Nero 127; De Angeli (1988) nr. 153.

98. Domitian: *RIC* 2: 180.277. Nerva: *RIC* 2: 226.52. Septimius Severus: *RIC* 4(2): 64; cf. 4(2): 135.

99. *BMCRE* Vitellius 47, pl. 62.13; *RIC* 1²: 275.131, 277.166; De Angeli (1988) nr. 157.

100. Naples, Mus. Naz. *Fiorelli* 15994; Breglia (1968) nr. 59. See also Beaujeu (1955) 326. Cf. also a *kistophoros* of Hadrian, which shows on the obverse the head of the first Augustus, while the reverse shows a seated Hadrian holding a bundle of wheat stalks in his hand: *BMCRE* Hadrian 1094. See Alföldi (1979) 585 – 586 and Beaujeu (1955) 169 for the interpretation of this type.

3. "Liminality"

1. Van Gennep (1960); original publication in 1909.

2. Chapple and Coon (1942) 397 – 415, 443 – 463, 484 – 528.

3. Vetter (1953) 247. On the Tablet of Agnone, see sec. 1.1.

4. Caldarelli (1982–1984) 35–42.

5. Cf. also Varr. *Rust.* 3.15.5; Cic. *Verr.* 2.5.187, *Leg.* 2.35–36; Ov. *Am.* 3.10.11– 14, *Met.* 5.341–344, *Fast.* 1.349–353.

6. For the connection of the *divisio agrorum* with Pliny *HN* 18.3.13, see Chirassi-Colombo (1981) 417.

7. Toynbee (1971) 43–61.

8. Watson (1971) 4.

9. So Le Bonniec (1958) 92.

10. The latter requirement is reflected in the ancient etymology of the term *praesentaneus*, which derives from *praesens*, meaning "being in the same place, bodily present." Some modern scholars, however, reject this etymology and with it Veranius' explanation. Radke (1965) 88–89 derives it from *praesementaneus*, "before the harvest," and argues that it refers to an agrarian lustration rather than a funerary rite (cf. the agrarian sacrifice of the porca praecidanea, sec. 2.2.1). This explanation seems a bit forced, particularly as there is no other attested occurrence of *praesementaneus*. Radke's rejection of the funerary significance of the porca praecidanea also seems unjustified. Latte (1960) 101 derives the term from *praesens*, meaning "immediate, without delay," and contrasts this sacrifice with the one offered eight days later, the *novendialis*. For the *novendialis*, see Toynbee (1971) 51. This explanation is plausible but unprovable.

11. So Le Bonniec (1958) 106.

12. Cato *Agr.* 134; Fest., s.v. *praecidanea agna*, 223 Müller; Gell. *N.A.* 4.6.7–9; Marius Victorinus in *Gramm. Lat.* 6, 25 Keil.

13. Cf. Le Bonniec (1958) 95–97, 106, who argues that the sacrifice was originally dedicated to both Ceres and Tellus. He bases this hypothesis on the fact that the most ancient cult of Ceres was closely linked with that of Tellus and on his own claim that the porca praecidanea has chthonic weight.

14. So Le Bonniec (1958) 103.

15. On the harvest sacrifice of the porca praecidanea, see sec. 2.2.1.

16. See Chirassi-Colombo (1981) 417.

17. Vatican 10.018, from the Via Labicana: De Angeli (1988) nr. 165.

18. Cf. also De Angeli (1988) nr. 152: Ceres with Hermes; nrs. 126–365: Ceres at the Rape of Proserpina, with Hades/Pluto and Proserpina.

19. For Ceres' connection with motherhood, see sec. 2.3.1.

20. Sardonyx, Paris, Bibliothèque Nationale: De Angeli (1988) nr. 149.

21. Birth of Dionysus: De Angeli (1988) nr. 150. Birth of Apollo and Diana: De Angeli (1988) nr. 151.

22. Vetter (1953) 204–208, 211. See sec. 1.1.

23. Serv. on Verg. *Aen.* 4.166; Plut. *Vit. Num.* 12.3. For Ceres and Tellus in association with weddings, see also sec. 2.3.2.

24. See Le Bonniec (1958) 114–115. The evidence is a poorly preserved fragment of the Augustan grammarian Sinnius Capito; for the text, see Funaioli (1961) 463, nr. 16. See also sec. 2.3.2.

25. On the wedding procession, see Treggiari (1991) 166–167.

26. Cf. also Varr. *Ling.* 5.61; Plut. *QR* 1; Serv. on Verg. *Aen.* 4.103, 339.

27. Treggiari (1991) 168.

28. For divorce as a rite of passage, see Van Gennep (1960) 141–145.

29. Cf. Corbett (1930) 222, who argues that "excessive" refers to the nonreciprocity of divorce. The context, however, works against Corbett. In what follows, Plutarch discusses the punishment Romulus established for homicide, and he therefore emphasizes the types and degree of punishment in the laws attributed to Romulus.

30. See Treggiari (1991) 441–442; Corbett (1930) 219–222.

31. So Watson (1975) 33.

32. See Watson (1975) 33. Interestingly, Cicero refers to a law of the Twelve Tables regarding divorce and also mentioning keys. The orator pretends that Antony's dismissal of his mistress was a divorce: illam suam suas res sibi habere iussit, ex duodecim tabulis clavia ademit, exegit ("He ordered her to have her things for herself; he took the keys from her according to the Twelve Tables; he left") (Cic. *Phil.* 2.28.69). The passage implies that depriving the wife of the husband's keys was part of the divorce ritual.

33. For this interpretation see Le Bonniec (1958) 86–87; Noailles (1948) 10ff. Cf. the view cited in the Loeb translation of Plutarch's *Lives* (B. Perrin, trans.) that ἀπο-δόμενον is to be read as a participle in the middle voice meaning "giving up of one's own will" and θύεσθαι as the middle infinitive meaning "to cause a victim to be offered, to make a sacrifice." The provision would then read: "The one giving up his wife of his own will is to make a sacrifice to the chthonic gods." According to this interpretation, Romulus' law has four provisions: (1) the nonreciprocity of divorce, (2) the legal grounds for divorce, (3) the prescribed punishment for illegal divorce, and (4) the prescribed ritual for divorce. The major objection to this interpretation, however, is that the middle forms of ἀποδίδωμι in all its attestations mean: "to give up or deliver to one's own profit, to sell."

34. For Ceres' connection with the underworld, see sec. 3.2.1. Cf. Noailles (1948) 14, who argues that the chthonic deities are the Manes, who are offended by the pollution brought on the family by the wife's crimes, and that the husband offers an expiatory sacrifice to them as part of the divorce proceeding. This suggestion, however, is based on the rejected interpretation of ἀποδόμενον. For Ceres as the recipient of the consecration of a person guilty of a crime, see also Pliny *HN* 18.3.13.

35. Cf. Le Bonniec (1958) 86, who rejects as absurd the idea that Ceres was a goddess of divorce. He sees in her only a divinity of marriage.

36. On Ceres' connection with "beginnings," see also sec. 1.5.

37. On the initia Cereris and its identity with the sacra Cereris, see Le Bonniec (1958) 423–437. Following Le Bonniec, I do not accept Wagenvoort's argument that

the initia Cereris originally were attached to the native Italic cult of the goddess. For this argument, see Wagenvoort (1956) 150–168 and (1960) 111–142. On the Greek cult of Ceres and Proserpina see also sec. 1.4 and 5.2.

38. Sulla: Plut. *Vit. Sulla* 26. Cicero and Atticus: Cic. *Leg.* 2.35.

39. For literary, numismatic, artistic, and epigraphic evidence for the initiations of the various emperors, see Alföldi (1979) 585–606.

40. The literature on the Eleusinian Mysteries is copious; see, e.g., Mylonas (1961) with bibliography.

41. On the Eleusinian Mysteries among the Romans, see also: Ov. *Met.* 5.341–571; *Fast.* 4.417–620; Sen. *Herc. Fur.* 845–847; Stat. *Silv.* 4.8.50–51; Juv. 5.15.140–142; Suet. *Aug.* 93; *Claud.* 25; Ap. *Met.* 6.2, 11.5; Hyg. *Fab.* 147.5.

42. Ceres with torch: figs. 5, 8, 13, 14, 16b, 17, 20, 21, 25, 34b, 35b, 41b; Ceres in chariot: figs. 5, 21; Ceres with *ciste*: figs. 8, 20.

43. On the *ciste*, see Mau (1899) col. 2592; Jahn (1869) 326–331; Kanta (1979) 12, 102–104.

44. On these sarcophagi, see De Angeli (1988) nrs. 126–134; Robert (1969) 450–495.

45. Aachen, Münster G3: De Angeli (1988) nr. 133.

46. De Angeli (1988) nrs. 145–148.

47. Marble cinerary urn from Rome near the Porta Maggiore. Rome, Mus. Naz. 11301: De Angeli (1988) nr. 145.

48. *EE* 4.866. Cf. also *CIL* 6.1779, 1780.

49. Chapple and Coon (1942) 507–508.

50. So Chapple and Coon (1942) 398: "In agricultural communities, important crises, that is, crises which involve relatively great changes of interaction rates, come . . . at planting time and . . . at harvest."

51. Much of the controversy revolves around whether the mundus associated with Ceres is the same as the one created at the founding of a city and connected for Rome with its founder Romulus (Plut. *Vit. Rom.* 11; Ov. *Fast.* 4.821). On a possible Etruscan origin for the mundus, see Pfiffig (1975) 84. For the controversy on the mundus, see Coarelli (1983) 208–226; Chirassi-Colombo (1981) 418–420; Verzar (1976–1977) 378–398; Rykwert (1976) 129–132; Le Bonniec (1958) 175–184, with references to earlier scholarship.

52. For the connection of the mundus with Ceres, see also Serv. on Verg. *Ecl* 3.105 and *CIL* 10.3926 = Dessau 3348.

53. For Ceres' connection with the underworld, see sec. 3.2.1.

54. For the festivals of the dead, see Frazer (1940) 4.2:51–83. For the Lemuria, see Frazer (1929) 4:36–46. For the Anthesteria, see Hoorn (1951) 15–57.

55. See Chirassi-Colombo (1981) 419 for a comparison of the *mundus patet* ritual with the Saturnalia, another festival of inversion in which the ultimate result is to reinforce the status quo.

56. On the social significance of prodigies, see MacBain (1982) 34–79. On the Roman attitude toward prodigies, see Bloch (1963) 77–86.

57. Cf. Le Bonniec (1958) 91 and 455, who explains Ceres' connection with these events as evidence of her chthonic associations or of the "exotic and mysterious" nature of her Greek cult.

58. Dion. Hal. 6.17.2–3; Pliny *HN* 35.154.

59. On the lectisternium, see also sec. 1.4.

60. On the *ieiunium Cereris*, see also sec. 1.4 and 4.4.3.

61. 182 B.C.: Livy 40.2.1–3 (unrest in Asia Minor and the death of Hannibal at the court of Prusias); 174 B.C.: Livy 41.28.2 (war in Spain, Latins sent home from Rome); 133 B.C.: Cic. *Verr.* 2.4.108 (murder of Tiberius Gracchus); 125 B.C.: Phlegon *Mir.* 10, in *FrGrH* 2B, p. 257, nr. 36 (Gracchan reforms at Rome, revolt of Fregellae); 104 B.C.: Obseq. *Prodig. Lib.* 43 (103) (defeat of Romans at Arausio by Cimbri and Teutones and slave revolt in Sicily); 99 B.C.: Obseq. *Prodig. Lib.* 46 (106) (revolt in Lusitania, rioting in Rome); 92 B.C.: Obseq. *Prodig. Lib.* 53 (113) (devastation of Macedonia, prelude to Social War); 84 B.C.: App. *BCiv.* 1.78.359 (unrest at Rome, murder of Cinna); 42 B.C.: Dio Cass. 47.40.5–6 (Battle of Philippi); 32 B.C.: Dio Cass. 50.8.1 (Battle of Actium); A.D. 64: Tac. *Ann.* 15.44.2 (Great Fire of Rome).

62. See Gagé (1963) 108–109.

63. Gagé (1963) 131.

64. For the role of Juno Regina and Apollo in the expiation of prodigies, see Le Bonniec (1958) 455; Gagé (1955) 155–220, 349–394.

65. See sec. 3.2.1. For the passage from Varro, see also sec. 3.2.3, 3.2.5, and 6.4.

66. For the rituals of the porca praecidanea and porca praesentanea, see sec. 3.2.1.

67. *BMCRE* Galba 140, pl. 57.8; De Angeli (1988) nr. 95a.

68. *BMCRE* Civil Wars 58, pl. 51.17.

69. Cf. also an aureus dated to this period, on the reverse of which appears the legend PAX above the wheat stalks and poppies of Ceres and the clasped hands of Concordia holding the caduceus of Pax (fig. 22: *RIC* 1^2:206.34; *BMCRE* Galba 6).

70. The argument contained in this section was first published in Spaeth (1990) 185–187.

71. Ogilvie (1965) 501.

72. Le Bonniec (1958) 346–347. See also Chirassi-Colombo (1981) 410. On the oath, see Ogilvie (1965) 313–314. The later date of this version may also be suggested by the mention of the triadic cult of the goddess, which traditionally was not founded until 494 B.C., and the addition of the other magistrates besides the tribunes who were to be protected by the law. On the problem posed by addition of these magistrates, see Fest., s.v. *sacrosanctum*, 424 Lindsay, and LeBonniec (1958) 346–347.

73. This argument contained in this section was first published in Spaeth (1990) 187–190.

74. On Spurius Cassius, see Lintott (1970) 18–22; Ogilvie (1965) 337–345; Le Bon-

niec (1958) 227–235; Oltramere (1932) 259–276. As Ogilvie has recognized, the story of Spurius Cassius has almost certainly been contaminated by the anachronistic inclusion of events of the Gracchan period. Nevertheless, it illustrates the association of Ceres with the punishment for attempted tyranny and indicates that this connection was still current at the time of our principal sources for the story, Livy and Dionysius.

75. For the ancient sources, see: Livy 2.41; Dion. Hal. 8.69–80; Pliny *HN* 34.13.30; Val. Max 7.8.2, 6.3.16; Cic. *Rep.* 2.35.60. On the agrarian proposal and the sources for it, see Basile (1978) 277–298.

76. There are three versions of the trial and punishment of Spurius Cassius. In the first, he was tried privately by his father as the paterfamilias (Livy 2.41.10; Pliny *HN* 34.9.15; Val. Max. 5.8.2). In the second version, he was tried publicly by the state (Livy 2.41.11; Dion. Hal. 8.78.5; Val. Max. 6.3.1). In the third, apparently a composite of the first and second versions, he was tried publicly by the state, but his father served as primary accuser and witness (Dion. Hal. 8.79.1). For further discussion of the various versions, see Lintott (1970) 19.

77. Livy (2.41.10) mentions this statue, and Pliny (*HN* 34.9.15) specifically states that it was dedicated to Ceres. Pliny (*HN* 34.14.30) has another rather confused account of a statue associated with Spurius Cassius. He indicates that Spurius erected a statue of himself before the Temple of Tellus, which was seen as representative of his tyrannical ambitions. The censors therefore had the statue melted down. This account does not reflect the common tradition regarding the statue. All other references to this statue indicate that it was erected out of the confiscated goods of Spurius and dedicated to Ceres (Pliny *HN* 34.9.15; Livy 2.41.10; Val. Max. 5.8.2; Dion. Hal. 8.79.3). Moreover, the erection of a statue of a living individual at this early period is unlikely. I propose that the account of Pliny *HN* 34.14.30 confuses the monument of the punishment of Spurius, the statue erected from his *consecratio bonorum*, with the crime for which that punishment was applied, the seeking of tyrannical power. On this matter, see also Ogilvie (1965) 344.

78. Pliny *HN* 18.3.12.

79. Livy 2.41.10; Val. Max 5.8.2.

80. Livy (2.41.12) and Val. Max. (6.3.1) both mention the state execution. Dion. Hal. (8.78.5) notes that it was carried out at the Tarpeian Rock. Dionysius (8.79.3) records the dedication of the goods of Cassius to Ceres.

81. On the cultic associations of the Tarpeian Rock, see Richardson (1992) 377–378; Nash (1968) 2:409; Platner and Ashby (1929) 509–510. The *rupes Tarpeia*, which is closely associated with the cult of Jupiter (e.g., Sil. *Pun.* 3.623; 10.360; Prop. 4.1.7; Firm. Mat. 1.10.7), is identified by Varro (*Ling.* 5.41) with the *saxum Tarpeium* from which criminals were cast.

82. E.g., Pliny *HN* 7.44.143. See also Strachan-Davidson (1912) 1:13–15.

83. The argument contained in this section was first published in Spaeth (1990) 182–195.

84. Those scholars who have treated the mission to Henna have generally interpreted

it as a conciliatory gesture made by the Senate to the plebs for the murder of their champion, Tiberius. See Le Bonniec (1958) 367 – 368; Astin (1967) 227; Stockton (1979) 87 – 88; MacBain (1982) 38 – 39. A variation of this theory suggests that under the pretext of conciliating the plebs for the murder of Tiberius, the Senate was actually trying to turn its attachment away from the older plebeian cult of Ceres with its dangerous political associations toward a new cult of the goddess, uncompromised by such connections. See Le Bonniec (1958) 368 – 369. The major objection to these proposals is that they are inconsistent with the evidence for the period immediately following the death of Tiberius. Rather than attempting to conciliate the plebs by showing remorse for the death of Tiberius, the Senate insisted that he had been put to death justly. Several decrees were passed not only condoning the act but even honoring it (Cic. *Dom.* 91). Moreover, the consuls of the following year, P. Popillius Laenas and P. Rupilius, conducted a formal inquisition of the supporters of Tiberius and had many of them exiled or put to death (Sall. *Iug.* 31.7; Vell. Pat. 2.7.3; Cic. *Amic.* 11.37; Val. Max. 4.7.1; Plut. *Vit. Ti. Gracch.* 20.3 – 4). In this context, the Senate's mission to Henna can hardly have been intended to atone for the murder of Tiberius. Rather, it must be connected with the attempts to justify that murder.

85. The college of priests in charge of the Sibylline Books could not consult them without specific authorization from the Senate (Cic. *Div.* 1.97, 2.112). The members of the college could presumably be convinced to find what the Senate wished in the books or at least to interpret the instructions found there in a manner that would accord with the Senate's wishes. In addition, the Senate had the final responsibility for determining the manner in which the recommendations of the college based on the instructions found in the books were to be put into effect (Front. *Aqu.* 1.7). See Bouché-Leclercq (1882) 4:294.

86. For political manipulation of the Sibylline Books in the Late Republic, see Bouché-Leclercq (1882) 307.

87. Cic. *Dom.* 123 – 125. On this passage, see Nisbet (1979) 209 – 211. Nisbet argues that *consecratio bonorum* alone did not require the presence of a pontifex.

88. Cf., however, Val. Max. 3.2.17 and Vell. Pat. 2.3.1, where Nasica covers his left arm with his toga, rather than his head. The sources agree that Nasica did something with his toga, but are somewhat uncertain as to what exactly this was.

89. Earl (1963) 118 – 119. Cf. Appian (*BCiv.* 1.2.16), who offers a number of different explanations for this action. He states that Nasica covered his head either to induce more men to follow him because of his odd appearance, or to make himself a helmet as a sign of battle, or to conceal himself from the gods because of what he was about to do. This variety of explanations suggests that Appian found the description of this incident in his source, and was unaware of its explanation. So Badian (1972) 725.

90. On the homo sacer, see sec. 3.3.5.

91. Badian (1972) 725.

92. Cic. *Dom.* 124. On the significance of *capite velato* in the *consecratio bonorum*, see Nisbet (1979) 173.

93. So Badian (1972) 726.

94. The bodies are reported to have been thrown into the Tiber by the aedile Lucretius Vespillo (Val. Max. 1.4.3; Plut. *Vit. Ti. Gracch.* 20.2; Livy *Periocha* 58).

95. Cf. Astin (1967) 227 and Stockton (1979) 87, who suggest that the Senate refused to allow Tiberius and his supporters to be buried in order to prevent possible political demonstrations at a public funeral.

96. Indeed, this was the charge the people levied against Nasica. See Plut. *Vit. Ti. Gracch.* 21.2.

97. In time, the accusation in certain sources takes on the aura of proven fact. For example, Cicero (*Amic.* 41) reports that Tiberius "tried to seize royal power or indeed ruled as king for a few months" (regnum occupare conatus est vel regnavit is quidem paucos menses). Cf. also Sall. *Iug.* 31.7; Cic. *Brut.* 212; *Cat.* 1.29; *Phil.* 8.13; *Offic.* 1.76; Val. Max. 3.2.17, 5.3.2e. Tiberius thus took his place in the canonical list of those who had attempted to seize a kingdom: Spurius Cassius, Spurius Maelius, and Marcus Manlius. For Tiberius' association with these other "attempted tyrants" see, e.g., Cic. *Mil.* 8.72; Val. Max. 6.3.1; Quint. *Inst.* 5.13.24.

98. For this inquisition, see also Sall. *Iug.* 31.7; Vell. Pat. 2.7.3; Cic. *Amic.* 11.37; Val. Max. 4.7.1.

99. For the date of Carbo's tribunate and the bill on immediate reelection to the tribunate, see Stockton (1979) 91, n. 24.

100. For further discussion of the incident, see Astin (1967) 233–234.

101. Cf. also Scipio's response when he first heard of Tiberius' death. He quoted from Homer (*Od.* 1.47), "So may anyone perish who does such things" (ὥς ἀπόλοιτο καὶ ἄλλος ὅτις τοιαῦτά γε ῥέζοι) (Plut. *Vit. Ti. Gracch.* 21.5). See Astin (1967) 226.

102. Vell. Pat. 2.4.4; Plut. *Vit. Ti. Gracch.* 21.5.

103. So Cic. *Verr.* 2.4.108. See also Val. Max. 1.1.1.

104. On the associations of the cult of Ceres with the First Secession of the plebs, see sec. 1.3 and 4.4.1.

4. "The Plebs"

1. See Mitchell (1990) 1–30 and sec. 1.3.

2. On the Temple of Ceres, Liber, and Libera and its cult, see also sec. 1.3 and sec. 2.2.2.

3. So Richardson (1992) 80; Coarelli (1988) 66–70; Platner-Ashby (1929) 110; Merlin (1906) 93–95. For the argument that the Temple of Ceres, Liber, and Libera was located in the Forum Boarium, see sec. 2.2.2 and Simon (1990) 45; Nash (1968) 1:227; Le Bonniec (1958) 266–277; Van Berchem (1935) 91–95; Giovenale (1927) 352–371.

4. *CIL* 15.7172. Cf. Richardson (1992) 152; Platner-Ashby (1929) 210.

5. For the First Secession of the plebs, traditionally dated to 494 B.C., see Livy

2.32.3, 3.54.9; Cic. *Rep.* 2.58; Sallust *Hist.*1.11M. For the Second Secession, tradition-ally dated to 449 B.C., see Dion. Hal. 11.43; Diod. 12.24; Pompon. *Dig.* 1.2.3.24; Sall. *Iug.* 31.17; Oros. 2.13.7. The Mons Sacer is sometimes named as the site of the first secession: Cic. *Rep.* 2.33.58; Aug. *Civ. D.* 3.17. On the problem of the location of the site of the first secession, see Ridley (1968) 538.

6. Livy 3.31.1, 32.7; Cic. *In Cornelianum* (Ascon., p. 77 Clark); Diod. 12.24.5; Dion. Hal. 10.32.2–4. On the significance of the law, see Alföldi (1963) 90–93, with references to prior scholarship.

7. See sec. 3.2.4, 3.3.5, and 3.3.6.

8. Livy 3.55.7: "that his goods should be sold at the Temple of Ceres, Liber, and Libera" (familia ad aedem Cereris, Liberi Liberaeque venum iret). Based on this pas-sage, Latte (1934–1936) 73–77 has argued that a market was set up at the temple for the purpose of selling these goods.

9. Livy 10.23.13, 27.6.19, 36.9, 33.25.3. See sec. 4.3.2.

10. For the Temple of Saturn as the public treasury, see: Solin. 1.12; Macrob. 1.8.3; Plut. *Vit. Ti. Gracch.* 10; App. *BCiv.* 1.31. For the use of temples as treasuries, see Vidal (1965) 545–587; Bromberg (1940) 128–131.

11. Cf. Livy 10.23.13, 27.6.19, 36.9. See Richardson (1992) 80–81; Platner-Ashby (1929) 110.

12. This is the second definition given in the *OLD*, s.v. *asylum*.

13. This is the first definition given in the *OLD*, s.v. *asylum*.

14. So Le Bonniec (1958) 345.

15. This is the first definition of the term in the *OLD*, s.v. *confugio*. Cf., e.g., Plaut. *Mostell.* 1135: quid confugisti in aram?; Cic. *Rosc. Am.* 27: confugiunt quasi ad aram in exsilium; Pliny *Tra.* 10.74 (16): confugisse ad tuam statuam; Gai. *Inst.* 1.53: qui ad fana deorum vel ad statuas principum confugiunt. On statues of the emperors as places of sanctuary, see S. Price (1984) 191–195.

16. For the use of ancient temples as places of asylum, see Schlesinger (1933) and Latte (1920) 106–108. On the problem of temple asylum in Rome itself, see Altheim (1938) 255ff. If indeed the Temple of Ceres possessed the right of asylum, then it would be one of only two temples in Rome known to have possessed it. The other was that of the Divus Julius, which Dio Cassius informs us served as a place of asylum (47.19.2). Servius tells us that the right of asylum was defined in the law of consecration of the temple: hoc autem (asylum) non est in omnibus templis nisi quibus consecrationis lege concessum ("This asylum, however, was not in all temples, but only those to which it had been conceded by the law of consecration") (Serv. on Verg. *Aen.* 2.761). Wissowa (1912) 474, n. 3, has suggested that this right was associated only with cults that were somehow "un-Roman." However, an ancient tradition connects Romulus with the es-tablishment of asylum in temples: Cal. Piso fr. 4, Peter; Ov. *Fast.* 3.430ff.; Plut. *Vit. Rom.* 9. Cf. Salvadore (1978) 287–290.

17. For the *annona*, see sec. 2.2.2.

18. See Alföldi (1965) 95, with further references.

NOTES·TO·PAGES 85 – 88

19. So Beloch (1926) 328.

20. The use of the plural *aedibus* is curious. Perhaps it applies to the Temple of Ceres by synecdoche, or it may refer to specific rooms in the temple. It may also refer to the temple of another divinity connected with the plebs, the Temple of Diana on the Aventine. We know that the *lex Icilia de Aventino publicando* was stored there (Dion. Hal. 10.32.4).

21. For the *lex sacrata* and sacrosanctitas, see sec. 3.3.5.

22. So Ogilvie (1965) 314.

23. Lengele (1937) cols. 2460–2462.

24. Cf. Cic. *Rep.* 2.58: contra consulare imperium tr. pl. ("against the *imperium* of the consuls, the tribune of the plebs").

25. So, e.g., Medicus (1964) 83. For a resume of the scholarship on the etymology of aedilis, see Le Bonniec (1958) 353–357. Le Bonniec argues for a wider interpretation of the term and believes that it refers to all plebeian sanctuaries.

26. Walde and Hofmann (1930), s.v. *aedes*; Ernout and Meillet (1959–1960), s.v. *aedes*. The ancient sources also associate the two terms, e.g.: aedilis qui aedes sacras et privatas procurat ("The aedile is the one who takes care of sacred and private buildings") (Varr. *Ling.* 5.81). Cf. also Fest., s.v. *aedilis*, 13 Müller; Dion. Hal. 6.90; Theophil. *Inst.* 1.2; Lyd. *Mag.* 1.35.

27. Cf. also Pompon. *Dig.* 1.2.2.21.

28. So Sordi (1983) 127. For the creation of the office of aedilis Cerealis, see also Rickman (1980) 59; Broughton (1952) 2:306.

29. Rickman (1980) 34–35. For the three duties, see Cic. *Leg.* 3.3.7.

30. On the aediles' administration of the ludi Ceriales, see later in this section. The control of the sacred games was finally transferred to the *praetor urbis* by Augustus. See Dion. Hal. 2.19; Mart. 10.41.4. Le Bonniec (1958) 352–353 has a different order of priorities and suggests that the cura ludorum grew out of the cura annonae, since their original duty to oversee the harvest led the aediles to take on responsibility for the games designed to insure a good harvest.

31. This function was in addition to their political duties. Roman magistrates traditionally carried out many of the duties of priests in the state cults. The cult of Ceres also had a functionary, the flamen Cerialis, specifically devoted to performing rituals dedicated to the goddess. This flamen celebrated the Cerialia, the sacrum Cereale, the sacrifice of the agrarian porca praecidanea, and the offering of the *sacrima*, the first fruits of the harvest. On the flamen Cerialis, see sec. 1.2. It seems practically certain that this minor flaminate was filled exclusively by members of the plebs. See Le Bonniec (1958) 342–343.

32. Fasti Praenestini. Cf. the Fasti Ostienses, which contain a fragmentary reference to the same festival. See *CIL* 14.4547; Le Bonniec (1958) 53.

33. So Mommsen in *CIL* 1², p. 336, and Le Bonniec (1958) 52–53.

34. Despite Arnobius' mention of Ceres alone in connection with this rite, it seems likely that Tellus also was honored by it, since the ritual took place in her temple on its

foundation day. Also *Tellu[ri]* in the inscription is surer than *[Cere]ri* epigraphically, though no one can doubt the restoration.

35. Cornificius Longus, frag. of *De etymis deorum*, in Funaioli (1961) 1:475.

36. So Le Bonniec (1958) 55.

37. On the ludi Ceriales, see Scullard (1981) 101–103; Le Bonniec (1958) 315–323; Sabbatucci (1954) 275–279; Bayet (1951) 354–357; Piganiol (1923) 87–91.

38. *RRC* 427.2; *BMCRR* Rome 3940.

39. So Le Bonniec (1958) 320–323.

40. Cf. also Juv. *Sat.* 14.262–264.

41. On the political significance of the celebration of games, see Quinn-Schofield (1967) 683.

42. *OLD*, s.v. *caerimonia*.

43. Frazer (1929) 3:325–330 provides comparative anthropological evidence for the use of games in religious festivals to promote the growth of crops. See also Frazer (1940) 3.1:92–112.

44. Cf. also Livy 27.36.9 (208 B.C.): Et plebeis ludis biduum instauratam a C. Mamilo et M. Caecilio Metello aedilibus plebis; et tria signa ad Cereris eidem dederunt ("And at the plebeian games there was a repetition for two days by C. Mamilius and M. Caecilius Metellus, aediles of the *plebs*; and these same persons also offered three statues at [the temple] of Ceres"). Although the source of the funds spent for the erection of the statues is not mentioned, presumably the aediles again used the fines they had collected.

45. Flora: Ov. *Fast.* 5.279–294. Faunus: Livy 33.42.10, 34.53.3. See Le Bonniec (1958) 348–349.

46. Hellebrand (1935) col. 554. Mommsen (1899) 1025–1026.

47. Mommsen (1899) 166.

48. Mommsen (1899) 902–904.

49. See sec. 3.2.4, 3.3.5, and 3.3.6.

50. Livy 3.55.7: ut familia ad aedem Cereris Liberi Liberaeque venum iret.

51. Latte (1934–1936) 73–77.

52. On the complex problem of the ethnic origins of this triad, see sec. 1.3.

53. Le Bonniec (1958) 323–326, 342.

54. So Sordi (1983) 135; Hoffman (1934) 100.

55. For the plebeian cult, see Alföldi (1963) 99. For the cult of Jupiter Optimus Maximus, Juno Regina, and Minerva, see Radke (1965) 158–160; Koch (1937) 121–134.

56. Le Bonniec (1958) 293.

57. For the location of the Temple of Jupiter, Juno, and Minerva, see Richardson (1992) 221–222; Nash (1968) 1:530; Platner-Ashby (1929) 297–302. For the location of the Temple of Ceres, Liber, and Libera, see sec. 4.2.1, with references.

58. On the pomerium see Richardson (1992) 293–296; Blumenthal (1952) cols. 1867–1876; Platner-Ashby (1929) 392–396; Antaya (1980) 184–189. On the intrapomerial status of the Capitoline temple, see Schilling (1949) 28–33. Both suggested

locations for the Temple of Ceres, Liber, and Libera are outside the pomerium. For the extrapomerial status of the Aventine location, see Sen. *De brev. vit.* 13.8; Merlin (1906) 53–68. For that of the Forum Boarium location, see Le Bonniec (1958) 232, n. 3.

59. So Ridley (1968) 547 and Pais (1923) 1 : 158ff. On the assimilation of Ceres to Demeter, see sec. 1.3 and 1.4. On the exclusion of foreign cults from the area enclosed by the pomerium, see Strab. 5.232; Serv. on Verg. *Aen.* 1.292; Vitruv. 1.7.1. See also Schilling (1949) 27.

60. Ridley (1968) 547.

61. So Alfödi (1963) 99–100.

62. So Sabbatucci (1953–1954) 77.

63. On this association see Aurigemma (1909) 31–65; Colin (1954) 346–355. The story of the importation of the cult to Rome is told in a number of ancient sources, including Livy 29.10–14; Ov. *Fast.* 4.247–348; Appian *Punica* 7.9.56; Dio Cass. 17.61; Herodian 1.11. The summary that follows is based largely on Livy's account.

64. Livy 29.10.8, 14.8. On Publius Cornelius Scipio Nasica, see F. Münzer, *RE* 4, 1494–1497, s.v. *Cornelius*, 350; Frazer (1929) 3 : 248.

65. Livy 29.14.12–13. On the significance of the association of the matrons with the cult, see Stehle (1989) 154–156.

66. On Claudia Quinta, see Ov. *Fast.* 4.305–349; Münzer, (1899a) col. 2899; Frazer (1929) 3 : 238–240. In some sources, it is a Valeria, not a Claudia, who performs the miracle. The Valerii also were an ancient patrician family. On the problem, see Schmidt (1910) 9. On the purity of the patrician gens Claudia, see Tac. *Ann.* 11.25.

67. On the establishment of the games, see Livy 36.36. For patrician privileges at these games, see Val. Max. 2.4.3 and 4.5.1.

68. For further discussion of the opposition of the rituals of the two cults, see Le Bonniec (1958) 365–367 and Sabbatucci (1954) 275–279.

69. The ludi Megalenses were celebrated on April 4–10; the ludi Ceriales on April 12–19. See Piganiol (1923) 87.

70. On the celebration of the ludi Megalenses by the curule aediles, see Cic. *Har. Resp.* 13.27; Livy 34.54; Dio Cass. 13.8, 43.48. On the creation of the curule aedileship for the patricians, see Livy 6.42.12–14. On the opening of this office to the plebeians, see Livy 7.1.6.

71. See sec. 4.3.2.

72. For the Megalensia, see: Ov. *Fast.* 4.353–356; *CIL* 1², p. 235.314; *ILS* 88449. For the Cerialia, see Plaut. *Men.* 101; Gell. *N.A.* 2.24.2.

73. For the Temple of Magna Mater, see Richardson (1992) 242–243; Nash (1968) 2 : 27; Platner-Ashby (1929) 324–325. For excavation reports on the site of this temple, see Pensabene (1978) 67–71; (1979) 67–74; (1980) 65–81. For the Palatine Hill, see Richardson (1992) 279–282; Nash (1968) 2 : 163; Platner-Ashby (1929) 374–379.

74. On the location of the Temple of Ceres, Liber, and Libera, see sec. 4.2.1.

75. The entire Palatine was within the pomerium: Tac. *Ann.* 12.24; Richardson

(1992) 280; Platner-Ashby (1929) 392. The Temple of Ceres was on the Aventine, outside the pomerium.

76. See Schilling (1949) 27–35. Cf. Lambrechts (1951) 54.

77. Graillot (1912) 57.

78. See Graillot (1912) 41–43.

79. See also Verg. *Aen.* 9.85, 10.156–158.

80. On the problem of the reliability of Herodian, see Hohl (1954) 1. On the confusion of the Trojans with the Phrygians, see Dion. Hal. 1.29 and Graillot (1912) 43.

81. See Vermaseren (1977) 39.

82. As Stehle (1989) 161, n. 60, points out, the Romans were using the Trojan legend for diplomatic purposes by the early second century. See also Galinsky (1969) 172–176 and Lambrechts (1951) 50.

83. Livy 29.14.14. This association was to be visually expressed in the coins of the Late Republic with the goddess on the obverse and Victoria, the personification of Victory, on the reverse. See the denarii of the gens Fabia dated to c. 90 B.C.: *BMCRR* Rome 1581–1610.

84. So Lambrechts (1951) 59–60.

85. Cf. Graillot (1912) 71, n. 2, who notes that Cybele was identified with Ops by the time of the Late Republic.

86. So Le Bonniec (1958) 448–449.

87. Later the festival became annual. See Vidman (1978) 87–95, Wissowa (1899*a*) col. 1978.

88. On the use of Roman coin types as propaganda, see most recently Evans (1992) 17–32.

89. Le Bonniec (1958) 370–378.

90. On the problem of the interpretation of coinage, see Crawford (1974) 2:726. Ceres' appearance on Late Republican coinage may also be connected with the growing popularity of the Eleusinian Mysteries or with concern for the grain supply. See sec. 1.5. I have accepted, in general, Crawford's dates for the coinage. Where a controversy over the date exists and has a bearing on the interpretation of the coin, I discuss it in the text.

91. *RRC* 321.1; *BMCRR* Rome 1725. Babelon (1885–1886) 1:326 and Grueber (1910) 1:236, n. 3, suggested that this coin referred to the foundation of a colony on two islands called the Caeiciae. The name of the islands is known from Pliny (*HN* 4.12.57) and suggests a connection with the cognomen Caeicianus. According to Babelon and Grueber, the moneyer issued the coin in memory of his ancestor who founded the colony. The yoke of oxen represents the act of foundation of the colony, and the bust of Ceres indicates the abundance and fertility of the new city. As Le Bonniec (1958) 370–371 noted, we know nothing of the history of these islands, the etymology of their name, or the existence of this putative ancestor of Caeicianus.

92. See sec. 4.2.3.

93. On the gens Cassia, see Tac. *Ann.* 6.15. Cf. Münzer (1899*b*) col. 1678.

94. *RRC* 427.2; *BMCRR* Rome 3940. For the interpretation of the coin, see Le Bonniec (1958) 320–323.

95. Groag (1932) col. 602.

96. This coin type may also have another meaning. It may be an "aedilician" type, referring to services the issuer could provide as aedile—in this case public games. The aedilician coins can refer to services already provided by the issuer or his family, services to be provided in the future, or even services that would have been provided had the issuer been elected aedile. The coin may therefore be interpreted as an attempt by the moneyer to suggest the games he would provide when he was elected to office. On the aedilician type, see Crawford (1974) 2:729.

97. *RRC* 351.1; *BMCRR* Rome 2463.

98. So Le Bonniec (1958) 372; Crawford (1974) 1:367; Grueber (1910) 1:314.

99. See sec. 2.2.2 and 4.2.4.

100. The coin thus represents another kind of aedilician coin series, in which the issuer emphasizes the services he has provided, will provide, or would have provided to the public as aedile. This interpretation may perhaps be applied to another coin bearing the image of Ceres. This coin, a denarius struck in 63 B.C. by L. Furius Brocchus, bears on its obverse a head of Ceres with a wheat stalk and barley grain and on the reverse a curule chair with fasces on either side: *RRC* 414.1; *BMCRR* Rome 3896. Babelon (1885–1886) 1:527 has suggested that the head of Ceres refers to the grain distributions conducted by the plebeian aediles. The curule chair and fasces, however, indicate the curule, not the plebeian, aedileship. Le Bonniec (1958) 375 finds the relation of obverse and reverse inexplicable. I believe that the explanation lies in the interpretation of the aedilician type. The head of Ceres and grain symbols refer to the largess that Brocchus would have provided to the public had he served as plebeian aedile. The curule chair and fasces probably refer to his actual service as curule aedile.

101. See sec. 4.2.4.

102. *RRC* 449.2; *BMCRR* Rome 3976.

103. *RRC* 449.3a; *BMCRR* Rome 3973.

104. On Pansa, see Gundel (1958) cols. 1953–1965.

105. So Le Bonniec (1958) 375. The coins may also refer to a family cult devoted to Ceres: so Crawford (1974) 1:465. We know, for example, that the father of this moneyer, also named C. Vibius Pansa, issued a denarius c. 90 B.C. with a reverse type of Ceres bearing torches in either hand, with a pig in front of her: *RRC* 342.3a–b; *BMCRR* Rome 2242, 2238.

106. On libertas, see Wirszubski (1950).

107. See Le Bonniec (1958) 375; Bruhl (1953) 42ff.; Wirszubski (1950) 31–65, 74–79.

108. For the coin of Pansa with the goddess Libertas, see *RRC* 449.4; *BMCRR* Rome 3983. Le Bonniec (1958) 373 has suggested that this same appeal to libertas is represented by a denarius issued by Marcus Volteius: *RRC* 385.3; *BMCRR* Rome 3160. It bears on its obverse a head of Liber with an ivy wreath, and on its reverse Ceres with

torches in a *biga* of snakes and the legend M. VOLTEI M. F. Le Bonniec argues that Liber and Ceres are again the patrons of libertas. Although this interpretation is possible, its likelihood is diminished by the fact that the coin appears as one of a series issued by Volteius with a single common theme. The other four coins of the series use patron deities to refer to the great public games of Rome: Jupiter (ludi Romani), Hercules (ludi plebeii), Cybele (ludi Megalenses), and Apollo (ludi Apollinares); see Crawford (1974) 1:402. A more likely interpretation is that Liber and Ceres on the coin in question also symbolize public games, the ludi Ceriales, as Crawford indeed suggests. If the coin does refer to the ludi Ceriales, it may still have a political significance, as an aedilician type.

109. *RRC* 467.1a–b; *BMCRR* Africa 21. See sec. 1.5.

110. So Crawford (1974) 1:93 and Le Bonniec (1958) 375–376. The legends COS. TERT. and DICT. ITER. provide the dating of the coin. The legends "*M*" (munus = "gift") or "*D*" (donatium = "donative") indicate that it was a special free issue.

111. So Grueber (1910) 2:576. Cf. Babelon (1885–1886) 2:14, who connects the donative with the victory over Pharnaces at Zela in 47 B.C. At this date, however, Caesar was consul for the second time, and dictator only for the first.

112. Le Bonniec (1958) 376. Cf. Grueber (1910) 2:509, who suggests that Ceres appears on this coin as a veiled reference to Africa, the location of the victory. She would stand for grain, a product in which Roman Africa (modern Tunisia and Algeria) abounded. This explanation seems contrived. Crawford (1974) 2:736 believes that the symbol of Ceres was used because she served as the goddess of donatives to the people. I presume that he refers to the grain distributions made from the Temple of Ceres, but the attempt to equate these distributions to a monetary donative seems problematic.

113. *RRC* 502.2; *BMCRR* East 41.

114. *RRC* 502.3; *BMCRR* East 46.

115. Crawford (1974) 1:515.

116. Le Bonniec (1958) 377.

117. For the use of the slogan of libertas by the tyrannicides, see Wirszubski (1950) 87–96. For this interpretation of the coin, see Le Bonniec (1958) 377. Cf. Grueber (1910) 2:472, who argues that Ceres appears on these coins to indicate Sestius' success in provisioning Brutus' army, especially in securing the grain that Ceres symbolized.

118. See, e.g.: *RRC* 501.1, *BMCRR* East 38 (labeled Libertas); *RRC* 505.1–5, *BMCRR* East 82–85 (unlabeled); *RRC* 506.3, *BMCRR* East 39 (labeled Libertas).

119. *RRC* 494.44a; *BMCRR* Rome 4233.

120. For this date, see Crawford (1974) 1:509–511; Sydenham (1952) 180; Babelon (1885–1886) 2:241–242.

121. Le Bonniec (1958) 378. Cf. Grueber (1910) 1:576, who dates the coins to 39–38 B.C., and suggests that they may allude to a treaty concluded in this period between Octavius and Sextus Pompey, in which Pompey agreed to supply Rome with grain. In this case the image of Ceres would refer to her role as the goddess of grain and the grain supply.

122. *RRC* 494.19; *BMCRR* Rome 4282.

123. Crawford (1974) 1:505, however, believes that the object is a branch, and so identifies the figure as Pietas.

124. *RIC* 1²:56.219; *BMCRE* Augustus 544. On this coin, see also appendix 2, nr. 1.11.

125. For the Tiberian type, see *RIC* 1²:95.25–29. For the Claudian type, see fig. 41: *RIC* 1²:128.101; *BMCRE* Claudius 224.

126. See sec. 6.4.

127. On the date of the foundation of the cult of Ceres, Liber, and Libera and its connection with the establishment of the Republic, see sec. 4.4.1.

128. See sec. 2.4.

129. So Chirassi-Colombo (1981) 422–423; Le Bonniec (1958) 458–462.

130. Temple of Ceres, Liber, and Libera: Cornificius Longus, frag. of *De etymis deorum*, in Funaoli (1961) 1.475; Pliny *HN* 35.24, 99, 154; Tac. *Ann.* 2.49; Pompon. *Dig.* 1.2.2.21. Cerialia: Juv. 14.262–264; Gell. *N.A.* 18.2.11; Dio Cass. 47.40.6.

131. *RIC* 2:229.80, 230.103; *BMCRE* Nerva 115. Cf. also Rickman (1980) 264.

132. For the connection of the plebs and the princeps in the Early Empire, see Yavetz (1969) 103–129.

5. *"Women"*

1. On this cult and its introduction to Rome, see sec. 1.4.

2. Cf. also Fest., s.v. *Graeca sacra*, 97 Müller. See sec. 5.2.3.

3. Peterson (1919) 1:64. See also Beloch (1890) 52ff. and Heurgon (1942) 333ff., 366ff.

4. On the association of Demeter Thesmophoros with women, see Zeitlin (1982) 129–157; Chirassi-Colombo (1979) 25–58; Chirassi-Colombo (1975) 183–213; Peterson (1919) 185.

5. On the flamen Cerialis, see sec. 1.2.

6. On the aediles of the plebs, see sec. 4.3.2.

7. On this priesthood, see also Chirassi-Colombo (1981) 422 and 426; Le Bonniec (1958) 397–399.

8. *CIL* 9.2670 (Aesernia); 9.3170 (Corfinum); 10.5073 (Atina); 10.6103 (Formiae); 10.2190 (Pompeii); 10.3912 (Capua). Cf. also the dual priesthood of Ceres and Venus, also held exclusively by women: *CIL* 9.3087, 3089, 3170 (Corfinum); 10.5191 (Casinum); 10.680 (Surrentum); *NSA* (1899) 399 (Corfinum); *EE* 8.315.855 (Pompeii). For more on the dual priesthood of Ceres and Venus, see Colonna (1953); Chirassi-Colombo (1981) 426.

9. The only exception to this rule comes from outside of Italy. According to inscriptions from cities in North Africa during the Early Empire, men as well as women served as the *sacerdos Cereris*. The cult that these priests and priestesses served was dedicated

to two goddesses, the Cereres. On the cult of the Cereres, see sec. 1.5. For male priests of the Cereres, see *CIL* 8.12318 (Carthago), 8.6709 (Tiddis in Numidia); *Ath. Mitt.* 14, 105 (Africa proconsularis). For female priestesses of the two goddesses, see *CIL* 8.112 (Capse in Byzacena); 8.1140 (Carthago); 8.6708 (Tiddis in Numidia); 8.580e (Saltus Massipias); 8.11826 (Mactar in Byzacena); 8.15447 (Ammaedara in Byzacena); 8.6359 (Mactar in Numidia); 8.11306 (Cillium in Byzacena); *EE* 5.947 (Saldae in Mauretania Sitifensis); 5.925 (Mila). The two divinities to whom the cult was dedicated are usually identified as Demeter/Ceres and Persephone/Proserpina, although some scholars have proposed Ceres and Tellus. Archaeological evidence suggests that local African divinities were assimilated to the Cereres. There is epigraphical evidence for both the Cereres Graecae and the Cereres Punicae, who seem to have been the same divinities (Cereres Graecae: *CIL* 8.10564 [from Vaga] and an inscription from Cuicuil cited in Carcopino [1942] 15 – 16; Cereres Punicae: Charles-Picard [1942] 183, Barbieri [1961] 32, n. 46). I propose that the native cult originally had male priests, who were retained by the cult after the assimilation of the local divinities to the Roman ones. In the Roman cult of Ceres and Proserpina in Italy, however, the officiants were always women.

10. *CIL* 1^2, p. 974 (Rome); 6.2181 (Rome); 9.4200 (Amiternum?); 10.812 and 1074 (Pompeii); 10.1812 and 1829 (Puteoli); 10.4793 and 4794 (Teanum Sidicinum).

11. Pomeroy (1975) 214.

12. The interpretation of female exclusivity is not necessary but is probable in my estimation, given the context of the passage. In the lines preceding the ones just quoted, Cicero is discussing certain nocturnal rites of women, which he states were disrupted by a man "who brought lust aforethought into the sacrifice" (qui in sacrificium cogitatam libidinem intulit). The reference is to Clodius, who disrupted the rites of the Bona Dea in 61 B.C. These rites were strictly limited to women, as Plutarch informs us in his life of Julius Caesar (10.3), and a man's presence desecrated them and was considered sacrilege. According to Cicero's law, in his ideal state the rites of the Bona Dea would be permitted since they were conducted for the public good. However, they would be conducted only under strict supervision, since their abuse could lead easily to illicit sexual behavior, which, as Cicero notes, may be amply illustrated from the comic poets. To prevent similar abuse, the rites of Ceres are to be conducted in broad daylight in front of many witnesses. The association between the passages suggests that in the rites of Ceres as well as in the rites of the Bona Dea, the initiates were women. It is just barely possible that men are excluded from Cicero's injunction regarding initiation in the cult of Ceres because their sexual behavior does not bring shame on them as a woman's does on her. However, the historical model of the Greek cult, which admitted only women participants, reinforces the grammatically simplest reading of the passage and suggests that only women were initiated into the Roman cult of the two goddesses.

13. Cf. also Cic. *Verr.* 2.4.102, 112; 2.5.187.

14. On the significance of the limitation of mourning, see sec. 1.4. Cf. also Val. Max. 1.1.15; Fest., s.v. *Graeca sacra*, 97 Müller; Serv. on *Aen.* 4.609.

15. On the term "matrona," see Gagé (1963) 7 – 8.

16. For the sources for the myth of Demeter and Persephone, see Farnell (1896−1909) 3:75−112 and Foerster (1874).

17. See Burkert (1985) 242−246; and Farnell (1896−1909) 3:75−112, who also provides the ancient sources for the festival.

18. The fast associated with the Thesmophoria may also be connected with the Roman sacrum anniversarium, if the ritual of the *castus Cereris* applies to such a fast. On the *castus Cereris*, see Le Bonniec (1958) 404−412.

19. De Angeli (1988) 907 and nrs. 80−81, 126−135.

20. Denarius of C. Vibius Pansa, dated to 48 B.C.: *RRC* 449.3a; *BMCRR* Rome 3973; De Angeli (1988) nr. 80.

21. Aachen Münster G3: De Angeli (1988) nr. 133.

22. Zeitlin (1982) 149.

23. Gagé (1963) 143.

24. Paris, Bibliothèque Nationale: De Angeli (1988) nr. 123.

25. Bieber (1977) 148−162.

26. Bieber (1977) 157.

27. Relief inserted into the small Metropolis at Athens. Bieber (1977) 154, fig. 718.

28. The two themes of chastity and fertility are generally the focus of matronal cults. See Gagé (1963) 6.

29. See Le Bonniec (1958) 407−408 and Lenz (1932) 299−313.

30. Fehrle (1910) 139.

31. Zeitlin (1982) 149.

32. On the contrast between the Bacchanalia and the cult of Ceres and Proserpina, see also sec. 1.4.

33. On the relationship of chastity and fertility, see Zeitlin (1982) 148.

34. Burkert (1985) 243−244.

35. The lack of mention of human fertility symbols in the sources on the sacrum anniversarium does not necessarily mean that such symbols were not employed in the ritual. The close connection of the Roman festival to the Thesmophoria suggests that similar symbolism was employed. The knowledge of such symbolism may have been restricted to the female participants in the cult and unknown to the male Roman writers (or perhaps such knowledge was suppressed by them). For the association of Ceres with human fertility, see sec. 2.3.

36. See sec. 2.2.2.

37. See, e.g., figs. 2−6, 10−11, 13, 20, 24, 27, 33a, 36a, 37a, 38a, 43, 45.

38. So Le Bonniec (1958) 408−410.

39. On the *primitiae* offered to Ceres, see sec. 2.2.2.

40. See Galinsky (1981) 126−144 and Kleiner (1978) 772−776.

41. Burkert (1985) 245; see also Lincoln (1981) 92.

42. Ernout and Meillet (1959−1960), s.v. *castus*.

43. See Lattimore (1942) 295−296.

44. Livy 10.23.5; Serv. on Verg. *Aen.* 4.166. On the *univirae*, see Lattimore (1942) 296 and Williams (1958) 23.

45. Williams (1958) 24.

46. On Lucretia, see Joshel (1992) 112–130; Joplin (1990) 51–70; Donaldson (1982) 3–20.

47. On the continuing interest in the story, see Donaldson (1982).

48. So Le Bonniec (1958) 411–412.

49. For the orifices of the body as symbolic of boundaries, see Douglas (1970) viii–x, 70.

50. See Chirassi-Colombo (1981) 425.

51. On the Vestal Virgins, see Beard (1980) 12–27.

52. See Dixon (1988) 71–103; Hallet (1984) 211–262.

53. Ernout and Meillet (1959–60), s.v. *materies*.

54. For Aeneas and Venus, see Verg. *Aen.* 1.314–417; 2.588–620. For Romulus and Remus and Rhea Silvia, see Livy 1.3.11, 6.1; Verg. *Aen.* 6.778–788; Plut. *Vit. Rom.* 2–3; Dion. Hal. 1.76.3–84. For the Sabine women, see Livy 1.13.1–4.

55. On Ceres and motherhood, see sec. 2.3.1, with references.

56. On the ancient Italic cult of Ceres and Tellus, see sec. 2.2.1.

57. For these distinctions in various artistic media, see Pollini (1978) 256–285.

58. *RIC* 3:70.356; *BMCRE* Antoninus Pius 395.

59. I have found no evidence for such an association in imperial coinage after Julia Domna, the wife of Septimius Severus.

60. Florence, Mus. Arch. 26: De Angeli (1988) nr. 172. See also Vollenweider (1966) 69, 118, pl. 76.4.

61. See, e.g., for Livia, Riewald (1912) nrs. 57, 58, 76, 305.

62. For the Ceres type, see De Angeli (1988) 907–908; Wrede (1981) 21–27, 213–219; Bieber (1977) 163ff. (1968) *passim*, esp. 3–4 and 14. For the related Herculaneum Woman type, see Bieber (1977) 163–167.

63. Bieber (1977) 164.

64. Paris, Louvre MA 1139; De Angeli (1988) nr. 190.

65. De Angeli (1988) 907–908 associates the practice with Eleusinian cult; Wrede (1981) 112 suggests the interpretation of the Ceres type as "the *sanctitas* and *pietas* of a *mater familias*; Bieber (1977) 165 interprets the Ceres type as representing a "priestess of Demeter."

66. *BMCRE* Claudius 109; De Angeli (1988) nr. 180.

67. *RIC* 1²:126.80; *BMCRE* Claudius 72.

68. *BMC* Alexandria 73, pl. 2.

69. Ephesus: *SEG* 4.515; Aphrodisias: Riewald (1912) nr. 57.

70. Berlin, Staatliche Museen, inv. FG 11096; Vollenweider (1966) pl. 84.2.

71. Vollenweider (1966) 73–74.

72. On private works of art as reflections of imperial ideology, see Veyne (1958–1959) 61–78.

73. See sec. 2.4.

74. On the moral role of the female members of the imperial household, see Beaujeau (1955) 420.

75. On the use of divinities of fecundity and maternity on coins for the purposes of dynastic propaganda, see Beaujeau (1955) 420 and Trillmich (1978) 1–6.

76. Temporini (1978) 44.

77. Beaujeau (1955) 420.

78. Fittschen has noted that the new portait types of Faustina the Younger on coins coincide with the births of her many children. According to Fittschen, the new types celebrated each new assurance of the dynastic succession. See Fittschen (1982) 126.

79. Livia as Mater Augusti: *CIL* 10.7501, 7340; *AE* 1938 no. 83; *IGR* 1.150, 4.144,5; J. Oliver (1965) 179. Agrippina the Younger as Mater Augusti: *BMCRE* Nero 422–427; *SIG* 1(3).809; *JOEAI* 26 (1930) 51–52; as Mater Claudii Neronis Caesar: *BMCRE* Nero 1–3. Domitia Longina as Mater Divi Caesaris: *BMCRE* Domitian 501–503. Faustina the Younger as Mater Caesaris: *AE* 1936 nr. 40; 1937 nr. 24. Julia Domna as Mater Augusti: *CIL* 6.419, 1035; *IRT* 404; *AE* 1934 nr. 35, 1937 nr. 239, 194 nr. 45, 1946 nr. 67, 1948 nr. 111, 1957 nr. 123, 969/70 nr. 699; *RIC* 4(1): 168.562, 208.858, 210.879; as Mater Augusti et Caesaris: *CIL* 8 suppl. 20986ff.; as Mater Augustorum: *CIL* 7.226; *IRT* 37, 394, 402; *AE* 1914 nr. 217, 1967 nr. 571.

80. On the title pater patriae and its significance, see Alföldi (1952) 204ff.; Berlinger (1935) 77ff.; Skard (1933) 42ff. On the title mater patriae, see Temporini (1978) 61–66, with further references.

81. Tac. *Ann.* 1.14.1; Dio Cass. 57.12.4.

82. Cohen (1880–1892) 1 : 165.807.

83. Coin from Romula: Vives y Escudero (1926) 4 : 124.3. Inscription from Anticaria: *CIL* 2.2038.

84. Temporini (1978) 61–62.

85. Faustina the Younger: *CIL* 14.40 (Ostia); *BMCRE* Marcus Aurelius and Commodus 700–705; *BMCRE* Marcus Aurelius and Lucius Verus 929–931, 988†, 1554–1557; cf. also Thierion (1967) 41ff. Julia Domna: *CIL* suppl. 26498; cf. *PIR* 4(2) (1958) 314, s.v. *Iulia*, nr. 663.

86. *Genetrix orbis terrae*: Romanelli (1926) 1929. Mater castrorum et senatus et patriae: *CIL* 6.1035, 14.2255; *AE* 1929 nr. 1, 1934 nr. 35, 1937 nr. 239, 1946 nr. 67, 1948 nr. 111; cf. Benario (1958) 67ff.

6. "Ceres in the Ara Pacis Augustae"

1. On the decorative program of the Ara Pacis, see most recently Kleiner (1992) 90–99.

2. The argument presented in this chapter is given in more detail in Spaeth (1994).

In this article I also discuss the relationship of the Ara Pacis relief to a very similar one from Carthage.

3. For the discovery of the relief, see Jahn (1864) 178–179. For its importance, see Kähler (1954) 84. Kähler argues that the east side of the Ara Pacis, which faced the Via Flaminia, was the primary facade seen by the public; its two panel reliefs are hence extremely significant for the message of the monument. On the restorations to the relief, see Moretti (1948) 232–237 and La Rocca (1983).

4. The identification of the central figure as Tellus seems to have been proposed first in a letter by Cardinal Giovanni Ricci da Montepulciano in February 1569: see Settis (1988) 402–403. This interpretation remains preferable for a number of recent scholars, including Settis (1988) 413–414; Hölscher (1984) 31; and La Rocca (1983). The identification of the figure as Italia (or Tellus Italiae/Saturnia Tellus) was first argued by van Buren (1913) 134–141 and is followed most recently by Canciani (1990) 808–810, nr. 10; Hannestad (1986) 71–74; and Simon (1986) 36. The Venus identification was originally offered by Benndorf (1869) pl. 77, 394, and Kalkmann (1886) 231–260. Galinsky (1966) 223–243 and Booth (1966) 873–879 revived this interpretation, and it has been approved by a number of recent scholars, including Freibergs, Littleton, and Strutynski (1986) 12 and Thornton (1983) 619–628. The Rhea Silvia identification was proposed by Berczelly (1985) 89–149, but has gained no other adherents. The Pax identification was first proposed by Gardthausen (1908) 14–16 and was recently revived by De Grummond (1990) 663–677. Today the most commonly accepted interpretation is that the figure is "polysemantic," that is, it refers to a combination of divinities. For this interpretation, see most recently Kleiner (1992) 96; Galinsky (1992) 457–475; and Zanker (1988) 172–179. For a comprehensive bibliography of the earlier identifications of the central figure of the Ara Pacis relief, see Spaeth (1994) 66–67, nn. 5–10.

5. For a comprehensive bibliography of these earlier identifications of the side figures of the Ara Pacis relief, see Spaeth (1994) 67, nn. 11–20.

6. The arguments generally focus on the identification of the central figure. For criticism of the Tellus and Italia identifications, see Galinsky (1969) 194–203. For criticism of the Venus identification, see Drummond (1972) 218–220. For criticism of the Pax identification, see Galinsky (1992) 458–460 and Spaeth (1994) 67, n. 21. For criticism of the polysemantic interpretation, see De Grummond (1992) 663–664.

7. Although some scholars have recognized the attributes of Ceres in this figure before, they have seen these attributes as secondary to the main identification of the figure. So Galinsky (1969) 238–239, who points out the similarities of this figure to representations of Ceres, only to conclude that the figure is Venus assimilated to Ceres. I argue below that the attributes of the figure point clearly to her primary identification as Ceres.

8. See sec. 1.4 and De Angeli (1988) 893 and 907.

9. Farnell (1896–1909) 3:272. For the type, see, e.g., the Demeter of Knidos: Beschi (1988) nr. 138.

10. The description that follows is drawn from Beschi (1988) 846.

11. The wheat stalks and poppy capsules are clearly visible in a close physical examination of the relief, although they are somewhat difficult to see in photographs of it. They were probably even more visible before the relief had been subjected to both the ravages of time and attempts at cleaning. The plants composing the crown have not been properly identified by a number of scholars who treat the relief. So, for example Berczelly (1985) 116, n. 101, identifies it simply as a "crown of flowers." Simon (1967) 26−27 refers to it as "the wreath of fruit," and specifically denies that it can be a corona spicea: "Neither Ceres appears nor the crown of ears of corn, so beloved a symbol in visual art."

12. See sec. 2.2.2.

13. For Demeter with the corona spicea on Greek coins, see Beschi (1988) nrs. 162−173, 176−186, 188. For Ceres with the corona spicea on Roman coins, see, e.g., figs. 3, 4, 6, 27, 33a, 36a, 37a, 38a, 43. The crown is a common attribute of the goddess; she is portrayed with it in 47 of the 191 representations cited by De Angeli (1988), that is, in c. 25 percent of these representations.

14. The addition of the legend on Greek types may be intended to distinguish her from her daughter, Persephone, who also wears the crown on Greek coins—so Beschi (1988) 881. Proserpina/Libera is infrequently represented in Roman coins, so the distinction between the two provided by the legend was unnecessary.

15. For the corona spicea of Demeter/Ceres in other media, see, e.g., figs. 2, 13, 20, 24. For the crown composed of wheat and poppy capsules, see, e.g., figs. 10 and 45. These latter examples are from the Roman Empire, and involve assimilation of Ceres to a female member of the imperial family. On this assimilation, see sec. 5.4.

16. See sec. 2.2.2 for references.

17. See, e.g., Hom. *Il.* 5.499−502. For the Greek festivals of Demeter connected with grain, see Brumfield (1981).

18. For the epithets, see Beschi (1988) 844.

19. For the wheat stalk crown, see nn. 13 and 15 above. For Ceres holding stalks of wheat or having wheat at her side, see, e.g., figs. 7−8, 11−16, 18−20, 25, 31, 34b, 40b, 41b, 44. Of the 191 representations cited by De Angeli (1988), the goddess is represented with wheat in 125 (c. 65 percent) (either holding wheat, wearing a wheat crown, or with wheat in the background). For Demeter's association with wheat, see n. 13 above; Wolters (1930) 284−301; and Muthmann (1982) 68.

20. Beschi (1988) nrs. 2, 4.

21. Mylonas (1961) 52. For the identification of the poppy capsules on the Ara Pacis as belonging to the *papaver somniferum*, see Seeberg (1969) 9.

22. Gow (1950) 169.

23. On the symbolic significance of the poppy, see Lembach (1970) 162; Hopkinson (1984) 119; Seeberg (1969) 11. On Ceres' association with death, see sec. 3.2.1.

24. See, e.g., fig. 31. See also De Angeli (1988) nrs. 5, 6, 7, 43, 46, 52−55, 97, 162, 174.

25. Cf. also Callim. *Cer.* 44.

26. In the Mediterranean the iris blooms in March–April, the poppy in April–July, and the narcissus in September–October. See Polunin and Huxley (1981) 74 (poppy), 219 (narcissus), 224 (iris).

27. *Hymn. Hom. Cer.* 5–18; Ov. *Fast.* 4.437–442; *Met.* 5.391–395; Claud. *Rapt. Pros.* 2.128–134.

28. See Richardson (1974) 143–144; Beschi (1988) 846; Lembach (1970) 86–88.

29. For references, see Richardson (1974) 141.

30. Copenhagen, Glyptotek Ny Carlsberg, inv. 1716. De Angeli (1988) nr. 8; cf. also nos. 1, 5–7, 9. On this relief, see further sec. 2.2.1.

31. See, e.g., figs. 13, 14, 16b, 17b, 20, 31, 34b, 40b, 41b, 49, 50, 54. Ceres is represented as a seated figure in 48 out of the 191 representations cited by De Angeli (1988), that is, in c. 25 percent of them.

32. For seated representations of Demeter, see Beschi (1988) nrs. 121–157. For Demeter seated upon a rock, see Beschi (1988) nrs. 122, 126, 129, 130, 364.

33. On the Mirthless Stone, see Richardson (1974) 219–221. For an example of Demeter sitting on a rocky throne that appears to be the Mirthless Stone, see I. and A. Raubitschek (1982) 115–117, pl. 15b. For further bibliography on this example, see Beschi (1988) nr. 364. Demeter is identified on this vase by an inscription, now difficult to read.

34. For the ancient sources and modern scholarship on this etymology, see Pease (1955–1958) 1:272; 2:722.

35. Van Buren (1913) 135–136.

36. So Berczelly (1985) 94.

37. See, e.g., figs. 8, 10, 12, 14, 18, 19, 20, 24, 25, 29, 36a, 37a, 42b, 44, 49, 50. Ceres is shown with the veil in 61 of the 191 representations cited by De Angeli (1988), that is, in c. 31 percent of them.

38. Galinsky (1969) 214–215.

39. Rome, Mus. Naz. 112375. See sec. 1.4 and De Angeli (1988) nr. 23. Note that the hairstyle of the Ariccia bust is also similar to that of the Ara Pacis figure: two strands of hair falling onto the shoulders.

40. In another representation of Ceres from a relief dating to the Augustan period, her garment has slipped even further, revealing her right breast. In this relief the goddess is recognizable as Ceres from the wheat that grows next to her. See De Angeli (1988) nr. 1.

41. For Demeter Karpophoros, see Farnell (1896–1909) 3:32, with references, and Muthmann (1982) 71. For Ceres Frugifera see Sen. *Phoen.* 219; Claud. *Rapt. Pros.* 2.138. For this epithet on Roman coins, see De Angeli (1988) nrs. 67, 107. For Ceres as Mater Frugum, see Ov. *Fast.* 1.671; *Met.* 6.118. Cf. also Ceres as *potens frugum*, Ov. *Am.* 3.10.35; and as *genetrix frugum*, Ov. *Met.* 5.490. On this series of epithets, see also sec. 2.2.1.

42. On the association of the pomegranate with both Demeter and Persephone, see Muthmann (1982) 67–77.

43. *Hymn. Hom. Cer.* 370−374, 405−413; Ov. *Met.* 5.535−539.

44. Palermo, Museo Regionale inv. 395.

45. See White (1967) 350.

46. On the problem of the interpretation of this epithet, see White (1967) 350; Zuntz (1971) 100; Hopkinson (1984) 185.

47. On the symbolic significance of the pomegranate, see Muthmann (1982) 77.

48. On Ceres and Liber, see sec. 1.4 and 2.2.2 and Le Bonniec (1958) 297−304.

49. Rossbach (1853) 347−349.

50. Funaioli (1961) 463, no. 16. See Le Bonniec (1958) 114−115.

51. On this role of Demeter/Ceres, see sec. 2.3.1, 3.2.3, and 5.3.2, with references to primary and secondary sources.

52. See Gàbrici (1927) pl. 59.8. Zuntz (1971) 151, pl. 21c, identifies this *kourotrophos* figure as Persephone, due to her apparent youth. An iconographic distinction between Persephone and Demeter, however, is notoriously difficult to make. For another statuette from the same site, showing a more mature female figure holding a child, see Zuntz (1971) 112 and pl. 14b.

53. Syracuse, Museo Nazionale. See Langlotz and Hirmer (1965) pl. 17.

54. Bonfante (1984) 21−24. For the native Italic goddesses associated with Ceres and their connection with motherhood, see sec. 1.1, 2.3.1, and 3.2.3.

55. For the possibility that the two children represent, on another level, Gaius and Lucius Caesar, see sec. 6.4. The two children may also signal a polysemantic reference to Venus as *geminorum mater Amorum* (Ov. *Fast.* 4.1). On the meaning of this phrase, see Wlosok (1975) 514−523.

56. Dietrich (1962) 140.

57. Cf. also Columella *Rust.* 6.praef.7.

58. Ov. *Fast.* 4.403−404; *Am.* 3.10.13−14.

59. Farnell (1896−1909) 3:220, pl. 4a.

60. Muthman (1982) 73−77, with fig. 55 on p. 74. Opposite Demeter on the relief appears another enthroned goddess, holding a flower and a pomegranate, who has been identified as Persephone.

61. The more common offering to Demeter, however, was the pig, which is not depicted in the Ara Pacis relief. Perhaps the reason for this lies in the appearance of this animal in the Aeneas panel opposite the one under discussion.

62. *API* 6.40 and 258. See Bevan (1986) 82.

63. Bevan (1986) 86.

64. So Bevan (1986) 246−247.

65. There is limited evidence for the sacrifice of sheep to Demeter. One of the Dedicatory Epigrams records the sacrifice of a ewe to Demeter (*API* 6.258). Sheep bones have been discovered in Demeter's sanctuary at Cyrene, although pig bones are more common. See Bevan (1986) 246 and 249.

66. For this argument, see Hopkinson (1984) 185, with references.

67. For the connection of the drapery arrangement with Aphrodite/Venus, see Galin-

sky (1969) 214 – 215. For Ge/Tellus' associations with fruits, children, and animals, see Strong (1937) 115 – 118.

68. On Ceres' connections with Venus, see sec. 1.1, 5.2.2, and Spaeth (1994) 77, nn. 93 – 95; on her connections with Tellus, see sec. 1.1, 1.2, and 2.2.1.

69. For a thorough discussion of polysemy in the Augustan Age, see Galinsky (1992) 468 – 475.

70. Galinsky (1969) 203 – 204.

71. For the distinction between the two types, see Ruge (1937) cols. 1533 – 1539.

72. See Spaeth (1994) 67 and nn. 11 – 13. For a refutation of the recent argument that these figures are Horae, see Galinsky (1992) 459 – 460.

73. De Grummond (1990) 669.

74. See, e.g., Simon (1967) 27, pl. 32.1: a skyphos from Taranto with a picture of a figure with *velificatio* labeled Aura (University of Sydney inv. no. 53.30).

75. For the *velificatio* motif, see Rizzo (1939) 141 – 159 and Matz (1952) 725 – 728. Other beings represented with *velificatio* in antiquity include: Nereids, Horae, Maenads, Lycomedids, Niobids, Niobe, Selene, Helios, Caelus, Europa, Dionysus, Ariadne, Poseidon, Amphitrite, and Aphrodite.

76. On the nymphs, see Ruge (1937) 1527 – 1590; Roscher (1884 – 1937), s.v. *Nymphae*, 500 – 567. For cult sites of nymphs during the imperial period, see Toutain (1967) 1 : 380.

77. On the *ketos*, see Shepard (1940) 29 and 94.

78. For the motif in Greek art, see Shepard (1940) 42; for its use in Roman art, see Levi (1971) 101.

79. On the crown, see Schreiber (1896) 94 and De Grummond (1990) 669 – 670.

80. On the nudity of the Nereids, see Herzog-Hauser (1936) col. 2. On their depiction with *velificatio*, see Lattimore (1976) 53.

81. Athens, National Museum, inv. 1737: Lattimore (1976) fig. 19; Karouzou (1968) 173 – 174.

82. Olck (1912) col. 732.

83. So Keller (1887) 291 – 292.

84. Gossen (1923) col. 788.

85. *BMC* Sicily 36 – 37.16 – 18.

86. Rizzo (1939) 150 – 159.

87. Westermark and Jenkins (1980) 59 – 71.

88. For representations of nymphs with urns, see Ruge (1937) cols. 1578 – 1580 and Roscher (1884 – 1937), s.v. *Nymphae*, 455 – 545.

89. For the crane as herald of ploughing and sowing time, see Hes. *Op.* 448 – 450; Ar. *Av.* 710; Theoc. *Id.* 10.31. For the crane as the signal of the coming rains, see Aratus *Phaen.* 1075 – 1081. See also Brumfield (1981) 20 – 23 and Gossen-Stier (1922) col. 1576.

90. For the nymphs and rain, see Roscher (1884 – 1937), s.v. *Nymphae*, 515.

91. Piccaluga (1974) 36 – 77.

92. Oceanids: *Hom. Hym. Dem.* 5; Naiads and Nymphs: Claud. *Rapt. Pros.* 2.55 – 61; Sirens: Ov. *Met.* 5.551 – 555.

93. Piccaluga (1974) 66 – 69.

94. For cultic worship of Demeter and the nymphs, see Theoc. *Id.* 7.147 – 157, schol. Pind. *Ol.* 13.74.

95. The cult sites of Demeter and Persephone were by springs (Pellene, Athens, Patrai, Platea, Andania); rivers (Argos, Triphyliaka, Lidia, Phigaleia, Trapezos in Arcadia); lakes (Kopais, Lerna); swamps (Artela); ritual baths (Lebadeia), and the sea (Attica, Phaleros, Mykalessos in Boeotia). See Piccaluga (1974) 62 – 64. Wells, springhouses, and drains are important elements of the physical plan of the sanctuaries of Demeter at Eleusis, Priene, Pergamum, Selinunte, and Kos. See Muthmann (1968) 37 – 41.

96. Piccaluga (1974) 62 – 65. Demeter's epithets include Hagne, Herkynia, Lusia, and Poteriophoros.

97. Berlin, Staatliche Museen, inv. Sk709. For other representations of Demeter and the nymphs, see Muthmann (1968) 24 – 44. See especially the votive relief from Megalopolis (second half of the fourth century) in the Athens National Museum, nr. 1449, on which the last of the dancing nymphs holds a poppy and wheat stalks: Karouzou (1968) 97, pl. 74.

98. See Roscher (1884 – 1937), s.v. *Nymphae*, 515 – 519 and Ruge (1937) cols. 1548 – 1549.

99. For the nymphs and fruit, see also Ov. *Met.* 9.85 – 88, where the Naiads create the *cornucopiae*.

100. For the nymphs and spring, see Hor. *Carm.* 1.4.5 – 12, 4.7.1 – 6. For the nymphs and flowers, see Prop. 1.20.33 – 38, 4.4.25 – 26; Nic. in Ath. 681D, 683A; Verg. *Ecl.* 2.45 – 50; Ov. *Met.* 14.264 – 267.

101. Drachman (1910) 113.

102. For the nymphs and grain, see also Ov. *Fast.* 5.261 – 272.

103. Drachman (1910) 373. See also Ruge (1937) col. 1569.

104. See Roscher (1889 – 1937), s.v. *Nymphae*, 515 – 519, and Ruge (1937) col. 1549.

105. Dionysus: Ov. *Fast.* 3.769 – 770; *Met.* 3.313 – 315. Hermaphroditus: Ov. *Met.* 4.287 – 288. Jupiter: Ov. *Fast.* 3.443 – 444, 5.111 – 128.

106. For the nymphs as *kourotrophoi*, see Hes. *Theog.* 347; Serv. on Verg. *Ecl.* 10.62. For artistic representations of nymphs as *kourotrophoi*, see Kenner (1981) 36.

107. Aratus *Phaen.* 909 – 912; Cic. *Div.* 1.13; Verg. *G.* 1.356 – 357; Pliny *HN* 18.359.

108. The appearance of the crane inland was generally thought to be a sign of rain: Verg. *G.* 1.374 – 375; Pliny *HN* 18.362.

109. For the flight of water birds from the marsh, see Pliny *HN* 18.362; Verg. *G.* 1.363 – 364. For their sportive play in the waters of lake, marsh, or sea, see Aratus *Phaen.* 942 – 943; Varro of Atax *apud* Serv. on Verg. *G.* 1.375; Verg. *G.* 1.383 – 387; Pliny *HN* 18.363.

110. Cf. also a fragment of the hymn to Demeter by Philico, in that Zeus promises

that if Demeter stops the rain that is destroying all the crops, she and the nymphs will be given a cult at Eleusis. See Gallovotti (1931) 51, n. 95.

111. Piccaluga (1974) 70–76.

112. Bailey (1935) 36–37.

113. For the contrast between the two types of nymphs, see Bailey (1935) 34–36. On the contrast between the native rivers and streams of Italy and the foreign waters of the sea, see also Prop. 3.22.23–29. Propertius identifies Rome by her benevolent rivers and streams, while he describes the waters of the sea as filled with foreign monsters.

114. Juturna: sister of Turnus; her shrine in the Roman Forum, where the Castores appeared after the Battle of Lake Regillus (Ov. *Fast.* 2.585–616; Verg. *Aen.* 12.138–159, 468–499, 783–785, 843–886). Egeria: wife and adviser of Numa; her shrine at the Porta Capenae with the Capenae and at Ariccia (Ov. *Met.* 15.479–551; *Fast.* 3.261–294). Carmentis: mother of Evander; her shrine at the Porta Carmentalis (Ov. *Fast.* 1.466–586; Verg. *Aen.* 8.337–341). Camenae: associated with Canens, daughter of Janus; their grove and spring outside the Porta Capena (Ov. *Met.* 14.320–434; Plut. *Vit. Numa* 13).

115. See sec. 1.1, 1.2, and 2.2.1.

116. See sec. 1.4 and 5.2.

117. See, e.g., Settis (1988) 416–417; Galinsky (1969) 218–237; Galinsky (1992) 468.

118. Cf. Galinsky (1969) 219 and 226, where he divides the Ara Pacis into a Trojan and a Roman half.

119. Cf. Livy 1.4.4–7. For discussion of the Lupercal panel, see Simon (1967) 24–25; Berczelly (1985) 99–114.

120. For the association of Romulus and Remus with the children of the Ceres panel, see Strong (1937) 118; Berczelly (1985) 131–132; De Grummond (1990) 668. For another interpretation of the children, see sec. 6.2.

121. On the Aeneas panel, see Simon (1967) 23–24; Canciani (1986) 391, nr. 165.

122. Verg. *Aen.* 9.77–122; 10.215–257. See sec. 6.3.

123. For the offering of a pig to Demeter in Greek cult, see Bevan (1986) 68–73.

124. On the agricultural rituals, see sec. 2.2. On the funerary rituals, see sec. 3.2.1. On the sacrifice of a pig at the Cerialia, see Ov. *Fast.* 4.414.

125. See, e.g., Moretti (1948) 216; Simon (1967) 24; Hannestad (1986) 74; Zanker (1988) 204. For the recipient as Juno, see Taylor (1925) 309–313; Ryberg (1949) 80; Toynbee (1953) 77.

126. See Zanker (1988) 204.

127. So Weinstock (1960) 57, n. 141. For the annual sacrifice to the Penates at Lavinium, see Macrob. 3.4.11; Serv. on Verg. *Aen.* 2.296, 3.12; Val. Max. 1.6.7.

128. Cf. also Verg. *Aen.* 8.641: "They were joining the peace treaty with the female pig having been slaughtered" (caesa iungebant foedera porca).

129. See sec. 3.3.4.

130. On Augustus' marriage legislation, see Galinsky (1981) 126–144. On the con-

nection of this legislation with the appearance of women and children in the processional panels of the Ara Pacis, see Kleiner (1978) 772–776.

131. See sec. 3.2.3.

132. See sec. 3.2.5.

133. So Weinstock (1960) 57.

134. For Ceres' connection with beginnings, see Cicero *Verr.* 2.5.187. See also sec. 1.5.

135. See sec. 1.3 and 4.4.1.

136. See, for example, the mention by Aulus Gellius in the second century A.D. of the reciprocal invitations (*mutitationes*) issued by patricians and plebeians to members of their own ordo during certain religious festivals (*N.A.* 18.2.11).

137. On the composition of the Roma panel, see Simon (1967) 29–30 and Torelli (1982) 40.

138. The side figures in the two reliefs may also have been contrasted. Since, however, the Roma panel is so fragmentary, this can remain only speculation.

139. Ceres' connection with the countryside arises from her association with agriculture. See sec. 2.2.1 and 3.3.1. For Ceres as a goddess of the countryside, see especially Verg. *G.* 1.1–23; *Ecl.* 5.74–80.

140. On the religious significance of Roma, see Mellor (1975), esp. 201 for the cult of Roma at Rome itself.

141. So Knoche (1952) 338.

142. For this formula, see *Res Gestae* 13; App. *BCiv.* 5.130; Livy 1.19.3; Suet. *Aug.* 22; Sen. *Apocol.* 10. For a discussion of the formula, see Gagé (1936) 70 and Momigliano (1942) 62.

143. See sec. 3.3.4.

144. On the contrast between two aspects of peace, see also Weinstock (1960) 50.

145. I have made use of the emendations discussed by Bowra (1957) 21–28. The poem has been dated variously, from the third century B.C. to the first century A.D. See Bowra, p. 28, on the problem of the date.

146. For a connection between Roma and Ceres, cf. also Tib. 2.5.57–64.

147. See Bonnano (1976) 28 and Pollini (1978) 100.

148. See Bonnano (1976) 28 and Kleiner (1992) 98.

149. See sec. 5.4 and appendix 2.

150. Florence, Mus. Arch. inv. 26. See sec. 1.6 and 5.4.

151. For the identification of the two children in the Ceres panel as Gaius and Lucius Caesar, see Rose (1990) 467; De Grummond (1990) 668; and Kleiner (1992) 98. De Grummond and Kleiner also suggest a possible identification with Tiberius and Drusus, which is less likely since they were already adults at the time of the erection of the Ara Pacis. De Grummond also proposes another connection with the divine twins Castor and Pollux. On the possibility that the children are also meant to be understood as Liber and Libera, the children of Ceres, see sec. 6.2. On their connection with Romulus and Remus, see above in this section.

152. On the problem of the identification of Gaius and Lucius Caesar in the processional frieze, see Rose (1990) 463–467 and Pollini (1987) 21–28.

153. Berlin, Staatliche Museen, inv. FG 11096.

154. Vollenweider (1966) 1 : 73–74, 2: pl. 84.2.

155. Cf. those scholars who argue that these reliefs recall the decoration of a temporary structure erected on the day of the *constitutio* of the altar, e.g.: Toynbee (1953) 72; Simon (1967) 14; Settis (1988) 406. Borbein ([1975] 244–245) views this argument as simplistic.

156. White (1967) 346–347.

157. For Ceres Frugifer and Demeter Karpophoros, see n. 41 above. For Demeter Horephoros, see *Hymn. Hom. Cer.* 54, 192, 492.

158. On this role of Ceres, see sec. 2.2.1.

159. So Zanker (1988) 185.

160. See Jucker (1961) 205.

161. Copenhagen, Glyptotek Ny Carlsberg, inv. 1716. See sec. 2.2.1. De Angeli (1988) nr. 8, pl. 599. See also De Angeli (1988) nrs. 1, 5–7, 9; Jucker (1961) nr. 130.

162. For the association of the garland and floral scroll friezes of the Ara Pacis with the Golden Age, see L'Orange (1962) 9–15; Sauron (1982) 81–101; Zanker (1988) 185; De Grummond (1990) 672; Galinsky (1992) 463–468. For the frequent use of the floral scroll motif in Augustan art, see Zanker (1988) 184–188. On Augustus' proclamation of the return of the Golden Age, see Zanker (1988) 167–172.

163. Galinsky (1992) 464–465.

164. Cf. schol. to German. *Arat.* 96: "Some say that she is Ceres, because she holds the wheat stalks" (Alii dicunt eam esse Cererem, quod spicas teneat). See Berysig (1867) 65, 11.18–19. Cf. also 125, 1.14, 22: "Some say that she is Ceres" (nonnulli eam aiunt esse Cererem).

165. For Virgo's association with the Golden Age, see, e.g., Hannell (1960) 118–119; De Grummond (1990) 673.

166. For this interpretation, see Breiter (1908) 2 : 129. Cf. also German. *Arat.* 103–104 and Verg. *Ecl.* 4.6.

167. Other scholars have also seen a connection between the goddess of the Ara Pacis relief and Virgo, although they have not recognized the former as Ceres. See Hannell (1960) 118–119; Simon (1967) 29; De Grummond (1990) 673.

168. Buchner (1982). On the problem of the relationship of the Ara Pacis to the Horologium, see most recently Schütz (1990) 449–450.

169. On Augustus' interest in astrology, see also Bowersock (1990) 385–387. On Manilius' poem, cf. Bowersock (1990) 393: "Even the long poem of Manilius, all of which was composed when Augustus was still alive, can now be seen not as a bizarre by-product of the early empire but as an integral and authentic reflection of later Augustan culture."

170. On the liminal significance of agricultural rites and their connection with Ceres, see sec. 3.3.1.

171. On the dating of Book 4 of Horace's Odes to 13 B.C. and on the connections between this book and the *constitutio* of the Ara Pacis, see Putnam (1986) 327–328.

172. On the theme of the return of Augustus and its revitalization of the land, see Putnam (1986) 30. See also the discussion of Vell. Pat. 2.89.4 by Woodman (1983) 255. Woodman notes that agriculture as a symbol of peace under an ideal ruler is an ancient topos, which can be traced back to Homer (*Od.* 19.109–114). I would point out, however, that the idea of *return*, both of fertility and of the person who brings it, is especially significant in the context under discussion.

173. On the connection between peace and Ceres, see sec. 3.3.4.

REFERENCES

Alföldi, A. 1979. "Redeunt Saturnia regna, VII: Frugifer-Triptolemos im ptolemäisch-römischen Herrscherkult." *Chiron* 9:553–607.

———. 1963. *Early Rome and the Latins.* Ann Arbor.

———. 1956. "The Main Aspects of Political Propaganda on the Coinage of the Roman Republic." In *Essays in Roman Coinage Presented to Harold Mattingly,* pp. 63–95. Ed. R. Carson and C. Sutherland. Oxford.

———. 1952. "Die Geburt der kaiserlichen Bildsymbolik." *MusHelv* 9:204–243.

Altheim, F. 1938. *A History of Roman Religion.* Trans. H. Mattingly. New York.

———. 1931. *Terra Mater: Untersuchungen zur altitalischer Religionsgeschichte.* Religionsgeschichte Versuche und Vorarbeiten 22.2.

Antaya, R. 1980. "The Etymology of *Pomerium.*" *AJP* 101:184–189.

Astin, A. 1967. *Scipio Aemilianus.* Oxford.

Aurigemma, S. 1909. "La protezione speciale della Gran Madre Idea per la nobilità Romana e le leggende dell'origine troiana di Roma." *BullComm* 37:31–65.

Babelon, E. 1885–1886. *Monnaies de la république romaine.* Paris and London.

Badian, E. 1972. "Tiberius Gracchus and the Beginning of the Roman Revolution." *ANRW* 1.1:668–731.

Bailey, C. 1935. *Religion in Virgil.* Oxford.

Banti, L. 1943. "Il culto del cosidetto 'tempio di Apollo' a Veii e il problema delle triadi etrusco-italiche." *StEtr* 17:187–224.

Barbieri, G. 1961. "Nuove iscrizioni di Marsala." *Kokalos* 7:15–52.

Basile, M. 1978. "Analisi e valore della tradizione sulla rogato Cassia agraria del 486 B.C." In *Sesta miscellanea greca e romana,* pp. 277–298. Rome.

Bayet, J. 1951. "Les Cerialia, altération d'un culte latin par le mythe grec." *RBPhil* 29:5–32, 341–366.

———. 1950*a*. "La déterioration des Cerialia par la mythe grec." *CRAI*: 297–302.

———. 1950*b*. "Les Feriae Sementivae et les indigitations dans le culte de Cérès et de Tellus." *RHR* 137:172–206.

———. 1926. *Les origines de l'Hercule romain.* Paris.

Beard, M. 1980. "The Sexual Status of Vestal Virgins." *JRS* 70:12–27.

Beaujeu, J. 1955. *La religion romain à l'apogee de l'empire. I: La politique religieuse des Antonins (96–102).* Paris.

Beloch, F. 1926. *Römische Geschichte bis zum Begin der punischen Kriege.* Berlin.

Beloch, J. 1890. *Campanien: Geschichte und Topographie des antiken Neapel und seiner Umgebung.* Breslau.

Benario, H. 1958. "Julia Domna *mater castrorum et senatus et patriae.*" *Phoenix* 12:67–70.

Benndorf, O. ed. 1868–1883. *Griechische und Sizilische Vasenbilder.* Berlin.

Berczelly, L. 1985. "Ilia and the Divine Twins." *ActaAArtHist* 5:89–149.

Berger, P. 1985. *The Goddess Obscured: Transformation of the Grain Protectress from Goddess to Saint.* Boston.

Berlinger, L. 1935. *Beiträge zur inoffiziellen Titulatur der römischen Kaiser.* Diss. Breslau University.

Berysig, A., ed. 1867. *Germanici Caesaris Aratea cum scholis.* Berlin.

Beschi, L. 1988. "Demeter." *LIMC* 4.1:844–892.

Bevan, E. 1986. *Representations of Animals in Sanctuaries of Artemis and Other Olympian Deities.* Oxford.

Bianchi, U. 1978. "Gli dei delle stirpi italiche." In *Popoli e civiltà dell' Italia antica.* Vol. 7:197–236. Ed. M. Palottino. 7 vols. Rome.

Bieber, M. 1977. *Ancient Copies: Contributions to the History of Greek and Roman Art.* New York.

———. 1968. "The Statue of Cybele in the Getty Museum." *Getty Museum Publications* 3.

Bloch, R. 1963. *Les prodiges dans l'antiquité classique.* Paris.

———. 1954. "Une lex sacra de Lavinium et les origines de la triade agraire de l'Aventine." *CRAI*: 203–212.

Blumenthal, V. 1952. "Pomerium." *RE* 21^2, cols. 1867–1876.

Bolen, J. 1985. *Goddesses in Everywoman: A New Psychology of Women.* New York.

Bonfante, L. 1984. "Dedicated Mothers." *Visible Religion* 3:21–24.

Bonnano, A. 1976. *Roman Relief Portraiture to Septimius Severus.* BAR Supplementary Series 6.

Booth, A. 1966. "Venus on the Ara Pacis." *Latomus* 25:873–879.

Borbein, A. 1975. "Die Ara Pacis Augustae. Geschichtliche Wirklichkeit und Programm." *JdI* 90:242–266.

Borda, M. 1951. "Flava Ceres." In *Studies Presented to David Moore Robinson*. Vol. 1:765–770. St. Louis.

Bouché-Leclercq, A. 1882. *Histoire de la divination dans l'antiquité*. Paris.

Bowersock, G. 1990. "The Pontificate of Augustus." In *Between Republic and Empire: Interpretations of Augustus and his Principate*, pp. 380–394. Ed. K. Raaflaub and M. Toher. Berkeley.

Bowra, C. 1957. "Melinno's Hymn to Rome." *JRS* 47:21–28.

Breglia, L. 1968. *Roman Imperial Coins: Their Art and Techniques*. Trans. P. Green. New York and Washington.

Breiter, T. 1908. *M. Manilii Astronomica*. 2 vols. Leipzig.

Bromberg, B. 1940. "Temple Banking in Rome." *Econ. Hist. Rev.* 10:128–131.

Broughton, R. 1952. *The Magistrates of the Roman Republic*. 2 vols. New York.

Bruhl, A. 1953. *Liber Pater: Origine et expansion du culte dionysiaque à Rome et dans le monde Romaine*. BEFAR 175. Paris.

Brumfield, A. 1981. *The Attic Festivals of Demeter and Their Relation to the Agricultural Year*. New York.

Buchner, E. 1982. *Die Sonnenuhr des Augustus*. Nachdruck aus *RM* 1976/1980.

Burkert, W. 1985. *Greek Religion: Archaic and Classical*. Trans. J. Raffan. Oxford.

Caldarelli, R. 1982–1984. "A proposito di un teonimo della Tabula Agnonensis." *QLF*:35–42.

Canciani, F. 1990. "Italia." *LIMC* 5.1:806–810.

———. 1986. "Aineias." *LIMC* 1.1:381–396.

Carcopino, J. 1942. "Les cultes des Cereres et les Numides." *Aspects mystiques de la Rome paienne*, pp. 13–37. Paris.

Chapple, E., and C. Coon. 1942. *Principles of Anthropology*. New York.

Charbonneaux, J. 1963. *La sculpture grecque et romaine au Musée du Louvre*. Paris.

Charles-Picard, G. 1954. *Les religions de l'Afrique antique*. Paris.

Charlesworth, M. P. 1939. "The Refusal of Divine Honors." *BSR* 15:1–10.

Chirassi-Colombo, I. 1984. "Cerere." *Encicloppedia Virgiliana*. Vol. 1:746–748. Rome.

———. 1981. "Funzioni politiche ed implicazioni culturali nell'ideologia religiosa di Ceres nell'impero romano." *ANRW* 2.17.1:403–428.

————. 1979. "Paides e Gynaikes: Note per una tassonomia del comportamento rituale nella cultura attica." *Quaderni urbinati di cultura classica* n.s. 1:25–58.

————. 1975. "I doni di Demeter: Mito e ideologia nella Grecia arcaica." In *Studi Triestini di antichità in onore di L. Stella*, pp. 183–213. Trieste.

Coarelli, F. 1988. *Il Foro Boario, dalle origini alle fine della repubblica*. Rome.

————. 1983. *Il Foro Romano: Periodo arcaico*. Rome.

Cohen, H. 1880–1892. *Description des monnaies frappés sous l'empire Romain*. 2nd ed. Paris and London.

Colin, J. 1954. "Les sénateurs et la Mère des dieux aux Megalensia: Lucrece 4.79." *Athenaeum* 32:346–355.

Colonna, G. 1953. "Sul sacerdozio peligno de Cerere e Venere." *ArchCl* 8: 216–217.

Consigliere, L. 1978. "*Slogans Monetarii e Poesia Augustea*." Università di Genova, Facoltà di Lettere, Pubblicazioni dell'Istituto di Filologia Classica e Medievale 56.

Corbett, P. 1930. *The Roman Law of Marriage*. Oxford.

Crawford, M. 1974. *Roman Republican Coinage*. 2 vols. Cambridge.

Curtius, L. 1934. "Ikonographische Beiträge zum Porträt der römischen Republik und der Julisch-Claudischen Familie. VI: Neue Erklärung des grossen Pariser Cameo mit der Familie des Tiberius." *RM* 49: 119–156.

De Angeli, S. 1988. "Demeter/Ceres." *LIMC* 4.1:893–908.

De Grummond, N. 1990. "Pax and the Horae on the Ara Pacis Augustae." *AJA* 94:669–670.

Devoto, G. 1967. "Il panteon di Agnone," *StEtr* 35:179–197.

Dietrich, B. 1962. "Demeter, Erinys, Artemis." *Hermes* 90: 129–148.

Dixon, S. 1988. *The Roman Mother*. London and Sydney.

Donaldson, I. 1982. *The Rapes of Lucretia: A Myth and Its Transformations*. Oxford.

Douglas, M. 1970. *Natural Symbols: Explorations in Cosmology*. New York.

Downing, C. 1984. *The Goddess: Mythological Images of the Feminine*. New York.

Drachman, A., ed. 1910. *Scholia Vetera in Pindari Carmina*. Leipzig.

Drummond, A. 1972. Review of K. Galinsky, *Aeneas, Sicily, and Rome. JRS* 62:218–220.

Dumézil, G. 1966. *Archaic Roman Religion*. Trans. P. Krapp. Chicago.

REFERENCES

Earl, D. C. 1963. *Tiberius Gracchus: A Study in Politics*. Coll. Latomus 66. Brussels.

Edlund, I. E. M. 1987. *The Gods and the Place: Location and Function of Sanctuaries in the Countryside of Etruria and Magna Graecia (700–400 B.C.)*. SkrRom 4.43.

Eichler, F., and E. Kris. 1927. *Die Kameen im Kunsthistorisches Museum*. Vienna.

Eisler, R. 1987. *The Chalice and the Blade: Our History, Our Future*. San Francisco.

Ellul, J. 1973. *Propaganda: The Formation of Men's Attitudes*. New York.

Erhard, P. 1978. "A Portrait of Antonia Minor in the Fogg Art Museum and Its Iconographical Tradition." *AJA* 82: 193–212.

Ernout, A., and A. Meillet. 1959–1960. *Dictionnaire étymologique de la langue latine*. 4th ed. Paris.

Evans, J. 1992. *The Art of Persuasion: Political Propaganda from Aeneas to Brutus*. Ann Arbor.

Farnell, L. 1896–1909. *The Cults of the Greek States*. 5 vols. Oxford.

Fehrle, E. 1910. *Die kultische Keuschheit im Altertum*. Religionsgeschichtliche Versuche und Vorarbeiten 6.

Fitschen, K. 1982. *Die Bildnistypen der Faustina Minor und die Fecunditas Augustae*. Abhandlungen der Akademie der Wissenschaften in Göttingen, Philol.-Histor. Klasse. Dritte Folge.

Foerster, R. 1874. *Der Raub und Rückkehr der Persephone*. Stuttgart.

Frazer, J. 1940. *The Golden Bough: A Study in Magic and Religion*. 3rd ed. 12 vols. New York.

———, ed. 1929. *The Fasti of Ovid*. 5 vols. London.

Freibergs, G., C. Littleton, and V. Strutynski. 1986. "Indo-European Tripartition and the Ara Pacis Augustae: An Excursus in Ideological Archaeology." *Numen* 33: 3–32.

Frymer-Kensky, T. 1992. *In the Wake of the Goddess: Women, Culture, and the Biblical Transformation of Pagan Myth*. New York.

Funiaoli, G., ed. 1961. *Grammaticae romanae fragmenta*. Stuttgart.

Furtwängler, A. 1900. *Die Antiken Gemmen: Geschichte der Steinschneidekunst im klassischen Altertum*. 3 vols. Leipzig and Berlin.

Gàbrici, E. 1927. "Il santuario della Malophoros à Selinunte." *MonAnt* 32.

Gadon, E. 1989. *The Once and Future Goddess*. New York.

Gagé, J. 1963. *Matronalia: Essai sur les dévotions et les organizations cultuelles des femmes dans l'ancienne Rome*. Brussels.

Galinsky, G. K. 1992. "Venus, Polysemy, and the Ara Pacis Augustae." *AJA* 96:457–475.

———. 1981. "Augustus' Legislation on Morals and Marriage." *Philologus* 125:126–144.

———. 1969. *Aeneas, Sicily, and Rome*. Princeton.

———. 1966. "Venus on a Relief of the Ara Pacis Augustae." *AJA* 70: 223–243.

Gallini, C. 1970. *Protesta ed integrazione in Roma antica*. Bari.

Gallovotti, G. 1931. "Inno a Demeter di Filico." *StIt* 9:37–60.

Gantz, T. 1971. "Divine Triads on an Archaic Etruscan Frieze Plaque from Poggio Civitate (Murlo)." *StEtr* 39:1–22, pls. 1–12.

Gardthausen, V. 1908. *Der Altar des Kaiserfriedens: Ara Pacis Augustae*. Leipzig.

Gascou, J. 1987. "Les sacerdotes Cererum de Carthage." *AntAfr* 23:95–128.

Gesztelyi, T. 1972. "The Cult of Tellus-Terra Mater in North Africa." *Acta classica Universitatis Scientarum Debreceniensis* 8:75–84.

Giovennale, G. B. 1927. *La basilica di S. Maria in Cosmedin*. Rome.

Gossen. 1923. "Schwan." *RE* 2², cols. 782–792.

Gossen-Steier. 1922. "Kranich." *RE* 11, cols. 1571–1578.

Gow, A., ed. 1950. *Theocritus*. Cambridge.

Graillot, H. 1912. *Le culte de Cybèle, mère des dieux à Rome et dans l'empire Romain*. Paris.

Grether, G. 1946. "Livia and the Roman Imperial Cult." *AJP* 67:222–252.

Groag. 1932. "Memmius." *RE* 15, cols. 602–626.

Gross, W. 1962. *Julia Augusta: Untersuchungen zur Grundlegung einer Livia-Ikonographie*. Abhandlungen der Akademie der Wissenschaften in Göttingen Philol.-Histor. Klasse 3.52.

Grueber, H. 1910. *Coins of the Roman Republic in the British Museum*. London.

Gundel, H. 1958. "Vibius 16." *RE* 16², cols. 1953–1965.

Hallet, J. 1984. *Fathers and Daughters in Roman Society: Women and the Elite Family*. Princeton.

Hanell, K. 1960. "Das Opfer des Augustus an der Ara Pacis." *OpRom* 2: 33–123.

Hannestad, N. 1986. *Roman Art and Imperial Policy*. Aarhus.

Hausmann, U. 1966. "Die Flavier." *Das römische Herrscherbild* 2.1. Berlin.

Helbig, W. 1963. *Führer durch die öffentlichen Sammlungen klassischer Altertümer in Rom*. 4 vols. Tübingen.

Hellebrand, W. 1935. "Multa." *RE* supp. 6, cols. 542–555.

Herzog-Hauser, G. 1936. "Nereiden." *RE* 17.1, cols. 1–23.

Heurgon, J. 1942. *Recherches sur l'histoire, la religion et la civilization de Capoue préromaine, des origines à la deuxieme guerre punique.* Paris.

Hoffman, M. 1934. *Rom und die griechische Welt in 4. Jahrhundert. Philologus* supp. 27.1.

Hohl, E. 1975. "Kaiser Commodus und Herodian." In *Studies in Cassius Dio and Herodian*, pp. 1–46. Ed. H. A. Andersen and E. Hohl. New York.

Holscher, T. 1984. *Staatsdenkmal und Publicum vom Untergang der Republik bis zur Festigung des Kaisertums in Rom.* Xenia 9. Konstanz.

Holst-Warhaft, G. 1992. *Dangerous Voices: Women's Laments and Greek Literature.* London and New York.

Hoorn, T. van. *Choes and Anthesteria.* Leiden 1951.

Hopkinson, N., ed. 1984. *Callimachus: Hymn to Demeter.* Cambridge.

Imhoof-Blumer, F. 1897. *Lydische Stadtmünzen: Neue Untersuchungen.* Genf and Leipzig.

———. 1890. *Griechische Münzen.* Abhandlungen der Philos.-Philol. Klasse der Kgl. Bayr. Akademie der Wissenschaften 18.

Jahn, O. 1869. "Die cista mystica." *Hermes* 3 : 317–334.

———. 1864. "Elementargottheiten auf einem florentinischen und kartagischen Reliefs." *AZ* : 177–185.

Joplin, P. 1990. "Ritual Work on Human Flesh: Livy's Lucretia and the Rape of the Body Politic." *Helios* 17.1 : 51–70.

Joshel, S. 1992. "The Body Female and the Body Politic: Livy's Lucretia and Verginia." In *Pornography and Representation in Greece and Rome*, pp. 112–130. Ed. A. Richlin. New York and Oxford.

Jucker, H. 1961. *Das Bildnis im Blätterkelch.* Istituto Svizzero di Roma. Bibliotheca Helvetica Romana 3.

Kähler, H. 1954. "Die Ara Pacis und die augusteische Friedensidee." *JdI* 69 : 67–100.

Kaibel, G. 1878. *Epigrammata graeca ex lapidibus conlecta.* Berlin.

Kalkmann, A. 1886. "Aphrodite auf dem Schwan." *JdI* 1 : 231–260.

Kanta, K. 1979. *Eleusis: Myth, Mysteries, History, Museum.* Athens.

Karouzou, S. 1968. *National Archaeological Museum: Collection of Sculpture. A Catalogue.* Athens.

Keller, O. 1887. *Thiere der klassischen Altertums in kulturgeschichtlicher Beziehung.* Innsbruck.

Kenner, H. 1981. "Das Tellusrelief der Ara Pacis." *ÖJh* 53 : 31–42.

Kleiner, D. 1992. *Roman Sculpture*. New Haven and London.

――――. 1978. "The Great Friezes of the Ara Pacis Augustae: Greek Sources, Roman Derivatives, and Augustan Social Policy." *MEFR* 90:753–785.

Knoche, U. 1952. "Die augusteische Ausprägung der Dea Roma." *Gymnasium* 59:326–349.

Koch, C. 1937. *Der römische Iuppiter*. Frankfurt Studien 14.

Köves-Zulauf, T. 1986. "Die Verehrung von Tieren in der griechisch-römischen Antike: Die römische Fuchshetze." In *Zum Problem der Deutung frühmittelalterlicher Bildinhalte*, pp. 57–65. Ed. H. Roth. Sigmaringen.

Kruse, H. 1968/1975. *Römische weibliche Gewandstatuen des 2. Jahrhunderts n. Chr.* Diss. Göttingen University.

Lambrechts, P. 1951. "Cybèle, divinité étrangère ou nationale?" *Bull. Soc. Roy. Bel. Anthro. et Prehist.* 62:44–60.

Langlotz, E. and Hirmer, M. 1965. *The Art of Magna Graecia*. London.

La Rocca, E. 1983. *Ara Pacis Augustae: In occasione del restauro della fronte orientale*. Rome.

Latte, K. 1960. *Römische Religionsgeschichte*. Munich.

――――. 1934–1936. "Zwei Excurse zum römischen Staatsrecht." In *NGG Philol.-Hist. kl. Altertums-wissenschaft*, pp. 73–77.

――――. 1920. *Heiliges Recht: Untersuchungen zur Geschichte der sakralen Rechtsformen in Griechenland*. Tübingen.

Lattimore, R. 1942. *Themes in Greek and Latin Epitaphs*. Urbana.

Lattimore, S. 1976. *The Marine Thiasos in Greek Sculpture*. Monumenta Archaeologica 3.

Le Bonniec, H. 1958. *Le culte de Cérès a Rome des origines à la fin de la République*. Études et Commentaires 27. Paris.

Lembach, K. 1970. *Die Pflanzen bei Theocrit*. Heidelberg.

Lengele, J. 1937. "Tribunus." *RE* 6², cols. 2432–2492.

Lenz, F. 1932. "Ceresfest, eine Studie zu Ovid Amores 3.10." *StIt* n.s. 10:299–313.

Levi, D. 1971. *Antioch Mosaic Pavements*. 2 vols. Rome.

Lincoln, B. 1981. *Emerging from the Chrysalis: Studies in Rituals of Women's Initiation*. Cambridge, Mass.

Lintott, A. 1970. "The Tradition of Violence in the Annals." *Historia* 19:8–22.

L'Orange, H. 1962. "Ara Pacis Augustae: La zona Floreale." *ActaInstRomNor* 1:9–15.

References

MacBain, B. 1982. *Prodigy and Expiation: A Study in Religion and Politics in Republican Rome*. Coll. Latomus 177. Brussels.

Mattingly, H., and E. Sydenham. 1923–1981. *Roman Imperial Coinage*. 9 vols. London.

Matz, F. 1952. "Der Gott auf dem Elephantwagen." *Akademie der Wissenschaft und der Literatur in Mainz* Abh. 10:719–763.

Mau, A. 1899. "Cista." *RE* 3, cols. 2591–2606.

Medicus, D. 1964. "Aedilis." *Der kleine Pauly* 1, cols. 83–84.

Mellor, R. 1975. θεὰ Ῥώμη: *The Worship of the Goddess Roma in the Greek World*. Hypomnemata 42. Göttingen.

Merlin, A. 1906. *L'Aventin dans l'antiquité*. BEFAR 97. Paris.

Michels, A. K. 1967. *The Calendar of the Roman Republic*. Princeton.

Mitchell, R. 1990. *Patricians and Plebeians: The Origin of the Roman State*. Ithaca and London.

Möbius, H. 1979. "Zweck und Typen römischer Kaiserkameen." *ANRW* 2.12.3:32–88.

Momigliano, A. 1942. "Terra marique." *JRS* 32:53–64.

Mommsen, T. 1899. *Römisches Strafrecht*. Leipzig.

Morretti, G. 1948. *Ara Pacis Augustae*. Rome.

Munro, H. ed. *T. Lucreti Cari: De rerum natura*. 2 vols. London.

Münzer, F. 1899*a*. "Claudius 435." *RE* 3, col. 2899.

———. 1899*b*. "Cassius." *RE* 3, cols. 1678–1753.

Muthmann, F. 1982. *Der Granatapfel: Symbol des Lebens in der alten Welt*. Bern.

———. 1968. "Weihrelief an Acheloos und Naturgottheiten." *AntK* 11:24–44.

Mylonas, G. 1961. *Eleusis and the Eleusinian Mysteries*. Princeton.

Nash, E. 1968. *Pictorial Dictionary of Ancient Rome*. Rev. ed. 2 Vols. London.

Nisbet, R. G., ed. 1979. *Marci Tulli Ciceronis de doma sua ad pontifices oratio*. New York.

Noailles, P. 1948. "Les tabous du mariage dans le droit primitif de Romains." In *Fas et Jus*, pp. 1–27. Paris.

Oberleitner, W. 1985. *Geschnittene Steine: Die Prunkkameen der Wiener Antikensammlung*. Vienna.

Ogilvie, R. 1965. *A Commentary on Livy, Books 1–5*. Oxford.

Olck. 1912. "Gans." *RE* 7, cols. 709–735.

Oliver, J. 1965. "Livia as Artemis Boulaia at Athens." *CP* 60:179.

Oltramere, A. 1932. "Sp. Cassius et les origines de la démocratie moderne." *Bull. de la Soc. d' Histoire et Arch. de Genève* 5:259–276.

Pais, E. 1923. *Italia Antica.* Bologna.

Pallottino, M. 1991. "The Religion of the Sabellians and Umbrians, Italics of Central and Southern Italy." In *Roman and European Mythologies,* pp. 46–49. Ed. Y. Bonnefoy. Trans. W. Donniger. Chicago and London.

Paribeni, R. 1930. "Ariccia: Rinvenimento di una stipe votiva." *NSc* 55: 370–380.

Parker, R. 1983. *Miasma: Pollution and Purification in Early Greek Religion.* Oxford.

Pease, A. ed. 1955–1958. *Marcus Tullius Cicero: De Natura Deorum.* 2 vols. Cambridge, Mass.

Pensabene, P. 1980. "La zona sud-occidentale del Palatino." *QuadAEI* 4: 65–81.

———. 1979. "Auguratiorium e il tempio della Magna Mater." *QuadAEI* 3: 67–74.

———. 1978. "Roma. Saggi di scavo sul tempio della Magna Mater del Palatino." *QuadAEI* 1:67–71.

Pestalozza, A. 1897. *I caratteri indigeni di Cerere.* Milan.

Peterson, R. 1919. *The Cults of Campania.* 2 vols. Rome.

Pfiffig, A. 1975. *Religio Etrusca.* Graz, Austria.

Phillips, K. 1993. *In the Hills of Tuscany: Recent Excavations at the Etruscan Site of Poggio Civitate (Murlo, Siena).* Philadelphia.

Piccaluga, G. 1974. "Il corteggio di Persephone." *Minutal: Saggi di storia delle religioni.* Rome, pp. 37–77.

Piganiol, A. 1923. *Recherches sur les jeux romains: Notes d'archéologie et d' histoire religieuse.* Strasbourg.

Platner, S., and T. Ashby. 1929. *A Topographical Dictionary of Ancient Rome.* London.

Pocetti, P. 1985. "Considerazioni sulle espressioni peligne per 'sacerdotessa di Cerere.' " *Studi e Saggi Linguistici* 25:51–66.

———. 1982. "Ancora sull'interpetazione di peligno An(a)c(e)ta alla luce di una nuova attestazione." *Studi e Saggi Linguistici* 22:171–182."

———. 1980. "Un nuova iscrizione peligna e il problema di An(a)c(e)ta." *RendLinc* 35:509–516.

Polaschek, K. 1973. *Studien zur Ikonographie der Antonia Minor.* Rome.

Pollini, J. 1990. "Man or God: Divine Assimilation and Imitation in the Late Republic and Early Principate." *Between Republic and Empire: Interpretations of Augustus and His Principate.* Ed. K. Raaflaub and M. Tober. Berkeley, Los Angeles, and Oxford, pp. 334–363.

———. 1987. *The Portraiture of Gaius and Lucius Caesar.* New York.

REFERENCES

————. 1978. *Studies in Augustan "Historical" Reliefs.* Diss. Univ. of California at Berkeley.

Polunin, O., and A. Huxley. 1981. *Flowers of the Mediterranean.* London.

Pomeroy, S. 1975. *Goddesses, Whores, Wives, and Slaves: Women in Classical Antiquity.* New York.

Poultney, J. 1959. *The Bronze Tablets of Iguvium.* Philological Monographs of the American Philological Association 18.

Pouthier, P. 1981. *Ops et la conception divine de l'abondance dans la religion romaine jusqu' à la mort d'Auguste.* BEFAR 242. Rome.

Preston, J. 1982. "Conclusion: New Perspectives in Mother Worship," In *Mother Worship: Theme and Variations*, pp. 325–343. Ed. J. Preston. Chapel Hill.

Price, S. 1984. *Rituals and Power: The Roman Imperial Cult in Asia Minor.* Cambridge.

Price, T. 1978. *Kourotrophos: Cult and Representation of the Greek Nursing Deities.* Leiden.

Pugliese-Caratelli, G. 1981. "Cereres." *PP* 36:367–382.

Putnam, M. 1986. *Artifices of Eternity: Horace's Fourth Book of Odes.* Ithaca, N.Y.

Quinn-Schofield, W. K. 1967. "Observations upon the Ludi Plebei." *Latomus* 26:677–685.

Radke, G. 1987. *Zur Entwicklung der Gottesvorstellung und der Gottesverehrung in Rom.* Impulse der Forschung 50. Darmstadt.

————. 1965. *Die Götter Altitaliens.* Münster.

Raubitschek, I. and A. 1982. "The Mission of Triptolemus." In *Studies in Athenian Architecture, Sculpture, and Topography Presented to Homer Thompson*, pp. 109–117. Hesperia Supplement 20. Princeton.

Reinach, S. 1905–1923. *Cultes, Mythes, et Religions.* 5 vols. Paris.

Richardson, L. 1992. *A New Topographical Dictionary of Ancient Rome.* Baltimore and London.

Richardson, N. 1974. *The Homeric Hymn to Demeter.* Oxford.

Richter, G. 1971. *Engraved Gems of the Romans.* London.

Rickman, G. 1980. *The Corn Supply of Ancient Rome.* Oxford.

Ridley, R. 1968. "Notes on the Establishment of the Tribunate of the Plebs." *Latomus* 27:535–554.

Riewald, P. 1912. *De imperatorum Romanorum cum certis dis et comparatione et aequatione.*

Righetti, R. 1955. *Gemme e camei delle collezioni communali.* Rome.

Rizzo, G. 1939. "Aurae velificantes." *BullGov* 67:141–168.

REFERENCES

Robert, C. 1969. *Die Antiken Sarkophag-Reliefs*. Vol. 3.3. Rome.

Romanelli, P. 1926. *Leptis Magna*. Africa Italiana Monografie 1. Rome.

Roscher, W., ed. 1884–1937. *Ausführliches Lexikon der griechischen und römischen Mythologie*. Leipzig.

Rose, C. 1990. " 'Princes' and Barbarians on the Ara Pacis." *AJA* 94:453–467.

Rossbach, A. 1853. *Untersuchungen über die römische Ehe*. Stuttgart.

Ruge, W. 1937. "Nymphai." *RE* 17.2, cols. 1527–1599.

Ryberg, I. 1949. "The Procession of the Ara Pacis." *MAAR* 19:79–101.

Rykwert, J. 1976. *The Idea of a Town: The Anthropology of Urban Form in Rome, Italy, and the Ancient World*. Princeton.

Sabatucci, D. 1972. "La 'trascendenza' di Ceres." In *Ex orbe religionum. Studia G. Widengren*, pp. 312–319. Numen Suppl. 21–22. Leiden.

———. 1957. "Di alcuni sacrifici romani alla luce del mito di Kore." *Studi e materiali di storia delle religioni* 28:53–66.

———. 1954. "L'edilità romana: Magistratura e sacerdozio," *MemLinc* 8.6.3: 255–334.

———. 1953–1954. "Patrizi e plebei nello svilluppo della religione romana." *SMSR* 24–25:76–92.

Salmon, E. T. 1967. *Samnium and the Samnites*. Cambridge.

Salvadore, M. 1978. "Varro *De Vita Populi Romani* fr. 4 Rip." *RivFil* 106: 287–290.

Sauron, G. 1982. "Le message symbolique des rinceaux de l'Ara Pacis Augusta." *CRAI*: 81–101.

Schilling, R. 1991a. "Ceres." In *Roman and European Mythologies*, pp. 121–123. Ed. Y. Bonnefoy. Trans. W. Donniger. Chicago and London.

———. 1991b. "Roman Festivals." In *Roman and European Mythologies*, pp. 92–93. Ed. Y. Bonnefoy. Trans. W. Donniger. Chicago and London.

———. 1991c. "Roman Gods." In *Roman and European Mythologies*, pp. 68–77. Ed. Y. Bonnefoy. Trans. W. Donniger. Chicago and London.

———. 1949. "Le temple de Vénus Capitoline et la tradition pomériale." *RPhil*: 27–35.

Schlesinger, E. 1933. *Die griechische Asylie*. Göttingen.

Schmidt, E. 1910. *Kultüberträgungen*. Giessen.

Schreiber, T. 1896. "Die hellenistische Reliefbilder und die Augusteische Zeit." *JdI* 11:89.

Schütz, M. 1990. "Zur Sonnenuhr des Augustus auf dem Marsfeld." *Gymnasium* 97:432–457.

Scott, K. 1936. *The Imperial Cult under the Flavians*. Stuttgart.

REFERENCES

Scullard, H. H. 1981. *Festivals and Ceremonies of the Roman Republic.* London.

Seeberg, A. 1969. "Poppies, not Pomegranates." *ActaInstRomNor* 4:7–11.

Settis, S. 1988. *Kaiser Augustus und die verlorene Republik.* Mainz.

Shepard, K. 1940. *The Fish-Tailed Monster in Greek and Etruscan Art.* New York.

Simon, E. 1990. *Die Götter der Römer.* Munich.

———. 1986. *Augustus: Kunst und Leben in Rom um die Zeitenwende.* Munich.

———. 1967. *Ara Pacis Augustae.* Greenwich, Conn.

Skard, E. 1933. "Pater patriae." In *Festskrift til Halvdan Koht*, pp. 42–70. Oslo.

Sordi, M. 1983. "Il santuario di Cerere, Libero, e Libera e il tribunato della plebe." In *Santuari e politica nel mondo antico*, pp. 127–139. Contributi dell' Istituo di storia antica. Pubblicazioni della Università cattolica del Sacro Cruore. Milan.

Spaeth, B. 1994. "Ceres in the Ara Pacis Augustae and the Carthage Relief." *AJA* 98:65–100.

———. 1990. "The Goddess Ceres and the Death of Tiberius Gracchus." *Historia* 39:182–195.

———. 1987. *The Goddess Ceres: A Study in Roman Religious Ideology.* Diss. Johns Hopkins University. Baltimore.

Starhawk. 1979. *The Spiral Dance: A Rebirth of the Ancient Religion of the Goddess.* New York.

Stehle, E. 1989. "Venus, Cybele, and the Sabine Women: The Roman Construction of Female Sexuality." *Helios* 16:143–164.

Stockton, D. 1979. *The Gracchi.* Oxford.

Stone, M. 1976. *When God Was a Woman.* New York.

Strachan-Davidson, J. 1912. *Problems of the Roman Criminal Law.* Oxford.

Strong, E. 1937. "Terra Mater or Italia?" *JRS* 27:114–126.

Sutherland, C. 1951. *Coinage in Roman Imperial Policy, 31 B.C.–A.D 68.* London.

Sydenham, E. 1952. *The Coinage of the Roman Republic.* London.

Talbert, R., ed. 1985. *Atlas of Classical History.* London and New York.

Taylor, L. 1925. "The Mother of the Lares." *AJA* 29:309–313.

Temporini, H. 1978. *Die Frauen am Hofe Trajans: Ein Beitrag zur Stellung der Augustae im Principat.* Berlin and New York.

Thierion, M. 1967. "Faustina Augusta, mater castrorum." *Schw. Münzbl.* 17:41–46.

Thornton, M. 1983. "Augustan Genealogy and the Ara Pacis." *Latomus* 42: 619–628.

Torelli, M. 1984. *Lavinio e Roma: Riti iniziatrici e matrimonio tra archeologia e storia.* Rome.

———. 1982. *Typology and Structure of Roman Historical Reliefs.* Ann Arbor.

Toutain, J. 1967. *Les cultes païens dans l'empire romain.* Vol. 1: *Les provinces latines.* Rome.

Townsend, J. 1990. "The Goddess: Fact, Fallacy, and Revitalization Movement." In *Goddesses in Religion and Modern Debate*, pp. 180–204. Ed. L. Hurtado. Atlanta.

Toynbee, J. 1971. *Death and Burial in the Roman World.* New York.

———. 1953. "The Ara Pacis Reconsidered and Historical Art in Roman Italy." *ProcBritAc* 29:67–95.

Treggiari, S. 1991. *Roman Marriage.* Oxford.

Trillmich, W. 1978. *Familienpropaganda der Kaiser Caligula und Claudius: Agrippina Maior und Antonia Augusta auf Münzen.* DAI Antike Münzen und Geschnittene Steine 8. Berlin.

———. 1971. "Zur Formgeschichte von Bildnistypen." *JdI* 86:179–213.

Turcan, R. 1971. "Les guirlandes dans l'antiquité classique." *JAC* 14:92–139.

Van Berchem, D. 1935. "Il tempio di Cerere e l'ufficio dell'annona a Roma." *BullComm* 63:91–95.

Van Buren, A. 1913. "The Ara Pacis Augustae." *JRS* 3:134–141.

Van Gennep, A. 1960. *The Rites of Passage.* Trans. M. Vizedom and G. Caffee. Chicago.

Vermaseren, M. 1977. *Cybele and Attis: The Myth and the Cult.* London.

Verzar, M. 1976–1977. "L'umbilicus urbis: Il mundus in etá tardo-republicana." *DialArch* 9:378–398.

Vetter, E. 1953. *Handbuch der italischen Dialekte* 1. Heidelberg.

Veyne, P. 1958–1959. "Tenir une buste: Un intaille avec le Génie de Carthage et le sardonyx de Livie à Vienne." *Cahiers de Byrsa* 8:61–78.

Vidal, H. 1965. "Le depôt *in aede.*" *Rev. Hist. Dr. Fr. Etr.* 44:545–587.

Vidman, L. 1978. "Ieiunium Cereris quinquennale (en marge des Fasti Ostienses)." *ZPE* 28:87–95.

Vives y Escudero, A. 1926. *La modeda hispanica.* Madrid.

Vogt, J. 1924. *Die alexandrische Münzen: Grundlegung einer alexandrin-ischen Kaisergeschichte.* 2 vols. Stuttgart.

Vollenweider, M. 1966. *Die Steinscheneidekunst und ihre Künstler in spätre-publikanischer Kaisergeschichte.* 2 vols. Stuttgart.

Wagenvoort, H. 1960. "De dea Cerere deque eius mysteriis Romanis." *Mnemosyne* 13:111–142.

———. 1956. "Initia Cereris." In *Studies in Roman Literature, Culture, and Religion*, pp. 150–168. Leiden.

Walde, A., and J. Hofmann. 1938. *Lateinisches etymologishes Wörterbuch.* 3rd ed. Heidelberg.

Walters, H. 1926. *Catalogue of the Engraved Gems and Cameos Greek, Etruscan, and Roman in the British Museum.* Rev. ed. London.

Warner, M. 1983. *Alone of All Her Sex: The Myth and the Cult of the Virgin Mary.* New York.

Watson, A. 1975. *Rome of the XII Tables: Persons and Property.* Princeton.

———. 1971. *The Law of Succession in the Later Roman Republic.* Oxford.

Weinstock, S. 1960. "Pax and the Ara Pacis." *JRS* 50:44–58.

Westermark, U., and K. Jenkins. 1980. *The Coinage of Kamarina.* London.

White, D. 1967. "The Post-Classical Cult of Malophoros at Selinus." *AJA* 71: 335–352.

Whitmont, E. 1982. *Return of the Goddess.* New York.

Williams, G. 1958. "Some aspects of the Roman Marriage Ceremony." *JRS* 48:16–29.

Wirszubski, C. 1950. *"Libertas" as a Political Idea at Rome during the Late Republic and Early Principate.* Cambridge.

Wissowa, G. 1912. *Religion und Kultus der Römer.* 2nd ed. Munich.

———. 1899*a*. "Ceres." *RE* 3.2, cols. 1970–1979.

———. 1899*b*. "Cerialia." *RE* 3.2, cols. 1980–1982.

Wlosok, A. 1975. "Geminorum Mater Amorum." In *Monumentum Chiloniense: Studien zur augusteischen Zeit. Kieler Festschrift für Erich Burck zum 70. Geburtstag*, pp. 514–523. Ed. E. Lefèvre. Amsterdam.

Wolters, P. 1930. "Gestalt und Sinn der Ähre in der antiker Kunst." *Die Antike* 6:284–301.

Woodman A. 1983. *Velleius Paterculus: The Caesarian and Augustan Narrative.* Cambridge.

Wrede, H. 1981. *Consecratio in formam deorum: Vergöttlichte Privatpersonen in der römischen Kaiserzeit.* Mainz.

Yavetz, Z. 1969. *Plebs and Princeps.* Oxford.

Zanker, P. 1988. *The Power of Images in the Age of Augustus.* Trans. A. Shapiro. Ann Arbor.

Zeitlin, F. 1982. "Cultic Models of the Female: Rites of Dionysos and Demeter." *Arethusa* 15:129–157.

Zevi-Gallina, A. 1973. *Roma Medio-Repubblicana: Aspetti Culturali di Roma e del Lazio nei secoli IV e III A.C.* Rome.

Zuntz, G. 1971. *Persephone: Three Essays on Religion and Thought in Magna Graecia.* Oxford.

GENERAL INDEX

Catena, 105, 106, 109

Cereres: 3, 17, 25, 115

Ceres: Augusta, 26, 47, 68; and cult of
Liber and Libera, xiv, 4, 7–9, 15, 28,
30, 39, 41, 81, 88, 90–96, 101, 104;
and cult of Proserpina, xvi, 3, 6–13,
15, 18, 20, 21, 22, 29, 59–60, 66,
103–113, 118, 140; Eleusinia, 21;
Frugifera, 130, 146; iconography of,
127–134; Italic cult of, xiv, 1–4, 24–
36, 39, 44, 52–53, 54, 56, 62, 87–88,
104, 118, 140; Mater, 21, 42, 56,
117–118, 122, 131; new, 120; and
Tellus (see Ceres, Italic cult of); and
Temple of Ceres, Liber, and Libera,
6–8, 15, 22, 28, 30, 39–41, 66, 70,
81–86, 90, 91, 93, 97, 98, 101, 143;
Ultrix (see Keri Arentikai)

Ceres-type sculpture, 29–31, 120

Cerialia, 22, 28, 34, 98, 101; Caesarian
coin and, 19, 99; calendar and, 4, 7;
other festivals and, 5, 18, 44, 93; rituals of, 15, 36–37, 46. See also ludi
Ceriales; ludi scaenici; ludi circenses

Cerus, 1, 34

chastity, 22, 57, 60, 112–116; cult of
Ceres and Proserpina and, 12, 13, 29;
definition of, 114; ritual practice of,
110–111, 112; women of family of
princeps and, 30, 119, 121

children, 41, 113, 131–132, 133, 145.
See also birth; fertility, human;
motherhood

chthonic divinities, 56, 59, 64

Cicero, M. Tullius, 18, 60

Circus Maximus, 28; Cerialia and, 4, 15,
36, 88; Temple of Ceres, Liber, and
Libera and, 7, 82–83

civilization, Ceres and, 17, 27, 53, 61

class, upper: cult of Ceres and Proserpina and women of, xvi, 13, 103, 105,
107, 108–110, 113; female virtues
and women of, 111, 113–114, 116,
119

Claudius: coinage of, 26, 30, 47, 100,
120; Eleusinian Mysteries and, 27,

60. See also Agrippina the Younger;
Antonia Minor; Livilla; Messalina

Claudius Gothicus, 30

Commodus, 27, 60. See also Bruttia
Crispina; Faustina the Younger

Concilium Plebis, 85

Concordia, 28

Conflict of the Orders, 6, 81, 143

consecratio: bonorum, 70, 71–73, 83–
84, 90; capitis, 70, 71–73

consecration, 28, 59, 69–70, 71–73. See
also consecratio

Cornelia, 117

cornucopia, 25

corona spicea: Antonia Minor and, 30,
47, 120; Augustus and, 23; Ceres and,
16, 21, 25, 38, 112, 127–128, 130,
133, 148–149; definition and origins
of, 11; Livia and, 23, 47, 119, 145;
princeps and, 26, 47; Tellus and,
134–135

countryside, Ceres and, 24, 29, 37

cow, 45, 132–133, 147

crane, 137, 138

crops: Ceres and, 16, 20, 24, 34–35, 37,
63, 112, 118, 139; Pax and, 68. See
also fertility, agricultural

crown, 127, 135, 137. See also corona
spicea

Cumae, 104

cura: annona, 40, 87; ludorum solemnium, 87; urbis, 87

Cybele. See Magna Mater

Cyprus, 112

Damophilus, 8

death: Ceres and, 3, 18, 21, 27, 53–56;
mundus Cereris and, 5, 63–65

Demeter, 41, 60, 103–104, 111; Ceres
and, xiv, 8–9, 11, 18, 21, 92, 127–
134; and cult of Dionysus and Kore,
7, 8, 91 (see also Ceres, Liber, and
Libera); and cult of Persephone, 8,
17; Demophöon, 42; Melaina, 129;
motherhood and, 42, 43, 118; new,

120, 121; Thesmophoria and, 12, 104, 107–108
Diana, 56. *See also* Artemis
Dido, 45, 56–57, 58, 114–115, 132
Dionysus, 28–29, 41, 42, 56, 138. *See also* Liber
Diva Genetrix, 2, 43
divorce, 5, 27, 58, 90, 93, 57–59
Domitia Longina, 122, 176
Domitian, 48. *See also* Domitia Longina
Drusilla, 174
Drusus Minor. *See* Livilla

earth, Ceres and, 16, 20, 37, 129–130
Eileithyia, 26, 43, 56
Eleusinian Mysteries, 17–18, 21, 27, 29, 60
Eleusis, 21, 129
Enna. *See* Henna
Etruscans, 3–4, 7

Faliscans, 1, 34, 37, 41
farming. *See* agriculture
fast of Ceres. See *ieiunium Cereris*
Fauna, 8
Faunus, 8, 90, 138
Faustina the Elder, 29, 47, 119, 120, 179–180
Faustina the Younger, 122, 123, 180
Feriae Sementivae, 5, 35, 44
fertility: agricultural, 34–41; in ancient Italy, 2, 3; and Ara Pacis, 126, 127–134, 138, 140, 141, 144, 148–149; in Augustan period, 20, 22, 23, 24; Ceres and, xiv, xv, 1–2, 33–49; and cult of Ceres and Proserpina, 12, 13, 111–113; in Early Empire, 24–26; in Early Republic, 9, 10–11; human, 41–47; in Late Republic, 16–17; in Middle Republic, 15–16; and plebs, 97; and princeps, 121; in regal Rome, 4–5; and women, 30, 67, 112–113, 118
Fides Publica, 28
fields, Ceres and, 20, 24, 37

Filia Cerealis, 2, 43
fillets, 115–116
fines, 89–90
first-fruit offering. *See* praemetium; sacrima
flamen *Cerealis,* 4, 25, 34, 35–36, 39, 104
Flora, 82, 89, 90; *Cerealis,* 2, 3, 34. *See also* ludi, Florales
flowers, 128–129
food, 16, 25, 39
Fordicidia, 5, 36, 44, 45
Forum Boarium, 7
fox, 36–37
fruit: Ceres and, 25, 130–131, 133; Demeter and, 127; nymphs and, 138; other divinities and, 28; Pax and, 68; Tellus and, 133
frumentatio, 6, 10–11, 16, 39–40, 84, 87, 98

Galba, 68
Gallienus, 27, 60
Germanicus. *See* Agrippina the Elder; Antonia Minor; Livilla
Golden Age, 146–149
goose, 136, 138
Gorgasus, 8
Gracchus, Tiberius, 19, 73–79, 117
grain: administrators of supply of, 40 (*see* praefecti annonae); in ancient Italy, 1; Ara Pacis and, 138, 146, 148; as attribute of Ceres, 29, 38, 112, 128, 133; as attribute of Demeter, 127; as attribute of other divinities, 28; as attribute of Pax, 68; in Augustan period, 20–21; Ceres and, xiv, 37–41, 101, 137; Christian saints and, 31; cult of Ceres and Proserpina and, 112; distribution of (*see* frumentatio); in Early Empire, 25–26, 29; importation of, 9; Magna Mater and, 96; in Middle Republic, 16; plebs and, 87, 98; princeps and, 101–102, 121; supply of (*see* annona); Temple of Ceres, Liber, and Libera and, 84–85

INDEX OF PASSAGES CITED